Benedetto Croce

PHILOSOPHER OF ART
AND LITERARY CRITIC

OTHER BOOKS BY GIAN N. G. ORSINI

La poesia di Alfred Tennyson, 1928
Milton e il suo poema, 1928
Bacone e Machiavelli, 1936
Studii sul Rinascimento italiano in Inghilterra, 1937
Fulke Greville tra il mondo e Dio, 1941

Benedetto Croce

1938

Benedetto Croce

Philosopher of Art and Literary Critic

By GIAN N. G. ORSINI

SOUTHERN ILLINOIS UNIVERSITY PRESS

CARBONDALE

Copyright © 1961, by Southern Illinois University Press
Library of Congress Catalog Card Number 61-6101
Printed in the United States of America by
Vail-Ballou Press, Inc., Binghamton, N.Y.
Designed by Andor Braun

ACKNOWLEDGMENTS

THE WRITING of this book was rendered possible by a leave for re-search and grants from the University of Wisconsin, and by a grant from the Institute for Advanced Study at Princeton, N.J.

I owe a special debt to Professor Lienhard Bergel of Queen's College, New York, for reading the manuscript in one of its earlier stages and for many other kindnesses, and to Dr. Alda Croce for important references.

Some chapters draw upon previously published articles: "Theory and Practice in Croce's Aesthetics" in *The Journal of Aesthetics and Art Criticism*, XIII (1955), 300–313, and "Croce and the Poetic Image" in *Symposium*, x (1956), 1–24.

CONTENTS

		Page
	ACKNOWLEDGMENTS	v
	ABBREVIATIONS	ix
	Introduction	3
i	The Making of Croce's Philosophy	12
ii	The Aesthetic Image	24
iii	The Lyrical Intuition	46
iv	The "Techniques" of Poetic Expression	64
v	The Question of Literary Genres	96
vi	Other Classifications of Poetry—the Theatre	112
vii	Taste or the Reproduction of Expressions	125
viii	The Function of Literary Criticism	140
ix	The Province of Literary History	166
x	Croce's Earlier Criticism	198
xi	The Cosmic Intuition	210
xii	Croce's Later Criticism	226
xiii	"La Poesia"	253
xiv	Croce and "Decadentism"	275
xv	Croce and the History of Criticism—Conclusion	282

APPENDIX 1: Biographical Notes on Croce 293

APPENDIX 2: Crocean Bibliography 299

NOTES 312

INDEX 368

ABBREVIATIONS

A   *Aesthetic*, transl. D. Ainslie, 2nd ed., 1922.

A¹   *Aesthetic*, transl. D. Ainslie, 1st ed., 1909.

Aneddoti   *Aneddoti di varia letteratura*, 2nd ed., 1953–54, 4 vols.

ASC   *Ariosto, Shakespeare e Corneille*, 1st ed., 1920.

Au   *Autobiography*, transl. R. G. Collingwood, 1927.

CC   *Conversazioni critiche*, serie I & II, 2nd ed., 1924; III & IV, 1st ed., 1932; V, 1st ed., 1939.

CVM   *Cultura e vita morale*, 2nd ed., 1936.

D   *La poesia di Dante*, 1921.

Discorsi   *Discorsi di varia filosofia*, 1945, 2 vols.

E   *Estetica*, 9th ed., 1950.

EA   *The Essence of Aesthetic*, transl. D. Ainslie, 1921.

G   *Goethe*, 4th ed., 1946, 2 vols.

Letture   *Letture di poeti e riflessioni sulla teoria e la critica della poesia*, 1950.

LNI   *Letteratura della nuova Italia*, I & II, 1914; III & IV, 1915.

LNI, IV²   The same, vol. IV, 2nd ed., 1922.

Logica   *Logica come scienza del concetto puro*, 2nd ed., 1909.

NPS   *Nuove pagine sparse*, 1948, 2 vols.

NSE   *Nuovi saggi di estetica*, 1st ed., 1920.

NSE²   The same, 2nd ed., 1926.

P   *La poesia*, 2nd ed., 1937.

P⁵   *La poesia*, 5th ed., 1953.

PAM   *Poesia antica e moderna*, 1941.

PdE   *Problemi di estetica*, 1910.

PdE[4]	The same, 4th ed., 1946.
PNP	*Poesia e non poesia,* 1923.
PPPA	*Poesia popolare e poesia d'arte,* 1933.
Pratica	*Filosofia della pratica: economica ed etica,* 3rd ed., 1923.
PS	*Pagine sparse,* 2nd ed., 1943, 3 vols.
Shak.	*Shakespeare,* nuova ediz. a cura di N. Orsini, 1948.
SS	*Storia della storiografia italiana nel sec* XIX, 1921, 2 vols.
Storia	*La storia come pensiero e come azione,* 2nd ed., 1938.
TPS	*Terze pagine sparse,* 1955, 2 vols.
TSS	*Teoria e storia della storiografia,* 2nd ed., 1920.
US	*Ultimi saggi,* 1937.

Benedetto Croce

PHILOSOPHER OF ART
AND LITERARY CRITIC

Introduction

MODERN LITERARY CRITICISM is feeling more and more the need of going back to fundamentals. In the critical analysis of poetry and of imaginative literature it is now considered necessary to bring up and discuss the basic assumptions upon which critical judgments are founded, to analyze the general concept of poetry and to redefine it in terms which are valid for contemporary experience. The question of what constitutes poetic quality, of the structure and texture of poetry, the relations between poetry and the drama, the foundations of judgment for the novel, and so forth, have been taken up as indispensable premises to the analysis of particular works and to the assessment of a writer's stature.

As a result, contemporary criticism, especially in the United States, seems to concern itself with general issues just as much as with practical criticism. This may be seen in the fact that most collections of modern criticism contain a considerable proportion of discussion of general principles besides analyses of single writers and single works. The critics seem to go more and more into what was once called poetics and into what is still called aesthetics.

Many of the barriers that fenced in traditional academic scholarship have been broken down. One of them was a big "No entry" sign posted over the road that led to philosophical speculation. The good scholar was supposed to deal only with "facts" and avoid "ideas." But in their search for ultimates, more and more modern critics feel that they have to venture upon

3

that forbidden path which leads to philosophy. Even the term "ontology," that word of awe, is now occurring in the works of literary critics. Furthermore, the domain of German philosophy, which was carefully shunned by academic scholars of the older generation, is now being increasingly explored by literary critics.[1] The notion that a view of poetry implies a view of life, and a view of life implies a view of the world—that is, a philosophy— is no longer as strange as it once was.

At the same time, one general principle has been affirmed by a large number of critics, so much as to become almost a universally accepted doctrine. That is the independent status of poetic creation. Poetry—or imaginative writing in general, including the drama and the novel—stands by itself. It is not subordinate or subservient to any other human activity, but it produces itself according to its own laws. It should therefore be judged by principles drawn from its own nature, and not from those drawn from the nature of ethics, or of science, or of politics, or of philosophical or religious knowledge, or any other human ideal or activity, however desirable. This general conviction assumes several individual forms and variations. Some formulate it as the "autonomy" of poetry, some as the "autotelic" character of poetry, others find yet other ways of asserting it. Poetry seems to have won its right to independence. The question still remains, upon what grounds is this freedom to be founded, what are the ultimate principles involved in it, and how do they bear upon the issues of practical criticism.

It is here that the work of Benedetto Croce may be of help to contemporary criticism.[2] For the essence of his aesthetic is the autonomy of the poetic faculty, and the essence of his criticism is the practical application of this principle. Croce has explored to the last degree the ultimate implications of this critical doctrine, and at the same time made aesthetics a highly developed instrument for the critical evaluation of literature. For him, critical theory existed only for the sake of critical practice. While investigating the implications of literary judgment and its relationship with other forms of reflective thought, he has shown extensively how much light is thrown by such discussions on the practical issues of criticism. His doctrine of aesthetics eschews abstract speculation on the Beautiful, and concerns itself with the theory of art and of artistic and literary criticism.[3] The function of literary criticism, its method, its procedure, its history and development from the Greeks down to our day, were discussed by him in a series of lucid analyses that never lost sight of concrete problems. He has both tested and exemplified his own doctrines in an extraordinarily wide series of critical essays, ranging over the whole territory of Western literature from Homer to Mallarmé. The extent of this critical work may be gathered by the simple arithmetical fact that the number of his books of criticism stands to those of aesthetic theory in the proportion of five to one, or five books of practice to one of theory.

Furthermore, Croce kept continually in touch with contemporary thought and took up discussion of new ideas whenever they appeared, at home or abroad. One of the fascinating aspects of his work is his keen and immediate awareness of contemporary issues, and his continual reckoning with different ways of thinking. There are few episodes of major importance in twentieth-century thought—from Marxism to Fascism, from symbolism to existentialism, from Spengler to Toynbee, from William James to John Dewey, from Pareto to Veblen—that were not discussed in his journal, *La critica*. His collected book reviews fill more than ten volumes of his works and constitute a running commentary on the last half-century of Western culture. In the field of French literature alone (and French was not his major interest) he discussed nearly one hundred new books, as may be seen from a recent account of his contributions to this area.[4]

The very range and extent of his work have tended to handicap its full appreciation even in his own country, and much more so abroad. Since Croce's first book on aesthetics goes back to 1902 and attained at once the status of a classic, some critics outside Italy are under the impression that it was his one and only contribution to the subject. Actually the book was only a beginning. For 50 years after its publication, Croce extended, revised and corrected, sometimes radically, his views on literature and on criticism. Some Italian students of Croce go so far as to speak of no less than four different aesthetics in Croce. There are actually four distinct phases in Croce's thinking on this subject, as he himself repeatedly acknowledged.[5] The first is the doctrine of intuition as expression, represented by the *Aesthetic* of 1902. The second is the doctrine of lyrical intuition, which was the foundation of his practical criticism for some two decades, and which was formally expounded in 1908. The third is the doctrine of the cosmic intuition, formally expounded in 1918 and represented in practical criticism mainly by his studies on Ariosto, Shakespeare and Goethe. The fourth and last is the doctrine of literature as distinguished from poetry, published in 1936 and similarily utilized in his later criticism.

It may perhaps be excessive to speak of four different doctrines. Croce himself maintained that the whole represented a single theory which developed consistently into richer and fuller formulations. The consistency has been challenged by critics of Croce. This is a moot point, and some attention will be given to it in Chapter XI. But whatever side is taken in this argument, it should be clear by now that there is much more in Croce than the *Aesthetic* of 1902, important as that book was. In 1923 Spingarn could already say: "Croce's youthful *Aesthetic* is a very slender basis for any judgment on Croce's contribution to philosophy, ethics, political and economic theory, history, aesthetics and literary criticism." [6] And yet in 1923 Croce was only half-way, having thirty more working years before him. So any discussion of Croce which fails to take account of his various interests and the various phases of his thought is bound to be nugatory.

In most of his investigations Croce, like everyone else, began by holding the accepted views. But he then subjected them to critical scrutiny and found them wanting, and so developed views of his own. Take for instance two of his most controversial doctrines: his rejection of genres as a critical standard and of the "medium" theory of the arts. They are rejected in his *Aesthetic*, but he began by holding them both. We find him subscribing to the genre theory in 1885 (PS, I, 471; see list of abbreviations at beginning of this volume), and to the "medium" theory—as well as to Lessing's correlative theory of the arts—in 1893.[7] Only in 1900, after mature reflection, did he find reason to discard them.

For causes which it would be too long to investigate and which relate in part to the barriers raised by the Fascist regime against free communication with democratic nations, in the years after the war of 1914–18 Croce's voice was listened to only occasionally in the free countries. And yet Croce himself kept in touch with what was going on outside Italy and took up many of the problems which were being discussed abroad. But the critics outside Italy who were discussing those problems and reaching conclusions which were similar to Croce's generally remained in ignorance of the fact.[8]

It was in any case difficult even for the best informed student of Croce to keep up with his tireless activity. Before an English translation of the *Aesthetic* of 1902 was ready in 1909, Croce had already passed into the second stage of his doctrine, that of the lyrical intuition, and before the incomplete and imperfect English translation could appear in a revised and corrected version in 1922, Croce had already formulated his third doctrine, the cosmic intuition. Each of these formulations was accompanied by a crop of critical essays on contemporary and classical authors, most of which are still untranslated. The fourth stage of his doctrine was published in 1936, at the height of the Fascist era, and has not been translated except for a few pages. The whole of Croce's later criticism remains untranslated to this day.

In the early twenties Spingarn spoke of finding one's way "through the jungle of Croce's forty or fifty volumes."[9] Today there are more than 70, the result of unceasing industry, good fortune and an unusually long life of 86 years. Confronted with such a voluminous production, the would-be reader of Croce is naturally perplexed and looks around for some guidance. The book by Raffaello Piccoli[10] is a compact summary in English of Croce's doctrines, but only up to the date of its publication,

1922. Sprigge's book, cited in the Biographical Notes, is a good portrait of the man and his political and social attitudes, but does not deal adequately with his aesthetic and philosophical views.

In Italian of course there are several aids to the study of Croce, including a full bibliography, completely indexed; see Appendix 2. But there are still a number of unsettled points concerning the development of Croce's thought and the chronology of his doctrines. The current view of this chronology as it refers to aesthetic theory is cited above, but each date may be pushed backwards. The theory of art as expression is already outlined in a book of 1893. The lyrical intuition, announced in the Heidelberg lecture of 1908, was already formulated in the first draft of the *Logic* (1905). The first formulation of expression as an a priori synthesis is dated, even by some Italian scholars, in 1912, but it is to be found in the *Logic* of 1908. The cosmic intuition is dated 1918, but it is already found in a book which goes back to 1915. My book gives some attention to chronology, but does not attempt to solve all the relative problems. A complete study of Croce's intellectual development still remains to be done.

However, the ultimate aim of this work is not biographical or purely historical but critical. The goal has been to see whether there is a practical theory of literary criticism in Croce. "Are the problems of criticism solved more clearly and satisfactorily when viewed from Croce's standpoint?" is the question I have asked myself throughout. Accordingly, I have endeavored to see things as much as possible from his point of view and to present his doctrines in the most favorable light. However, dissent will appear on three main points of doctrine: Croce's handling of the image in his theory of practical criticism (Chapters III and VIII), his third or universalistic aesthetics (Chapter XI) and his later criticism of contemporary writing (Chapter XIV).

In other words, Croce in this book has been criticized only from within, when his conclusions appeared to be inconsistent with his premises. Of course these premises themselves are subject to discussion. But this discussion is profitable only when it arises out of complete knowledge of what Croce had to say.

Several of the objections which arise spontaneously in the mind of a reader of Croce were taken up and answered by him in one of his many minor writings. It is therefore very hazardous to assert (as some critics are prone to do) that Croce neglected this or that thinker whom he should have known. A few instances, drawn from recent American discussion of Croce, will show this. One critic complains: "Croce never deigned to take notice of Freud!" But he did; he reviewed Freud's book on dreams, and had other things to say about him later; see below, Chapter viii. "Croce never discussed phonetic laws!" complains another critic, who is interested in language. But he did; he wrote a whole paper on the subject (*PdE*, 177–84). "Croce never took notice of Max Weber" is another complaint. Now Croce introduced Weber in Italy as far back as 1918, spoke of him several times later and wrote a review of him in 1948 (TPS, ii, 130–33). Croce's philosophy has been unfavorably contrasted with H. Poincaré's views, whereas Croce made Poincaré's theory of science a cornerstone of his own *Logic* (see Chapter i). These instances (none of which is imaginary) refer mainly to Croce's philosophical and social doctrines; but examples from aesthetics will be cited throughout this book. And finally, when it comes to fundamental issues, one should remember Croce's warning that no philosopher can be "transcended"—or shall we say, superseded—until his doctrines have been completely digested and absorbed.[11]

A special effort has been made in this book to correlate the ideas of Croce with those of English and American literary criticism. In spite of differences there is a much broader area of agreement than is generally suspected, and an attempt has been made to bring out this agreement by quotation of parallel ideas from English-speaking critics. Unless there is specific mention to the contrary, all references to English and American writers (both critics and poets) will be my own, and Croce should not be held responsible for them.[12]

The arrangement of the material presented another problem. Croce's doctrines can be arranged either chronologically or topically. According to the first method Croce's ideas would be presented in their successive phases. Following the second, they would be arranged according to subject: the concept of intuition, the question of genres, the problem of technique, the function of criticism, and so forth. In both cases a certain amount of repetition would result. For in the first alternative one would have to go through all the topics over again for each phase of Croce's thought, and show what formulation Croce gave them in each phase. In the second way, the topics would be treated separately, but one would have to go through all the four phases of doctrine for each of them, and there would be no saving of space.

The arrangement finally followed in this book is one that seems to involve the least amount of overlapping. It is a compromise between the two alternatives, being partly chronological and partly topical. The chronological order is preserved on the whole. After a chapter on the development of Croce's philosophy, his different aesthetic phases are presented successively, beginning with the first, expounded in its main principle in Chapter II. The second phase follows in Chapter III. But the third phase is dealt with later in the book, in Chapter XI, and the last in Chapter XIII. In between these chapters a certain number of important topics, such as technique, genres, criticism and history, are dealt with, once and for all, in Chapters IV to IX. A chronological account of Croce's practical criticism is divided into three chapters, X, XII and XIV, according to the phases of his doctrine; but relevant examples of his criticism may be given in any chapter. Finally Chapter XV attempts a quick survey of Croce's contributions to the history of criticism and a summary and conclusion to the whole argument.

By and large, this book deals with literary aesthetics and has little to say on the aesthetics of the other arts. The translations from Croce's works in quotations have generally been made anew, with the help of the previous ones when they existed. But for the reader's convenience references have been given to the pages of some current translations. Differing from some others like Vincent Sheean who have translated Croce,

I have not hesitated on occasion to break up his long sentences into shorter English ones, to ensure smooth reading.

When this book was nearing completion, there appeared a study of Croce's earlier aesthetics and criticism by Calvin G. Seerveld.[13] This lively and circumstantial monograph takes Croce only up to 1915, but within that limit it is generally more detailed than the present book in the discussion of Croce's philosophical attitudes. However, both my divergencies and my agreements with Seerveld are unintentional, since his book appeared when mine had already reached final form. Further references to it will be made in the notes.

CHAPTER 1

The Making of Croce's Philosophy

CROCE'S PHILOSOPHICAL INQUIRIES began when the dominant school of thought was Positivism, or the view that all inquiries into philosophy and the humanities should follow the methods which had been successfully adopted by the sciences of nature. At the beginning of the twentieth century in Italy a positivistic school, whose acknowledged leader was R. Ardigò, held sway in the academic world. "Facts, not ideas" was the watchword, and the only facts that counted were those classified by the sciences of nature. Spencer's philosophy of evolution was extolled, while most of the philosophies developed before the triumphant advance of modern science were rejected as fanciful speculations. When the positivists applied their methods to the investigations of human society and of history, they produced results which can fairly be described as grossly materialistic. Human intelligence became the mechanical effect of casual associations, and human effort the working of blind instinct, animal appetites or selfish delusions (CVM, 63). Civilization was only the survival of savage customs and art a form of neurotic behavior. The psychiatry of the time was represented by men like C. Lombroso, who maintained that genius was a form of mental disease and won international acclaim in his own day, as Freud did in ours.

Now Croce was a scholar carefully trained in the methods of investigation developed by critical history in the nineteenth century, or in what is known as the historical method. He, too, was keenly interested in facts and their accurate observation and

interpretation, but they were the facts of history and not those
of the natural sciences (cvm, 53–56). For Croce history was
never mere antiquarianism; it was the record of human intelligence building up civilization in all its forms, social, intellectual
and artistic. All these activities were for Croce unintelligible
save as an effort to realize ideals—the ideals of beauty, of truth
and of ethics—and history itself was unintelligible unless one
assumed the capacity of human beings to be guided by ideals
and even to sacrifice themselves for them. Human action had
been so interpreted by thinkers of the idealistic school, and
Croce noted that as a consequence those thinkers produced a
series of brilliant histories, especially of literature and of the arts
(cvm, 64).

On the other hand, Croce observed that the positivistic
school broke down completely when it dealt with history. What
shocked Croce was the superficiality of the positivists when
they handled subjects that were accessible to the historian and
the humanistic scholar, the second-hand quality of their knowledge, their haste in jumping to conclusions, their gross inaccuracies, their lack of psychological perception and the crudity
of their judgments in matters of taste.[1] He was equally offended
by the Hegelians' arbitrary "Philosophy of History" (*Au*, 90).
Croce's ideal was that of a philosophy that united logical rigor
and keenness of discrimination with an educated approach to the
humanities. He ended by producing such a philosophy himself,
but it was the result of a complex intellectual development
which took about twenty years (1893–1913). We shall now
give a summary of his development as a philosopher, reserving
for Chapter ix an account of his growth as a critic and literary
scholar.

Croce's earliest philosophical questionings were aroused by
his instructor in theology at the high school, who gave a course
in "the philosophy of religion" which had the unintended
result of destroying the pupil's religious faith (*Au*, 34). But
systematic study of philosophy began in 1885, in his university
days, when he came under the influence of Antonio Labriola,
who taught moral philosophy at the University of Rome (*Au*,

41). Labriola acquainted Croce with German thought and guided his readings in philosophy, including aesthetics.[2] He also infected young Croce with his faith in the philosophy of Herbart, a theory of moral ideals based upon a realistic metaphysics and a strong hostility to Hegel.[3] Croce's first philosophical orientation was definitely anti-Hegelian.

His earliest statement on aesthetics was a review, published in 1886 when Croce was only 20, of a book by the Neapolitan professor Antonio Tari, whose sparkling lectures on aesthetics Croce had occasionally attended as a youth.[4] In it Croce describes aesthetics as a "German science" but adds immediately with characteristic caution that sciences do not really have a nationality, although they have a birthplace. So in Germany aesthetics was fathered by Baumgarten and developed by Kant and others. Croce noted that in his own day the field was divided between the aesthetics of content, or of Hegel, and the aesthetics of form, or of Herbart.[5] There is no mention as yet of Vico.

Croce then went through a period of purely historical research which lasted from 1886 to 1892 (*Au*, 48). In 1893 he was aroused by the hotly debated argument whether history was a science or an art. At first, Croce inclined to the opinion of most historians of his own day (especially the positivists) that history was a body of knowledge and therefore a science (PS, I, 207). But the more he thought about it, the more he was assailed by far-reaching questions: what is art? what is science? what is knowledge? This marks the real beginning of Croce as a philosopher. To answer these questions he undertook a far more extensive study of philosophy. He read many German books, especially in the field of aesthetics and criticism. German aesthetics, he acknowledged in 1884, was difficult, obscure, pedantic and sometimes even absurd. But it represents a great intellectual effort which modern criticism must master, hard though the labor be. He also read Vico for the first time (*Au*, 52), noting his conception of poetry as a form of elementary cognition.[6]

The result of this first philosophical inquiry was published in a short monograph, *History assigned to the general concept of Art* (1893). Croce noted that four principal answers have been given to the question "What is beauty?": 1) the sensualistic, 2) the intellectualistic, 3) the formalistic and 4) the idealistic. The first maintains that beauty is mere sensuous pleasure and the second that beauty is an embodiment of the True and the Good. Both, says Croce, were refuted by Kant in the *Critique of Judgment*. The third is the Herbartian theory that beauty consists of purely formal relations. This theory, never fully developed by its author, has since worked itself out in his followers and is also dismissed by Croce. The fourth consists in the view of "concrete Idealism" developed by E. von Hartmann in 1887 (this was the latest German aesthetic). It holds that beauty is the embodiment of the Idea, which Croce interprets as "beauty is the expression of a content." Art is a special way of attaining beauty by representing the particular as such. This is the only view that still stands up for Croce, so in 1883 he had already reached his famous conclusion that expression is the essence of beauty.

His answer to the question "what is history?" was now that history was not a science, since science deals with laws and generalities while history deals with individual fact. As cognition of the individual, history comes under the general category of art, but it is a special kind of art because it provides knowledge of actuality,[7] whereas pure art only gives knowledge of possibility. This theory of history was later considerably modified. But we have here the kernel of Croce's future philosophy and the gist of his answer to positivism.

The aesthetics of Hegel had reached Croce also through other channels, in the transformations that it underwent in two very different minds: the above-mentioned aesthetician Tari and the critic and historian of literature Francesco De Sanctis (*Au*, 37). Croce's convictions at the time of his first philosophical engagement were described by him later as follows: he was "a De Sanctis idealist in aesthetics," "a Herbartian in ethics," "an anti-Hegelian and anti-metaphysician in the conception of history" and "a naturalist or intellectualist in epistemology" (*Au*, 91). In 1894 he wrote another short monograph, *Literary Criticism: Questions upon Theory*, in support of De Sanctis (*Au*, 55). It was published in 1895.

But in 1895 Croce under the influence of Labriola went through a Marxist phase, which brought him in closer touch with Hegel (*Au*, 92).[8] Emerging from Marxism, Croce returned to aesthetics [9] and made in 1899 his greatest systematic study of the subject, which resulted in the first draft of his treatise, entitled *Fundamental theses of an Aesthetic of Expression and General Linguistics* (*Au*, 63–65). This was printed in 1900 and is now known as the *Theses of Aesthetics*.[10] He then made a study of the history of aesthetics and in 1901 published a paper acknowledging Vico as its founder, on account of his conception of poetry as elementary cognition. This paper was absorbed in Chapter v of Part II of the final version of his treatise *Aesthetics as the Science of Expression and General Linguistics* which appeared in 1902. This famous book, which was to undergo further revisions, is usually referred to by its author and others as his "first *Aesthetic*." The second part of the book is a history of aesthetics, written according to principles which Croce had earlier discussed in a paper "Upon certain laws which govern the History of a Science" (1901).[11] We shall return to it in our last chapter.

In the *Aesthetic* Croce developed his theory of art as pure intuition, or as a cognitive process whose object is the individual and is distinct from the logical process which grasps the universal. This theory will be discussed in detail in the following chapters. Croce then extended his philosophical inquiries into logic and ethics, and came to grips finally with Hegel's philosophy in 1905 at the suggestion of Giovanni Gentile (*Au*, 93), a younger philosopher who in these years (1895 ff.) urged Croce in the direction of absolute idealism (cf. *Logica*, 227).[12] The result of this study was the famous critique of 1906, *What is alive and what is dead in the philosophy of Hegel* (*Au*, 97–98).

As the title indicates, this book performs a drastic operation upon the body of Hegel's system, which the Hegelians have never forgiven Croce. For him, "what is alive in Hegel" is his theory of philosophy as science of the concept and his concept of reality as development. "What is dead in Hegel" is his erroneous extension of the dialectic of opposites to things which

are not opposite but only distinct from each other (such as Art
and Philosophy) and the consequent triadic march of categories
to the absolute Idea. In his *Aesthetic* Croce had already rejected
Hegel's view of the Beautiful as the sensuous manifestation of
the Idea, as well as that of a theory of Art which was at the
same time a dialectical deduction of the history of art. He now
gave his general reasons for rejecting Hegel's a priori construction of the facts of experience, mercilessly lopping off the attendant "sciences" of Philosophy of Nature and Philosophy of
History. Indeed Hegel's whole construction is vitiated by what
Croce calls his "panlogism," or the translation of all human activities—including the practical and the aesthetic—into logical
terms, which Croce utterly rejects. So he could later claim that
his own philosophy, far from being Hegelianism, was "the most
complete overthrow" of that school of thought (*Au*, 100).

But on the other hand Croce preserved certain features of
Hegel's doctrine of the concept, or of thought as dealing
with the universal. Hence Croce's correlative rejection of all
conceptions of truth as an inductive generalization [13] or as a
practical instrument, as well as those that made it an object of
intellectual intuition or the revelation of a transcendent God.
He held firmly to the rigor of logical thinking by means of pure
concepts, and rejected empirical generalizations as based upon
an arbitrarily limited field of observation (cvm, 54–55) and resulting in what Croce calls "pseudo-concepts." [14] He found this
logical rigor in the works of the great classical philosophers from
Plato and Aristotle to Kant and Hegel. He did not find it in the
positivists and was not an admirer of J. S. Mill or H. Spencer.
He held that philosophy must have as its foundation the history
of philosophy, and that no philosophical problem could be
profitably discussed without relating it to its antecedents in the
classical philosophies (cvm, 15–16). Hence Croce's often-
avowed contempt for the improvisations of half-baked theorists,
such as the positivists, or of scientists and scholars who venture
upon philosophical questions ignoring the history of philosophy,
in the fond belief that thought begins with themselves.

At this point Croce's basic philosophical reasoning may be
summed up as follows. In order to understand history he found

it necessary to conceive the spirit of man as free, conscious and creative. And in order to establish a concept of man as free, conscious and creative, he found it necessary to adopt the logic of the concrete universal.[15] For Croce, the ultimate goal of philosophy was not to solve the riddle of the universe or to attain once and for all absolute Truth, but simply to provide an understanding of history or of the course of human events. There actually is, he believed, a "touchstone," an objective test, which enables us to determine the validity of a philosophy, and that is the question: "does it help us to understand history?" (CVM, 62). In so far as it does, it is true; in so far as it does not, it is false. From this one might formulate the principle of Croce's metaphysics (even though he disclaimed having one) as "the real is what is historically knowable."

So although Croce himself in his earlier period designated his philosophy as "idealism" (e.g., *Logica*, 186–87; CC, II, 355), it has peculiarities of its own which mark it off sharply from other idealistic systems. Its central concept is that spirit is realized only in history, or in ascertained and verifiable fact. In the rejection of a priori deduction and acceptance of the historical method, Croce may even be said to share common ground with positivism.[16] Although he fully acknowledged his debt to Hegel, Croce's aversion to orthodox Hegelianism was a permanent feature of his intellectual life.[17] It is symptomatic that he did not reach his conclusions through the traditional approaches of nineteenth-century idealism, which are epistemology and metaphysics. To metaphysics especially he was always averse and repeatedly gave his reasons for rejecting it.[18]

In the place of metaphysics or of a philosophy of nature we find in Croce a theory about the nature of scientific thought, which is another characteristic feature of his philosophy. He adopted the so-called "economic theory of science" which had been originally developed by scientists like Mach and Poincaré and which considers scientific concepts to be logical fictions produced for practical convenience.[19] So according to Croce the sciences of nature deal with fictions and abstractions, while concrete reality can only be reached through perception of the indi-

vidual fact, or historical knowledge. Only history provides us
with true knowledge, and philosophy is its foundation. Croce
was well aware that the originators of the "economic theory"
did not favor philosophic idealism, but he attached more weight
to their ideas on the method of the sciences than to their opinions
on philosophy, in which he did not consider them competent.[20]

While rejecting traditional metaphysics and epistemology,
Croce did rely to some extent upon the metaphysical and epistemological discussions of the great idealistic philosophers.[21] He
specifically relies upon Kant for his concept of the a priori
synthesis, which plays such a large part in Croce's philosophy
after 1908 (*Logica*, 153–61) and upon Hegel for the metaphysical interpretation of that concept (*Logica*, 322). But his critique
of Hegel's logic makes the dialectic of opposites subordinate to
the dialectic of "distincts," Croce's own conception of the life
of the spirit.[22] This conception (which we shall explain) was
worked out in the four volumes on aesthetics, logic, ethics and
historiography that make up the "Philosophy of Spirit." The
Logic was written in 1908 and published in 1909, and so was the
Philosophy of the Practical: Economics and Ethics; the *Theory
and Practice of Historiography* was added in 1917. Being written over a period of 15 years (1902–17), these volumes sometimes present different stages of thought in the discussion of the
same problems. The outline which we will now give of Croce's
system is therefore inevitably something of a simplification of a
complex and developing train of thought.

For Croce the activity of mind takes two basic forms: cognition and volition or theory and practice; knowing what the
world is like or taking action to introduce an alteration in it.
This distinction is fundamental and irreducible. Croce has been
sometimes criticized for not giving the logical grounds for this
distinction. In his earliest statements on it, he simply took it for
granted as a matter of common sense. In his later statements,
Croce would argue that Spirit is unity, but unity involves distinction, just as distinction implies unity; so both cognition and
volition are forms of the one Spirit, but at the same time irreducible to each other.[23] In his recognition of will as a distinct

spiritual activity, equal in status to thought, Croce differs from most idealistic systems, and from Hegel's in particular. Idealists like Hegel and Gentile make Thought or the Idea the supreme and all-embracing form of reality. The problems of practical action—of politics, economics, the law and the state—are interpreted by them solely in terms of logic. Croce believed on the contrary (and it does seem a matter of common sense) that there is a whole sphere of conscious activity, the practical or volitional, to which the rules and processes of logic do not apply and which can only be formulated in its own terms. These terms are emotion, feeling, passion, impulse, effort, volition, decision, choice, aim, goal, etc.; all that leads up to action and is connected with it. Feeling is not for Croce, as it is for some philosophers, a third form of mental activity, distinct from thought and action, but is included wholly in the sphere of the "practical." [24]

Just as there is a distinction in the sphere of theory between logical thought and intuition, there is a similar distinction in the sphere of the practical. Volition, too, can be directed either toward the particular or toward the universal. In the latter case it constitutes ethical action; in the former, it is purely economic, political or utilitarian action. The volition of the particular constitutes for Croce a single and autonomous sphere of spiritual activity, to which all passions, impulses, and what other philosophers might call self-regarding actions are assigned. He calls it, in a broad sense, "economic" (a by-product of Croce's discussion of Marxism). This represents another distinctive doctrine of Croce's, to which he gave increasing developments in his latest speculations.

In addition to the aesthetic there are therefore three other forms of spiritual activity for Croce: the logical, the "economic" and the ethical. Each arises upon the foundation of its antecedent in the order given. Having reached the last form, spirit then returns to the first: action, once completed, becomes the object of thought. So the system of forms moves with a circular motion, each form arising upon its antecedent [25] and becoming the condition and the material of its successor. [26] None is actually first and none is last (NSE², 304): there is no primacy of thought over action or of action over thought, no supremacy of logic and no "aesthetic primitivism." [27] The four forms are coexistent and correlative in their distinction, which is not separation. This is the dialectic of "distincts" which Croce substituted for the Hegelian dialectic of opposites, while incorporating some of its features.[28]

The forms of spirit also determine the different branches of historical inquiry. As Croce now saw it, this inquiry aims ultimately at assigning a particular event to the sphere of spiritual activity to which it belongs. Hence there are as many branches of history as there are spiritual forms (*Logica*, 209). And as the forms are distinct from each other and not to be confused with each other, so the kinds of history must also be carefully kept distinct from each other: the history of art must be kept distinct from the history of thought and from the history of political or economic action, and so on. Each branch of history interprets its own set of facts according to its own basic principle, as action or as thought, directed either toward the particular or toward the universal, and does not invade the limits of the other branches. Strictness in following and enforcing this principle is an outstanding feature of Croce's critical method.

Croce's *Logic*, where these arguments are developed, may therefore be considered in its essence a general theory of the humanities. He there comes to the conclusion that history is the most complete form of knowledge, as the synthesis of the particular with the universal. In keeping with his view about the "touchstone" of philosophy, Croce argued that all philosophies arise to solve intellectual problems presented by particular historical situations, and find their consummation in the light they throw upon these situations. This leads to another characteristic doctrine, viz. that philosophy is in the last analysis the methodology of history, or a systematization of general principles to solve specific problems of historical inquiry (TSS, 135). Since there is no end to historical problems, there is likewise no end to the systematizations of philosophy. Each systematization is provisional,[29] conditioned by its specific historical problem, and there is no final system, no immutable body of doctrines, no "eternal philosophy."

In this view Croce found an answer to the conflicting claims of absolutism and relativism. This answer involves the denial of the existence of a single, fundamental problem of philosophy, which can be solved once and for all, thus rendering all future thinking unnecessary (or which is never solved, thus rendering all philosophy futile).[30] Such a theory is held by idealists who identify the fundamental problem of philosophy with the problem of the relation between thought and reality or between the subject and the object. But for Croce the number of philosophical problems is unlimited and philosophical inquiry never ends. On the other hand, philosophy is a science; it does provide a solution to its problems, and the solution to each problem is final—for that problem, and for that problem only. "Every philosophy is final for the present problem which it solves, but not for that which arises immediately afterwards and for others that will arise from that one" (TSS, 143).

To this view Croce sacrificed without compunction his own history of aesthetics, which forms the second and longer part of his treatise of 1902. This history related the progressive solution of the fundamental problem of aesthetics, which was finally achieved by Croce's own doctrine.[31] He now rejected this view and replaced it by the conception of innumerable particular problems of aesthetics, each thinker to be discussed in terms of his own problem or problems and not in terms of later problems and solutions (NSE², 112; *Discorsi*, II, 102–3).[32] On similar grounds Croce rejected all closed systems of philosophy, like Hegel's, and maintained the "nondefinitive character of philosophy." [33] This doctrine cannot be refuted by saying that it presents itself as a final philosophy, since it is final only for the particular problem that it solves, viz. the problem of the "definitive" character of philosophy.[34] According to Croce, "life"—i.e., the events of social and political history and the ever new developments in art and in poetry—will always provide fresh problems for history and therefore for philosophy.[35]

And indeed as long as he lived Croce was stimulated by new events to ask new questions and to find solutions to them. No sooner had he completed his "system" (or "systematization") than he began tinkering with it. It is not the purpose, however, of this book to follow the full development of his philosophy, but only of his aesthetics and criticism. We will add that in the later stages of his thought Croce's aversion to closed systems led him to abandon even the designation of "idealism" for his own philosophy. Instead, he preferred "historicism." [36]

What has been given above is merely the skeleton of Croce's philosophy. We have had to omit the arguments, the historical and literary illustrations, as well as the epigrams and historical anecdotes which abound in Croce's philosophical books. The complete system provided him with various insights into the more complicated workings of the human spirit, of which he made good use in his many judgments on men, movements and books. The independence of the sphere of art was defended by him all the more effectively since he had provided a proper sphere for every other kind of activity. If philosophy was excluded from art, it could reside in a substantial mansion of its own with several divisions: the system of philosophical sciences, aesthetics, logic, economics, ethics and historiography. If moral ideals were denied rule over poetry, they were shown to rule over the whole course of the history of civilization, or what Croce later called "ethico-political history," giving remarkable specimens of it in his *History of the Kingdom of Naples* (1925), his *History of Italy from 1871 to 1915* (1928), and his *History of Europe in the 19th Century* (1932).[37] For although devoted to aesthetics, Croce never was an aesthete. He never identified art with life. The philosophy of the distinct forms of spirit is reflected in his work by a balanced discrimination of all kinds of men—poets and philosophers, critics and scholars, heroes and adventurers, men of thought and men of action, saints and sinners—each judged on his own merits and assigned his rank in the cosmos of history.[38]

We shall now trace in detail the various stages of Croce's aesthetic philosophy, beginning with the basic concept of his first aesthetic: the theory of art as pure intuition or the aesthetic image.

CHAPTER ii

The Aesthetic Image

THE FIRST PHASE of Croce's thought, as expounded in the *Aesthetic* of 1902, centers in the theory of the aesthetic image, or pure intuition. Croce's contention here is that all creative literature—indeed, all art—consists in the production of an image. The image is not to be identified with the figures of traditional rhetoric, but it is the whole poem, or the whole work, conceived as a single picture which brings together many details into a complex unit. What this unit is, what mental processes are involved in its production, reproduction and evaluation, and what relations it has with other mental processes, are the main problems of Croce's aesthetics.

The conclusions he arrived at in his first treatise are summarized in the opening sentences of the book: "Knowledge has two forms: it is either intuitive knowledge or logical knowledge; knowledge by means of the imagination or knowledge by means of the intellect; knowledge of the individual or knowledge of the universal; of single things or of their relations; it is, in brief, productive either of images or of concepts" (E, 3; A, 1). To analyze these conclusions, let us see first what are images and then what are intuitions.

AN IMAGE for Croce is a mental picture of something concrete and specific, of a particular object or an individual person. Its material is drawn either from what are called "sense data" or from "inner experience." It is drawn ultimately from sense data

24

when it is a picture like the vivid ones that we find in Coleridge's *Rhyme of the Ancient Mariner:*

> . . . Beyond the shadow of the ship
> I watched the water-snakes:
> They moved in tracks of shining white
> And when they reared, the elfish light
> Fell off in hoary flakes.

This is all light and color, movement and action: no abstraction or generalization, but a picture of something happening in the world of sense and motion.

On the other hand, an image may be drawn from "inner experience" when it is the presentation of a mood or the expression of a feeling. Emotions are as concrete as sensations, but they may be expressed by words which grammarians classify as abstract nouns. For instance, T. S. Eliot says in *Burnt Norton:*

> What might have been is an abstraction
> Remaining a perpetual possibility
> Only in the world of speculation.

Here the language is almost completely abstract; there is even the word "abstraction" itself. But this does not make the passage a piece of reasoning; it is rather the expression of a mood, felt by an individual poet in a particular situation. The abstract terms become concrete when they are part of a poem: they convey an image. It is the context, or the whole unit of expression, that determines the function of the words used (*PdE*, 155).

Now images, so defined, are not merely the ornaments of poetry, "like cherries on a cake"; [1] they are the stuff and substance of poetry. They are also the stuff and substance of all other imaginative literature, including fiction and the drama. The characters of fiction and of drama are individuals: their presentation is an image. The idea we form of Clytemnestra or of Othello, of Francesca da Rimini or Madame Bovary, of Uncle Toby or Mr. Pickwick, is for Croce a poetic image just as much as a vivid metaphor in a poem. But also the whole work in which the character appears is an image, for it is a single, unified and individual presentation. "Unified" means for Croce that several

minor images are included in it: "What is known as an image is always a tissue of images" (NSE, 29; EA, 32). A long work of literature is a synthesis of many secondary images, some of which have an identifiable provenance: "He who conceives a tragedy pours into the crucible, so to speak, a large variety of impressions: even the expressions produced on previous occasions are fused together with the new ones into a single mass, in the same way as one may cast into a smelting furnace both formless pieces of bronze and elegant statuettes" (E, 24; A, 20). So works like the *Divine Comedy* or *Hamlet, Paradise Lost* or *Faust,* if we believe in their artistic unity, are to be seen as single images, admittedly of great richness and complexity, but still radiating from one center and forming one picture. The fact that many images unite to form a single image is a basic principle of Croce's aesthetic, and we shall often have occasion to refer to it. For reasons of convenience we will call it henceforth "the principle of Integration."

It may here be objected that there is more to a play and to a novel than the portrayal of individual character, important as that is. There is such a thing as plot, or the relation in which the various characters stand to each other, presented in a succession of situations that develop to a climax. There are therefore such things as construction, perspective, atmosphere, tension, visual angle, setting, dialogue, and so forth, through all their technical divisions and subdivisions.

Let us take plot first as perhaps the most important. If it is admitted that each of the characters of a play or a novel is an individual, then the relations in which the characters stand to each other are also something individual and particular, concrete and specific, and so they also constitute a poetic image. For instance, the relationship of Madame Bovary to her husband and to her lovers is something as particularized and as unique as Madame Bovary herself. No one else before her got into just such a tangle of emotions. Therefore the plot, with all its subdivisions of situation, complication, climax and catastrophe, and all its appurtenances of atmosphere, setting, visual angle, etc., is also on the whole an image, a single concrete and particularized picture. We shall return to this in Chapter IV.

It may be objected that a great novel includes a number of abstract and general ideas: psychological observations, analyses of characters and motives, even philosophical reflections. But if these observations and reflections tend to carry the plot forward, they are also part of the image, and the fact that they are expressed in abstract terms does not invalidate this, for as we have seen abstract terms become concrete in concrete contexts. Or it may be objected that fiction and the drama include dialogue, which is an art in itself. To invent appropriate dialogue for imaginary individuals is certainly a difficult task, but no more difficult than to invent an imaginary individual, complete in all significant detail. His (or her) speeches must present the concrete reality of that character in the shape of conversational utterance. To find adequate words for this may be one of the most exacting feats of the creative imagination. But the feat still consists of bringing out specific traits of a concrete individual. It is still image making.

At this point it may be asked: What is there to be gained from the knowledge that all the various stages and processes of literary composition are at bottom only a single process, that of making images? We already know these methods by various names, such as invention, construction, character portrayal, art of dialogue, etc. What is the advantage of calling them all by a single name? The answer is of course that little will be gained if it is only a change of name. But much will be gained if there is a corresponding change in thinking, i.e. if we learn to look at what is individual in the work of art. In general, the advantage of reducing all processes to one by logical analysis is that of getting down to what is basic, fundamental and indispensable—in other words, of defining the philosophical concept or concrete universal of art. This advantage will become apparent in the help it gives us for practical criticism and for the solution of such general questions as: what is the relation of poetry to truth? what is the function of the intellect in poetic creation? is the poetic image a symbol or a sign? what is the place of art in human society? etc. In this way we are laying the foundations of what will be a genuine science of literature —not a science in the naturalistic or positivistic sense, but in the philosophical sense of a body of organized knowledge, a system of principles and of applications. This is why Croce did not hesitate, as some moderns do owing to what Croce calls "the superstition of natural science" (E, 71; A, 63), to call his aesthetic theory a science, viz. the "science of expression."

IN THE OPENING PARAGRAPH of the *Aesthetic*, quoted above, Croce speaks of the image as a form of knowledge which he also calls intuitive knowledge. Now the faculty by which images are produced is usually called imagination, a term also employed by Croce. Why does he then bring in intuition, as he calls it henceforth? We reach here a point in which we can see some of the deeper implications of the term "image" as used by Croce. These implications may be summed up in the following three propositions: 1) art is a form of spiritual activity; 2) it is specifically a cognitive activity 3) consisting in the cognition of the particular as such.

Let us take the first proposition. By it Croce means that art is a part of the general process through which man acquires consciousness of himself. "Spirit" implies self-consciousness, the absolutely free and spontaneous act by which mind makes itself its own object and becomes aware of its operations and of their results. In this process, mind first acquires consciousness of its energy in the form of a dark ocean of tumultuous impulses, which are made objective in the bright visions of art and of poetry. As these visions are the creations of a power active in all forms of consciousness, they possess universal value. To say therefore that art is a spiritual activity is not only to make it indispensable to any way of life that aims at the full development of the human personality, but also accounts for its being acknowledged one of the great civilizing forces of history.

But what, if anything, lies below or beyond consciousness?

In the first *Aesthetic* Croce answered: "On the hither side of the lower limit of intuition we find sensation, which our spirit can never grasp in itself as mere matter. This it possesses only in form and with form, but postulates the notion of it as a mere limit. Matter, in its abstraction, is mechanism and passivity; it is what the spirit of man suffers, but does not produce. Without matter no human knowledge or activity would be possible: but mere matter gives us animality, what is brutal and impulsive in man, not the spiritual domain which constitutes humanity" (E, 8; A, 5–6). This is one of the traces of what Croce later called his "early Kantianism" (*Au*, 95), for the notion of matter as a "mere limit" recalls Kant's "limiting concepts." [2] Shortly afterwards Croce abandoned this view for a more completely idealistic view of sensation, which we shall see later in this chapter.

The second proposition listed above states that art in general, and poetry in particular, is a kind of knowledge. What kind of knowledge is specified in the third proposition. But it may be seen at once that to conceive art as a theoretical activity is to exclude it from the sphere of action and of all conative impulses, of will, desire, passion and emotion. And this not because art is too noble or too pure, but simply because of its essentially cognitive function. Art presents a picture and does not further an aim. The sphere of the practical mind includes all activities which aim at changing real conditions in the world, viz. all forms of economic, political and ethical activity. To create a work of art—specifically, a poem—is not to alter any of the social or economic conditions of mankind, but only to gain a certain kind of insight. Art builds up a pattern of relationships (i.e. an image) that have existence only in the mind that contemplates them, and have no meaning whatever as practical values.

Of course the insight provided by a work of art may be of absorbing interest to its possessor, it may arouse all his energies and call for the complete dedication of the artist to his task, and the vision obtained may induce deep spiritual satisfaction in him and in others who share it. But this is also true of other forms of knowledge, such as the intellectual vision obtained through philosophy or history. Like these forms of knowledge, art may have important consequences in the life of man. But, like them, it will not directly achieve any practical aim. An editorial full of clichés may influence an election more than a specimen of perfect prose; a blustering speech full of repetitions and crudities may provoke a crowd to action in a way a good poem never will; a garish advertising poster may influence people to spend their money more effectively than the *Virgin of the Rocks*. But art is essentially an "ideal" activity. And by "ideal" Croce does not mean "absolutely perfect" or "beyond this world," but simply "theoretical," existing primarily in the mind as a form of awareness.[3]

To the upholders of the social significance of art, who may be loath to acknowledge such a purely theoretical function for it, one can point out that according to Croce society needs purely theoretical activities for its very existence. Such activities should be pursued for their own sake and not for the eventual benefits that may accrue from them. Otherwise there is the danger of a predetermined conclusion being imposed upon an investigator, be he in search of truth or of beauty, be he an artist or a scientist or a philosopher or a "social thinker." Just as there can be for Croce no predetermined conclusions to intellectual inquiry, so there can be no predetermined contents or forms imposed upon the artist.

Finally, the third proposition states that art is knowledge of the individual and not of the universal. This means that poetry does not deal primarily or directly with concepts or abstractions, but with presentations of concrete images of individual reality, such as we have seen in our discussion of the question: "what is an image?" Therefore all art, including poetry, is not a doctrine or a philosophy, nor does it convey a doctrine or a philosophy. In fact poetry according to Croce does not make statements of any kind. It does not make statements of principle and it does not make statements of fact. It simply provides the picture of something individual in all its concreteness, and does not make any assertion about its reality or unreality. It is a vision which bears evidence only to itself and not to any external fact.[4]

When Coleridge wrote "The lightning fell with never a jag," he was not recording meteorological observations or contributing to the scientific study of electric storms. He may of course have seen sometime such flashes of lightning in a real sky, but even if he did not it makes no difference to the truth of the image. For he does see such a storm in his imagination, and sees it so vividly that he is able to convey it to us and that we see it too. That is the truth, and all the truth that is contained in a poetic image: its integrity of vision.

It may be objected that while the *Rhyme of the Ancient Mariner* does not contribute anything to science, it does contribute something to ethics, for it ends with a statement about God's love for His creatures, enjoining the reader to follow His example. This is true, but that statement is part of the speech of the Ancient Mariner, i.e. of a poetic character, and therefore part of the image in which that character consists.

Not only poetry, but all imaginative literature results from a spiritual activity which produces an individualized image, or the cognition of a particular. This activity Croce calls by the name of "intuition," so that intuition and image for him are synonymous. Some readers are puzzled by the use of the term "intuition," which usually has a different meaning in English. Why should the image-making process be called intuition? We shall try to answer this question in the following section.

THE WORD "INTUITION" is often used colloquially for "the instinctive knowledge of a fact," "instinctive" meaning "immediate" and "without reason or evidence." But for Croce intuition, as we have seen, is not the statement of a fact. In philosophy the term has often the meaning of "knowledge of self-evident truths," such as the axioms of mathematics, for which no reason can be given but which are indubitably true. This may be called Cartesian intuition,[5] and it is certainly not Croce's, for his "intuition" is not the statement of a truth, indeed it is not a statement at all. So some English readers have complained that "Croce's intuition is entirely different from what is called intuition in everyday talk." [6] But the term has a place, and a distinguished one, in the history of English criticism.

This is due to the fact that the term has another meaning in philosophy, which may be called the Kantian meaning, since it is to be found in Kant. In German it is represented by the word *Anschauung*, which has, as we shall see, no exact correspondent in English. The definition of *Anschauung* in a German philosophical dictionary is as follows: "the immediate cognition of a concrete object in its determinations of space and time." [7] This broadly corresponds to Croce's *intuizione*. Croce himself gives as instances of intuitions a landscape in a painting or the outline of a country on a map (E, 4; A, 2). We may take a still more familiar example, the desk upon which I am now writing. It is, as the German definition has it, a concrete object, it has a determinate location in space and in time, and it is the object of a kind of knowledge. In English one would not call that knowledge an intuition, but in the terminology of classical German philosophy it is an *Anschauung*.

If it is asked "why not use the word *perception* for that kind of knowledge, the immediate cognition of a concrete object?", the answer is that perception implies the presence of the object, whereas the cognition of the desk can remain in the mind, even in the absence of its object, as a memory. Perception also implies the reality of the object perceived, whereas we can form in our minds the idea of a concrete object such as a desk which has no real existence. This imaginary desk may possess a specific color, shape, weight, hardness, volume and other concrete qualities, to the extent that a sketch or a description may be made of it, and a real one constructed on that model. So even the picture of an imaginary object may be a perfectly good intuition, as long as it is particularized and concrete. Coleridge's *Rhyme*, in fact, presents us with several striking instances of such purely imaginary objects. Then why not speak of an "idea," as we have done above? Because the word "idea" has had too many different meanings attached to it in the course of two thousand years of philosophical speculation. Another term, somewhat less vague and equivocal, is needed. This has been recognized repeatedly by English philosophers, whom we shall quote in a minute. But first let us note that, in spite of its apparent unfamiliarity, the Kantian meaning of intuition is so far from being unknown in philosophy, that the French philosophical dictionary of Lalande concludes its discussion of the various uses of the term "intuition" by recommending the Kantian meaning as the only one to be given to the term, using "evidence" or some other word for the Cartesian meaning.[8]

Indeed the term has been used in the Kantian meaning by a number of philosophical writers in English. For one, it was used as meaning "knowledge of the individual" by John Dewey in his early textbook on *Psychology* (1891) and defended by him as the sole legitimate meaning.[9] Even earlier it was used in a very similar way in a classic of English criticism by Coleridge who found precedents for it in English theology and claimed credit for having revived it: "I have restored the words, *intuition* and *intuitive*, to their original sense—'an intuition,' says Hooker, 'that is, a direct or immediate beholding or presentation of an object to the mind through the senses or the imagination.'"[10]

So there is very good precedent in English for the use of "intuition" in Croce's sense. However the contact with Kant and with German thought which was close in Coleridge became looser during the course of the century, and so not long after him we find an erudite philosopher, Sir W. Hamilton, discussing the difficulty of rendering *Anschauung* in English, in a passage that anticipates much of what we have had to say for Croce: "We are, likewise, in want of a general term to express what is common to the presentations of Perception, and the representations of Phantasy, that is, their individuality and immediacy. The Germans express this by the term *Anschauung*, which can only be translated by *intuition* (as it is in Latin by Germans), which literally means *a looking at*. This expression has, however, been preoccupied in English to denote the apprehension we have of self-evident truths, and its application in a different sense would therefore be, to a certain extent, liable to ambiguity."[11] Hamilton himself suggested the use of "representation" for "the immediate object, or product, of Imagination," but he acknowledged that the word had already acquired a more specialized meaning. The translation of the term *Anschauung* is discussed by the English interpreters of Kant, who suggest one or the other of the already cited English terms as its representative.[12] But there does not seem to be any general agreement.[13]

Since there is no satisfactory English equivalent, we will continue to use "intuition," as the translators of Croce have done up to now.[14] But the above discussion should make it clear, once and for all, that Croce uses the term for the *cognition of the individual as such*, and not for "the apprehension of self-evident truth." For "intuition" in the sense of the *immediate awareness of a philosophical truth*, Croce makes use of a convenient Italian synonym, viz. *intúito*, and he has discussed that form of apprehension in a paper entirely separate from the *Aesthetic* (cvm, 217–22; cf. *Logica*, 89).

Another ambiguity has been found in this term; it may designate both the process and the result of an act of intuition: "it is no longer clear whether intuition, as a term or concept, designates the epistemological faculty of intuiting, or the object intuited by this faculty." [15] We must begin by setting aside the term "faculty," which is not Croce's, since it belongs to a psychological theory, the doctrine of the faculties of the mind, which Croce rejects.[16] Croce's term is "form of spiritual activity."

Now if it is claimed that Croce has created ambiguity in a previously unequivocal term, the answer is that the term has always had those two meanings and they have been used interchangeably. It is a fact that this is true not only of "intuition," but of all similar terms relating to the imagination and the fancy. Even of Aristotle's term *phantasia* it has been observed that it "is used by Aristotle to mean both the faculty of imagination and the product of imagination." And so also for Kant's use of *Anschauung*. This fact was also observed by that unsuspected predecessor of Croce, Coleridge, in a remarkable passage: "I have followed Hooker, Sanderson, Milton, &c., in designating the *immediateness* of any act or object of knowledge by the word *intuition*, used sometimes subjectively, sometimes objectively, even as we use the word *thought*, now as *the* thought, or act of thinking, and now as *a* thought, or the object of our reflection; and we do this without confusion or obscurity." [17]

Nor is this a case of ambiguity peculiar to philosophers. It is instead an instance of a regular linguistic shift of meaning, which affects not only philosophical terms like *intuition* or *imagination*, but a host of common English words, innocent of any philosophical intention, including such familiar words as "work" and "play." This shift was observed by I. A. Richards, who called it the "part-whole shift" and gave as an instance the common word "addition." It may mean a process, as in "addition is easier than multiplication," and it may also mean "what is added": "the porch was a later addition." [18]

And finally it may well be asked: what difference does it make to the theory of intuition whether the term is taken to indicate the process or its object? The process of intuition, as Croce has defined it, is the act by which an image is formed. The image is a mental picture which exists only when so produced, and the process is enacted only for the sake of producing the picture: neither exists without the other, and the object, as Hamilton noted, is also the product. However the distinction between the two meanings becomes necessary whenever there is a tendency to take one of the two without the other. For instance, if a philosopher discusses the aesthetic process without ever giving an instance of it, it is well to remind him that the process involves a product, and if he is really able to define the art process, he should be able to select some instance of its products from the storehouse of world history. On the other hand, if there is a tendency to take the image by itself as something existing independently of the imagination that produced it, it will be well to call attention back to the producing process, or the imagination. The well-known fallacy of discussing dramatic characters like Shakespeare's as if they were real people arises out of this tendency, and so does the idea of speech or language existing independently of the speaker and of all speakers.

In discussions to which we shall come later, in Chapter xi,

it will also be necessary to stress that the object of intuition is the particular, while the act itself, or the process, is universal. In other words, intuition is not a purely private affair, it is a universally human process. What one man has intuited (if we may use ourselves the verb "to intuit") any other man will be able to intuit. This is what is often spoken of as the universal character of art, its appeal to men of all times and of all countries. The organization which the particular content receives from the unifying power of the imagination makes it permanently accessible to all men. So the Homeric poems and the lyrics of a Sappho are still things of beauty today, even though the experience which is the content of their verse belongs to dead centuries and bygone societies.

THE INTEGRITY of the aesthetic intuition, however, is challenged by two powerful opponents: traditional epistemology and traditional logic. For traditional epistemology the aesthetic intuition possesses no real unity: it is merely an aggregate of sensations, or of memories of sensations. It will be recollected that in our own discussion of intuition we spoke of it as drawing its material ultimately from sensations. But this was given only as the traditional view, not as the last word on the subject. The traditional view was still held to a certain extent by Croce when he wrote the earliest version of his *Aesthetic*. But it implies an empirical or realistic theory of knowledge which he soon afterwards abandoned. In Croce's later view the ultimate unit of knowledge is the intuition, and the so-called sensations and impressions are *ex post facto* dissections of this unit, or mutilated fragments of the original act of awareness. Whoever in actual experience sees only a single color or hears only a single sound? Single colors and single sounds are deliberately cut out from the rich and complex whole with which experience provides us, or what is called *Gestalt* in modern psychology.

Even assuming that there are impressions and ideas which the poet receives completely from the outside, yet the poet must add something to them which was not there before: he must produce at least the *link* that connects the pre-existing elements, the *nexus* that binds them into a whole. But the whole is an individual, that is to say something which cannot be further analyzed without destroying it. When the so-called pre-existing elements are so brought together, they are no longer the same: they become details of a new picture and are themselves created anew in that relationship. So that the poet is actually the creator both of the parts and of the whole.

At this point the connection, which Croce stressed, between belief in the creative imagination and a philosophical view of mind as active and productive becomes apparent. It is not intended to go further into this question which would require a much fuller discussion, but it may be of interest to see the theory of sensation held by Croce affirmed in the words of a modern physicist, Hermann Weyl: "Consciousness reacts with an entirety that is not merely a mosaic composed of sensations; on the contrary, these so-called sensual data are a subsequent abstraction. The assertion, that they alone are actually given and the rest is derivative, is not a description that carefully pictures what is given in its full complexity, but rather a realistic theory arising from a realistic conviction that 'only sensations can be given.' " [19]

But the integrity of the poetic image is also challenged by another powerful opponent, traditional logic. There is a view of long-standing in logic that the individual (i.e. particular) is merely the sum of abstract qualities, an aggregate of general concepts. This is based on the Aristotelian belief that true knowledge is only of universals or of general ideas, so that there can be no knowledge of the individual as such. All we can know are the qualities of which an individual is possessed, and those qualities are universals. The individual as such remains beyond the reach of knowledge, an unfathomable mystery, an inexpressible reality. We may perhaps refute this view by asking what are universals? According to this view, they are the common element that we may discern in a number of single instances. But if this act of discernment is to be valid, it must be based on valid knowledge of the single instances, i.e. of individuals. So there must be knowledge of the individuals as such. Now this knowledge of the individuals as such is, as we have seen, what Croce designates as intuition.

So for Croce it is not true that the individual can never be known as such. The reverse is true: the individual is known all the time, and is the object of intuitions which we are continually making. Croce replaces the traditional view that the individual is something ineffable, something inexpressible, by the view that *only* the individual is expressible or effable: *solum individuum effabile* (NSE, 81; EA, 93).

In an ulterior stage of reflection the individual represented by the intuition becomes (as we have seen in Chapter I) the object of another form of knowledge, which is perception or the awareness of something as real. This is effected by the introduction of the concepts of real and unreal, existent and nonexistent. Through these concepts we reach the level of historical knowledge, as Croce defined it in his first *Aesthetic* (E, 32; A, 28): the individual is not only seen in all its particularity, but also discriminated as to its existence or nonexistence. For instance, Iago is a fully particularized individual but fictitious, whereas Alcibiades is also fully particularized, but he really existed. This judgment involves the use of concepts which are entirely absent from intuition. The image, as we have seen, makes no assertion as to its reality or unreality. "The poet," as Sidney said, "nothing affirmes and therefore never lyeth." [20]

Croce now puts this more abstractly, in a proposition which calls for further elucidation: "intuition is the undifferentiated unity of the real and the simple image of the possible" (E, 6; A, 4). This means that perception has something in common with the ideas that we have of objects which do not exist but are only possible, and that is the concrete mental picture or intuition. This is the positive side of the "unity of the real and the possible." But this unity has also a negative side: it is undifferentiated. This aspect of art is often noted by critics who praise imaginative creations because they seem to be neither completely real nor completely unreal, but something in between. As Alexander said, "the artist and the spectator do not ask if the Hermes is really alive, they raise no question of true or false: they see it so." Or to take an example from literary criticism, here is how M. Baring praises the heroine of Tolstoy's *War and Peace:* "There is nowhere in literature . . . a more vital and charming personality than Natasha; a creation as living as Pushkin's Tatiana, and alive with a reality even more convincing than Turgenev's pictures of women, since she is alive with a different kind of life; the difference being that while you have read in Turgenev's books about noble and exquisite women, you are not sure whether you have not known Natasha yourself and in your own life; you are not sure she does not belong to the borderland of your past in which dreams and reality are mingled." [21] "The borderland in which dreams and reality mingle" is what Croce means by "the undifferentiated unity of the real and the possible." Artistic intuition is therefore what Croce calls "pure" intuition, i.e. an intuition which is not categorized, not interpreted by the intervention of a concept or category, such as *real* and *unreal*, and—we may add—*good* or *bad*. Its truth or untruth, goodness or badness, lie solely in its being (or not being) genuinely itself, a pure intuition.

In his contention that the imagination presents the fully particularized individual, Croce is far from being alone among the critics. Setting aside for the time being Croce's Italian predecessors, like Vico and De Sanctis, one may refer to what G. Santayana said in 1896 on this subject: "the great characters of poetry—a Hamlet, a Don Quijote, an Achilles—are no averages, they are not even a collection of salient traits common to certain classes of men. They seem to be persons—that is, their actions and words seem to spring from the inward nature of an individual soul. Goethe is reported to have said that he conceived the character of his Gretchen entirely without observation of originals. And, indeed, he would probably not have found any. His creation rather is the original to which we may occasionally think we see some likeness in real maidens." [22] When we have reached the point that Santayana attained in that statement, the view of the individual as the sum of qualities has been completely abandoned. If critics still return to it, it is through forgetting De Sanctis and Santayana and Croce, and slipping back into acceptance of the traditional opinion.

This whole discussion may appear to be a purely abstract argument, but it has an important bearing on the practical issues of criticism. For if we accept the theory of poetry as pure intuition we do away, once and for all, with the Didactic Heresy, the Biographical Heresy, and the Realistic Heresy. Croce's doctrine comes in this way to support some of the basic assumptions of contemporary criticism. And he has put his theories to very practical use by rejecting such things as the didactic interpretation of the *Divine Comedy*, the biographical criticism of Goethe and the psychological analysis of Shakespeare's characters as if they were real people (this in 1919, long before the present reaction to Bradley had set in).

The Didactic Heresy still flourishes among scholars who are accustomed to move in the region of general ideas relating to religion, philosophy or sociology. These scholars are naturally reluctant to conceive a mental sphere from which the general ideas which are their daily pasture are completely eliminated and where pure unadulterated individuality, which seems to them the most slippery and elusive thing in the world, reigns supreme. They feel that art must possess intellectual content of some sort—perhaps not in purely abstract form, but in some other, intermediate form. But if these critics are asked: "Intermediate between general ideas *and what?*" they can only come up with some recognition of imagination, or of "the music of verse" or of "sensuous imagery"—in other words, of intuition—as the point of reference at the other end of the scale. But they hold that imagination should be strictly governed by general ideas and be guided by "judgment." [23] These critics should try the experiment of considering pure imagination as the very essence of poetry. There is good precedent for it. Even Dante drew a sharp distinction between concept and image, and ascribed poetic beauty only to the latter—i.e., to the sensuous shape, the poetic vehicle of verse and rhyme and stanza and canzone, which can be appreciated even by readers who miss the underlying concept:

> Give heed at least how beautiful I am! [24]

There is a somewhat similar attitude in critics with a very different tendency who accept wholeheartedly the idea of poetry as pure image, but would limit it to modern poetry. For these critics, only contemporary writing can be "pure poetry"; all previous literature—all writing anterior to Baudelaire, according to the French version of this theory—is more or less intellectualized or didactic, and romantic poetry blurs its images because it is over-emotional. Critics with this tendency should try a different experiment: they should look for pure poetry in the great literature of the past, and try to see *The Faerie Queene* or *Paradise Lost* as a pure image, or group of images, as Croce saw the *Orlando Furioso* and the *Jerusalem Delivered*. In the process they might, of course, come across some complex amalgams of poetry and intellectual elements, as Croce did in the *Divine Comedy* and in *Faust*. But he still was able to show the essence of their poetry in a clear nucleus of pure images in each.

Croce's criticism of the older poems met with opposition at the other end of the line, from historical scholars who made the often-urged claim that the poetry of the past must be judged by the standards of the past, and not by some modern theory. This is a claim which runs into serious logical difficulties: is the claim itself based upon a standard of the past? Of course it is not, being based upon the modern historical approach. But if the claim is not based upon a standard of the past, it fails to meet its own requirement. Croce has repeatedly answered this "historical" objection, pointing out the fallacies it involves, as we shall see in Chapter VII.

Critics who believe in the intellectual function of poetry insist that general ideas are to be found in poems and point out maxims, propositions and concepts occurring in masterpieces of poetic art. Croce does not deny the fact, but argues that concepts then become integral parts of an image and are in effect no longer universals but particulars: "Philosophical generaliza-tions placed in the mouth of a character in a play do not perform there the function of concepts, but of characteristics of the speaker. In the same way, the color red on a figure in a painting is not there as the concept a physicist has of the color red, but as a characteristic trait of the figure. The whole is that which determines the quality of the parts" (E, 4–5; A, 2). The last sen-tence is an explicit formulation of the principle of organic unity, which is one of the guiding concepts of Croce's thinking. We shall meet it again in the following section and in the following chapter.

THE NEXT STEP in Croce's theory of the aesthetic image is its identification with expression. A fully formed poetic image is a verbalized image, set out in its appropriate words in their ap-propriate order, neither the words nor the order being de-terminable in advance. In a poem or a novel multiple impressions are unified in a single concrete image—and an image is not concrete until it is expressed in words (or in colors, lines, masses or tones). In Croce's terms, the particular is not only the ob-ject of an act of cognition: it is also, and at the same time, the object of an act of expression, and the two acts are one.[25]

Stated in such categorical terms, this identification often arouses opposition. It seems possible that thought and expres-sion may occasionally blend so perfectly as to be in effect one; but it also seems that thought more frequently does not reach such complete unity with expression and falls more or less short of it. This objection is really an admission, for Croce does not affirm that all and any intuitions are identical with expressions, but only perfectly realized ones. There are many that never come quite through, and indeed most of the expressions of ordinary speech and writing are approximate and imperfect. To the claim that one's thought exists in the mind before it has been put into words (or lines, colors, tones, etc.), Croce answers that if it actually exists in our consciousness it must already possess expression to some degree. The fuller expression our

thought receives after the pains of writing (or drawing, or painting, etc.) corresponds to a fuller thinking out of the original
intuition. The clear-cut intuition or *Anschauung,* of which we
spoke in a previous section, was something that could be put into
words, and therefore expressed.

For instance, let us take one of the poetic images quoted at
the beginning of this chapter. In the Coleridgean line, "They
moved in tracks of shining white," the image is in the words,
and the words are the image. They are not something super-
added to a mental picture which existed independently of them
and which could be expressed equally well by some other
words. It is a picture of color in movement, and of just that
color and that movement which is expressed by "tracks of
shining white."

The process of actual expression may be of course long and
laborious. In the case of some poets, it may even take a whole
lifetime.[26] What counts aesthetically is the quality of the total
image expressed, not the time it took to express it. Revisions and
alterations, if they bring out better the intuition, are integral
parts of it. Sometimes the supposed revision is really a return
to the original version, which had been provisionally abandoned
(NPS, I, 190). But expression does not consist in imposing a
ready-made mould upon an otherwise independent and extraneous matter. All doctrines that claim to define the forms of
expression before the actual expression takes place fall into this
fallacy, which was denounced long ago by A. W. Schlegel.[27]
This we shall see in detail when we come to discussing "technique" in Chapter IV.

Among the earlier critics of Croce's identification of intuition and expression were logicians who could see in it only
an interchange of abstractions.[28] Such critics seemed unable to
discern the bearing of general statements upon particular cases—
in this instance, upon the issues of literary criticism. For this
identity is only another instance of the principle of organic
unity of form and content, upon which so much modern criticism relies.[29] In poetry, form consists not only of the words of
the poem, but of all the special patterns that the words may

assume: rhythm, meter, cadence, rhyme, sentence-structure, etc. A poem for Croce it not a "prose discourse" which is afterwards "reduced into the phonetic pattern of the meter." [30] To use Ransom's terms again, it is a discourse which achieves determinate meaning only when it achieves determinate sound. In Wimsatt's terms, the "making" is identical with the "saying" [31] and the meter is just as much part of the thought as the words are. The form of a poem is an organization of words, stresses and rhythms which is not identical with that of any other poem, but is the carefully fashioned individual shape of that individual thought.

A remarkable anticipation of this organic concept of expression is to be found in Pater's essay on Style (1888). For Pater "all beauty is in the long run only fineness of truth, or what we call expression, the finer accommodation of speech to that vision within." [32] And expression, for Pater as well as for Croce, consists in giving an individual form to an individual content: "the unique word, phrase, sentence, paragraph, essay, or song, absolutely proper to the single mental presentation or vision within." [33] This phrase which Pater repeats, the "vision within," seems to correspond with the *endon eidos*, the "inner form" or *das innere Bild*, which is the central concept of organic aesthetics from antiquity to the Romantics and thence to Croce.[34]

But according to a different view which is current nowadays and which may be called, purely for convenience, the atomistic view, images are independent units which pre-exist to the poem. An image is thought to be made up of ideas, each of which has the power of arousing certain well-defined emotions in the psyche of the reader. The poet's job, according to this view, is to arrange these units in such a way as to produce the maximum concentration of such emotions. Followers of "depth psychology" consider these ideas and images to be rooted in the subconscious of the individual or of the race. The emotions aroused will be therefore all the more overpowering. Hence the doctrine of "archetypal images" and similar entities.

Now Croce as a level-headed historian of civilization and as a lucid philosopher of the spirit has never felt the Romantic yearning towards the dark, the subliminal and the inchoate, for the "secret chaos which lies at the heart of the universe," as A. W. Schlegel put it.[35] Croce has always shown a preference for the luminous, the fully-fashioned and the conscious. Of course he did not believe that all mental processes are governed by logic. But he assigned the less rational, or nonrational, impulses to the practical side of the mind, and specifically to its elementary form, the "economic" will or vital impulse. His main objection to the atomistic theory of images would be that, like traditional rhetoric in this respect, it makes the poetic image pre-exist to its expression.

However, there is still another aspect of the relation between art and emotion which is yet undetermined. To account for it Croce formulated later his concept of the "lyrical intuition." In order to come to it immediately, we shall forego a point-by-point exposition of the other doctrines contained in the first *Aesthetic*, the most important of which—such as the theory of technique and the critique of literary genres—will be taken up in later chapters.

CHAPTER *iii*

The Lyrical Intuition

CROCE TURNED TO LITERARY CRITICISM in 1902 pro-
fessedly in order to exemplify and illustrate his aesthetics. During the years 1902–13, as we shall see in Chapter x, he
wrote a series of critical essays on the contemporary writers of
Italy, which constitutes his first major critical engagement. In the
exercise of practical criticism Croce soon found himself judging
works of literature according to principles which he had not
fully recognized in his *Aesthetic*. It was borne in upon him
that the poetic quality of the image in literature was due to its
expression of emotion.[1] This was called to his attention in 1907
by another scholar, Giulio Augusto Levi. Croce immediately
acknowledged the truth of Levi's observation; that was indeed
his critical practice.[2] But he also noted that there was a philosophical problem involved which had not been formulated by
Levi, viz. why *should* intuition be the expression of emotion?
on what philosophical grounds was this proposition based?
(PS, I, 160–63).

Croce took up this problem in a paper entitled "Pure intuition and the lyrical character of art" which he read at the
Philosophical Congress of Heidelberg in 1908. A translation of
it appeared as the appendix to the first edition of the English
version of the *Aesthetic* in 1909 (A¹, 371–403), but was omitted
in the subsequent edition of 1922 to make room for the badly
needed revised translation of the second part of the *Aesthetic*.
In Italian it was included in the mainly untranslated *Problems
of Aesthetics* of 1910 (*PdE*, 1–30).

46

Here Croce formally introduces an alteration in his previous doctrine. He makes what he calls a philosophic deduction of the lyrical character of art from his previously formulated concept of pure intuition. As he put it later, "through a speculative process . . . the sentimental meaning and lyrical character of the intuition is made to issue from its very purity" (cc, I, 21–22). Students of philosophical reasoning may follow this deduction in detail in the original text. Here we will summarize the argument in general terms. Granted that intuition is knowledge of particulars, one may still ask: what are the particulars of which knowledge is gained in intuition? They are not sense data, for the reasons stated in the previous chapter. Nor, obviously, can they be ideas or concepts, since art is the knowledge of particulars. What else is there? "No other psychic content remains," answers Croce, "but what is known as appetition, tendency, feeling, volition. All these are one, and constitute the practical sphere of the spirit in its infinite gradations and in its dialectic of pleasure and pain" (A¹, 394; *PdE*, 23). In this manner the practical spirit becomes the material to which the theoretical spirit gives a form, and the circular motion of the spiritual forms, mentioned in Chapter I, is established.

Hence for Croce all art becomes the expression of emotion, of feeling, of "a state of mind." Art is therefore always "lyrical" in the sense that is expressive of the author's emotion. Croce here quotes the famous aphorism of Amiel, "A landscape is a state of mind," which he interprets as meaning "a painting is the expression of a mood," and then proceeds to make an hyperbolical extension of the same idea, the consequences of which he was later to deplore: "a great poem might be all contracted in an exclamation of joy, of sorrow, of admiration or of regret" (A¹, 395; *PdE*, 24). This paradox was taken up by some of the Italian Futurists and other avant-gardists and turned into a recipe for exclamatory writing and "fragmentism." [3] This was the last thing that Croce intended, and he protested strongly against it. Bluntly addressing these poetasters, he said in 1915: "when I stated that art was lyrical, I meant that art which is of all times, the art of Aeschylus or of Shakespeare, of

Dante or of Manzoni, of Rabelais and of Racine: certainly not an art still to be produced, and much less an art such as might be expected from yourselves. Your deliberate and manufactured 'lyricism' deserves another name . . . viz., charlatanism and histrionics" (PS, I, 369).

Arising from the doctrine of lyricism, the concept of "poetic personality" was next introduced in the Heidelberg paper. The lyrical function of art is to express the personality of the artist —not, be it carefully noted, his "practical personality" as evidenced in his biography, but what Croce calls here the "soul" of the man: "a personality of some kind, with the sole exclusion, in this case, of the strictly ethical meaning: let it be sad or glad, enthusiastic or despondent, sentimental or sarcastic, benevolent or malevolent; but it must be a soul. Art criticism seems to consist altogether in determining whether there is a personality in the work of art, and of what kind. A work that is a failure is an incoherent work: i.e., a work in which no single personality emerges, but a number of disjointed and conflicting personalities, that is really none at all. This is also the only correct meaning of verisimilitude, truth, logic, and necessity in a work of art" (A¹, 389; *PdE*, 18).

Croce then turns to practical criticism for confirmation, and notes that literary critics and art connoisseurs often find the artistic quality of a poem or of a picture in the liveliness of the feeling expressed, rather than in the formal perfection or consummate clarity of the image produced. But the feeling belongs to a poetic and ideal personality, not to the practical personality of the artist.[4] Croce explicitly condemns as inartistic "the intrusion of the empirical or deliberate personality of the artist into the spontaneous and ideal personality which is the subject of the work of art." He excludes from the domain of art "rhetorical and sensational writers who introduce in the work of art an emotion extraneous to the work itself." He thus anticipated certain parts of T. S. Eliot's plea for the impersonality of the poet in "Tradition and the Individual Talent" (1920). But Croce was also aware of the fact that sometimes the hostility shown towards the "personality" of an artist is merely a cloak for "the misunderstanding and intolerance of certain spirits against other spirits differently constituted (of calm spirits against excitable spirits, for instance)" (A¹, 390–91; *PdE*, 19)— and he might have added, of Neo-classical writers against Romantic poets.

In Croce's own day, however, impersonality was the slogan of naturalistic art, and he had little difficulty in showing that the self-styled impersonal naturalists exhibited in their works a definite personality of their own. Croce concluded that both the image and the emotion are essential constituents of a work of art. "An image that does not express a state of mind has no theoretical value" (A¹, 397; *PdE*, 25). "It is impossible to portray artistically a rose or a cloud unless poetry transforms emotion into a rose or a cloud" (*La poesia di Dante*, 1st ed., p. 31).

The traditional dichotomy of "Classic" and "Romantic" is now given a new meaning. The terms are here taken not in their historical reference, as rival literary schools, but as constituents of the aesthetic process: "Classic" is the phase of representation and expression or the fully-shaped image, and "Romantic" is the emotional content. Both being necessary to art, Croce concludes that a perfect work is classic and romantic at the same time (A¹, 391; *PdE*, 20).[5]

A new meaning is also given to that other famous dichotomy, Imagination and Fancy. English-speaking readers of Croce should note that in Italian critical terminology these two terms are reversed: *immaginazione* usually corresponds to "fancy," and *fantasia* to "imagination." [6] The English translator of Croce was at first not aware of this fact (A¹, 396–97), with the result that a very interesting parallel between English and Italian criticism was thoroughly obscured. Coleridge's distinction between the Imagination and the Fancy was closely paralleled in nineteenth-century Italian criticism by De Sanctis' *fantasia* and *immaginazione*. Croce took up this distinction which he found in De Sanctis and in his German predecessors, and redefined it. Imagination remains the creative faculty, or intuition. But Fancy is excluded from the theoretical sphere and assigned to the practical sphere; it is the arbitrary combination of already formed images: "it may be said that the fancy is a practical activity or diversion, played upon the store of images which the soul possesses; while the imagination, i.e. the transformation of practical into theoretical values, of states of mind into images, is the *creation* of that store itself" (*PdE*, 25).[7] We begin to see here some of the complex interrelations to which the dialectic of the distinct forms of mind lends itself. This is the first instance we have met; we shall meet several others.

In the course of this discussion Croce makes another remark which is of considerable critical importance. He observes that "great artists have often preferred to treat groups of images which had been used many times before as material for works of art. The novelty of these new works has been solely that of art or of form—that is to say, of the new accent which they have known how to give to the old material, of the new way in which they have felt and intuited it, thus creating new images upon the old ones" (A[1], 396; *PdE*, 24). This of course is merely another instance of what we have called in Chapter ii the principle of Integration: images absorb previous images and make them the material of a new synthesis. As stated here the principle tends to support what might be called traditional poetry, or poetry that deals with traditional themes. However, for Croce it is not the old tradition that makes it beautiful, but the new spirit infused in it. Croce's doctrine may therefore be said to support traditional poetry, but not for the traditional reasons, for the ultimate test is innovation. This is noted because it has been claimed that Croce later underwent a critical conversion, and after having started as a supporter of radical innovation, became after World War I a supporter of traditionalism. Neither statement is correct, and there was no such conversion. Croce's doctrine, being a philosophical view of poetry and not a partisan argument, justifies both tradition and innovation, showing that they are both to be found in all genuine works of art.

Since this is a basic point in Croce's theory and practice of criticism, we shall give now some further references to the principle of Integration from later writings.[8] In 1912 Croce wrote: "the poet particularizes his inspiration under certain conditions of time and place, i.e. of history, and therefore cannot but channel it into certain established forms, which are the traditional language, metres, arrangements by stanza, acts or chapters, and in a word by 'genres' . . . But . . . the true poet, while apparently respecting (and to some extent he does respect) established forms, actually is always modifying them, or creating new forms which replace the previous ones. He seems to guide his inscription into the existing channel (and to some extent he does guide it), but he is actually opening up a new channel. Indeed, if things did not go in this way, how were the preexisting channels opened and how could new ones be formed?" (CVM, 193).

So in 1924 he could well say to a critic: "I have never affirmed that the poet or the painter or the architect could compose, paint or build without reference to the historical conditions under which he arises, i.e. out of this world . . . When the artist has formed his image, the previous language, syntax, metre, psychology, etc., i.e. all that history, *are already within the new image* and at the same time transcended by it: the language is the old language, and yet it is new; the metre is the old metre, and yet it has a new movement . . . the poem is at the same time old and new" (CC, III, 141–42).

As regards the doctrine of lyricism, critics who are opposed to the recognition of an emotional element in art may still object:—quite apart from Croce's own experiences as a critic, cannot the first *Aesthetic* stand as it was, without the addition of the lyrical element? cannot the poetic image be entirely unemotional and purely iconic? But the fact is that the first *Aesthetic* does not exclude emotion; indeed it refers to it continually. Even in the very first sketch of the *Aesthetic*, the *Fundamental Theses* of 1900, intuition is defined as the expression of impressions, and impressions are assigned to the general class of psychological phenomena which definitely includes emotions, being made up of the three categories of "sensations, feelings and appetitions." These three are traditionally distinguished, but Croce already tended to merge them together: "every sensation implies a certain feeling of pleasure or pain, and a tendency to preservation or elimination." [9] In the *Aesthetic* of 1902 this argument is tacitly assumed and the various psychological categories are used indifferently: e.g. the material of intuition is described as "impressions, sensations, feelings, impulses, emotions or whatever name one uses" (p. 14). And on page 19 we find the general statement: "matter (in art) has been understood as emotionality not yet artistically elaborated, the *impressions*." The main change after the Heidelberg lecture is that emotion, instead of being one of the possible materials of poetry, became the only possible content. Croce could reasonably claim that the doctrine of the lyrical character of art was implicit in the first *Aesthetic*, although it was not given there the relief which he gave to it later.[10]

In the succeeding editions of the *Aesthetic* (which ran to nine during the life of the author) a number of changes were gradually introduced. The most important changes were effected after the Heidelberg lecture, in the third edition (1908), upon which the second edition (1922) of the English translation is based. In that edition, Chapter x on "aesthetic feelings" was entirely rewritten and corresponding alterations, of minor extent, were made throughout the book. The result of all these changes was to make it clear that there are no "impressions" besides the emotions, the only possible content of art according to the Heidelberg lecture.

This lecture began with an interesting survey of aesthetic theories, which is not merely a classification of them but a deduction and a logical development, according to which each doctrine improves upon the preceding and in turn paves the way for the successive. This incidentally is a much more comprehensive and also more liberal presentation than most classifications of aesthetic theories which are to be found in books of criticism. Shortly afterwards it was replaced by Croce's theory of the "necessary forms of error" (*Logica,* 277 ff.) which includes the forms of aesthetic error or the critical heresies, and is also a very comprehensive and liberal doctrine. The classification in the Heidelberg lecture was never referred to again by Croce.

THE FIRST RESTATEMENT of the whole doctrine of aesthetics in the light of the lyrical concept was a short book entitled *The Breviary of Aesthetics*. It consists of four lectures, originally intended to be read at the inauguration of the Rice Institute in Texas (one of Croce's links with the United States). The English translation by Douglas Ainslie was published in 1912 [11] and a revised edition appeared under the title *The Essence of Aesthetic* in 1921. Like Ainslie's other translations of Croce, this one is at times brilliant, at times erroneous. The Italian original (1913) was reprinted in the (partly translated) *New Essays on Aesthetics* of 1920 (NSE[2], 1–87). The *Breviary* provides a vivid summing up of Croce's thought up to 1912. However, since it is often the only book by Croce besides the *Aesthetic* known to English-speaking readers, it is well to note that there are 40 more years of work by Croce to be reckoned with, during which he went well beyond the point reached in 1912. In a selection "from all his works" made by Croce in the last year of his life he did not include a single page from the *Aesthetic* or from the *Breviary;* although the section on Aesthetics runs to 250 pages, all of it was written after 1912.[12]

The *Breviary*, owing to its terseness, may have contributed to an opinion which one hears sometimes from the critics of Croce, that of his "dogmatism." To a critic who once made this objection, Croce answered that his philosophical propositions were of the kind that in logic is called "apodictic" (CC, III, 18; cf. *PdE*, 245). As regards the *Breviary*, it should be remembered that Croce by 1912 had already dedicated three substantial volumes to systematic discussion of aesthetics, logic and ethics, where his theories are expounded in detail with continual examination of divergent and opposing views; in addition, he had been answering critics and reviewing books on all these subjects in his journal. Anyone who wants to know the reasons behind Croce's sometimes startling and paradoxical conclusions may find them fully set out in these volumes, together with historical accounts of the problems discussed.

In the *Breviary* Croce approaches the concept of lyricism in the following manner. He begins by defining art again as the creation of an image, theoretical in character and particular in content. He then raises the question: What is the function of the pure image in the life of the spirit? To answer it, he turns to the traditional Classic-Romantic dichotomy, and gives it a new meaning. Its two terms are now taken as symbols of two general theories, one that stresses the formal element in poetry, and the other which calls for emotion in poetry. But Croce reaffirms that the great works of poetry are neither purely formal nor purely emotional, neither Classic nor Romantic but a synthesis of both. Poetry consists of "a vigorous emotion [*sentimento*] completely transformed into a crystal-clear representation." These propositions, illustrated by specific instances, lead to the further inference that "what confers coherence and unity to the intuition is emotion [*sentimento*] . . . an intuition is truly such when it represents an emotion, and can rise only from it and above it. . . . Not the idea, but the emotion is what confers to art the ethereal lightness of the symbol: a longing [*aspirazione*] enclosed within the circumference of an image: that is art; the desire is there only for the representation, and the representation only for the desire. Epic and drama, or drama and lyric, are scholastic divisions of the indivisible: art is always lyrical, or if preferred, it is the epic and the drama of emotion" (NSE,[2] 27–28).

On the other hand, bad art consists in a mechanical combination of several images not animated by any feeling. It may even consist of a single image, which however is felt to be "frigid" even though carefully worked out (NSE[2], 27). The ultimate justification of the pure image in the total life of the mind appears then to be its expressive function. Through poetry we become acquainted with new states of mind, unfamiliar ways of feeling, rare and subtle and deep moods, crystallized in perfectly fashioned images. Indeed, this is the cognitive value of art in all its forms, according to Croce.

However, the idea of poetry as the expression of emotion or feeling, while accepted by some critics,[13] meets with resistance from other directions, particularly from the modern dislike of emotionalism in all its shapes. To some it seems debasing—and in some sense almost a violation of good manners (cf. PNP, 267–68)—to make poetry, and creative literature in general, a mere vehicle for emotion. Is all the art which is lavished on the fashioning of a great poem to result only in the expression of what the poet happened to be feeling at the moment? Isn't that a purely personal matter? This school of thought usually prefers to conceive the poetic image as something devoid of emotion and beautiful in itself, or beautiful in the manner in which it is linked to other images in a pattern which is also devoid of emotion or "abstract." But can a man who is totally devoid of feeling write poetry? At least from the time of Longinus, the possession of deep feelings has been considered a requisite for great writing. To the modern cult of "impersonal art," Croce objected that it is impossible for the human mind not to react with like or dislike to a picture presented to it, so that the image inevitably becomes impregnated with feeling while the artist is fashioning it (LNI, III, 104).

On the other hand, aesthetic expression, or the expression of emotion in art, must not be confused with the so-called "expression" of emotion in ordinary life. This kind of expression is practical and not theoretical, since it usually aims at influencing the conduct of other people, or else is part and parcel of the emotion itself, like a cry or a blush, a snort or a growl. Croce called the latter "naturalistic" or "symptomatic" expression, distinguishing it carefully from artistic expression, which is spiritual and theoretical.[14]

Furthermore, Croce defined the nature of the emotion that finds expression in art still more precisely in a little-noted chapter of his *Philosophy of the Practical* (1908). For Croce, there is only a distinction of degree between emotions and actions. They are both made "of the same stuff": an emotion is an impulse that tends towards action, and an action is an emotion which has realized itself. Now poetry is not the expression of emotion, as distinct from action. Rather it is the expression of something intermediate between emotion and action: "desires and actions are, as we know, of the same stuff; and art takes this stuff in its identity, unconcerned with the further elabora-

tion which it will receive in an ulterior stage of reflection"
(*Pratica*, 172). The emotional content of poetry is thus found
in the undifferentiated unity from which both desire and volition
develop, or the indistinct region of the soul from which inclina-
tions and appetitions well up towards the luminous regions of
clear-cut representations and logical judgment. By this qualification, emotion loses its too definitely purposeful character and
becomes a mood without a determinate object. For it, Croce
prefers to emotion the term *aspirazione*, which we have translated "longing," or *stato d'animo*, translated "state of mind" or
"mood."

IT WILL NOW BE CLEAR that for Croce the connection between
image and emotion is not a series of automatic responses to
previously formed associations, as claimed by the atomistic
theory discussed in the preceding chapter. For Croce we have
here an absolute identification. In a genuine poetic creation
neither the image nor the emotion may be said to have existed
before; they appear together in one and the same act, the act of
expression. This is another total identification which arouses
perplexity and hesitation in those who are not accustomed to
the categorical character of philosophic reasoning. Yet we have
here only another appearance of the familiar principle of organic unity. If one believes in this principle, one cannot at the
same time believe that emotion and expression are two separate
things.

The idea of this separation has been rejected well before
Croce. Among the various thinkers who rejected it, was an
Oxford philosopher of the nineteenth century who affirmed categorically the unity of emotion and expression which seems to
have given so much trouble to some English critics of Croce: "It
would be truer to say that the expression *is* the completed feeling:
for the feeling is not truly felt till it is expressed, and in being
expressed it is felt but in a different way. What the act of expression does is to fix and distinguish it finally; it then, and then
only, becomes *a* determinate feeling." [15] The author of these

words, R. C. Nettleship, was a philosopher of the idealistic school. He may therefore have been acquainted with statements by Hegel that lead to a similar conclusion. Croce himself in later writings stressed the connection between this aesthetic doctrine and broader philosophical issues.[16]

A more recent English aesthetician, who differed on other points from Croce, repeated the same identification: "The poem is not the translation of the poet's state of mind, for he does not know till he has said it either what he wants to say or how he will say it." [17] Later still Collingwood, following Croce, stressed the theory that art is the expression of emotion. However in his hands the statement, carelessly repeated, became at times indistinguishable from a very different theory: the view that poetry is a mere vent or effusion of unrestrained feeling. For instance, he once speaks of the poet as one who "makes a clean breast of experience, concealing nothing and altering nothing." [18] This is too much like the "confession" theory of poetry, popular among the Romantics, and it was rightly condemned by a thinker like Cassirer; [19] but it is entirely alien to Croce, since it eliminates the image altogether and takes emotion in the raw. In Chapter xi we shall see how strongly Croce condemned the literature of "confession" from Rousseau to his own day.

Furthermore Croce has given the unity of form and content, of image and emotion, a philosophic foundation by defining it as an "*a priori* synthesis" in his *Logica*.[20] This formulation takes care also of the objections advanced by realistic schools of thought (which include neo-scholastic ontology), such as the following: that the thing expressed, "the idea or feeling," "remains entirely outside the word that expresses it by so referring to it, and entirely distinct from it in its ontological constitution." [21] The a priori synthesis is a deliberately Kantian formula which means nothing more metaphysical than what we have already seen affirmed by the English philosophers: that image and emotion come to exist in one and the same act, the act of aesthetic expression.

This concept of expression as an a priori synthesis, first

formulated in 1908 (*Logica*, 155), involves three factors: the image, the emotion, and the synthesis thereof. But according to the doctrine of the a priori synthesis, the first two factors are abstract or, as A. C. Bradley put it, they are never found *in* the poem, but only out of the poem,[22] and only the last factor is concrete, i.e. the synthesis or the poem itself. At other times, Croce conceived expression as an Aristotelian form, to which emotion provides the material. But it is not easy to assimilate this logical pattern to the previous one. For while there are three factors involved in the synthesis, there are only two in the form-and-matter relationship, and they cannot be made to fit the three others with a one-to-one correspondence. If we attempt to identify aesthetic form, which is an active principle, with one of the factors of the synthesis, then it should be with the synthesis itself, or the unifying factor. And this is what Croce apparently did on one page of the *Breviary* when he spoke of art as "an aesthetic synthesis *a priori*, of emotion and image in the intuition." Here the abstract elements are distinct from the synthesis, which alone is "concrete and alive" (NSE[2], 33).

But in the following page Croce apparently slipped into a different identification, which was to have a curious consequence in his theory of criticism (NSE[2], 34). He there proceeded to identify, as it seems, aesthetic form with the image, which is only a constituent of the synthesis.[23] This was not only bad theoretically, but it was also to have the effect of eliminating the image almost completely from the scope of practical criticism. Once the image is identified with form, which is a universal dynamic principle, the only thing that can be said of it by the critic is that it is there or that it is not there, according to a doctrine that we shall discuss when we come to the problems of literary criticism in Chapter VIII.

Some modern critics consider images almost as material objects, beautiful in themselves but with no emotional significance. They usually interpret "image" in the restricted rhetorical meaning, as metaphors or similes or other figures of speech. These images are supposed to be endowed with an intrinsic power, which does not depend so much upon the words used as upon the ideas conveyed. But if it were so, they could be transferred from one poem to another without variation of poetic effect, and this simply does not happen. Poets borrow images, but in so doing they transform them. A curious instance of this is to be found in Baudelaire, who once made a poem by borrowing images from two of the best known poems in the English language. He made some changes, but the main difference is in the poem as a whole. Take a stanza from one of the most conventional poems of Longfellow, "A Psalm of Life":

> Art is long, and Time is fleeting,
>> And our hearts, though stout and brave,
> Still, like muffled drums, are beating
>> Funeral marches to the grave,

Add to it a stanza from Gray's "Elegy":

> Full many a gem of purest ray serene
>> The dark unfathom'd waves of ocean bear;
> Full many a flower is born to blush unseen,
>> And waste its sweetness on the desert air,

Filter them through the mind of Baudelaire, and you get "Le guignon":

> Pour soulever un poids si lourd,
> Sisyphe, il faudrait ton courage!
> Bien qu'on ait du coeur à l'ouvrage,
> L'Art est long et le Temps est court.
>
> Loin des sépultures célèbres,
> Vers un cimitière isolé,
> Mon coeur, comme un tambour voilé,
> Va battant des marches funèbres.
>
> —Maint joyau dort enseveli
> Dans les ténèbres et l'oubli,
> Bien loin des pioches et des sondes;
>
> Maint fleur épanche à regret
> Son parfum doux comme un secret
> Dans les solitudes profondes.[24]

The images of the English poems have passed into the French one: the heart beating like a drum, the pulse sounding like a funeral march, the gem unnoticed at the bottom of the ocean and the flower wasting in the desert; but the poetic effect is entirely different. The images have become vehicles for the expression of a mood of gloomy intensity which is as far from Gray's sentimental melancholy on one side (the side of poetry) as it is from Longfellow's brisk little homily on the other (the side of didacticism). Some details of course have been added; but it is the new mood which gives unity to the poem and carries everything along with it. The "elegant statuette"—to use a phrase of Croce's mentioned earlier—represented by the stanza from Gray's "Elegy" has become completely absorbed in a new intuition.

So it is futile to consider the rhetorical image as an objective semantic unit which confers significance to a poem, instead of receiving it from an emotion. This is confirmed by the earlier history of the pulse-drum-funeral march simile. It can be traced long before Longfellow, being found in Bishop King's famous "Exequy" on his dead wife:

> But heark! My pulse, like a soft Drum,
> Beats my approach, tells *Thee* I come;
> And slow howere my marches be,
> I shall at least sit down by *Thee*.

Here again the poetic effect of the image is different because the emotion expressed is different. To some readers it may convey a desire to join the lost one. But T. S. Eliot quotes it in his essay on "The Metaphysical Poets" with the remark: "In the last few lines there is an effect of terror which is several times attained by one of Bishop King's admirers, Edgar Poe." [25] Still later the simile was considered again by John Crowe Ransom, who quoted it from Eliot and observed: "it may seem jaunty for the actual occasion, or even wrenched." [26] If an image were a solid semantic unit, such a difference of opinion could not be possible. But the case is different when it comes to defining an emotion expressed in poetry, a problem which requires delicate handling and for which Croce developed a special method, which we shall see in Chapter VIII.

Another point made currently in regard to the expression of emotion is to extol understatement, which almost makes artistic expression a question (as already mentioned) of good manners. The standard textbook example of the virtue of understatement is the scene of military justice in Hemingway's *Farewell to Arms*. This is praised on the grounds that the author has said "less" than he might have said on the subject. It should rather be praised because the author said *all* that he needed to say for his purpose: nothing more, but nothing less. The defect which is the opposite of understatement is considered by the same text-book to be "sentimentality," which it defines as "emotion in excess of the occasion." [27] This again sounds like a moral pre-scription rather than an aesthetic observation. In artistic com-position the emotion can be considered excessive not because it goes beyond the bounds of some moral or social code, but be-cause it emerges beyond the limits of a completed image, in the shape of repetitions, rhetoric, clichés, etc. Apart from the poem itself there is no standard of measurement by which an excess of emotion can be determined.

At this point we may consider an objection which is some-times raised against the theory of expression. It is asked: how can we determine the adequacy of the image to the emotion that it is supposed to express, since we have only the image and the poet alone knows what his emotion was really like? What this objection does is to question the very fact of expression. The expression of an emotion consists precisely in the process of put-ting it into words so that it can be known through them. If emo-tions can never be known through words, then the theory of expression certainly falls to the ground; but do we not also re-ject a fact of common experience? Do we not convey every day our thoughts and emotions by means of words? And do we not continually meet with expressions which clearly are either in excess or in default of the meaning intended? In every-day speech we do not find it impossible, or even difficult, to evaluate the degree or failure of an expression, and to tell that somebody is either saying too little or saying too much. For the analysis of a complex work of art a more elaborate procedure may be required, as we shall see in Chapter VIII; but the process of expressing emotion and evaluating its expression goes on all the time.

Expression cannot be ultimately analyzed into something else or defined in terms of another process because, as Croce claims, it is something basic and fundamental. A French critic of Croce recently gave a definition of expression, which in effect is little more than a paraphrase of it. However, the paraphrase may be found useful by those who still have difficulty with the concept. É. Souriau noted that "expression" is something very different from "sign," because it involves "the idea of bringing out [*efférence*], of exteriorization, either voluntary or spontaneous; in particular, the idea that expression is a kind of symbolism in which the symbolizing proceeds from the symbolized." [28]

This definition brings up again the term "symbol" which is one of the most fashionable terms of modern poetics. It may be asked why does not Croce use the term "symbol" rather than image or intuition. Certainly an aesthetic centering on that term can be very close to Croce, as may be seen by the following quotation from a contemporary English critic, Sir Herbert Read,[29] who is not a disciple of Croce: "The form of the work of art is inherent in the emotional situation of the artist: it proceeds from the apprehension of that situation (a situation which involves either external objective phenomena or internal states of mind) and is the creation of a formal equivalence (i.e. symbol) for that situation. It resists or rejects all attempts to fit the situation to a ready-made formula of expression, believing that to impose such a generalized shape on an unique emotion or intuition results in insincerity of feeling and artificiality of form."

Croce would have subscribed entirely to the last sentence, but he would not have said that the form is "inherent" in the emotion nor that the image is a "formal equivalent" or symbol for the emotional situation.[30] We can now see why he usually avoids the term "symbol." A symbol means something which stands for something else, and poetry does not stand for something else; it stands for itself. The image does not "stand for" the emotion; it is inseparably united with it. This idea was also vigorously expounded by another French critic, similarily without apparent influence of Croce: "Expression in art is simply incarnation. The language of the poet expresses his thought not by making it understood in no matter what fashion, or in a way that is neutral or indifferent, but in giving it a body from which it can never be henceforth separated." [31]

Indeed the concept of expression is so central to modern poetics that we find a modern American critic, not a Crocean, obviously working his way toward it. This is Cleanth Brooks: "the poem is not only the linguistic vehicle which conveys the thing communicated most 'poetically,' but . . . it is also the sole linguistic vehicle which conveys the things communicated accurately. In fact, if we were to speak exactly, the poem itself is the *only* medium that communicates the particular 'what' that is communicated. The conventional theories of communication offer no easy solution to our problem of meanings: we emerge with nothing more enlightening than this graceless bit of tautology: the poem says what the poem says." [32] To that "problem of meanings" Croce offers a solution by conceiving the poem as the expression of an emotion by means of an image.

So we find nineteenth- and twentieth-century writers of the most diverse origins—English, American and Continental—converging on the concept of expression for a definition of poetry.[33] Croce's full articulation of that concept in his doctrine of the lyrical intuition provides the literary critic with three points to work on: the image, the emotion, and their adjustment. The critic characterizes the image, identifies the emotion and evaluates the degree of their adjustment.

CHAPTER IV

The *"Techniques" of Poetic Expression*

THE PRECEDING CHAPTERS have already touched incidentally upon some points concerning the so-called
"techniques" of literature. These "techniques" will now be discussed systematically, in the following order: 1) Language and
Diction, 2) Rhetoric and Style, 3) The Technique of the Novel,
4) Prosody and Metrics, and 5) The Technique of the Arts in
General, or Croce's Doctrine of Externalization.

We will begin by defining what Croce calls the "rhetorical
theory" of literary composition. This is the traditional view of
the art of writing which makes the means of expression pre-exist
to the act of expression. First, the words that a writer uses are
thought to pre-exist to the writer, each word as a separate unit
with its own separate meaning and proper usage already defined
and established. Next, these units are arranged in sentences, "like
stones in a wall" (*PdE*, 178), according to a variety of pre-
established patterns, which extend from the rules of grammar
and syntax to the prescriptions of rhetoric and the "laws" of
stylistics. Then there is a set of ornamental devices, called
tropes and figures of speech, which may be added for embellishment. In the case of poetry there is still another form, viz. metre,
also consisting of a series of set patterns, each with its own laws
and prescriptions. From the accumulation of all these forms
beauty of expression is supposed to result.

Against this view of the art of writing (with its attendant
doctrine of literary genres, to which the next chapter will be
dedicated) a revolt has been brewing for several centuries,

which may be said to culminate in Croce's critique of rhetoric. According to Croce all these forms, patterns, modes and "norms" are abstractions from actual utterances and not their law or governing principle. For Croce an actual utterance, or poetic expression, is a thing of the kind that T. E. Hulme called an "intensive manifold." [1] In other words, it is an object possessed of such a unity that a part of it cannot be removed from the whole without destroying it. This according to Croce is what happens to poetic expression when it is dissected into the traditional rhetorical forms. He does not mean of course that words do not have meanings, that sentences do not have shapes, or that verses do not have melody, but that they are in each case individual meanings, individual shapes and individual melodies. And of course he does not mean that points of resemblance may not be found between individual expressions. But he argues (and this is the crucial issue) that "expression is from the whole" (*PdE*, 155): so a classification that is made out of one point only, and leaves out all the rest, is a meaningless abstraction.

If rhetorical forms nevertheless seem to have a meaning, it is because of something real which lies behind their assumed pre-existence. That is the pre-existence of other complete expressions. As we have seen more than once, every expression arises out of previous expressions. Not the set forms, but the individual expressions or works of art from which the set forms are abstracted, pre-exist, and the new expression will make use of them, incorporating in the new work a part of one in one place and of another in another, but it will take what it does take according to its individual character and not according to a general rule. So the reality behind "technique" may be defined as "the previous artistic history out of which the new work rises and, subjectively, the culture of the artist" (cc, v, 148; cf. cc, iii, 48 and us, 18). As we saw in Chapter iii, Croce speaks of the poet expressing his intuition by "channelling it into certain pre-established forms, i.e. traditional language, metre, etc." But he goes on to say that the poet modifies the old channel in the very act of using it, so that the result is something different (cvm, 193).

We reach here a point of convergence of several aesthetic systems. The patterns of rhetoric, the laws of stylistics, the "structural principles" of drama and fiction, and all norms and conventions are abstract forms, or mental constructs of the kind that Coleridge attributed to the Understanding as distinct from Reason, Hegel to the Abstract Intellect and Bergson to the practical Intelligence.[2] As we shall see in detail in the following chapter, Croce adopts a similar view and calls them "pseudo-concepts," abstractions made for practical convenience but with no cognitive value. Of such abstractions the natural sciences are made, according to the "economic theory" of science which Croce adopted from Mach and Poincaré, as we saw in Chapter I. So grammar, syntax, rhetoric, stylistics and metrics may be said to constitute the "natural sciences" of the art of speech (*Storia*, 301; NPS, II, 148), but this designation in Croce's doctrine far from exalting them reduces them to pure fictions. As aesthetic standards they become fruitful sources of error: e.g. when metres, sentence patterns, figures of speech and individual words are thought to be beautiful in themselves and not as parts of an expression which is beautiful as a whole (NSE[2], 285). So rhetoricians will think that they can write beautifully without vision or inspiration, simply by adopting those forms.

These abstract forms have been produced in such quantity and in such complicated systems that their complete critique would be correspondingly extensive and laborious. The field is so vast that it will be impossible to cover it all, and something will have to be left to the understanding of the reader.

CROCE'S DOCTRINE of poetic language was one of the first parts of his *Aesthetic* to appear in print. It saw the light in a discussion of the stylistic theories of Professor Gröber in 1899. The draft of the *Aesthetic* known as the *Theses of Aesthetics* followed in the succeeding year, which also saw the publication of a rejoinder to Gröber. The doctrine of language was finally formulated in the XVIIIth chapter of the *Aesthetic* of 1902, and afterwards received a number of extensions and developments which were collected, together with the papers on Gröber, in the untranslated *Problems of Aesthetics* of 1912 (*PdE*, 143–223). Later Croce was to write still more on the general problem of linguistics, and he published a total of 35 papers and reviews on this subject in his lifetime.[3]

One of his earlier papers was a discussion of a famous popular book on the correct usage of the Italian language, the *Idioma gentile* by Edmondo de Amicis (1905). Croce's ensuing controversy with de Amicis may be said to parallel the controversy on somewhat similar issues between Rémy de Gourmont and A. Albalat in France at about the same time, although it never reached the proportions of the latter. Croce's discussion with de Amicis provides a clear statement of his opposition to the traditional doctrine of language and we shall take it as a convenient starting point (*PdE*, 203–14).

For Croce, language is not a sign or a system of signs, a sign being something which has only referential value, obtained from the external objects that it supposedly refers to; language has its object within itself, the representation or thought which is identical with its expression.[4] Nor is language a material object existing independently of a speaker. Rather it is a process which is being continuously enacted at every instant of our conscious life. This is the process of expression, which as we have seen in Chapter II is essentially an aesthetic process. So language and poetry are basically identical. All genuine speech is poetic, whether it is a word or phrase that renders a single impression, or a great poem embodying the thought of a lifetime. On the other hand, expression may take the shape not only of articulate sounds but also of tones, lines and color, mass and volume. It may be music, painting, sculpture, architecture or some other art. If all speech is expression, all expression is not speech. We come here upon the question of the unity and distinction of the arts, which is beyond the scope of the present book. However, some reference will be made to it in the last section of this chapter.

In the last chapter of the "Theory" of his first *Aesthetic*, Croce maintained the unity of speech and aesthetic expression, hence of aesthetics and what he calls "general linguistics" or the philosophical theory of language. He argued that all the questions that arise in aesthetics find their counterpart in general linguistics. For instance: is expression primarily physical or spiritual? is it an intellectual or a practical activity? All these questions are answered for linguistics in the same way as for aesthetics: speech is a spiritual activity, it is theoretical and not practical, it is imaginative and not logical. In particular, words are not general terms and language is not governed by logic; words are images and they are ruled by imagination, although they may be used by reflective thought as signs or symbols.

Croce claims for language the same "irreducible individuality" that he claims for art: "two truly identical words do not exist" (E, 160; A, 146), every word is different every time it is pronounced.[5] "My language of today is not the same as my language of yesterday, and the language that suits me does not suit another" (PdE, 205). Like art, "language is a perpetual creation . . . The ever-new impressions give rise to continual changes of sound and meaning, that is, to ever-new expressions" (E, 164; A, 150).

Just as the aesthetic unit or poem is an integral whole which is indivisible into material parts, so the linguistic unit of expression is indivisible into separate words. Speech, at least in its original reality, "is a *continuum,* devoid of any consciousness of the division into words and syllables, which are imaginary entities fashioned by the schools" (E, 163; A, 149). The ultimate unit of speech is the sentence; however, "not the sentence understood in the usual grammatical way, but as an expressive organism whose meaning is complete—therefore extending from a single exclamation to a long poem" (E, 159; A, 146).[6] Croce is here maintaining a theory which is similar to the contextualist theory of recent linguistics and psychology.[7] This theory affirms that separate words have no real existence; words exist only as part of a sentence. When we find words apparently standing alone, as in such expressions as "Stop!", "Go!" or "Fire!", that is because they themselves constitute a complete sentence, or "holophrase," as the current term goes.[8]

However, Croce's theory differs from similar statements in linguistics and psychology in being philosophical and involving value concepts. Croce studies language not as an empirical fact, abstracted from all other facts, but as a spiritual act, a concrete universal, or something that is present in every form of consciousness and the recognition of which implies a value judgment. From this point of view his problem is: "does the single word possess aesthetic value (and therefore spiritual reality) independently of the poem it occurs in?" and his answer of course is No. Historically, Croce's antecedents in his theory of language are not the positivistic investigators of the late nineteenth century, but the philosophers of the preromantic age, such as Vico and Hamann, Herder and von Humboldt (*PdE*, 209; E, 274 ff., 361 ff.; A, 220 ff., 324 ff.). It is hardly necessary to stress that in denying that words are general terms Croce is completely at variance with Hegel (*Saggio sullo Hegel*, 86).

If separate words do not really exist, it may be asked, why do we speak of them as separate? Croce's answer is that speech, like all other spiritual activities, is, once produced, subject to a process of dissection for practical and mnemonic convenience, as described at the beginning of this chapter. What was originally a continuous whole, an "intensive manifold," is split up into separate words and written down as such. The process of writing actually does not record words themselves but a series of reminders of the articulatory movements to be performed for the production of certain sounds (E, 110; A, 100). After being so recorded, words are collected in dictionaries or further dissected in books on grammar and on etymology. But what is so dissected is the dead word. The living word is only to be found as part of actual speech, in a particular historical situation (*Saggio sullo Hegel*, 87; US, 24–25). After being abstracted from living speech the separate word may still return to it, in the same way (to adopt a simile that Croce uses in another linguistic discussion, *PdE*, 196) that water frozen into ice may be melted by reimmersion and become again a flowing current. The principle of Integration is again involved: "expressions already produced must descend to the rank of impressions before they can give rise to new expressions. When we utter new words we generally transform old ones, varying or widening their meaning: but this process is not associative, it is *creative*": something is produced which did not exist before (E, 158; A, 144–45).

Croce would not limit himself to saying as Blackmur does that "good poets gain their excellence by writing an existing language *as if* it were their own invention." Croce would go further and say that it *is* their own invention. Nor is there for him such a thing as "an existing language." What exists is a multiplicity of individual expressions: "Languages have no reality beyond sentences and groups of sentences really written and pronounced by given peoples at definite periods; that is to say, they have no existence outside the works of art (whether little or great, oral or written, soon forgotten or long remembered, does not matter) in which they exist concretely" (E, 160; A, 147). Nor would Croce have gone on to say, as Blackmur does: "and as a rule success in the effect of originality is best secured by fidelity, in an extreme sense, to the individual words as they appear in the dictionary." [9]

For Croce, only dead words are to be found in the dictionary, which is "a collection of abstractions, or a cemetery of corpses more or less skilfully embalmed" (E, 164; A, 151). He explained later in more detail how this process of "embalming" a language is performed: "A dictionary takes out of the living sentences of speakers or writers the articulate sounds, or words, that are similar. They thus become abstract sounds, void of the individual meaning which they derived from, and conferred upon, the whole of which they are constituents. The dictionary-maker then fills the vacuum which he has produced in these sound-groups with a general meaning, obtained by abstraction from the meanings which the words had in the sentences of which they were part. These meanings are often so different and so disparate that they cannot fit into a single generalization, so several generalizations are made by the same process and lined up under the heading of a single word" (P, 168).

The contextualist theory is today widely known and several critics and students of language refer to it. But few seem to be aware of the fact that it was formulated by Croce as a philosophic proposition as far back as 1899 (*PdE*, 146). Also, some critics pay lip service to it, and then fall back easily into the old atomistic view of speech as an aggregate of independent units. For instance, they speak of words as exerting "pressures" upon each other, producing tensions, stresses and controls, and acting and reacting upon each other, which is to think of them atomistically. We may take as an instance a critic who has frequently asserted in recent years the contextual theory, I. A. Richards. He has poured scorn upon the atomistic view that "takes the senses of the author's words to be things we know before we read him, fixed factors with which he has to build up the meaning of his sentences as a mosaic that is put together of discrete independent tesserae." But then he goes on to speak of "the interinanimation of words" which is to return to the notion of words as independent entities.[10]

This notion is so hard to get rid of because, like all processes of abstraction, it is performed for a practical use. In effect it makes single acts of expression, which are innumerable and infinitely various, more easily classified and kept in memory. It is therefore of special use in teaching and in learning a language, a use of which Croce was well aware and had no intention of discouraging or condemning (E, 162, A, 148; *PdE*, 216–17; US, 24–25). This transition from the expressive to the practical is another instance of what Croce calls the circular movement of spiritual activities: each arises in turn over the other, and then becomes the material or the occasion for another form, continually and endlessly.

Just as Croce denies the validity of genres or kinds of poetry, he denies that words or expressions can be classified as "parts of speech." Nouns, verbs, adjectives, and all similar classifications, ancient and modern (such as "morphemes" and "phonemes"), are mere abstractions, forged for practical convenience, but which have no concrete existence and no aesthetic value.[11] So Croce cannot place any reliance upon the kind of stylistic criticism which turns upon such concepts, and asserts the special poetic value of certain kinds of adjectives or the artistic effect of certain moods or tenses of the verb (for an instance of the latter see TPS, II, 39). On the other hand, these pseudo-concepts may be useful to define certain kinds of bad writing, simply because bad writing tends to be mechanical and to rely upon clichés and set forms: e.g., D'Annunzio's artistic weakness is shown at times by his tendency to use vague "negative" expressions (LNI, IV, 42).

From this point of view all disputes about what constitutes correct "poetic diction" cease to have any relevance. All diction is poetic if it is expressive. Abstractly considered, words or phrases in a poem may be classified as colloquial or literary, popular or learned, modern or archaic; but then, they are abstractly considered. Such disputes, when they are taken up by poets who have actually something new to say (such as Wordsworth), actually turn upon the subject-matter or the emotional content of the poem, expressed by verbal patterns to which exception is made by critics and which are defended by the author. But a subject, once invested by the shaping power of the imagination, brings along with itself its own appropriate verbal form. When a poet uses a word or a phrase belonging to the so-called colloquial vocabulary to express his intuition, then that is the word or phrase required; to resort to it is not so much an act of audacity, as of necessity (LNI, IV, 171–72). The only test of diction is its appropriateness to the individual mood expressed by the poet, as shown by the failure of all attempts to establish a diction which will suit all poets.

A theory which seems to enjoy a certain vogue at present considers language in general as possessing a reality independent of the speaker or writer, as an "objective or material thing." [12] The effort of the speaker or writer to achieve expression is seen as a struggle with a material obstacle existing outside him. But how can language, which is an effort of the thinking subject to express himself, be at the same time an objective reality existing outside him and independently of him? Is not this idea merely the projection of a mental process into the external world? Yet this idea is sometimes carried to the point that successful expression is counted as a victory gained *against* language, and not *by* language.

This idea may be supported by means of a distinction, which is current in modern linguistics since Saussure as the distinction between *parole* and *langage,* speech as individual expression and speech as a collective or social product. It may then be affirmed that the speech of the individual must conform to the linguistic usage of the group he belongs to, that *parole* must conform to *langage:* so there is an external obstacle, or check, to individual expression. But according to Croce, individual expression or *parole* alone possesses concrete reality: linguistic usage or *langage* is a fiction (*PdE,* 159–60). What does exist are the previous individual expressions which provide the material for the new in the manner described above and which are schematized in the abstraction of "linguistic usage" with its grammatical and syntactical rules.

The struggle for expression can certainly be something very real and very painful, but it is a struggle within the mind of the speaker or writer and not between it and an external reality. Difficulty in expression may appear in two ways: either the speaker cannot find words for his thought, or conversely he cannot find thought for his words. In the first case it is not language that offers an obstacle to expression, it is the thought itself which is not sufficiently clear and articulated. The struggle then is to clarify the thought, not to get hold of mere words. In the second case words and phrases offer themselves in abundance but the thought seems to be lagging behind. But this is not due to an innate antagonism between thought and language, or the sinister power of clichés against original thinking. It is rather due to the fact that the speaker's memory alone is active and continues to bring up recollections of past expressions, while his expressive power is inactive and does not impart a new meaning to the flow of words supplied by memory. Achieved expression may be described as the convergence between a meaning which is coming to be and a pattern of words which is also coming to be at the same time. The point of convergence between the two processes is crucial and elusive: once missed it is hard to pick up again, but it is a point of spiritual synthesis and not a mechanical juxtaposition.

The struggle for expression is sometimes viewed, especially in schools, as the struggle of good usage in a certain language against bad usage, or the ignorant handling of that language. Croce's claim that linguistic usage is a myth seems to abolish the discrimination between good and bad usage, and to cut the ground from under the feet of teachers who are striving to maintain the standards of good English (or good French or good German etc.). But as we have already seen the abstractions which are excluded from aesthetics have a recognized function in education. "Good usage" is generally an abstraction from good writing, and good writing is achieved expression. The abstract framework of grammatical rules serves to bring up specific examples from the works of good writers, and so to develop the taste of the pupil. "Good or bad speech is judged not by the extrinsic yardstick of objective usage, but by the intrinsic and entirely intuitive yardstick of taste" (*PdE*, 206). ("Taste" will be more fully discussed in Chapter VII.)

The doctrine of good usage was vigorously attacked by I. A. Richards in his *Philosophy of Rhetoric* (1936), also upon the grounds of contextualism: "no word can be judged as to whether it is good or bad, correct or incorrect, beautiful or ugly, or anything else that matters to a writer, in isolation." This, he pointed out, "flies straight in the face of the only doctrine that for two hundred years has been officially inculcated. . . . I mean the doctrine of Usage. The doctrine that there is a right or good use for every word and that literary value consists in making that good use of it." [13]

Richards does not seem to realize that Croce had drawn the same conclusion from the same principle and consistently held to it (*PdE*, 146, 159–60, 178–79, 184; US, 25; *Discorsi*, II, 24). At least he refers to Croce in an obscurely indirect manner. After criticizing the traditional views of the relation between thought and expression (language as a "dress" or as a container), he observes: "These are obvious inadequacies; but as the history of criticism shows, they have not been avoided; and the perennial efforts of the reflective to amend or surpass them—Croce is the extreme modern example—hardly help." [14] Not only had Croce provided a complete theory of art to replace the traditional conceptions of rhetoric, but he was also more consistent than Richards. For having once refuted the doctrine of separate words, Croce did not surreptitiously reintroduce it into his next sentence. Whereas Richards had no sooner proclaimed the principle of contextualism, than he fell back into speaking of words as separate entities that have "powers" to "exert" and "back up" or "cooperate" with each other.[15] So hard it is to get rid of the prejudice of separate words, especially with Richards' positivistic tendency to reduce all mental processes to the mechanical operation of discrete material units.

Croce's doctrine qualifies the view of language sometimes found among critics of the symbolistic school, while acknowledging its core of truth. It is the view that language has been little more than cliché and convention in the literature of the past, but that now, since the appearance of this new school of writing, poems are written in which every word embodies a new and individual meaning.[16] But this is true of good poetry, at whatever time composed: Villon is as unique as Mallarmé, and Catullus is as unique as Verlaine. Every poetic utterance, as we have seen, creates its own language, and words and rhythms are used in a unique way every time a poet achieves expression, whether in the fifth century B.C. or in the twentieth century A.D. When Aeschylus saw the sea "flowering" with corpses after a battle, or spoke of Ares as the "moneychanger" of war, he was being as bold and imaginative as any modern poet, and possibly more. When Catullus said "Odi et amo," his own emotional conflict found perfect expression in the Latin words he used. When Dante spoke of "il tremolar della marina," Shakespeare of "the dark backward and abysm of time," Coleridge of "the elfish light" falling off "in hoary flakes," something was being done with language that had never been done before.

Conversely, writers who use second-hand imagery for second-hand emotions are bad, whether they imitate the ancient Alexandrines or the modern coterie of the rue de Rome.

The concept of individuality in expression is to be found both in Croce and in symbolism, but in the latter it is the programme of a poetry to be written, in the former a universal quality of poetic expression. The points of agreement between the two doctrines have been stressed by some critics,[17] but there is a world of difference between a philosophic theory of art and the programme or manifesto of a school of poetry, which includes a small group of writers and excludes all others.

The categorical identification of poetry with language means for Croce that language is the expression of an intuition and not a set of counters to be played with or of formulas with which to perform magic incantations. In *La poesia* Croce observed: "There is a famous statement by Mallarmé, often cited admiringly: 'one does not make poetry with ideas, but with words.' To which it must be answered, very simply, that poetry is not made with 'words' nor with 'ideas' but with poetry itself—with that imaginative creation which is at the same time living speech" (p[5], 260).

The statement that "poetry is language" was made by Heidegger in his commentary to Hölderlin, which Croce found both vague and rhetorical (*Discorsi*, I, 68–69; TPS, II, 164–65, 193). From such writers as Mallarmé and Heidegger the formula has passed into a number of contemporary critics, who seem to be unaware of the problems it raises (TPS, II, 38). One of these problems concerns the use of language in ways which are not poetic: e.g. for practical purposes, to effect persuasion and influence action, or for logical purposes, to convey concepts. The latter use was recognized fully in the first *Aesthetic*. In this particular case verbal expression is not identical with thought, but stands to it in the relation of a sign or symbol (E, 48; A, 42). So there is for Croce a symbolic use of language, but it occurs in what is known as expository prose and not in poetic expression. The fact that expression is not identical with the concept, as it is with the intuition, is proved by the observation that the same concept may be expressed by different words.[18] Hence "the quality of the expression is not deducible from the nature of the concept." "There must be expression, it cannot be absent; but what it is to be, this or that, is determined by the historical and psychological conditions of the person speaking." From this Croce draws a conclusion which is inescapable but which goes against the grain of the ordinary conception of language: "There is no such thing as the true (logical) sense of a word. The true sense of the word is that which is conferred upon it on each occasion by the person forming a concept" (E, 48–49; A, 42). This conclusion refutes the idea that insight into concepts may be obtained through the analysis of verbal forms, such as is made by the contemporary "analytical" school of philosophy, and Croce answered by anticipation those critics who claim that he should have built his theory of expression by deriving it from the meaning of "expression" in ordinary usage.[19] In his *Logic* Croce argued the impossibility of deriving a theory of reasoning from the analysis of verbal forms (Part I, Section II, Chapters 1–3).

So besides aesthetic expression there is also the expression of concepts, which proceeds by signs or symbols. Furthermore, there is also what is known as naturalistic or symptomatic expression, which has been discussed in the previous chapter. In later writings, culminating in *La poesia* (1936), Croce explored the area of nonaesthetic expression even more fully, as we shall see in Chapter XIII. Here it will be sufficient to note that the nonaesthetic uses of language are commonly called expression but for Croce are something very different. In other words, he held to his original conception of language: "born as poetry, language was afterwards twisted to serve as a sign" (TPS, II, 164; cf. *Discorsi*, I, 236).

The value of Croce's conception of language for literary criticism is that it eliminates mere verbalism and the pedantic discussion of classes of words, grammatical categories and all such abstractions, as well as the sterile debates on "correctness" and "poetic diction." Instead, it directs the attention of the critic to language as living speech. It abandons the task of breaking up the poem into verbal fragments to the empirical linguist, and turns criticism to the definition of the central theme or poetic motif of the work. In this process the critic may single out from a poem individual lines or words or phrases, but they are always referred back to the generating theme of the poem or the total poetic image.

THE DOCTRINE OF FIGURES OF SPEECH and of style is another traditional view which is incompatible with the principle of organic unity of thought and expression. This incompatibility was formulated by Croce as the "indivisibility of expression into modes or grades" in Chapter IX of the *Aesthetic*, Part I. Croce here points out that the whole system of rhetoric rests upon the underlying assumption that there are two ways of saying things: one is the "plain" way and the other the "ornate" way. It is assumed that the ordinary speaker can put his thought into plain words which will convey his meaning adequately, but with no beauty or distinction. Instead, the trained rhetorician will go beyond the plain word or phrase, and use the fine word or phrase that will convey exactly the same meaning, but with added beauty and elegance. In particular, there are certain ornaments called tropes or figures of speech which can be superimposed to the meaning in order to embellish it.

To the doctrine of tropes and figures of speech Croce makes this fundamental objection: "No satisfactory definition can be given of any of these terms. Those that have been attempted, when not obviously erroneous, are words without meaning. A typical instance is the very common definition of metaphor as 'a word used in the place of the proper word.' But why give oneself the trouble? Why substitute the improper word for the proper and take the worse and longer road when the better and shorter is known to us? Perhaps, as is commonly said, because the proper word is in certain cases not so *expressive* as the so-called improper word or metaphor? But in this case the metaphor is the proper word and the so-called 'proper' word, if it were used in its place, would be deficient in expression and therefore most improper" (E, 77; A, 69). Poets do not use metaphors to say in a different way what could have been said plainly, but they use them to say something different.

The elaborate and complicated classifications of tropes and figures of speech, which occupy such a large place in traditional rhetoric, all rest on a comparison of the poetic expression with a prose paraphrase, which is considered its equivalent and is then used to define the poetic expression. The traditional classifications are rivalled by some more sophisticated modern ones, such as the Subjective Image and the Objective Image, the Sunken, the Radical, the Intensive, the Expansive, the Animistic Image, etc. But once we have renounced the Paraphrastic Heresy, i.e. the doctrine that the meaning of a poem can be adequately represented by a prose paraphrase, all these must go too. It is therefore absurd to charge Croce with "theoretical paralysis" because he "denies the validity of all stylistic and rhetorical categories." [20] This is like accusing a modern scientist of "theoretical paralysis" because he rejects the doctrines of medieval astrology on the influences of the stars.[21] But just as astrology seems to survive in some quarters, so does the belief in words and figures of speech as material units, endowed with unique powers of their own.[22]

Croce gives a detailed critique not only of metaphor but of other rhetorical categories. For instance, take "ellipsis." This is defined as the omission of some word or phrase which would be expressed if the meaning were "fully set out." [23] But if the thought is completely expressed without the omitted phrase, then the sentence is already "fully set out" and any addition would spoil it. On the other hand, if the sentence is incomplete or obscure or in any way aesthetically inadequate without the omitted phrase, then the omission is an expressive deficiency and not an embellishment (*PdE*, 151–52). The converse argument applies to the opposite figure or "pleonasm." A pleonasm is a word or phrase added to an already completed expression. The dilemma rises again with no less force: either the addition is really necessary to the full expression of the thought, and then it is no addition, but an integral part of the expression; or

it is unnecessary, and it is an artistic blemish (*ibid.*). Word order provides the opportunity for other figures, such as "inversion" (*PdE*, 168). But if the so-called "inverted order" is
the one best suited to express the poet's intuition, then it is the
only "regular" order for that expression. The so-called Latinized
word order found in a poet like Milton was really indispensable
to the complete expression of his poetic vision, and no other
word order would have been adequate.[24]

The doctrine of figures of speech is sometimes dressed up in
modern critical terms by contemporary historical scholars, in
order to make it more acceptable to modern palates. For instance: "the figures are the sum of all resources (other than
metrical) by which poetry conveys its emotional overplus of
excitement or stimulation; they are the sum, expressed in Elizabethan terms, of the types of ambiguity, the obliquities, the
transferences, the echoes and controlled associations, which lift
poetry above statement and by which the poet lets odd and unexpected lights into his subject." [25]

This comes down to the assumption that poetry consists of
"statements" with an "overplus," or the traditional dichotomy
of plain and ornate style. It is therefore subject to the same
criticism. But the doctrines of rhetoric have a perennial fasci-
nation for a certain type of mind as a simple and easy way to
pry into the secrets of poetic art. In the hope of discovering by
this method the "key" to the poetry of an age like the Renaissance, scholars have delved into the dark and murky regions of
rhetorical theory, and laboriously dug up the complicated classifications of the ancient rhetoricians and their Renaissance disciples. One of the most painstaking of these labors consists of the
application of rhetorical analysis to the works of Shakespeare.[26]
Shakespeare's plays are split up into innumerable small pieces
and distributed under the full catalogue of rhetorical figures
and tropes: dictyposis, apomnemonysis, epicrisis, chria, enche,
eusthatia, asphalia, paraenesis, ominatio, systrophe, synecodoche,
merismus or partitio, eutrepismus, epanados, synathroesmus,
peristasis, taxis, hypotyposis or enargia, prosopographia, proso-
popoeia, characterismus, ethopoeia, dialogismus, pragmatogra-

phia, chronographia, topothesia, antanagoge, epitrope, homeo-
sosis, paradiastole, charientismus, catacosmesis, epanarthosis,
exargasia—and others still.

Now such a catalogue (together with the lucid exposition
that accompanies it in the work referred to) is no doubt useful
for the history of rhetorical theory. But to think that it helps us
to understand the art of Shakespeare is complete misunderstanding of the expressive process. These are abstractions, and the
characters of Shakespeare are no abstractions. They are full,
concrete, particularized images, and their speeches are not mu-
seums of rhetorical devices; they are images in action, developing and manifesting themselves in words.

For instance, in this classification Iago's speech on the will
as the gardener of the body is brought under the same category
as Jaques' "All the world's a stage." Quite logically, they are
both bracketed under "the figure allegory" defined as a metaphor
continued "through an entire speech." [27] But poetically speaking, Jaques' speech is merely the imaginative embroidering of a
moral commonplace, undertaken to round out pleasantly a
romantic episode, while Iago's speech is one of the most sardonic
representations of hypocrisy in all Shakespeare. The arguments
of virtue are paradoxically placed in the mouth of an evil character, who uses them with complete cynicism. The speech does
at times have a rhetorical flavor, as in the artfully protracted
series of antithesis: "plant lettuce or sow nettles, set hyssop and
weed up thyme, supply it with one gender of herbs or distract
it with many" etc., but this is again character-drawing, and
rhetorical artifice is a clue to the insincerity of the speaker, as
elsewhere in Shakespeare. The art of both these speeches consists in the way they particularize an imaginative situation, not
in their conformity to pre-established schematizations.

If traditional rhetoric were really as illuminating as some of
its modern advocates maintain, one would expect to find classical
scholars enthusiastically using it to expound the beauties of the
Greek and Latin poets. For classical scholars can reach rhetoric
at its sources and hence presumably at its purest. But this is not
exactly so. The ancient commentaries on Aristophanes are sim-

ply brim-full of rhetorical observations, but the scholar who made the most thorough study of them summed up his judgment in one uncomplimentary word—"rubbish": "This rubbish is the product of *rhetoriké* . . . the same sort of comments are meant to rank as literary criticism in the Fourth Book of Macrobius. There they are intended to prove that Virgil is rhetor no less than poet, so scrupulously does he observe the rules of rhetoric. Such is the monstrous view of these late doctors, which make comments of this order so perverse and worthless." [28]

To scholars trained in the traditional system of classical education, the tropes and figures or rhetoric are nothing new or glamorous. They may come as novelties and appear priceless technical secrets to men who have not been drilled in them at school, and so have not learnt by experience how little they contribute to good writing. An amusing instance of Croce's own early training in rhetorical categories was quoted by him in answer to a formalistic art critic: "This kind of bad criticism was well known to De Sanctis, who emancipated himself from it in his teaching at Naples before 1848, and I have also known it in my adolescence, when I was made to study the *Rhetoric* of Capellina. (Some time ago, I came across a copy of Dante which I read and annotated following the guidance of that doctrine, and I burst into laughter when I found the line 'See there Farinata who has risen' with the marginal note in youthful and calligraphic writing: 'Admirable hypotyposis!' What a critic of pure form was I then, at the age of thirteen, and did not know it!)" (cc, v, 45). When recording similar marginal notes on "agnition" and "peripety" actually made by a critic of the Renaissance, Croce observed: "this is always rhetorical criticism, whose aim is classification . . . its error . . . lies in making art consist in something other than the personality itself of the artist, his feeling and therefore his imagination." [29]

However inapplicable to the definition of poetic art, rhetorical terms may be used appropriately in certain other ways, which Croce defines carefully and which apparently have been misunderstood or forgotten by some of his critics: "1. as *verbal variants* of the aesthetic concept; 2. as designations of the *un-aesthetic;* or lastly (and this is their most important use) 3. no longer in the service of art and aesthetic, but of science and logic" (E, 78; A, 70). An instance of 1. is when an expression is praised as a metaphor or some other figure of speech when all that is meant is that it is an artistic expression. So "clarity," "vigor," "grace," "elegance" and all the other traditional qualities of style may be employed as verbal variants of "achieved expression." But these terms are very ambiguous, "so that the same word sometimes serves to proclaim the perfect, sometimes to condemn the imperfect." Hence they may come under the second class, "designations of the unaesthetic." E.g. "ellipsis" may designate deficiency, "pleonasm" excess, and "metaphor" the use of an unsuitable term.[30]

Finally, rhetorical terms may have (3) a positive use in logical analysis. Since the same concept may be represented by different words, a writer may select one term as the fixed sign for that concept. Then all other words that he may come to use for it, for the sake of variety or for some other reason, become synonyms or metaphors, synecdoches or ellipses for it. Croce was well aware that he himself in the course of his treatise made use of rhetorical terms in this manner. "But this procedure, which is of value in the critical discussions of science and philosophy, has no value whatever in literary and artistic criticism. In scientific discourse there are such words as metaphors and proper terms. . . . But in aesthetic expression there are only proper words, and the same intuition can be expressed in one way only, just because it is an intuition and not a concept" (E, 80–81; A, 72–73).

It is therefore unwarranted to accuse Croce of contradiction because he makes use of rhetorical terms in logical analysis.[31] Furthermore, Croce repeatedly declared that he was not trying to wage war upon words and expressly reserved his right to use traditional terms whenever convenient (*PdE,* 163–64, 217; NSE, 97). But he does not use them in the traditional way, i.e. as "principles of composition and standards of judgment" (*PdE,* 218).

The concept of *style* is another pseudo-aesthetic concept that Croce analyzed in connection with rhetoric: "Sometimes it is said that every writer must have a style, and then this style is synonymous with form or expression. At others, style is said to be absent from the form of a code of jurisprudence or of a mathematical work. Here one falls back into the error of admitting two different forms of expression, a bare form and an ornate form, because, if style is form, the code and the mathematical treatise must also, strictly speaking, be acknowledged to have each its own style. At other times one hears the critics blaming a writer for having 'too much style' or 'writing a style.' Here it is clear that style signifies, not form nor a mode of it, but improper or pretentious expression, a form of the inartistic" (E, 79; A, 71). Style, or artistic quality, in expository prose consists in the expression of emotion, just as in any other kind of writing. But the emotions expressed will not be those of the man who is not a thinker and does not deal with concepts, "not the hate or love for certain objects and individuals, but *the very effort of thinking*, with the pain and the joy, the love and the hate joined to it" (E, 26–27; A, 22; cf. PdE, 125–30).

In later writings Croce discussed more fully modern attempts to establish a method of stylistic analysis. But all such attempts proceed by means of classification of expressions, and since all such classifications for Croce are abstractions, they were all rejected by him.[32] Today many of the older classifications are no longer taken seriously, but attempts are still made to analyze the forms of expression or construction in the novel or the drama. However, under their modern garb they turn out to be close kindred of the old rhetorical classifications, with attendant Rules of Composition, guaranteed to make anyone write well. We shall consider one of them in our next section.

THERE IS A TWENTIETH-CENTURY TRADITION of analysis of narrative technique which seems to originate from statements made by Henry James on the writing of his own novels. In such statements it is possible that James, by adopting a detached "craftsmanlike" attitude to his own work, may have been a little less than just to some of his own creations, such as Miss Gostrey in *The Ambassadors*. However that may be, a whole series of books on the technique of the novel developed from the study of James' work.[33] A friend and admirer of James, Percy Lubbock, wrote in 1921 *The Craft of Fiction*, in which he pointed out the importance of the point of view of the narrator in the novel: "The whole intricate question of method, in the craft of fiction, I take to be governed by the question of the point of view—the question of the relation in which the narrator stands to the story." [34] Not long afterwards J. W. Beach wrote *The Twentieth Century Novel: Studies in Technique* (1932), and others followed him.

Croce reviewed the Italian translation of Beach's book in 1948. He observed that on Beach's own showing the main difference between the nineteenth-century novel and the earlier novel was not a difference in technique, but in the very ideal of the novel. The traditional ideal was that of a didactic tale written to expound some ethical or political teaching. In the nineteenth century this was superseded by the ideal of a narrative that aimed solely at the artistic presentation of human nature. This is a shift from a didactic ideal to a poetic ideal, and novels composed under the inspiration of the latter ideal are for Croce to be judged as works of poetry, while the others belong to the history of ideals or of culture. "Technique has nothing to do with all this: the didactic and controversial novel did not possess a technique which was inferior to, or different from, the artistic novel, but it differed because it had a different soul." Croce concluded that Beach "allowed himself to be dominated by the 'Rules of the Genre' (is it not this old acquaintance of ours, the Genre and its Rules, that he venerates as technique?), as if the essence of art consisted in them. But the lover of poetry will readily forget the 'Rules of the Genre' for a beautiful page, a living character, a felicitous trait." [35]

Another turn was given to the discussion of technique in 1948 by Mark Schorer's paper "Technique as Discovery," [36] in which he argued that for the artist "technique is the only means he has of discovering, exploring, developing his subject, of conveying its meaning." In a series of analyses he then showed how certain novelists apparently used technique to discover their subjects, or failed to discover them through neglect of technique. But "technique" can assume the appearance of producing such far-reaching results only because it has been previously endowed with all the powers of what is traditionally known in aesthetics as Form, i.e. the powers of objectification, organization and catharsis. It is the concept of Organic Form, or Inner Form, as developed by Shaftesbury, Schiller and their successors that logically possesses these powers and achieves those results.[37] But the devices referred to as "technique" are basically empty abstractions. Take the much-discussed "point of view" of the narrator. This, too, can be shown to be void of a positive content. For obviously a "point" without anyone in it and a "view" without anything to see are empty abstractions. But if there is already in the mind of the writer a story to be seen, and a character who sees that story, then the constituents of the novel are already there, and the "point of view" is only one of the relations that subsist between them, arbitrarily cut off from all the others and erected into a category.[38] This of course does not mean that the identity of the narrator and the point of view of the narrative may not involve considerable study at some stage or other of the composition. But at what stage, and in what manner, depends upon the particular novel, its plot, theme, characters, etc. Nor does it mean that the choice of an incongruous narrator or of an inconsistent point of view may not be a fault (Croce himself noted an instance in 1911 in LNI, 1, 132–37). But so will any other incongruity and inconsistency. And since every case is different, no general rule can be given. All technical devices that are extolled as infallible nostrums for the construction of the perfect novel or the perfect poem are a delusion and a snare.

THE NEXT CONSEQUENCE that Croce draws from the principle of organic unity is the denial of aesthetic validity to Prosody and Metrics. In other words, there is nothing *intrinsically* beautiful about verse, nor are there metres that are more beautiful than others. Beauty results from the total expression. The patterns of metre, of verses and stanzas etc., are abstractions of the kind that we have described at the beginning of this chapter. The metrical "form" which supposedly makes verse different from prose results from a dissection of the "intensive manifold" of poetry and destroys it. It abstracts from all those other constituents of a line which make it a real utterance: the sounds and syllables used, the tone and degree of accent, and the meaning of words, which is inseparable in poetry from their sound.

Like the other abstractions we have met, the abstraction of metre is made for practical convenience and if used in a purely descriptive way is harmless. But aesthetically it is beside the point. Yet whole systems of criticism are still built on the assumption that there is an aesthetic difference between verse and prose and that poetry can only be composed in verse. As J. E. Spingarn put it, "not only there is no sharp dividing line between prose and verse, but whatever distinction exists between words in metre and words without it exists in exactly the same way between verses written in the same metre." [39] It is pointless to argue that a pentameter is not the same as an Alexandrine, for no pentameter is exactly the same as any other pentameter. All that one can say is that some lines are more or less like others. But on such a vague relationship it is not possible to base an aesthetic judgment. A line cannot be judged good or bad because some of its elements are like, or unlike, those of another line. A line is good or bad in so far as it is, or is not, expressive.

Nor is this a denial of the musical quality of verse. Of course there is music in good verse, but each poet makes his own music, which is unique and unrepeatable, as becomes painfully apparent when attempts are made by imitators to duplicate it. However, it is sometimes argued that there is an aesthetic quality in recurrence. By "adopting" a certain metre at the beginning of a poem, a poet (it is claimed) arouses in the reader an expectation which, being gratified by the continuance of the metre through the whole poem, produces aesthetic satisfaction. But the reader will not be satisfied by the mere repetition of rhythm without meaning—by a mere rum-ti-tum. The metre must not only be regular, it must be expressive. There must be in the poem that particular union of sound with sense, of metre with feeling, which only the poet of genius manages to hit upon and which is beyond the reach of rules. Therefore one may multiply endlessly the metrical patterns of lines and stanzas and arrange them systematically in treatises on prosody and metrics, but one gets no nearer the secret of poetic composition. It is an a priori synthesis which we recognize when we see it, but for which no prescription can be given.

It may be objected: suppose a poet at the beginning of a poem arouses in us the expectation of a certain metrical recurrence, and then suddenly shifts to another in the middle of a poem. Will not this be an artistic deficiency? It might if the shift does not fit in with anything else in the poem. Then it will indeed be bad, but only because it is not expressive of anything, and not because it is an "irregularity."

Furthermore, a recognized metre is usually not an empty form but the full form or concrete reality of some previous poem that the poet liked. The very name of certain famous metres, like the Petrarchan sonnet or the Spenserian stanza, refers to specific poems and poets. The writers who adopted those metres in later times—i.e. who tried to make poems which sounded like the originals—were admirers of the *Canzoniere* or of *The Faerie Queene*, and their appearance marks a date in the history of the reputation of those poems. And when English poets in the nineties of the last century began writing *rondeaux* and *villanelles*, was it not a sign of a certain orientation towards French culture which was then manifesting itself in England? It is not the empty form which is the object of admiration, but a particular poem or group of poems.

Poets sometimes claim that they are "experimenting" with metre and trying to produce a new form. Metre would thus seem to be a concrete element of poetic art. But a poet who reaches the point of wishing to experiment is already saturated with previous poetry, and does not work in a void. No verse form exists in the abstract and each poem achieves its own individual metre which fits that poem and no other. This view, while on one side making metrical regularity unessential to poetry, on the other side is equally indifferent to irregularity and does not see any particular virtue in "free verse" for its own sake, because all good verse is always "free"—i.e. spontaneous expression (G, I, 89–91).

Croce's critique of metrics—or rather, of literary judgment based on abstract metrics—was ably presented in English by J. E. Spingarn in an essay on "Prose and Verse" from which quotation has already been made and to which the reader is referred for detailed discussion of the problem in terms of English metre.[40] Spingarn also made it clear that Croce's critique referred to metrics when taken as prescriptive or evaluative and not as descriptive. "It will always be convenient and proper to identify and classify the new rhythms by their superficial resemblance to the old ones: and so we shall continue to speak of 'anapaests', 'trochees', 'heroic couplets' or 'blank verse', at least until better terms are invented, just as we speak of tall men and short men, large books and small books, without assuming that adjectives imply fundamental distinctions of quality or character." But when we consider the poem as a work of art, then "rhythm and metre must be regarded as identical with style, as style is identical with aesthetic form, and form in turn is the work of art in its spiritual and indivisible self." [41]

Anyone who suspects that Croce's system led him to neglect metre should read his remarks on Dante's *terzina* or, better still, on Ariosto's *ottava* (to be quoted in Chapter XII) or his analysis of Goethe's lyrical metres, already referred to (G, I, 89–91). In the case of a contemporary poet, G. Pascoli, Croce based his negative judgment upon the poet's lack of rhythmical power, seen as a symptom of imaginative weakness.[42] But rhythm and metre are always considered as particularized instances of expression and not in the abstract.

HOWEVER, apart from these abstractions, there is for Croce something in works of art which may be properly designated "technique." It is the practical process through which the physical concomitants of the expressive act are preserved for future reproduction.[43] Most discussions of this idea of Croce's proceed in ignorance of his view of the mind-body relation, which is completely monistic. For Croce, the mind is the body and the body is the mind. The two are really one, and appear to be separate entities through the operations, which should by now be familiar, of the practical spirit, which splits up the intensive manifold of reality and separates the internal from the external, the spiritual from the material, etc. (*Pratica*, 52; US, 15). So for Croce every spiritual act has its physical side, or, to be more precise, "may be physically constructed" (*PdE*, 468). Every act of expression, even if it is "purely mental," has its counterpart in bodily movements (E, 106; A, 97). But these movements are essentially transient, so if one wants to preserve an expression, a way must be found to record these movements. And of course many methods have been found for this purpose. The sound waves of speech can be recorded in a number of ways which is increasing, and the physical movements which go along with other expressions can also be preserved—by the laying of pigment on canvas, or by the fashioning of clay or of some other material. These processes are called "technique" by a general usage which Croce accepts, while defining their function as that of preservation or "externalization" (*estrinsecazione*, E, 106; A, 97). In the case of poetry, "externalization" consists in the articulation of the vocal organs, or speech. Writing is an ulterior process which sets down symbols to remind us of the articulations required to produce sounds, so it is externalization at the second remove (E, 110; A, 100). In any case, externalization for Croce is a practical action and therefore does not belong to art. It has no aesthetic value.

This doctrine as applied to the fine arts often meets with opposition. Art is thought to be essentially skill in handling a material medium. The laying of paint upon canvas, or the fashioning of clay into a statue, are thought to be essential parts of the creative process, whereas for Croce they are merely a recording of it. In the *Aesthetic* he went so far as to say: "The work of art is always internal, and what may be called external is no longer a work of art" (E, 57; A, 51). However, he also affirmed that an artist may use externalization as an aid to composition, "as a kind of experiment and to have a starting point for further thinking and inner concentration" (E, 113; A, 103). Externalization, as J. Hospers observes, does not have to begin only after the inner creative process is completed, but may begin at the same time and proceed simultaneously throughout.[44]

The concept of the material medium is the cornerstone of the theory of the separation of the arts, which Croce also rejects: for him there is only one creative process in all the arts, and that is expression. Since we are not dealing here with the fine arts or music, but with literature, we will not go into this vexed question. This is also rendered unnecessary by the fact that Croce's theory of technique in the arts has been recently defended by contemporary American aestheticians.[45] Only two remarks, mainly historical, will be made here. One is, that the doctrine of the inwardness of artistic beauty may well be traced back to the aesthetics of Plotinus, who held that the real work of art existed in the mind of the artist and not in the external object—a doctrine revived early in the eighteenth century by Shaftesbury. These historical connections, of which Croce does not seem to have been fully aware, were noted by a German scholar.[46] The other remark is, that somewhat similar statements on the ideality of art, although based on a different philosophy, may be found in the writings of a contemporary thinker, J. P. Sartre.[47]

It is now possible to understand Croce's criticism of literary "technique" in all its logic. On the one side, he believed that technique in art is a purely recording process, and not a creative one. On the other hand, he had shown that so-called literary technique, the "arts of language" and the "structural principles" of the novel or the drama, consist of empty abstractions. So he came to the conclusion that strictly speaking a technique of aesthetic expression was impossible. "Sometimes a certain writer is said to have invented a new technique of fiction or of drama, or a painter is said to have discovered a new technique for distributing light. The word is here used indiscriminately, for the so-called *new technique* is really *that new novel itself*, or *that new picture itself*, and nothing else. The distribution of light belongs to the vision of the picture itself, as the technique of the dramatist is his new dramatic conception itself" (E, 123; A, 112).

Strangely enough, on account of this doctrine Croce has been accused of denying that poetry has a physical medium in language. But if it is meant that Croce denies that language has a physical side, this is refuted by the preceding exposition. If it is meant that poetry for Croce consists of thought without words, that seems an amazing criticism to make in view of Croce's repeated statements that identify poetry with language and aesthetics with general linguistics. But a serious misunderstanding to that effect seems to prevail among some English critics of Croce. The reason is that these critics believe that language is an external object. Since Croce denies that an external object is necessary to the aesthetic process, they assume that Croce also denies that language is necessary to poetry.

For instance, Bernard Bosanquet, who was a supporter of the theory of the external object or "aesthetic medium," apparently believed that for Croce language belonged to the process of externalization and that words were not part of poetic expression.[48] The dramatic critic of *The Times*, A. B. Walkley, answered him in two lively articles, showing that he had completely misunderstood the theory of externalization in the arts, but did not correct the specific misunderstanding about words in poetry.[49] This may account for the fact that later S. Alexander labored under a similar misapprehension, holding that for Croce art had "no physical embodiment" and that he denied that "the sound of words, the metre etc." were "the material of the art" of poetry.[50] In 1926 the general question of externalization was raised again by an English scholar, Mrs. E. Dodds, to whom Croce gave a detailed answer.[51] But Croce's elucidations seem to have been unnoticed in England.

Possibly influenced by the English critics, even a brilliant thinker like E. Cassirer in his *Essay on Man* advanced the same objection against Croce, arguing that "for a great painter, a great musician, or a great poet, the colors, the lines, rhythms and words are not merely a part of his technical apparatus; they are necessary moments of the productive process itself." [52] But that was precisely what Croce believed about poetry. Should still another reference be needed, here is one from the *Breviary:* "If one takes away from a poem its metre, its rhythm, and its words, one is not left, as some believe, with its thought, as something underlying these things, one is left with nothing at all. The poem was born as those words, that rhythm and that metre" (NSE, 39; EA, 44).

Croce's theory of technique met with a different objection from some of his artist friends in Italy: viz., that technique was a necessary stage of artistic training.[53] The objection was answered by Croce in an important untranslated paper of 1905 on "The mastering of technique" (*PdE,* 247–55), from which we shall now make some quotations, since the question is connected with the technique of literature. The artists' argument was that a painter must be trained in technique before he can attempt original work. When the student has finally mastered technique, in drawing or some other art, he may get an original idea, and then the technique which he has made himself master of will enable him to make a work of art. As long as he knows only technique, he will be only a craftsman; but he cannot become an original artist without craftsmanship.

Croce answered that this argument had long been familiar to him—he could have added that he himself had begun by assuming the truth of the theory of the separation of the arts according to the medium.[54] He then proceeded to challenge the very distinction between training and original creation: "what appears to be technical training and the acquisition of purely material skill is from the beginning nothing else but creation. The poet or the painter who is considered to be still in the process of formation, is already a poet or a painter: the painter has visions and expressions, a world of figures, attitudes, profiles, movements, color combinations, 'patches' [*macchie,* see Chapter VIII], which are to be found in part in his book of sketches and in part only in his memory. The poet has rhythms, similes, words, outlines of plays and novels, germs of lyrics, which are to be found partly in his notes and partly in his memory. These productions are already so much a work of art, that in certain cases many connoisseurs would exchange several large pictures for a collection of sketches and drafts: such things are perfect in themselves, and appear imperfect only when removed from their isolation and placed in juxtaposition with larger and more complex works. Many writers have given their best in letters and other writings not meant for publication, in which they have set down the formative process of their spirit, which did not reach a fuller attainment."

The principle of Integration is then called into play to account for the masterpiece: "What happens when one passes from these sketches to the greater work, to the masterpiece? . . . The vision of a great work seems to rise all of a sudden before the artist. In reality, what rises suddenly is a new connection, a new image in which innumerable preceding images are unified, each of which has already required an effort and was a creation of genius. Since the new connection presupposes the innumerable images to be connected, it is easy to fall into the illusion that those images are not art, but the means or *media* of art; not syntheses, which become subjected to a broader synthesis, but *inanimate material* which has to be possessed and mastered to make way for a masterpiece. Certainly, *in the instant of the new vision* all the previous ones lose their own life and receive the afflatus of a new life." These quotations have been made with the object of showing how carefully Croce went into the question of technique. The paper ends with the conclusion that "technique, conceived as something mechanical, is never to be found in the work of genius, genius being artistic creation" (*PdE*, 253).

An ingenious attempt to get around Croce's critique of externalization was made by an American aesthetician, Milton C. Nahm. Professor Nahm argues that Croce, on his own assumptions, should admit that externalization is an integral part of the expressive process. For Croce acknowledges that an intuition may be "impregnated" with concepts (E, 4; A, 2); so "there appears to be no reason why there may not be intuitions 'impregnated' with 'practical activity', technical dexterity, and artistic skill, as well." But if this is so, then Croce has "presupposed" externalization within the intuition and acknowledged it as part of the expressive process.[55]

Certainly on Croce's assumptions, concepts and volitions, or truth and morality, as well as utility, pleasure, number, measure, and indeed "everything else" may be found in art—but only as an antecedent, "submerged and forgotten in it" (NSE, 63; EA, 72–73).[56] If the process of externalization were ever to become part of an intuition—e.g. if a poet were to write about elocution or typography—it would cease to be externalization, and would be reduced to the rank of an impression or a passive material of intuition, instead of being its shaping power, as the supporters of the theory of "technique" would have it.

It may finally be objected that if we give up the traditional tools of formal and technical analysis the critic is left with nothing to work with. On the contrary, Croce's critical method provides a number of critical tools, such as definition and characterization, discrimination and differentiation, which we shall see in Chapter VIII.

CHAPTER V

The Question of Literary Genres

CAN POETIC EXPRESSIONS be classified? Are there affinities among them that group them together in families, kinds or species? The question is of primary interest to literary criticism. For if works of literary art are subject to classification, such a classification would constitute a real "science of literature" and afford a solid foundation for the critical judgment.

This "science" of literature of course exists already and has been known for centuries. It is the theory of genres that was once the foundation of judicial criticism and is now the customary historical approach. There is no single authoritative statement of the classification of genres or kinds, but the epic, the drama and the lyric are supposed to be the principal ones, and there are several subdivisions, such as (for the drama) tragedy, comedy, tragicomedy, farce, historical drama, social drama, melodrama, mystery plays, moralities, etc. etc. Other kinds have been added more or less systematically, such as the novel and the essay, or been considered descendants of the old ones: e.g. the novel is derived by some critics from the epic.

One of Croce's most distinctive and most controversial doctrines is his denial of the genres both as principles of composition and as critical or historical categories (US, 22). For him, genres are not separate forms of expression and works of literature are not to be evaluated according to their genres, but to be judged singly as individual expressions. No genuine history of literature should be conducted by genres. This is an important question, so we will devote a chapter to it, bringing together his variously dated arguments.[1]

First of all, it should be noted that Croce denies genres as aesthetic categories, but not as empirical classifications. He denies that they are separate forms of expression, but he does not deny that works of literature can be grouped together for convenience into kinds and genres. He even acknowledges that poems are "to some extent" composed within pre-established forms or genres (CVM, 193), but he denies that they derive their artistic quality from that fact. Again, he rejects them as standards of judgment, but acknowledges fully the fact that they exist as generalizations or ideas which are current in literary discussion. As such they are frequently productive of critical error, but sometimes they may be symptoms of more valuable things.

Croce's discussion of genres takes three forms: 1) *theoretical,* in which he refutes genres as aesthetic categories; 2) *historical,* in which he appeals to the history of literature and of criticism to prove that they are extrinsic and contingent classifications and not "natural divisions" of literature; and 3) *practical,* in which he demonstrates by actual criticism what should take the place of criticism by genres.

To begin with the first, Croce's main argument against genres as critical standards is that they lack universality. The definition of a genre includes a certain number of works but excludes all others. Prose is not verse, tragedy is not comedy, novels are not odes. Now critical judgment should be based upon as broad a foundation as possible. Since there are certain aesthetic qualities which are to be found in all works of literature, whatever their genre, it is those qualities that make them works of literary art, and they should be judged upon those qualities and not upon the restricted generalizations provided by genres. We already know what the universal qualities of works of art are for Croce. A work of art for him is a conscious production, it is cognitive, it is an image, and it is so unified that it expresses an emotion through the image. Therefore the critical judgment in literature as in the other arts should be based upon unity, ideality and expressiveness.

It may be objected that this definition covers only the most general qualities of a work of art and that we have defined, at best, the genus of literature or of poetry, but not its species. Genres are the species of which literary art or poetry is the genus. But the method of classification by genus and species (or ' by subordination and coordination, as it is also called) is subject to certain objections in Croce's logic, as we shall see in the next chapter. Here it will be sufficient to state that for Croce no one has been able to prove conclusively that poetry should be divided into genres, or that the genres can be logically deduced from the nature of poetry. On the contrary, it can be shown that genres are accidental and extrinsic classifications. They were originally based on the circumstances of recitation. The epic was poetry recited by a rhapsode, the lyric was poetry sung to the music of the lyre, and drama was poetry recited by a group of actors. Whatever the details involved, these are all extrinsic circumstances of recitation and not intrinsic qualities of poetry. The fact that a poem is sung or recited does not make it a good or a bad poem, and critical judgment cannot be based on that fact. The Greek theatre was certainly a ritualistic institution before it became the vehicle for poetry. But the poetry composed for the benefit of that institution was the result of a series of creative acts, each complete in itself, and to be evaluated as such by the critic of literature.

It is claimed, however, that there are intrinsic differences between works belonging to different genres, differences pertaining to the formal structure of the composition. These structural differences go back ultimately to the Aristotelian classification of genres in the *Poetics*, which in turn was derived from one of Plato's. This classification is based on an extremely superficial criterion: that of the "person speaking," or whether a story is told in narrative or dialogue, which provides two fundamental genres. A third or "mixed" genre was then added to account for the epic, which contains both narrative and dialogue. Such a scheme is strictly limited to storytelling and obviously has no place for the expression of the poet's emotions, or the lyrical genre. Most modern definitions of the "structure" of genres are elaborations or refinements upon the Aristotelian, and suffer from the same basic deficiency: they are founded on restricted generalizations and not on the universal nature of poetry.[2]

On the other hand, when the definition of a genre attempts to be intrinsic, it tends to resolve itself into a definition of good writing in general (NSE, 48; EA, 55). For instance, Poe's law of the "short story"—a genre he is supposed to have codified—is a definition of the art of writing in general: "in the whole composition there should be no word written, of which the tendency, direct or indirect, is not to the one pre-established design."[3]

It may be urged by the supporters of genres that their classification is based upon an objective circumstance which we have not yet considered: the emotional effect upon an audience. To put this at its crudest, a tragedy makes the audience weep and a comedy makes it laugh, so they are different genres. An improved form of this theory was formulated by Aristotle himself with his doctrine of the tragic emotions, pity and fear, and the beneficial effect of "catharsis" upon them—if such is the import of that extremely disputed term. In later times the emotional scheme was developed much more fully and elaborately. But to all these doctrines of emotional effect Croce has a fundamental objection: they deny the ideal nature of art. "Ideal," as we have seen in Chapter II, simply means cognitive, theoretical. To arouse emotions in others is not theory or contemplation, it is action, and very practical action. Hence for Croce it falls under the category of *praxis*, together with economic and political activities, and belongs to the history of those things, not of art. To arouse the emotions of the audience is propaganda, and propaganda is politics, or commercial advertising, or possibly preaching, but not poetry.

In the first *Aesthetic*, Chapter IV, Croce showed how genres are derived from individual works by the process of abstraction, so that it is impossible to deduce from them the individual acts of expression. There can be no predetermined way of expressing the ideals of chivalry or the emotions of domestic life, or the love of nature. Hence the fallacy of criticizing works according to the presumed laws of the genre to which they are assigned. In the second phase of his doctrine, that of the lyrical intuition, Croce expanded and transformed the concept of the lyric until it was no longer a genre among other genres, but the universal definition of art, or the expression of emotion through an image. In the *Breviary* we find a kind of interpenetration of the genres: "art is always lyrical, that is, the epic and drama of emotion" (NSE², 27). The rejection of genres is confirmed by the lyrical theory: "Since every work of art expresses a state of mind, and the state of mind is individual and always new, intuition implies infinite intuitions, which it is impossible to bring into a pigeon-hole classification by genres" (NSE, 49; EA, 56).

In later statements Croce stressed the interpenetration of all genres into one, which is not a genre but a universal (US, 23), and criticized the traditional tripartition: "A lyric which is not also epic and dramatic will be mere effusion and 'lyricism', not poetry. An epic in which the narrator is distinct from what he narrates will be historical thought and not poetry. A drama which is not generated by emotion will be, according to the case, either a dialogue or a debate or a mere counterfeit of real life, i.e. bustle and noise, animated in appearance but not genuinely and inwardly alive" (*Poeti e scrittori del . . . Rinascimento*, II, 117. Cf. NSE², 322–24). In *La poesia* (1936) he saw the concepts of genres arising out of otherwise innocent empirical generalizations and practical advice to artists, and later being "stiffened" into philosophical categories and definitions, with all their attendant evils in judicial criticism (P, 174).

It has been claimed for the theory of genres that it defines the permanent and fundamental types of literature, its "natural history" subdivisions.[4] It is also claimed that the classification in its broadest form—the tripartition of epic, drama and lyric —goes back to the ancient Greeks and bears the stamp of the Greek genius. To which it is perhaps sufficient to oppose what a great classical scholar, Wilamowitz, had to say about the way in which the concept of genres was applied to the history of Greek literature: "The origin of Greek literature and its types were identified with the absolutely normal and natural . . . what had been effected by definite, concrete conditions, and by the individual will of important men, became the product of immanent natural laws. The types of Greek poetry and artistic prose—epic, elegy, ode, tragedy, comedy, epigram, history, dialogue, oration, epistle—appeared as natural forms in the arts of discourse." [5] It is also a fact of history that the standard tripartition does not go back to the Greeks, but appears much later, as Croce showed in his history of aesthetics.

The example of Shakespeare is sometimes cited in support of the view that the genres represent natural and inevitable artistic divisions. It is argued that he composed his plays within well-defined genre divisions on the strength of the distribution of his plays into the clearly-marked partitions of Comedies, Histories and Tragedies. But that distribution is notoriously posthumous, and was effected, more or less confidently (for they were uncertain about the status of *Troilus and Cressida*) by the editors of the First Folio. If we go back to the editions of Shakespeare's plays published during his lifetime, the "quartos," we find the interesting fact that two of his most famous tragedies, *Hamlet* and *Lear*, were designated "Histories," while two of his histories, *Richard II* and *Richard III*, were labelled "Tragedies," and one of his most famous comedies, *The Merchant of Venice*, was labelled a "History." [6] This does not support the idea that there was a clear-cut genre division in Shakespeare's day, while it does support the idea, which was taken for granted by critics until the present revival of the genre theory by historical scholars, that Polonius' famous catalogue of dramatic genres is a satire on classification by genres.[7]

Historical scholars point to traditional narrative and dramatic devices as evidence in support of the genre theory. For instance, without genres how does one account for the fact that there are such things as the protasis and the invocation in Ariosto's *Orlando Furioso* and Milton's *Paradise Lost?* Are they not due to the persistence of the tradition of the epic poem? Indeed they are; and so are other features of those poems. But accounting for

facts, as we noted at the beginning of this chapter, is not determining values. Does the fact that a poem begins with an invocation and a protasis make it *necessarily* beautiful? Of course
not; neither are those things beautiful in themselves; their beauty,
if any, will depend on the individual quality of the diction, the
individual quality of the style, and the individual quality of the
verse, as argued in the preceding chapter. All the features of the
epic structure will not make a poem beautiful: for poem after
poem could be quoted from the mass of Renaissance epics which
is fully provided with all those features and yet was born dead.

But there seems to be a lurking tendency in historical scholarship to redeem these artificial poems of the Renaissance, and
similar ones of other periods, from the condemnation they have
long received, while admitting that they do not possess any of
the qualities that might commend them today as poetry. To support the genres, historical relativism is now called upon: it is
argued that Renaissance epics were considered beautiful in their
own day, according to the system of criticism then prevalent,
i.e. the didactic and Aristotelian. It is inferred that we should
therefore acknowledge their beauty in spite of the fact that
they have nothing in them that is imaginative or expressive.
The general issue of relativism will be taken up in the next
chapter; here we may note in this attitude another reason for
Croce's firmness in rejecting genres in connection with critical
standards: being inadequate, they tend to mislead the judgment.
A poor work is praised simply because it fits into a genre and
satisfies its rules or "conventions." Since with a little effort anything can be made to fit into one genre or another, and thus into
what is claimed to be an "art form," so any piece of writing
can be passed off as a work of "art" and its author recognized
as an artist. Hence the necessity of keeping exclusively to the
universal qualities of art and rejecting the restricted categories
of genres.

In the case of Ariosto—and of Tasso, and of many others—
what is the epic genre but the long shadow of Homer? Protasis
and invocation, and most other epic features, go back to what
Homer happened to say at certain points of his poem. An in-

dividual work of art has been erected into an absolute model. Virgil probably had even more than Homer to do with the establishment of the concept of the epic in the Renaissance, but his own imitation of Homer was due to the general attitude of Roman culture towards Greek, i.e. to a particular historical situation which can never be repeated. The fallacy of classicism is to perpetuate an historical condition which has long gone by, after schematizing it into abstract classes and destroying the life of its poetry.

The reliance of classicism upon the genres and their rules is also responsible for the converse critical error—good works condemned because they did not fit into the genres or follow their rules. Such was the condemnation of the *Divine Comedy* because it did not fit into the definition of the epic genre (or of any other), the condemnation of the *Orlando Furioso* because it was not a "regular epic," the similar judgment passed upon the *Jerusalem Delivered* which tortured its author into rewriting it in a much inferior but more "regular" form, the condemnation of Shakespearean (and even Cornelian) drama because it did not fit into the genre of regular tragedy—and so on, through the long list of errors due to the use of genres as critical categories. No wonder that Croce concluded in his first *Aesthetic* that: "Every genuine work of art has violated some established genre, thus upsetting the ideas of the critics, who were then obliged to enlarge the genre, but without being able to prevent that even the enlarged genre should prove too narrow, owing to the rise of new works of art, followed of course by new scandals, new upsets, and—new enlargements" (E, 42–43; A, 37). This statement was supported by the special chapter dedicated to the doctrine of genres in the second, or historical, part of the *Aesthetic*. That chapter presents the historical side of Croce's argument against the doctrine of genres. There Croce traces the main lines of its development and shows (for instance) how the definition of the epic was upset by the appearance of the *Orlando Furioso* and how the definitions of drama were upset by the appearance of plays that were neither regular tragedies nor regular comedies, etc.

In Renaissance poetics the genre theory also gave rise to that famous absurdity, the doctrine of the Dramatic Unities, which Croce describes as being not so much unities as "shortness of time, straitness of space, and limitation of tragic subjects" (E, 492; A, 438). The Romantic revolution swept them away as rules for practical writing, but with the advent of the historical point of view the genres were revived as "stages of development." In the older theory of genres the individual work was merely an instance of a general class; in the later idea of historical development, a work was only a stage in a process. In neither view does the work stand on its own merits.

Another attempt to give the genre theory a broader basis were the metaphysical systems of aesthetics that flourished in the Romantic and post-Romantic era. In them, the genres were dialectically deduced one from the other, or fitted into genetic schemes and identified with stages of intellectual development. According to Croce that was the error of Vico, and even more of Hegel. Metaphysical aesthetics were swept away by the positivist reaction, and attempts were made to set up a Darwinian evolution of genres, such as Brunetière's, which nobody takes seriously today. It may be added to Croce that the Aristotelian theory of tragedy then split up into two separate directions. One, stemming from Chapter XIII of the *Poetics*, speculated on the qualities of the "tragic hero" and the nature of the "tragic guilt": whether it was adequate or inadequate, whether it depended on the individual or on the nature of the universe, etc. (Hegel, Schopenhauer, Hebbel, etc., down to Jaspers). The other, stemming from Chapter XVIII, studied the formal structure of the play, and culminated in G. Freytag's celebrated analysis of the "rising" and "falling" action, etc., used by A. C. Bradley in his Shakespeare studies.

But the doctrine of genres has been challenged ever since its formulation in Renaissance poetics. It was not only Romantic criticism, with its "caprice" and "self-indulgence," that objected to genres as standards of judgment, but critics of the sixteenth and seventeenth centuries. The objections of Giordano Bruno and of Gravina, as well as those of Montani and Dubos, are part of a story that seems too little known to the historical scholars who still follow the genres theory today (E, 490–504; A, 436–49). The final result of the long debate was the breaking down of all genre partitions and the prevalence in modern writing of the so-called "mixed" genres, such as the modern play, which is neither entirely comedy nor entirely tragedy, and the modern novel, which can be practically anything. After all these discussions "one did not speak any more of genres, but only of art" (E, 502; A, 447).

Croce's general account of the development of the doctrine of genres was later supplemented on particular points by Croce himself and by other scholars. There has been one important contribution to the general history of the doctrine: the monograph by Irene Behrens on the history of the tripartition of genres from the origins to the nineteenth century.[8] In it she shows how the tripartition was finally crystallized only in the sixteenth century with the elevation of the lyric (at last recognized as a main genre) to the same rank as the epic and the drama. Behrens argued that the first critic to do so unmistakably was Minturno in 1559, although the lyric did not really come into its own until the Romantic movement. Croce, who does not appear to have been acquainted with the Behrens monograph, came shortly afterwards to the same general conclusion, viz. that the lyric had been added to the other two main genres by Renaissance criticism. However, he noted a fact that had escaped Behrens: that the lyric had been the object of a systematic critical justification by Angelo Segni in 1581 (*Poeti e scrittori del . . . Rinascimento*, II, 108–17).

In modern times, genres became a part of *Literaturwissenschaft* or the Theory of Literature, a more cautious and more scholarly form of traditional poetics cultivated in Germany.[9] They survive today in the histories of genres, or the history of literature by genres, which is one of the main areas of historical scholarship. But Croce of course firmly denies that it is possible to write the history of literature by genres, since genres are abstractions and not the historical reality of art, which is individual expression. Croce has pointed out more than once the absurdities into which the history of literature by genres necessarily falls: "the work of a single artist, which always possesses unity of development, whatever form it may take, lyrical, narrative or dramatic, is split up into as many pigeonholes as there are genres. So for instance Ariosto appears once among the writers of Latin verse of the Renaissance, a second time among the vernacular lyric poets, a third time among the writers of the first Italian satires, a fourth among the writers of comedy, and a fifth among those who brought the chivalric epic to perfection: as if in his Latin and vernacular verse, his satires and his comedies, he was not always the same poet Ariosto, in his various experiments and forms and in the logic of his historical development" (NSE, 47; EA, 54; cf. P, 178–79).

Croce did not limit himself to general statements but made a particular analysis of more than one genre history to show its intrinsic fallacy. He reviewed, as occasion offered, histories of the novel (CC, II, 163–67),[10] of comedy (CC, V, 125–26), of autobiography (CC, I, 193–96), and of the dialogue (*Poeti e scrittori del . . . Rinascimento*, II, 120–21). Such books are at best works of reference, bibliographical catalogues (CC, V, 126), the value of which depends upon the rarity and inaccessibility of the material collected (CC, I, 196). It seems beside the point to suggest that since Croce's argument histories of genres have reached such perfection that they are no longer subject to that argument. Croce's critique is directed to the very principle of the history of genres and not to shortcomings in its application, which might be made good by a more exact following of the same principle. In any case, it is doubtful whether there is a history of a genre more scholarly and more comprehensive than W. Creizenach's *Geschichte des neueren Dramas*, yet Croce found it a dull work, because essentially lacking in unity (PPPA, 240).

But if the concepts of genre have no value as guiding principles for the judgment and for the history of literature, yet they exist, and if they exist, according to Croce, they must have some positive function. Since this function is not to be found in the intellectual sphere, Croce looks for it in the sphere of *praxis*.

Their primary function is as a mnemonic aid. Since intuitions are innumerable and infinitely various it is impossible to keep them all in mind, so they are bundled together roughly and approximately into separate groups and provided with a label, which is the concept of genre. In this manner whole groups of intuitions can be called back to mind by means of a single word instead of being sought out laboriously one by one (*Logica*, 25–26).

So Croce never dreamt of trying to abolish the useful terms of tragedy and comedy, epic and lyric, novel and satire and the like. They are all useful for purposes of storage and of preservation, much as the arrangement of books on library shelves (E, 44; A, 38) or of the works of a prolific author in the volumes of a collected edition (US, 22). They are useful as shorthand designations for groups of works in speaking about literature in the bulk, provided no critical value is ascribed to them. For instance, as Croce said in his *Logic:* "If I mentally review the material that is to become a part of the history of Italian painting or of Italian literature, I must necessarily arrange it as major and minor works, plays and novels, religious painting and landscape painting, and so forth; with the proviso that these partitions will be abandoned when I will turn to an historical understanding of those facts. They will be abandoned in the act of historical understanding, but they will be resumed immediately, if I wish to expose the results of my historical research. In this exposition it will be impossible not to say that Manzoni, after having composed five *Sacred Hymns* and two *tragedies*, then turned to write an *historical novel*, or that in the seventeenth century *landscape painting* developed: words which are necessary instruments for a quick understanding and that only a philosophical pedant would attempt to suppress" (*Logica*, 127).

In an essay of 1916 on the history of aesthetics Croce noted that genres as well as rhetorical categories, though aesthetical fallacies, have a practical use in education and are indispensable to teaching literature.[11] He also stressed the services that the rhetorical critics of the ancient times and of the Renaissance had performed in fashioning them: "Notwithstanding the Romantic revolt against them, we all continue to speak of tragedy and comedy, of epic and lyric, poetry and prose; we all resort to the distinction between proper and metaphorical terms, and synecdoches and metonomies and hyperboles . . . and what is more, we all fashion new empirical concepts of the same kind, on the model of the old ones and in correspondence to the new conditions of culture and the new facts that we have to deal with. Of course these concepts old and new we handle with a caution that was formerly unknown, with a proper regard for their limitations, and with a consciousness of their function, which is practical and not critical or philosophical" (NSE, 97; cf. US, 32–33).[12]

It will be noted that Croce speaks of making new genre concepts. In a paper of 1922 entitled "Towards a modern Poetic" (NSE², 315–28), Croce actually proposed the building up of a new classification by genres, after repudiating once more the traditional tripartition, based as it was on "the external conditions of recital, theatrical production and musical accompaniment." He noted again the tendency of traditional genres to distort judgment: "Belief in the epic or the dramatic genre may operate today only to foment prejudice against the narrative form, to encourage the belief that works for the theatre have a logic of their own (which made Flaubert's wrath rise) and may be mediocre or null as poetic creations but perfect as plays; for instance, to undervalue a work of genius like *Adelchi* [Manzoni's tragedy] because of its supposedly defective dramatic structure, and to overvaluate an artificial work like [Kleist's] *Prinz von Homburg* because its dramatic construction is faultless; to lament the loss of true narrative poetry, which is calm and benevolent, when presented with a masterpiece like *Madame Bovary* or a short story by Maupassant, the impersonal and dramatic form of which appears a violation of the epic manner" (NSE, 323).

Croce noted that new empirical classifications of literature or genres were spontaneously rising in modern criticism as part of the characterization of new works, in a descriptive and not a judicial function, and encouraged their collection and expansion into a "modern Poetic." As instances of such classifications of poetry he gave the following: "tragic, disconsolate, despairing, serene, light-hearted, gay, brave, kindly, indulgent, affectionate, realistic, fantastic and so forth, as well as minor or idyllic (in the etymological sense) and grand or solemn poetry" (NSE[2], 326). All these classes refer to the emotional content of poetry and not to its formal structure. Croce gave them with no claim to finality, and he himself later effected a synthesis of two of them, the heroic and the idyllic, in the general concept of poetry (PAM, 177–84). Furthermore, Croce never hesitated to make use of empirical classifications, including genres, for the descriptive purpose of "characterization," which will be further discussed in Chapter VIII. As Mario Fubini notes in his perceptive study of the question of genres, Croce made use of a genre concept when he characterized the Don Juan play by Tirso de Molina as a mystery play or "sacra rappresentazione" (*Letture di poeti*, 45), while duly characterizing and qualifying it in the rest of his essay on that play.[13]

If genres are not real divisions of creative literature, they are certainly real as ideas or beliefs about literature, and as such they belong to the history of critical thought. Croce also notes that their emergence in critical discussion at certain times is indicative of significant changes in thought, or in taste, or in manners, or in culture, changes which are genuine objects of historical inquiry. Hence genres have also a place in the history of ideas, of manners or of culture, as clues to some underlying shift which it is the business of the historian to identify and bring to light (PPPA, xi–xii, 244, 303–4, 349–52, 438, 487–88; P, 182, 333, 336; *Poeti e scrittori del . . . Rinascimento*, I, 308–9). But most of these things have little to do with poetry.

With this important qualification in mind, we can take note of the fact that Croce formulated his own history of genres. The Greek "New Comedy," with its intellectually constructed types of characters, turned into the comedy of the Renaissance, which persisted as a type until the eighteenth century, when it received from political revolutions and the new interest in history the impulse to present historically and socially determined characters. At the same time these interests also made themselves felt in the prose romance, which turned into the "social novel" of modern times. However, both the ancient comedy and its modern descendants are not forms of poetry, but of didactic writing; they do not present individuals, but abstract schematizations. In the nineteenth century it so happened that some of the writers who took up the genre were predominantly artists and made works of poetry out of it; but then it was no longer a didactic scheme (PNP, 241–43).

We have already seen the rest of the story in Croce's discussion of Beach quoted in the preceding chapter. In the course of the century the ideal of the social or didactic novel gave way to the ideal of a novel that was entirely poetic, such as was actually written by the genuine artists, and this ideal still persists in the modern idea of the novel as a work of art. Needless to say, novels of this quality are to be judged by the same standards as all works of art: unity, imagination and lyrical power, and not as mechanical contrivances of plots and narrative devices.

What does Croce set up as a critical procedure for the study of such works in the place of the traditional history of genres? He provides a series of individual portraits. The subject of the critical portrait is the artistic personality of the poet, as defined above in Chapter III. The portraits may be presented singly, as individual essays, and collected in volumes which do not claim any intrinsic unity, such as Croce's later collections (*Poetry Ancient and Modern, Readings from Poets*). Or they may be gathered into chronological periods, such as Croce's *Literature of Modern Italy* (LNI), but without a general framework that includes them all. Or they may even be collected in essays which bear the title of a genre belonging to a certain period: as in Croce's essays on Renaissance comedy, tragedy, lyric poetry and narrative prose (in PPPA). This last grouping is actually the final blow against the genre theory, for in it Croce dissociates the writers sharply from each other and from the genre to which they are assigned by tradition.[14] To begin with, the writers of artificial comedy in the already mentioned didactic tradition are completely excluded. Then the genuine artists are presented as distinct personalities, each different from the other, each expressing his own individual intuition in his own manner. So instead of the monotonous picture presented by genre histories, of a group of genre operators all going through more or less the same motions, we have a brilliant gallery of individual portraits: Machiavelli, Aretino, Grazzini, Bibbiena, Bruno, etc., and justice is done to the individual achievement of each.[15]

Hence it may be said that all of Croce's work in criticism is a practical refutation of the genre theory. In later chapters we shall see how he interpreted Dante and Ariosto without having recourse to the concept of the epic, Shakespeare, Corneille and many other dramatists without having recourse to dramaturgy or the craft of the dramatic genre, and Flaubert, Maupassant and Verga without having recourse to the concept of the novel.

Croce's elimination of genres from aesthetics was deplored by some scholars who lamented that some of the most "luxuriant gardens" of criticism were abandoned (E, 155; A, 142; *PdE*, 245; TPS, II, 185). But, as an English student of Croce said, there are some serious surgical operations which are "followed by an inpouring of healing influences, not merely restoring equilibrium but bringing new strength and power." [16] And more than one critic of Croce has accepted his critique of the genre theory.[17]

CHAPTER VI

Other Classifications of Poetry—the Theatre

RELATED TO LITERARY GENRES are the aesthetic categories of the tragic and the comic, as well as the
similar concepts of the pathetic and the laughable, the sublime
and the beautiful, the graceful and the terrible, the picturesque
and the idyllic, the humorous and the ironic, the satirical and
the grotesque, the realistic and the symbolic, etc. To these may
be added the period concepts, such as classic and romantic,
baroque and mannerist, Renaissance and naturalistic, etc., which
are sometimes taken as aesthetic categories or varieties of the
beautiful in art. Under the name of "modifications of the Beautiful," many of these terms had for nearly two centuries an
honorable place in systematic aesthetics, where they were the
objects of many definitions and classifications. The Beautiful
was distinguished from the Sublime, the Sublime from the
Pathetic, the Tragic from the Terrible, the Humorous from the
Comic. Hegelians saw them as different stages in the dialectical
development of the concept of the Beautiful, the latter generating the Ugly by antithesis and thus paving the way for a higher
synthesis or branching out into several "moments" by dialectical
process (E, 96–97, 382–89; A, 87–88, 342–49). But in Chapter
XII of the *Aesthetic*, Part I, Croce argued that all "modifications
of the Beautiful" were to be banished from criticism as "pseudo-
aesthetic concepts" or, as he phrased it later, aesthetic "pseudo-
concepts" (*Logica*, 26–27). Like the genres, they represent
limited generalizations and not universals, and are made out of a
few instances erected into general classes. Like the terms of

rhetoric which we saw in Chapter IV, and the genres in Chapter V, they are sometimes used as synonyms for the universal aesthetic category: a work is praised as "symbolic," or conversely as "realistic," as "sublime" or as "ironic," when all that is meant is that it is a perfectly achieved aesthetic expression (E, 78–79; A, 70). And like all other pseudo-concepts, the "modifications of the Beautiful" emerge sometimes in history as indications of some underlying shift in matters of taste or of culture, as for instance "picturesque" which has an important place in the history of ideas in the eighteenth century. Otherwise, they are mere names, and Croce can say of them: "the sublime (or the comic, the tragic, the humorous, etc.) is *everything* that is or shall be so *called* by those who have employed or shall employ the terms" (E, 99; A, 90). Herein lies Croce's "nominalism" which has been an object of concern to aestheticians who still believe in the validity of those concepts, and to whom Croce's nominalism in their regard appears to be contradictory, for it employs abstraction in the very act of repudiating it.[1] But Croce was a nominalist only in regard to empirical concepts. He was not a nominalist when it came to philosophical categories or concrete universals, in the validity and actuality of which he was a firm believer.[2] Indeed for Croce the categories are logically prior to the empirical concepts, which are abstractions from individual acts of perception, in which the categories are present and operative. As we have seen, Croce's categories are the basic forms of spiritual activity: asthetic, logical, economic and ethic. "These forms are not empirical classes, in which several single acts are grouped, but the categories which stand as the foundation of judgments, by abstraction from which said classes are made."[3] In other words, Croce is a skeptic when it comes to the traditional concepts of rhetoric and of metaphysical aesthetics, but not when it comes to basic values, such as Beauty, Goodness and Truth.

As an instance of the "modifications of the Beautiful," let us take the Comic: a concept which has given rise to many ingenious speculations, and which is also of interest because it enters into definition of one of the great genres of drama, Comedy. If the Comic is simply identified with the laughable, as in common parlance, then it becomes confused with mere buffoonery, and ceases to be art. However, it is usually acknowledged by critics who make use of this concept that the comic in art is not the merely laughable, but laughter mixed with something else that is serious, or even tragic: so that the comic turns out to be not a separate species but a constituent, never alone and unmixed.

Nevertheless, philosophers ranging from Aristotle to Kant, from Hobbes to Vico, from Hegel to Bergson, have attempted to formulate a definition of the Comic in itself. Croce has discussed this problem more than once. In Chapter XII of the *Aesthetic*, Part I, one of the most elaborate and ingenious modern theories of the Comic was analyzed (E, 100–102; A, 91–92). This theory was constructed by the German aesthetician T. Lipps (E, 459; A, 410). In a later essay Croce investigated the history of a special variety of the Comic, the concept of Humor (*PdE*, 274–85), and also wrote a critique of Pirandello's 1909 book on the subject (CC, I, 44–48). In 1910 he made a study of the "Doctrine of Laughter and Irony in Vico" (*Saggio sullo Hegel*, 283–89). Later still, he dedicated an essay to what he called "An example of unmethodical construction of concepts: the theory of the Comic" (US, 280–89). So Croce cannot be said to have neglected this aesthetic concept. We will take his last essay as representing his most mature thinking on the subject.

The theme of this essay is that "the unmethodical character of the theories of the comic consists precisely in its claim to give a philosophic definition of something which due to its origin admits only of a nominal definition." Hence attempts to define this undefinable essence end by introducing surreptitiously in the definition the very term to be defined. "One says, e.g., that the comic is 'the contrast between the ideal and the real,' but it is understood that it is a contrast which is 'comic'; or that it is 'the relaxation of a tension, which is followed by a laugh'; or that it is 'a feeling of superiority,' but it is implied of a superiority that makes what is considered inferior appear laughable. And so forth. Try to think out any of the many definitions . . . and you will find . . . that one must always insinuate into it this unidentified term" (US, 284).

Croce's observations in the paper on "Humor" concluded with a statement which applies also to the Comic and to all the modifications of the Beautiful: "The literary critic must go beyond these general conceptions: he must individualize. For him, it is not 'Humor' that exists, but Sterne, Richter, Heine. There exists no 'Sublime,' but there are Aeschylus, Dante, Shakespeare. There is no 'Comic,' but there are Plautus, Molière, Goldoni" (*PdE*, 284–85). It is interesting to compare Croce with Bergson on this point. In Bergson's book on the Comic (1900), recently republished in an English translation, one may find an explicit definition of art as the cognition of the individual, very close to what Croce was then formulating in his first *Aesthetic:* "Art always aims at what is individual . . . What the poet sings of is a certain mood which is his, and his alone, and will never return . . . Nothing could be more unique than the character of Hamlet. Though he may resemble other men in some respects, it is not on that account that he interests us most. But he is universally accepted and regarded as a living character. In this sense only is he universally true. The same holds true of other products of art. Each of them is unique, and yet, if it bears the stamp of genius, it will come to be accepted by everybody." [4]

And yet Bergson on the next page proceeds to build up a theory of Comedy, referring it to the opposite type of cognition: generality. "The very titles of certain classical comedies are significant in themselves. The *Misanthropist,* the *Miser,* the *Gambler,* the *Absent-Minded Man,* etc., are names of whole classes of people." This abstract character may be true enough of "classical comedy"—that is, of certain French comedies of the seventeenth and eighteenth centuries, built according to Neo-Classical (i.e. intellectualistic) standards. But even Molière's Misanthrope is an individual character, who like Hamlet, if to a smaller degree, interests us for his own sake. If one goes outside French classical comedy and turns (say) to Shakespearian comedy, one will find a great comic character like Falstaff who is a concrete individual and no type, or only the type of other

Falstaffs (as Croce says of Don Quijote, E, 39; A, 34). As for titles, Shakespeare's comedy titles are often frankly noncommittal: *As You Like It, Twelfth Night or What You Will*, or purely suggestive, as *A Midsummer Night's Dream*. So even as an empirical generalization Bergson's theory of comedy falls short. For Croce of course generalities, types and abstractions do not constitute the essence of art, which is basically the intuition of the individual.

To the Tragic Croce gave much less attention than to the Comic. In the *Aesthetic*, Part II (historical), he surveyed critically various doctrines that attempt a definition of the Tragic and of Tragedy, from Aristotle to the end of the nineteenth century (E, 490–504; A, 436–49). He was instrumental in the publication of an Italian translation of Nietzsche's *Birth of Tragedy* and in a preface to it he evaluated its contribution to aesthetic theory. He found Nietzsche's dichotomy of Apollonian and Dionysiac useful as an introduction to the dialectic of opposites, but did not otherwise subscribe to Nietzsche's theories (*Saggio sullo Hegel*, 423–27). On the theory of the "Tragic Guilt" as formulated by German aesthetics (Hegel and Hebbel), he later wrote a short note, observing that this guilt lies in "the unilaterality of the individual"—which, Croce says, is "the guilt of life itself. . . . Hence all art, if any, would be tragic art: which, in a certain sense, is true" (CC, III, 175). In what sense all art is tragic for Croce may perhaps become apparent in some of the later doctrines which we shall discuss in Chapter XI.

Since both the genres and the modifications of the Beautiful are often justified by means of the traditional logical scheme of classification by kinds and species, it may be well to explain here Croce's objection to this scheme. In the *Breviary* he criticizes it as "building up pyramids of empirical concepts, which become more and more empty the higher one ascends and the more rarified they become" (NSE, 52; EA, 60). The method of coordination and subordination, by kinds and species, meets with this objection, which Croce derives from Hegel: "In ordinary classification, a concept is taken as a foundation; then another concept, extraneous to the first, is introduced, and is assumed as the ground for classification, like a knife used to cut a pie (the first concept) into so many pieces, each separate from the other. This procedure results in a complete destruction of the unity of the universal" (*Saggio sullo Hegel*, p. 58–59). Hence all subdivisions of art into kinds and species, subordinate and coordinate concepts, is rejected by Croce.

Does this mean that it is impossible according to Croce to effect *any* grouping or classification of intuitions or works of art? The only possible grouping of intuitions is "that genetic and concrete classification which is not really a 'classification' and is called 'history.' In history each work takes the place that belongs to it, that and no other" (*Breviary, loc. cit.*). He had already argued in the *Aesthetic* that the resemblances which admittedly exist between different works "consist wholly of what is called a *family likeness*, derived from the historical conditions in which the various works have appeared and from spiritual affinities between the artists" (E, 81–2; A, 73). The Principle of Integration accounts for these resemblances: parts of the previous works are incorporated in the later. But it must be repeated that the genetic connection does not afford the basis for a critical estimate, which can only be provided by aesthetic analysis, or the critical judgment upon the new individual created.[5]

ANOTHER PROBLEM is that of the aesthetic value to be assigned to the art of the theatre. This problem, as we have seen in the previous chapter, is connected with the definition of the dramatic genre. Is drama a kind of writing that owes its specific features to the fact that it is the subject of a stage performance? Is the performance itself merely an "execution" of the poet's work, or is it an interpretation of it, or does it belong to an independent form of art to which the poet's text provides only the occasion? Are the form and structure of a good play determined mainly by the conditions of performance—the theatre, the company, the audience? All these questions arise in connection with Shakespeare's dramatic works, and have prompted a multitude of investigations on the stage conditions of Shakespearean drama, on theatrical traditions and company organization, methods of production and styles of acting, in the hope of finding by this method the key to Shakespeare's art and solving thereby the problems of Shakespearean criticism and exegesis. In my opinion these hopes will be disappointed for the reasons which follow.

Seen in the light of Croce's aesthetic, a Shakespearian play is primarily a piece of writing, to be judged as literary art, and not merely a script for a particular company in a particular theatre before a particular audience. If the value of a play can only be judged by its performance under the original stage conditions, then it is impossible to judge Shakespeare's plays, or any other play that was performed in theatres of past ages by companies and before audiences which have long ago crumbled into dust. Hence the total lack of reference to any stage condition in Croce's critical discussion of Italian Renaissance drama, to which reference was made in the previous chapter. This of course cannot be attributed to ignorance of theatrical history in a scholar who spent so many years of his life investigating the history of the theatres of Naples and made signal contributions to it. Nor is it to be attributed to any indifference to the art of the living theatre. Not in Croce, who had loved the theatre in his youth, and in his later years recalled nostalgically the acting of contemporary plays by Bernhardt and Duse, seen on Neapolitan stages during the same period when he was investigating the history of the old theatres.[6]

Nor did Croce underestimate the historical significance of the theatre of the Renaissance. In the same volume with the discussion of Renaissance comedy, there is a paper on the *Commedia dell'arte*, in which Croce claims that "the modern theatre, as theatre, is an Italian creation." The Italian players of the Renaissance effected "the industrialization of the theatre, with companies organized by contract and by regulations, with masters and apprentices, with families that carried on the profession from father to son, from mother to daughter, with professional travel from one city to the other, etc." (PPPA, 503). To them are also due "the multiplication of permanent theatres, the intro-

duction of women as actresses, the mechanisms for scene-shift-
ing, the establishment of schools for dramatic art, and analogous
institutions for the musical theatre" (PPPA, 504–5). This claim
may be challenged or qualified by other historians, but it certainly does not show indifference to stage conditions.

And lest Croce, one of the most internationally-minded of
scholars,[7] be accused of nationalism in his claims for the Italian
theatre of the Renaissance, it will be well to note that for him
there was no such thing even as "Italian" poetry, since poetry
is something "supranational" (NSE, 275). One should also recall
Croce's full recognition of the part played by foreign scholars
and critics in the investigation of Italian literature: Italian folk
poetry was practically discovered by the Germans (PPPA, 26),
the Renaissance playwright Ruzzante by the French (PPPA,
290), and the poet Boiardo by English scholarship (*Poeti e scrittori . . .* , II, 261). Referring to Ruzzante, Croce noted: "This
is not the only case in which an aesthetic value is recognized by
an unprejudiced foreigner sooner and more easily than by men
of letters of the same nation as the author" (PPPA, 290–91; cf.
CC, II, 356 and *PdE*, 426–27). How many critics in the English-
speaking world are willing today to acknowledge the German
contribution to Shakespeare criticism?

Highly as Croce thought of the theatre, when he came to
judge a written text, the only values that counted for him were
aesthetic, i.e. the image built up by the text in the mind of the
reader. If the text failed to present a consistent or an harmonious
image, then it could be turned over to other branches of investigation and used as an historical document of some sort—as an
autobiographical confession, or a record of manners, or a tract
or pamphlet, or a mere scenario for the exercise of the skill of
the actors, such as were produced by the Renaissance play-
wrights. But none of these approaches has the right to impinge
upon the aesthetic judgment in the exercise of *its* functions.

But is the skill of the actors just mentioned merely a craft,
or is there an art of the theatre which can produce aesthetic effects just as much as poetry or painting or music? Notwithstanding his early love for the theatre, Croce never made a

systematic discussion of this question, but expressed incidentally various opinions on different occasions. In the *Aesthetic* the theatre is seen merely as a form of externalization for dramatic poetry, and the actor as one of its instruments, on a par with scenery, stage architecture and painting (E, 127; A, 116). In later statements Croce recognized the special status of the actor. But he never made up his mind definitely as to what this status was, and oscillated between the conception of acting as a purely practical (i.e. unaesthetic) arousal of emotions in the audience (PPPA, 301), and acting as a form of artistic expression. When holding the second alternative, he oscillated between the concept of the actor as a translator of poetry and the actor as a creative artist. Of course, actors can be any of these things at different times; but if it is acknowledged that acting at its best can be creative activity, then the poetic text used by the actor becomes the material to which the actor gives a new form, just as tales or poems may become the material out of which a play is fashioned, according to the principle of Integration.

The way is then open for a clear distinction between the work of art produced on the stage by the actor, the stage manager, the director, etc., and the work of art produced by the poet in his text. The latter cannot determine the former, for the stage requires a different artistic personality. On the other hand, the stage cannot determine the poetic quality of the text, since the latter precedes it.

In 1922 a brilliant critic, Piero Gobetti, who was later to die a victim of Fascist violence, came out with the view that the actor should be fully recognized as a creative artist, a view that Croce summarized as follows: "the work of the poet is complete in itself, and the work of the actor is to be judged in itself and not as the execution of a mandate received from the collaborating poet." From this statement, however, Croce then inferred that the art of the actor was "identical with the art of the translator." As such it is, like all translations of poetic works, "intrinsically impossible, and yet necessary and useful . . . to make the work of the poet known to those who cannot read it or do not know how to read it; to make it of easier and pleasanter apprehension, in hours of relaxation; to underline certain parts and to stimulate a better understanding of it, etc." (CC, III, 71–72). Besides these cases of "interpretation" or translation of a fully-fashioned poem, there are also others "in which actors present works which arise out of a sort of cooperation with the authors, and in which the poet's work is not organically formed, but a mere scenario and outline" (CC, III, 72).[8]

Theatrical productions of fully-fashioned poetic texts were also characterized as "translations" in 1936 (P, 103–4). But in the study of Shakespeare (1919) Croce had come to recognize acting as a work of art: "Theatrical performances are not interpretations, as people say, but variations, i.e. *creations of new works of art* by the actors, who always bring to them their own individual feeling. There is no third term of comparison in a presumed authentic and objective interpretation, and they possess the same status as works of music and painting inspired by dramatic works, which are music and painting, and no longer those dramatic works" (ASC, 212; italics mine).

We may formulate the difference between the work of art of the actor and that of the musician or painter as lying merely in the technique of preservation that renders more or less permanent a piece of music or of painting, while the actor's work is more ephemeral. This is a confirmation of Croce's theory that externalization is not essential to artistic creation. Until the invention of photography and voice recording the work of the actor was completely ephemeral, and yet was presumably no less a work of art.

The "translation" theory was abandoned by Croce in 1948 (NPS, I, 200). In the same year, stimulated (as before by Gobetti) by a younger critic, Carlo Ragghianti, who was developing an aesthetic of the cinema, Croce recognized that: "diction and mimic and scenery become one in the performance, become a single act of artistic creation, in which they cannot be distinguished" (TPS, II, 267–68). His last word seems to have been, in 1950, the recognition of two tendencies in the theatre: one towards mere emotionalism, the other towards art (TPS, II, 301; cf. in 1948, *Varietà di storia letteraria e civile*, II, 82).

The reason for this oscillation between different views is perhaps to be found in a statement of 1941: the theatre is a pseudo concept, hence incapable of rigorous definition: "The theatre as such does not provide a unified point of view in history because it is, so to speak, a collective name for aesthetic facts and for other facts which are variously cultural and moral, and in this second aspect it is comprised in the various histories which deal with each kind of fact" (ps, III, 66), i.e. social and economic history, the history of mechanical techniques, etc.[9]

It will be clear by now why Croce does not believe in the doctrine that I have elsewhere called "theatricalism," or the view that a play written for production is necessarily determined in its aesthetic form and structure by so-called "stage conditions."[10] The furthest that Croce went in that direction is his recognition, quoted above, that there are certain plays which result from a sort of collaboration between the author and the actor(s): the author provides a scenario or skeleton dialogue, which is filled out and given artistic shape by the speech, motion and personality of the actors. This is certainly true of such special cases as the *Commedia dell'arte*, but then the surviving text or scenario is a dull piece of routine writing which could never rank as literature, whereas the plays of Shakespeare and of Molière do. It might even be added that Shakespeare rose to his full stature as an artist only after he had ceased to be just a part of the theatrical repertoire and become a printed text, to be read as literature, as he did in the course of the eighteenth century.

Since J. E. Spingarn is the best-known representative of Croce's aesthetics in the United States, one may forestall any remark of the "this-is-not-the-Croce-that-we-knew" type by pointing out that the views given above on the theatre go beyond Spingarn and clearly diverge from him. In his well-justified reaction against the "theatricalism" of his own day, or the view which he described as "the actor and the theatre do not merely externalize the drama, or interpret it, or heighten its effect, but that they *are* the drama," Spingarn was perhaps less than just to the art of the theatre at its best.[11] He did not seem to acknowledge that the actor (not to speak of the director) could be an arist in his own right. Croce, as we have seen, came to recognize that in statements made from 1919 onwards, i.e. later than Spingarn's first efforts at propagating Croce's views in the United States.

It may be asked whether the recognition of the actor or of the director as an artist does not involve the admission of a distinct form or kind of art, separate from the art of poetry, which of course contradicts Croce's basic tenet of the unity of art. But the recognition is given to the actor as an individual artist, if and when he proves himself to be such, and not to the "art" or to the "medium." Indeed the art of the theatre obviously breaks down several partitions, since it makes use of so-called "media" supposedly belonging to separate arts, such as words like poetry, sound like music, motion and gesture like dancing, and color and form like painting and architecture. Yet the ultimate result, if it is artistic, will be a single picture, a poetic image, built up bit by bit in the mind of the audience as it takes in the total performance.

Spingarn took up again his thesis in 1923 in a paper entitled "The Growth of a Literary Myth," [12] in which he mentioned the fact that "A. B. Walkley once filled two columns of the London *Times* with proofs that my theory is not good Crocean doctrine, and perhaps he is right." The Walkley referred to is the brilliant dramatic critic whom we have already met in Chapter IV defending Croce's theory of externalization. The article referred to was published anonymously under the title "The Theatre.—Criticism and Croce." [13] It argues that production belongs to externalization, thus substantially agreeing with the early statement of Croce in the *Aesthetic,* Chapter xv, and with Spingarn's point of view. But it then goes on to argue that this externalization through the stage production is the only evidence we have of the author's intuition, and that it is subject to the influence of "stage conditions." So "no one has ever known, save Shakespeare himself, no one ever can know, the 'pure intuition' as Croce would say, or the 'creative art,' as Professor Spingarn would put it, behind any of Shakespeare's plays." This of course was written years before Croce himself attempted to define the "pure intuition" of Shakespeare's drama. Hence neither Walkley nor Spingarn may be said to fully represent Croce's thought on this question.

But whatever be the conclusion reached on the status of the art of the theatre, Croce held that classifications of the arts or of literature cannot be logically maintained. They usually involve, according to him, the use of pseudo concepts or logical fictions, brought together within the traditional framework of genus and species, or of Hegelian dialectic, which also break down upon critical examination. We are therefore left with only two basic concepts, the universal and the particular, or poetry and the poem: "No intermediate element interposes itself philosophically between the universal and the particular, no series of kinds or species, no *generalia*. Neither the artist who produces art, nor the spectator who contemplates it, has need of anything but the universal and the individual, or rather, the universal individualized: the universal artistic activity, which is all contracted and concentrated in the representation of a single state of mind" (NSE, 49; EA, 57).

_____

CHAPTER vii

Taste or the Reproduction of Expressions

> O Callicles, if there were not some com-
> munity of feeling among mankind, however
> varying in different persons,—I mean, if every
> man's feelings were peculiar to himself and
> were not shared by the rest of the species—I
> do not see how we could ever communicate
> our impressions to one another.
>
> PLATO, *Gorgias,* 481

ACCORDING TO CROCE, the act of expression, once completed, can be recorded in a physical object, such as
the pages of a written text. It then becomes possible to reproduce the original expression by re-enacting it with the help of
the signs impressed on the physical object. This may be done
by the artist himself in a later or an altered mood, or by any
other person who makes the necessary effort. But it may be
asked: Is such a reproduction possible in terms of Croce's theory
of expression? Since all expressions are unique, how can an expression ever be re-enacted? Will not the reader's or the critic's
attempted re-creation be in reality a new creation? Croce was
well aware of the possibility of this objection, and he met it in
Chapter xvi of the *Aesthetic,* Part i.

Stated in more general terms, this is simply the old problem
already discussed in Chapter iii: how can a critic know what
actually went on in the mind of the poet and say: "this poem
is the expression of such and such a feeling"? The modern doctrine of symbolism, too, seems to lead in a negative direction,
since poetic language is assumed by it to be something not only

unique but also magical, without any connection with ordinary experience. All the symbolist critic can do is to juggle with words himself and produce another such incantation. Finally, the impossibility of reproducing intuitions was urged against Croce with special force by philosophers of absolute subjectivism, such as Gentile. Whatever their initial assumptions, all these attitudes lead to some form of aesthetic skepticism or at least of critical relativism. The latter is a position which Croce knew well from the inside, for he himself had adopted a relativistic position in his very earliest attempts at a critical theory.[1] But in the *Aesthetic* he abandoned it, and since criticized relativism more than once.[2]

In the *Aesthetic* Croce gives the following account of the process of aesthetic re-creation: an individual, A, has expressed an intuition and left a record of it in a physical object. "If another individual, whom we will call B, is to judge that expression and decide whether it is beautiful or ugly, he must necessarily place himself at A's point of view, and go through the whole process again, with the help of the physical sign supplied to him by A" (E, 131; A, 119). Now for what reasons should B believe that, once he has so placed himself to obtain the point of view of A, he is able to re-enact A's intuition and obtain the same expressive image that A produced?

For two fundamental reasons: 1) There is only one way in which a given problem of expression can be solved (*ibidem*); 2) the activity that reproduces the expression is the same that produced it (E, 132; A, 120).

Suppose we take as an example Keats' *Ode to a Nightingale*. The first proposition asserts that there was only one way in which the state of mind that Keats entered into after listening to the nightingale could be put into words, and that the *Ode* is it. The second proposition asserts that when we read the *Ode*, placing ourselves in the same mental position that Keats occupied, we go through the same expressive process as the poet, and build up the same image that he saw. This is perhaps Croce's most cogent argument in support of his thesis of the reproducibility of the work of art. Once we have accepted his premises, it is hard to deny his conclusion. But what reasons does Croce give for his two premises?

To begin with, it should be remembered that they are by no means exclusive to Croce. They are accepted by aestheticians of other tendencies, as the conclusion also is. The first proposition, that there is only one solution to a given artistic problem, is necessarily maintained by all doctrines that take art seriously. For it affirms that art is not a matter of arbitrary choice or of caprice, but of severe calculation and direction. Art has a logic of its own, an inner necessity, which does not admit of approximations or makeshifts; so artists are exacting and fastidious, for they are well aware that there is only one solution to their problem, while there are innumerable ways of going wrong. This proposition is all the more true for the doctrine of expression. *Le mot juste* has always been singular; there is only one right word or phrase for each thought.

The second proposition is also well known to aestheticians, and its historical name is "the identity of genius and taste"—not of course empirical identity, but identity of essence (E, 133; A, 121). It was formulated as such by some of the critics who developed the concept of "taste" in aesthetics (E, 529; A, 470). The sympathetic reader's pleasurable participation in the creative process of the artist has been known since the seventeenth century as taste, or *gusto*.[3] In this sense taste is by definition "good" and does not need the addition of that epithet to its name. So it is not to be confused with the "good taste" of neoclassical doctrine, which implied conformity to a pre-established model or rules, but it is a spontaneous reaction of pleasure in the presence of a good work and of displeasure when faced with bad. It is not a critical judgment, for it does not judge, but simply feels; it can give no reason for its pleasure, but simply enjoys. In Croce's doctrine this process ceases to be at all mysterious: it is merely the process of expression repeated in another mind, or in the same mind after a change in the point of view from which the work was created.

The question now becomes, how can the conditions in which

the artist created his work be reproduced? Croce answers that this is exactly the service that is performed by historical scholarship, which labors at the preservation and elucidation of works of art: "the physical object is continually changing, and in like manner psychological conditions. Oil paintings grow dark, frescoes fade, statues lose noses, hands or legs, architecture becomes totally or partially a ruin, the tradition of the execution of a piece of music is lost, the text of a poem is corrupted by bad copyists or bad printing." As for psychological conditions, there is "the fundamental, daily and inevitable changing of society around us and of the inner conditions of our intellectual life. The phonetic manifestations or words and verses of the *Divine Comedy* must make a very different impression on an Italian citizen who is involved in the politics of the third Rome, from that experienced by a well-informed and congenial contemporary of the poet" (E, 136; A, 124).

It may be noted incidentally, *à propos* of this passage, that if art were for Croce (as some critics seem to believe) merely a matter of impression, there could be no reproduction of art such as Croce maintains does occur, for impressions, as implied here, are not only transient but all different. But art for Croce is not *im*pression but *ex*pression, that is, a spiritual activity that takes place within history and leaves a record of itself which is reconstructed and interpreted by historical scholarship: "As regards the physical object, palaeographers and philologists, who restore texts to their original integrity, restorers of pictures and statues and other industrious workers strive precisely to preserve, or restore all its primitive energy to, the physical object. . . . Historical interpretation labors for its part to reintegrate in us the psychological conditions which have changed in the course of history. It revives the dead, completes the fragmentary, and enables us to see a work of art (a physical object) as its author saw it in the moment of production."

Of course this process is not always easy, and sometimes meets with serious difficulties: "A condition of this historical labor is tradition . . . Where tradition is broken, interpretation is arrested." But this arrest is not necessarily final, for under different conditions the lost data may come to light again and the process of reconstruction may be resumed. Or, as in every human activity, mistakes may occur: "erroneous historical interpretation sometimes produces . . . new impressions superimposed upon the old, artistic fantasies instead of historical reproductions." But, as in all human activities, the recognition of the possibility of error only leads to greater vigilance and does not authorize the abandonment of effort: "*historical criticism* tends precisely to circumscribe fancies and to establish exactly the point of view from which we must look" (E, 138–39; A, 126–27).[4]

Croce was well aware that "variety of judgments" on works of art "is an indubitable fact" (E, 135; A, 123). In the *Aesthetic* he accounted for this fact either by shortcomings in the preservation of the work of art or shortcomings in its reproduction. As an instance of the latter, he takes the case of a poet who differs with the critic on the value of his poem: the critic may see in it only superficiality, while the poet may claim that it is the expression of high thoughts and deep feelings. For Croce either of them may be wrong, both being subject to human failings. "Haste, vanity, want of reflection, prejudice" may influence the poet in favor of his own work, and make him blind to its faults. "Haste, laziness, want of reflection, critical prejudice, personal sympathy or antipathy" may distract the critic. But if each performs his function properly there should be no discrepancy in the result. Such a conclusion is normally accepted without question in the case of other mental operations, e.g. an arithmetical calculation or a piece of scientific reasoning. Why should it not be so in the case of poetry?

"Because poetry is a matter of taste, and tastes differ" is the answer often given. This statement is obvious when it refers to the physical sense of taste and its pleasures, about which the proverb says that there is no disputing (and which in Croce's philosophy belongs to the individual sphere of will, or pure vitality). But art is a theoretical activity, and in aesthetics "taste" means the controlled re-enactment of the expressive process by the informed observer. This re-enactment also produces a kind of pleasure, but it is aesthetic pleasure, enjoyment of the beautiful, of the fully-fashioned image and its perfect expression. In this process no concept is involved, only the intuitive apprehension of a particular. "The only difference (between the poet and the reader) lies in the diversity of circumstances, since in one case it is aesthetic production, in the other reproduction" (E, 132; A, 120).

This brings us to a further distinction which is of capital importance to Croce and to any aesthetic system: the difference between taste and criticism. The critical judgment operates by means of something which is absent in the act of reproduction, i.e. a universal concept, that of art. This point was made clearly and definitely by Croce in an untranslated paper of 1909, in which he corrected the doctrine of literary criticism given in the *Aesthetic*, that criticism was merely taste.[5] From 1909 to the end of his life, he maintained instead that when an expression is reproduced, we have only the process of "taste" "but not yet *art criticism* or literary criticism. The work of art is then *re-created*, but one is not yet able to *judge* it. For judgment something is lacking, which may seem of small but is of great importance, may seem nothing and is everything. It is necessary that the aesthetic fact, reproduced in the imagination, be *characterized*, that is to say, *conceived* as an aesthetic fact; that from being contemplation it become a logical act (subject, predicate and copula). In this very simple act of adding a predicate to the subject of contemplation consists literary criticism" (*PdE*, 52).[6]

The distinction now made between taste and criticism affords the explanation for another conflict of opinion in regard to works of art. There is the possibility of disagreement between taste and criticism, between the sympathetic reader and the formal critic. Indeed, Croce noted that it was of frequent occurrence: for instance, the case of the *Decameron*, which was admired by many readers but denounced by some critics as immoral, and of Tasso's *Jerusalem* and Shakespeare's plays, which readers enjoyed but critics condemned as irregular and inartistic. The taste of the readers in these cases was sound, but the judgment of the critics went astray. "To extricate judgment from its quandary and harmonize it with taste, there is, was and shall always be needed a theoretical process that distinguishes art from what is not art, from other forms of the spirit, speculative, scientific, economic and moral. Judgment implies the possession of a concept of art, and whenever this is lacking, or is more or less obscured by doubt and confusion, art criticism will be defective. The concept of art, or an aesthetic, is still a condition of criticism. Criticism without a corresponding aesthetic is not conceivable, one develops out of the other together with the other" (*PdE*, 52–53).

It is therefore quite possible according to Croce to be familiar with works of art and of poetry and to have a lively feeling and appreciation for them, without possessing a critical theory. This is the stage of "taste"; many art lovers, connoisseurs, readers and lovers of poetry and literature remain in it all their lives and are perfectly happy in it. They do no harm to poetry or to art; on the contrary, they keep it alive. But if they attempt to give a reasoned judgment upon the works they love, they will reason weakly and inconclusively. On the other hand, it is not possible to have a critical judgment without taste, or the direct enjoyment of art, supported by a definite critical standard or aesthetic concept.

Croce's distinction between taste and criticism helps to settle the once hotly debated question whether the English neoclassical critics of the seventeenth and eighteenth centuries did or did not justly appreciate Shakespeare. Expressions of admiration for Shakespeare's characters and for his poetry as well as strictures on his lack of art may be quoted from several of these critics, and sometimes from the same critic, as in the case of Dryden. Dryden said that he loved Shakespeare, but when he came to choose the model of a regular play he chose one of Ben Jonson's: "I admire him, but I love Shakespeare." These neoclassical critics were precisely in the predicament described above by Croce: they *liked* Shakespeare—i.e. their taste was sound—but they could not make his work fit into their theory of regular drama—i.e. their judgment went astray, being grounded upon an erroneous doctrine. It may be added that these critics evaded their dilemma by resorting to a famous compromise formula, echoed by critic after critic from the days of Jonson to those of Dr. Johnson, that Shakespeare was the poet not of "art" but of "nature": i.e. an unconscious genius who composed poetry without knowing what he was doing, so that his work was necessarily uneven and irregular, a mixture of "great beauties" and "great faults," as the phrase went. This flimsy compromise was discarded when a sounder concept of artistic creation emerged from the aesthetic doctrines of the romantic era.[7]

In the historical part of the *Aesthetic* Croce showed that aesthetic relativism is a form of sensualism ("taste" as a sensation), and is therefore subject to the same uncertainties and contradictions as all forms of aesthetic sensualism. This is brought out by the analysis of such theorists as Batteux, Hume and Home (E, 524–26; A, 466–67). The old argument about the difference of tastes brings us back to fundamental issues: is art merely a question of impressions, of transient sensations, or does it possess some principle of permanence and of universal validity? Whatever the conclusions of empirical or sensualistic aesthetics, Croce's view was that art is a function of the theoretical spirit and therefore universal in its operation.

But in the present temper of modern thought, relativism is very attractive. It seems so obvious that the world is made up of an innumerable quantity of separate persons, each with his own different point of view, and that therefore no point of view can claim universal validity. But what about the world-view involved in relativism itself? For the relativist assumes that he, and he alone, is in possession of the truth about the universe: *he* knows that the universe is made up of innumerable separate minds, each with its own limited point of view, etc. etc. By what miraculous privilege is the relativist himself exempt from this limitation? He *knows*—so that even the relativist turns out to be at bottom an absolutist. This of course involves him in a logical contradiction, from which the way out is to look for a philosophy, as Croce does, that reconciles both the facts of variety and plurality, or the flux of history, and the logical requirement of universality and necessity. In effect, the relativist is arguing that there is not one work of art, but that there are as many works of art as there are observers. And the answer to that, in simple terms, is that in the case of controlled re-creation the mind of the observer is at one with the mind of the artist.

IN THE *Breviary* Croce took up again the question of aesthetic skepticism, and met it with a series of arguments, some of which he designated as intrinsic and some as extrinsic. Croce's main "intrinsic" argument is that he who denies the possibility of the reproduction of expressions denies also the very fact of communication, which is an obvious absurdity. Such a denial can only arise logically out of a philosophy (similar to the relativist's) that views individual minds as separate monads "without windows." How then can the thoughts of one monad ever be apprehended by the mind of another? Given the premises, there is only one solution: that of some overwhelming external force, such as the will of a Creator, that miraculously imposes a "pre-established harmony" on the workings of the separate minds, like clocks all set to the same hour by the hand of a human being. In other words, this leads us back to Leibniz.

If one does not accept that philosophy, what is the alternative? We must give up the idea that separate minds have nothing in common and conceive humanity, following Pascal's suggestion, as a single individual "who always subsists and continually learns." We must acknowledge a principle of unity in experience, otherwise the experiences of one man could differ so completely from those of all others that no correlation would be possible. How to conceive such a unity of experience is of course one of the basic problems of modern philosophy (cf. CC, V, 78–79).

In the *Breviary* Croce stated his view of the question in these terms: reality is not a chaos of monads, "reality is spiritual unity, and in spiritual unity nothing is lost, everything is an eternal possession" (NSE, 81; EA, 92). (Lest the sentence about "eternal possession" be considered a piece of romantic mysticism, it may be recalled that it is an echo of Thucydides, the most hardheaded of Greek historians.) Croce proceeds: "not only the reproduction of art, but in general the recollection of any fact (which is in effect always the recollection of an intuition) would be inconceivable without the unity of reality." Philosophers, it is true, assert the impossibility of ever reproducing the individual, but they are the philosophers of scholasticism "who separated the universal from the individual, and made the latter an accident of the former (the dust, that time sweeps away), and ignored that the true universal is the individualized universal, and that the only true *effable* is the so-called ineffable, the concrete and the individual" (NSE, 81; EA, 92–93; cf. *Hegel*, 86 and CC, III, 103).

Leaving for the moment the fundamental problems of philosophy, we come to Croce's "extrinsic" observation: "the very same critics who deny the possibility of reproduction in abstract theory—or, as they put it, deny the absoluteness of taste—are on the other hand extremely tenacious in upholding their own judgments of taste" (NSE, 80; EA, 91). As a contemporary instance of the attitude described, one could perhaps quote I. A. Richards. Being an empiricist, he denies the possibility of what he calls "actual transference and participation": "all that occurs is that, under certain conditions separate minds have closely similar experiences." [8] But how do we know that they are "closely similar" if we cannot compare the original with the reproduction? And once a gap is admitted between the original and its reproduction, how can one prevent it from expanding to infinity and making all communication impossible?

Whatever the answer to these questions, we find Richards as a critic answering Croce's description of the critical relativist: he is "tenacious" in maintaining his own judgments on poetry. For instance, in the same book he maintains that the poetry of T. S. Eliot is a genuine "music of ideas" (p. 293) and asserts categorically: "Only those unfortunate persons who are incapable of reading poetry can resist Mr. Eliot's rhythms" (p. 294). In another essay he makes this statement on Eliot: "He has given a perfect emotive description of a state of mind which is probably inevitable for a while to all meditative people." [9] How can Richards tell that Eliot's description of his state of mind is "perfect" unless Richards knows exactly what Eliot's state of mind was? in other words, unless he can reproduce Eliot's state of mind in his own?

Croce here refers again to the demonstration of the universal value of aesthetic judgment made by Kant "in a classic analysis" of the *Critique of Judgment*. Even empiricists, in spite of their theories, must feel the difference between the statement that "wine pleases me or not because it conforms to my physiological organism, and the statement that one poem is beautiful and another is ugly" (NSE, 80; EA, 91). As we have seen in Chapter I, Croce's aesthetic presupposes Kant's, and any criticism of Croce should reckon with Kant too.

Croce concludes: "The complete reproduction of the past is, like the goal of all human effort, an ideal which is realized only in infinity—and which therefore is always realized, at every moment of time, to the extent allowed by the actual situation. Is there some nuance in a poem the full meaning of which still escapes us? No one can affirm that that nuance, of which one possesses now dim and unsatisfactory knowledge, will not be better understood in the future, through the efforts of research and analysis, and through the emergence of favorable conditions and sympathetic trends" (NSE, 81; EA, 93).

THIS PROCESS OF RE-CREATION which precedes the critical judgment may meet with special difficulties when the ideas and beliefs of the poet are involved. As we have seen, ideas may get into poetry as the sources or occasions for the emotional state which is the content of the poem and the object of expression. These beliefs must be taken for granted during the process of re-creation, to avoid such things as the sophomoric objection that the *Divine Comedy* is "all out" because it implies Ptolemaic astronomy. The intelligent reader must suspend his objections, however well-grounded, to the views involved, and even try to adopt them imaginatively for the time being. This temporary suspension of one's cherished convictions should be made easier by the reflection that after all there is always something true at the bottom of most of the beliefs which have been held by mankind; indeed, there is as much truth in them as was permitted by the conditions of the time in which they arose.

This way of looking upon past beliefs is what is known as the historical point of view—but it should not be confused with the so-called historical or purely factual approach to literature, with which it has little in common. To look upon a doctrine or a belief from the historical point of view means to see it in relation to the historical conditions under which it was developed, the most important of which, according to Croce, is the problem to which the doctrine was framed as an answer (*Logica*, 145–47). It means seeing the past doctrine as a positive effort to overcome a difficulty rather than as a dead fact among other dead facts. It is assumed by Croce that his ideal reader of poetry is so much imbued with this point of view that he extends it automatically to all aspects of past history and that he is able to see the beauty of Greek poetry with its references to ancient polytheism and pagan ethics, to see the beauty of medieval poetry even if, like Dante's, it refers to scholastic philosophy, and to see the beauty of Renaissance poetry with its references to Renaissance politics, religious controversies, and so forth (cf. NSE², 226). All these things may get into poetry, and it is well to know them when they do, but they are not the substance of poetry. Readers not trained in the habit of mental adjustment to different civilizations and different political and religious ideas usually find it very hard to appreciate the poetry of the past, which they are not able to dissociate from their contemporary ideas and beliefs. Then they may wax enthusiastic over the poetry of the present, or of the immediate past, in the illusion that being nearer to them in time it is nearer in spirit, or in poverty of spirit. Hence also, in modern criticism, such inconclusive controversies as that between T. S. Eliot and I. A. Richards upon belief in poetry.[10]

But as far as poetry is concerned, the answer to the problem of belief is that the imagination has a truth of its own which carries conviction to the perceptive reader and calls for no further apology. We may not believe in the afterlife or in the river Styx, but Dante's Charon is a living figure which requires no justification. Nobody believes in Zeus any longer, but Prometheus' defiance of him in Aeschylus is still great poetry. And we may not believe in Catholicism, but Cardinal Federigo in Manzoni's *Betrothed* is a great character, a beautiful presentation of saintliness in a hard, hostile world.

The reproduction of past expressions may therefore be designated as "historical" not only because it is rendered possible by historical information, but also because it calls for the historical point of view in the reader. In a paper of 1933 entitled "The theory of aesthetic judgment as historical judgment," Croce investigated the philosophical genesis of that theory itself. He began: "What is more familiar to us, as critics or as simple lovers of art and of literature, than the theory that to judge a work of art or of poetry one should transfer oneself into the conditions in which the work was born and into the mind of the author?

"Yet it is a theory of relatively recent date, laboriously developed in the course of the eighteenth century and established only in the nineteenth.

"I stress the word 'theory', for it is not to be thought that the corresponding form of judgment came into the world only with the formulation of the theory. Whenever one judges a work of art, or a thought, or an action, the mind transfers itself, in a manner as necessary as it is spontaneous, into the fact to be judged and into its genesis, which is its very nature. . . . But judgment is sometimes prevented or deviated in its process by contrary forces that enslave it to the passions of the judge, to the narrowness of his personal tendencies, to the prejudices that reside within him, to his inertia, and so forth" (us, 134–35).

Croce then shows how it was only possible at the end of the eighteenth century to conceive the idea that works of art are produced under definite national and historical conditions. This is not critical relativism, as Croce shows by bringing up a representative of relativism, the German critic F. G. Riedel, and expounding his views. These views, published in 1758, were

refuted by Herder in his *Fourth Critical Sylva* (1789), and
Croce introduces Herder as the representative of the correct
critical view that takes into account historical conditions but
does not make the aesthetic judgment subordinate to them.

"Everything returns," and historical relativism returned with
the advent of positivism, assuming the shape that Croce calls
"philologism" or the belief that the factual and philological approach is the only way to study literature (US, 135–60). Under
this trend the old skeptical objections to aesthetic judgment
assumed a speciously "historical" garb, and the history of criticism was used to prove that the aesthetic standards of various
ages differ widely from each other, and that very different
things have been praised as poetry in different epochs. Croce
of course acknowledges the latter fact, but he infers from it
that it is not the concept of poetry, but only the *name* that has
changed its meaning in different epochs. He notes that people
in the past have given that name to things like "emphatic preaching, or cleverness, or wit, or the skilful manipulation of traditional forms, the heated passions of patriotism or politics, or the
material reproduction of sensuous objects." But none of these
things are really poetry.[11] In all ages, whatever the dominant
trends or fashions in literature, there have been poets who have
written poems not according to fashion but according to the
eternal idea of poetry (US, 27–28). It is the critic's job to grasp
this idea and to discover these genuine poems, however little
known or despised in their own day. Conversely the critic should
identify the poetasters who rhyme only according to fashion
and dominant conventions and turn them out of the history of
poetry. Historical thinking involves judgment, or the operation
of all categories: each historical event, as we have seen in Chapter I, is to be related to its category, the poetic to poetry and
nonpoetic to the intellectual or the practical.

Croce therefore rejected the doctrine of historical relativism,
or the view that the poetry of the past should be judged according to the ideas that prevailed in the past: that Dante should be
judged according to the didactic and allegorical poetics of the
Middle Ages, Renaissance poetry according to the formalistic

or genre theories or the didacticism of Renaissance criticism, seventeenth-century poetry according to the idea of the Baroque, and so forth. For him poetry of all ages is to be judged according to the universal category of art, which it is the object of aesthetics to determine.[12]

A particular form of this historical relativism is the claim that a poet is best judged by his contemporaries because they shared his beliefs and his historical background. It follows that a poet's contemporary reputation must be accepted without question by the modern critic, however artificial and conventional his verse appears today. According to another version of this view, Shakespeare's plays are to be interpreted solely according to the beliefs of his audience, and no interpretation of his characters or of his plots is acceptable that is beyond the assumed capacity of that audience. Croce's answer to arguments like these was that there is no reason to believe that earlier critics were better judges than the moderns, or the reverse, "since critics are not to be evaluated by chronological standards, as 'contemporary' or 'more recent', but only as understanding or not, as sensitive to the beautiful or not." [13] The requirement of "placing oneself from the poet's point of view" refers, as we have often noted, to the stage of re-creation of the expression, or "taste" and not to the stage of critical judgment, which Croce as we have seen sharply differentiates from it.[14] According to him, this re-creation is always possible in virtue of the unity of all human experience, and the aesthetic judgment is always valid in virtue of the universality of the aesthetic concept.

CHAPTER *Viii*

The Function of Literary Criticism

B Y THIS TIME the reader should have an idea of what literary criticism is and is not for Croce. It is the exercise of critical judgment based upon the complete re-creation of the poetic act of expression. When that re-creation is achieved through the process of taste and with the help of historical knowledge, the critic asks the question: Is the work which I have now before me a work of poetry? And he may answer "yes, this is a work of poetry" or "no, this is not a work of poetry," pronouncing a judgment which involves a universal category, that of poetry or of art in general. Without the category there is no judgment; where there is no judgment there is no criticism.

It should be equally clear what criticism is *not* for Croce. It is not the evaluation of a work by means of a genre concept, or of any other of the subdivisions of Art or Beauty; for the category of judgment must be a universal and not a limited generalization or pseudo-concept. Neither is it the analysis of the external form of a work according to the systems of "technique," as we have seen in Chapter IV. Nor is it the kind of criticism that picks out a beauty here, a fault there, points out a simile at one point and a metrical deficiency somewhere else, and then ends by striking the balance of beauties and faults and pronouncing judgment accordingly. Croce's criticism aims at defining the central quality of a work and deriving both its beauties and its shortcomings from this unitary concept (*PdE*, 441).

But how can such a complete result be obtained from the bare critical judgment, "*A* is a work of art"? First of all, it should be remembered that this formula, bare as it seems, has behind it the complete re-creation of the work. Secondly, the critical judgment in order to assert itself concretely must deal with a number of particular questions. As Croce said in 1919: "The critic, at the beginning of his work, has his mind and his imagination full of the work of art which is his subject. Upon the foundation of this full possession he asks questions, formulates problems and solves them in relation to the intellectual moment in which he finds himself" (NSE², 223; cf. *Discorsi* II, 93 and TPS, II, 189). What are these problems? It is a fact that every work of literature presents itself to the observer already covered with judgments and interpretations, definitions and descriptions (NSE², 295). It may be characterized as a masterpiece or a failure, as a work of cold craftsmanship or intense feeling, as original or conventional, gay or melancholy, subtle or sophisticated, etc. etc. The critic's job is to check these characterizations by reference to the work itself, duly re-created. He will then accept them, or qualify them, or reject them altogether and replace them with better ones.

In this process of revision, the question may arise: is this a work of art at all? or does it not belong instead to some other sphere of mental activity, to philosophy or politics or religion, to the history of ideas or to the history of culture? We all know that a work may be written in verse or in the external form of a novel or of a play, and yet exist mainly as a vehicle for religious or political or other ideas. The critic's job is then, according to Croce, to remove the work from the domain of poetry or of literary art in general, and assign it to its place elsewhere, by means of appropriate analysis and discussion. Although this is a terminal case, there are many intermediate cases requiring a more complete analysis which Croce carries out with particular rigor.

Once a work is definitely assigned to the aesthetic sphere, it can be studied as the embodiment of an image expressing an emotion or a state of mind. As already noted, this gives the critic three points to work on (or rather three directions from which to approach the same object): the image, the emotion, and their reciprocal relation. The critic characterizes the image, defines the emotion and evaluates their adjustment to each other.[1] The conclusion that the image affords a perfect expression of the emotion constitutes the aesthetic judgment true and proper. The critic then pronounces the verdict: "This work *is* a poem," subsuming the individual work under the universal category of poetry (or of art).

Let us now consider the three points in succession, beginning with the image. To "characterize an image" embodied in a work of art includes as we have seen many of the processes of analysis and description that critics devote to the plot and the characters of a novel or a play. Or it may include the progression of thoughts and emotions in a lyric, with its similes and metaphors and other figures or movements (e.g. PAM, 171–75). The characters of a story, as we have seen in Chapter II, are secondary images within the total image, just as in a lyric the individual "images" are parts of the greater image presented by the whole poem. All these images may be unified or fragmentary, sharp or faint, fully rounded or half-formed, original or conventional. It is up to the critic to make the decision and to pronounce judgment accordingly, either favorably or unfavorably. In this discussion Croce allows the use of all the terms of traditional criticism and of rhetoric, provided they are employed descriptively and not judicially, i.e. to point out a detail to which attention is called for its expressive function ("this epithet, this simile, this stanza") without any implication of a pre-established pattern to which it should conform (NSE[2], 285).

Both character analysis and analysis of imagery have therefore a recognized place in Croce's critical method, as long as images and characters are not treated in the abstract, or as independent entities. For instance, characters are treated in the abstract when they are discussed as if they were real persons: e.g. if the critic attempts to determine what they did in episodes which are not part of the work. Such is a well-known fallacy in Shakespearean criticism of the Victorian age, when critics wrote books on "the girlhood of Shakespeare's heroines" or came shortly afterwards to investigate such problems as "how many children had Lady Macbeth." But the twentieth-century critic, who deals with the characters of Shakespeare as if they were patients on the psychoanalytic couch and discovers the Oedipus complex in Hamlet, falls into the same fallacy. So, at the opposite extreme, does the "formalistic" critic who speaks of words and images in a poem as if they were independent realities endowed with powers of their own and acting and reacting upon each other. But as long as words, metaphors, characters and plots are considered strictly as parts of an individual whole and exercising therein a purely expressive function, there is for Croce no harm, and much convenience, in designating them by traditional terminology.[2]

The function of the image being to express an emotion, the critic then defines the emotion expressed. This is our second point. The various details of the total image analyzed in the previous discussion are now shown to be vehicles of various phases of emotion or movements of a mood. Here, too, the mood must not be taken in the abstract, separated from the image in which it is expressed. This leads to the fallacies of biographical and psychological criticism. It is the emotion as crystallized in the image that the critic should define, and not as it may appear in the poet's known behavior or in his correspondence or in other historical evidence. How the critic should proceed in this definition, which Croce calls by the name of "characterization," will be discussed in detail later in this chapter.

Finally, the critic may direct his attention to the degree of success in the expression of the emotion through the image, and make it the subject of his evaluation. He may then conclude with an affirmative or with a negative judgment as we have seen, and say "this *is* a poem" or "this is *not* a poem." Negative judgments are not only possible but frequent. Croce has always acknowledged that there are few really perfect works of poetry, that great poets are rare, and even that there have been whole ages devoid of poetry (NSE[2], 142, 305; PNP, 206). Most works of literature exhibit maladjustment in various degrees, which it is the critic's job to assess. To take an instance from Chapter III, excess of emotion over the image is the shortcoming of romantic literature, whereas classicism exhibits the opposite shortcoming.

Whatever their point of departure, all these critical discussions converge on one focus—the work as an individual synthesis of form and content, of image and emotion. Since the constituents of the work form an organic unity, judgment on one of them implies judgment on the other, and a judgment on the synthesis implies a definition of its constituents. So it does not matter which constituent is discussed first, or even if only one is discussed and the other is left implicit, provided the critic does not leave it out of the picture altogether and does not fall into one of the abstract positions criticized above. Croce himself stressed now the one and now the other, as occasion offered. In some of the early criticism attention is directed mainly to the image; in some of his later, to the emotion.[3] One reason why it is convenient to discuss the image and the emotion separately is that in the course of centuries of reflective thought a rich and varied terminology has been developed for each of them, and many critical problems centre on such terms. As we have seen, it is the critic's job to discuss these formulations, to reject them if necessary or to change them into a more adequate characterization of the work.

Now is this so different from what literary critics have always been doing? If a poem consists of an image, in the sense that Croce gives to this term, then the test of the poem lies in the unity, consistency and shapeliness of that image, and critics from time immemorial have dealt with the unity, consistency and shapeliness of poems. If a poem is an intuition, as Croce argues, then the test of the poem lies in its individuality; and again, critics of all ages have discussed the individual quality of poems, differentiated them from analogues and imitations, and extolled original creations.[4] If an image expresses an emotion, then the test of the poem lies in its expressiveness; and even this is not a novelty in criticism, for critics have often discussed the expression of emotion, at least in lyrical poets, rejecting those that were cold and artificial and praising those that were vivid and intense. So it does not seem that Croce was a radical innovator. Nor did he claim to be. After offering his definition of criticism as judgment, he observed: "such is the criticism of art in its essence; and as such it is to be found in all books of criticism, however various the forms that it assumes in books. The form of a book is determined by contingencies; and according to these a book of criticism may contain one or the other constituent of criticism in larger or smaller proportions" (*PdE*, 55; cf. cc, III, 83–84 and 102).

And indeed Croce as a practical critic proceeds most of the time in the same way that other modern critics do. He endeavors to determine the range and compass of a writer, to fix on his predominant talent, to trace his development, to distinguish different periods and stages in his work, and to single out, if possible, his masterpiece. He will discuss the plot of a play or of a novel, point out its imperfections and inconsistencies, and analyze its characters and situations, praising the good and condemning the bad. One of his best pieces of character analysis is the study of the pedant Wagner in Goethe's *Faust* (G, 1, 24–32). The character is at first described as he appears when he is alone, and then in his relations with his master Faust. The aesthetic effect arising from the conflict between the contrasting personalities of Faust and Wagner is brought out by Croce with full appreciation of its humorous overtones. Croce does not hesitate to discuss style and texture, vocabulary and metre, and he can be an unsparing critic of sloppy composition and lack of finish, of sentimentalism and conventional devices.[5] But for Croce all these critical discussions converge on one basic issue: the aesthetic image presented by the work in its totality, and its function as the expression of an individual state of mind.

THIS BEING SO, it is strange to find that the two notions about Croce's critical method which seem to be current in the United States are that a critic who works upon Croce's principles will never pronounce a judgment but merely express his impressions, or that he will say nothing at all about the work. These notions are so far from the truth that it may well be asked how they ever came to be held.[6] The first was mainly put forward by the New Humanists in their attacks on Croce. The second is more recent, but it is hard to find support for it in Croce's theoretical discussions [7] and it obviously ignores the whole of his critical work, which is both ample in extent and explicit in statement.

As to the first opinion, the blame for it must be shared by the scholar who did most to propagate Croce's views in America in the early part of the century—namely J. E. Spingarn. Spingarn went on expounding a superseded phase of Croce's doctrine long after Croce had abandoned it—viz. the theory that criticism is only the re-enactment of the expressive process, or "taste." As we have seen in the previous chapter, this was Croce's view in the first *Aesthetic*, but he rejected it in 1908 and never returned to it afterwards, holding instead the view that criticism is judgment, that it involves a category or universal concept, and that it arises only after the process of re-creation is completed.[8] As he put it in 1919 in words that seem a direct correction of Spingarn, "far from reproducing art, criticism implies that this reproduction is already accomplished" (NSE², 223). Even in his first *Aesthetic*, Croce recognized the judgment of a work of art by means of a category, but assigned this function to literary history (E, 144; A, 131). We shall see in the next chapter how he dealt with literary history afterwards.

But Spingarn in his famous lecture on "The New Criticism," first delivered in 1910 and republished later with revisions, maintained firmly that criticism was identical with "taste." [9] In later articles he went on repeating, as he did in 1922, that "criticism is essentially an expression of taste." Although he then added that taste "becomes criticism in its highest sense only when taste is guided by knowledge and rises to the level of thought," [10] and although as we have seen "taste" in the Crocean sense is far from being impressionism, Spingarn never made it clear that "thought" consisted in the formulation of a logical judgment, as Croce did. The closest Spingarn came to this was in 1923: "the critic must immerse himself in the creative spirit

of the poet before he can rise above it to the level of judgment," [11] but he never elaborated this hint and apparently left
American readers with the impression that for Croce criticism
was merely re-creation. Only one voice seems to have been
raised in protest against this misrepresentation of Croce.[12] A
fuller and more correct exposition of Croce's theory of criticism
was made in the United States by Lionello Venturi in 1936 [13]
but that also seems to have passed unnoticed by the literary
critics.[14]

Criticism for Croce not only implies a philosophy; it is a
philosophy, as he argued in a paper of 1918: [15] "Criticism is
judgment, judgment involves a standard of criticism, a standard
of criticism involves thinking a concept, thinking a concept
implies the connection with other concepts, and the connection
of concepts is, finally, a system of philosophy." Opposition to
this argument can only come, according to Croce, from " 'impressionistic' or 'relativistic' criticism" which resolves itself into
philosophical skepticism and is subject to the same objection
that applies to all skeptical philosophies: it is self-contradictory
(NSE², 201).

Croce's argument may be opposed on the grounds that literary
criticism is not a matter of philosophy but of common sense,
that it should be an unprejudiced and unsystematic judgment
of literary works apart from any system of philosophy. Croce
answered that what is known generally as "common sense" is
merely popularized philosophy "made up of the thoughts of
Plato and of Aristotle, Descartes and Kant, even of Jesus of
Nazareth, and is continually enriched by the addition of thoughts
from more recent thinkers" (NSE², 202). On the other hand, if
"common sense" is understood to be a natural capacity for
judgment independent of all training and tradition, then Croce
answers that there is no such thing. For there can be for Croce
no thought "outside of history" (NSE², 202–3). Even French
literary criticism, which seems so alien to philosophy, is ultimately philosophical, as Croce shows in a discussion of the main
French critics of the nineteenth century—Lemaitre and Brunetière, Sainte-Beuve [16] and Taine [17]—a discussion from which

Flaubert emerges as one of the greatest aesthetic thinkers of his nation (NSE², 210–11).

Since it is impossible for the critic to avoid having a philosophy, he should endeavor to follow a sound philosophy rather than accept blindly any current trend of thought. For Croce, a philosophy is sound when it is built up "methodically and with full knowledge of its historical antecedents" (NSE², 211). This for Croce rules out positivism and scientism which are notoriously weak in historical knowledge. It also rules out any system that will not enable the critic to understand individual works of art, for a concept of art is not valid if it proves "impotent to penetrate the intuition" (NSE², 212). This is a corollary of the doctrine of philosophy as methodology of history which we saw in Chapter 1. Belief in the unity of critical theory and critical practice separates Croce from those philosophers of art who look upon criticism as a kind of exemplification that anyone can perform, once the general principles have been ascertained by the philosopher. When these abstract philosophers venture to pronounce a judgment upon a work of art, they usually reveal signal weakness or utter incapacity (*Letture*, 229).

In connection with philosophy, it may be added that there is another kind of criticism which Croce provides, but which he keeps clearly distinct from aesthetic criticism, and that is philosophical and ethical criticism of writers in their extra-aesthetic, practical or intellectual activity. There is a kind of "aesthetic" critic for whom everything that a great writer does is sacrosanct, be it committing a felony or propounding a fallacy. But for Croce the fact that no moral judgment can be pronounced upon art does not mean that no moral judgment can be pronounced on the artist's conduct. On the contrary, Croce was firm and explicit in judging the conduct as well as the theoretical pronouncements of writers. He often put his finger unerringly on the sources of human and intellectual weakness that lurk behind the showy façade of an imposing literary edifice, as he did in his penetrating essay on Barrès, and he cut with a sharp knife through the fogs of confusion and sophistry that sometimes pass for "modern thought" and "modern poetics." [18]

He also encouraged research into the moral content of literature: e.g. in the wealth of "psychological observations or moral problems" that lies in nineteenth-century writing, most of it still awaiting analysis (*Teoria e storia della storiografia*, 147). Such analysis should proceed on the principle that psychological observations are easily convertible into rules of conduct (*Pratica*, 69): so it is possible to determine from the observations which abound in modern literature the character—ethical or unethical —of the ideals that guide modern societies (*Pratica*, 73). Here again Croce can be quite explicit in his moral judgment of a whole society, as we shall see in Chapter xiv. But this inquiry takes us into the history of manners and morals, or of culture, and out of aesthetic criticism.

THE SPECIFIC PROCEDURES of aesthetic criticism were worked out by Croce in considerable detail, yet always with flexibility and a sense of proportion. In one of his early critical essays we find him stating the fundamental principle that "a work of art must have a central motif, a character, an action, a situation, or—to put it more exactly—an emotion [*sentimento*]: the musician's motif, the painter's *macchia*, the architectural line, the poetic wave" (LNI, II, 161–62). The goal of criticism is thus to define the motif, or *macchia*. What Croce meant by this term is explained in a very suggestive untranslated essay which goes back to 1905 and has an important bearing also on the sister arts. It calls attention to the theory of the *macchia*—meaning roughly "patch of color"—which was developed in 1868 by the Neapolitan critic Vittorio Imbriani. The theory is that every good painting has an original cell or nucleus, called *macchia*, from which it develops and which confers artistic life and unity to it. This nucleus consists of a simple combination of a few lines or colors, which in the artist's hands is capable of expanding into a whole picture, but which possesses an intrinsic beauty of its own. For instance: "In the studio of the painter Palizzi, among many pictures and sketches, there hung on the wall a small piece of cardboard only a few inches large, splendidly framed, and on which there were only four or five brush strokes. 'These few brush strokes, which did not represent anything specific, were so happily harmonized that no other painting in those rooms, however perfect in its composition and interesting in its subject, could equal it: that harmony of color induced intense delight' " (*PdE*, 241).

Croce's quotation is from Imbriani, and incidentally provides a justification for abstract art well *avant la lettre*. The theory was extended by Croce to poetry without any qualification: "Every poet knows that inspiration comes to him precisely as a *macchia*, as a motif, a rhythm, a psychic motion, or whatever you call it, in which nothing is determinate and all is determinate: in which there is already that meter and no other, those words and no others, that arrangement and no other, that extension and those proportions and no others. And every poet knows that his work consists in working out that *macchia*, that motif, that rhythm, to obtain at the end—in a shape that is fully developed and may be recited aloud, and transcribed in writing—the selfsame impression that he had received, as a flash, in his first inspiration. The value of the poem, as of the painting, lies in the *macchia*, in the lyrical impulse, and not in the abundance and importance of the thoughts, emotions and observations, or in its capacity to reveal secrets" (*PdE*, 245; cf. *Pratica* 54). It follows that the critic's job is to discover the *macchia*, the "poetic motif," out of which the poem arises and then to trace its development in the completed composition. For Croce the "poetic motif" is a lyrical or emotional impulse, expressed by the image, which the critic defines in his analysis.

Within the limits of the individual work, the critic also decides how far it achieves expression and how far expression is impeded by extra-aesthetic tendencies, such as practical urges or the promotion of political and other interests. The critic points out the places in the work in which this happens and explains why they are not poetic. This is Croce's famous discrimination of "poetry and non-poetry," which he employs within the poem itself whenever necessary, wielding a blade as sharp as Occam's razor even upon the most acclaimed masterpieces.[19] For as Croce said in his second study of Carducci: "The spirit of man is at the same time one and various, and its so-called poetic, intellectual, emotive and practical impulses are all active at every moment, all at once, and yet each is distinct from the other. From this distinction conflict and struggle arise, and from the struggle spiritual development and productivity. . . . So to understand a poet critically is to understand the dialectic of his soul, the practical and emotional forces no less than the poetic and contemplative which are operating in him, and to show how the struggle between these forces now favors and now impedes his poetry; how the nonpoetic elements in his soul can now nourish the poetic, and now devour them, using them for their own nourishment" (LNI, II, 34).

This "dialectic of the soul," which is a reaffirmation of Croce's dialectic of the distinct forms of spiritual activity described in Chapter I, marks off again Croce's criticism from the purely aesthetic or formalistic or imagistic, which sees in poetry only the operation of abstract formal elements, images and devices. The critical characterization of a poet or an artist for Croce is not the static definition of a single theme, but the portrayal of dynamic conflicts between aesthetic and nonaesthetic forces in all their various configurations.

The theory of "characterization" (*caratterizzazione*) was developed by Croce in his middle period. It is therefore not to be found in the first *Aesthetic* or in the *Breviary*. But it will be found in a paper on "The extra-aesthetic concept of Beauty" dated 1919 and included in the untranslated portion of the *New Essays on Aesthetics* (NSE², 293–95). Characterization was taken up again in a paper of 1924 (CC, III, 82–84; cf. CC, IV, 303–4). Finally, in *La poesia* (1936) two full sections are dedicated to it (P, 121–28 and 145–54), one of which has been translated.[20] Characterization is not a process which is separate and distinct from that of the critical judgment which pronounces whether a work is an achieved act of expression or not.[21] The conscious re-enactment of the act of expression involves awareness of the emotion expressed and hence the possibility of giving an account of it. If a poem expresses joy or sorrow, passion rising to anguish or anguish subsiding into serenity, the critic who has re-enacted the expression will be able to identify the mood expressed.

The next, all-important question is: what name shall he give it? or by what terms shall he describe the emotions expressed by the poet? Should they be terms of some system of psychology, or of anthropology or of some other natural science? Croce of course rejects all of these. While acknowledging that the object described by the critic may be called "psychological" in a broad sense of the word, he is satisfied to make use of such terms as have been used for ages by critics and by moralists, or by non-technical students of human nature.[22] They are such terms as we have been using already throughout this discussion: joy and sorrow, anguish and serenity, love and passion, feeling and emotion, and so forth. These terms arise from the observation and analysis of every-day experience which was successfully practiced long before modern psychology was thought of, and they constitute a *corpus* of distinctions and classifications which are always at the service of the critic. From the philosophical point of view they are to be considered empirical, but they do not form a closed system of water-tight compartments. They are loose generalizations which tend to assume a specific meaning every time they are used concretely. On the other hand, scientific psychology tends to make a closed system out of them, turning them into something more abstract that better suits the purpose of that science, which seems to be the reduction of human nature to a simple mechanism that can be easily operated. Literary criticism has no such operational concerns and is content to take human nature in all its unresolved complexities and with the innumerable varieties of individual character.

It must be added that Croce has not hesitated to make use on occasion of the deeper insights which his own philosophy afforded him for his analysis of psychological content. This may be seen for instance in his interpretation of Maupassant, to which we shall come later in this chapter. Or in his interpretation of Shakespeare's histories as the expression of an interest in "practical activity" in the Crocean sense. Shakespeare's so-called "villain-heroes"—e.g., Richard III and Iago—were defined by

Hegel, in his own terminology, as "formal" characters; [23] for Croce they are "economic" characters. But in his characterizations Croce usually avoids technical terms, and does not stress the purely philosophical implications of his analysis.

It may be suggested that today we possess a scientific psychology (or rather, psychologies, for there is more than one school) and that we should use it in literary criticism for the analysis of the emotional content. Psychoanalysis, in one form or another, has been often so used. Did Croce ever take notice of Freud and Freudian methods? In 1925 Croce reviewed a French translation of Freud's book on the interpretation of dreams. He found nothing objectionable in the concept of dreams as the embodiment of repressed desires. But he observed that dreams, so understood, cease to be "a singular phenomenon and become an instance of the general tendency to proceed from desire to phantasy, that is to say, of the general theory of the fancy considered as a manifestation of vitality or of the practical spirit. . . . And here one sees the difference, indeed the abyss, that gapes between dreams and art, between imagination and fancy. In the imagination, the fundamental quality is contemplation . . . hence, although it has within itself both fancy and the desire which generated it, it has them as matter, which it overcomes by fashioning it into a cosmic image" (CC, III, 29–31).

But as psychoanalytic concepts penetrated more and more into literary criticism, Croce's reaction became sharper. In 1936, in *La Poesia*, he aligns psychoanalysis with what he calls "the decadent concept of personality"; the vogue of both these doctrines "is evidence of lost or perverted consciousness of man's spirituality. For it, the poetic image is the hidden or disguised means to satisfy certain impulses of eroticism or violence, of which conscience prevents the realization in ordinary life." And he referred the reader to critiques of psychoanalysis by G. de Ruggiero and by F. Flora (P, 319). In 1946 he wrote to the editor of a symposium on Freudian theories: "of course I cannot help agreeing with you on the importance of Freud's work, both as a psychological and naturalistic inquiry and as therapeutics: as long as it does not go beyond those limits, which it sometimes does. But I would like to see it clearly stated that Poetry has nothing to learn or to change as a result of these theories, because Poetry, as everyone knows, has for its matter love (and therefore the so-called sexual irrational or unconscious), hence it has been said innumerable times that Poetry is born of love. But at the same time it is also full of the aspiration to the elevation and the overcoming of that irrational in the religious and moral life" (NPS, I, 258). And he attacked psychoanalysis in literary criticism as "Freudian methods, devised for the cure of neurotics and psychotics, which are foolishly transferred to the interpretation of men who are not in those pathological conditions" (NPS, I, 220; cf. US, 280; NPS, II, 127).

The descriptions of psychological states that Croce makes use of in the definition of the poetic theme are not meant to be "scientific." They are approximate and instrumental. "And what is the proper use of these instruments? Solely to direct attention to the specific and the individual, and as such logically ineffable, character of a poem or of any other work of art" (NSE^2, 294). We come again upon the philosophical problem already met in Chapter II: the individual is "logically ineffable" or inexpressible in terms of concepts. But it is not poetically ineffable, for the poet, by his choice and arrangement of words and phrases, succeeds precisely in doing this, expressing the individual.[24]

However, a critic is not a poet, and he should not attempt to duplicate the work of art in intellectual or imaginative terms. Croce has repeatedly argued against this view of criticism, or the idea that the critic should produce something that will give in different terms the same aesthetic pleasure as the original work (PdE, 54; NSE^2, 79; CC, IV, 304; Discorsi, II, 93; Letture, 230; TPS, II, 188–89). This is the fallacy of so-called "aesthetic" criticism, with its flamboyant parallels of poems with paintings or with symphonies, and other "evocative" devices. But for Croce all poetry is untranslatable and nothing can give the equivalent of a poem. The critic moves in an entirely distinct sphere from the poet: he does not produce art objects, he discusses them, operating at the intellectual and logical level. Croce's "characterization" is not therefore an impossible attempt at repeating the magic effect of poetry, but the intellectual analysis of critical problems. He has even argued that De Sanctis' famed imaginative "re-creations" of Dante's characters actually resolve themselves into a discussion of critical propositions and aesthetic theories (NSE², 223–24).

The alternative to the use of "characterizations," with all their limitations, is to give up altogether the discussion of a work of art—or, as Croce adds, of anything else, "for all things are ineffable individuals" (NSE², 294). This would result in a condition of absolute silence, pending the mystical communion of the ecstatic reader with the ineffable poem. Such an ideal, which is sometimes advanced by critics of a mystical turn, was never attractive to Croce, who always manifested a strong antimystical attitude in all questions, philosophical (cf. *Logica*, 11) as well as critical. Against the mystics he brings forward an argument which he considers conclusive (NSE², 95): even those who advocate silence, like the mystics, cannot avoid speech, and sooner or later will eagerly attempt to communicate their raptures by means of discourse—i.e. by a stream of concepts and pseudo-concepts. Even concentration on the Self is speech, or thinking of the "Self" (NSE², 295). Hence the manifest error of attributing to Croce a critical method which results in mystical silence.

While the theory of characterization was developed after World War I, the relativity of all descriptive terms in criticism was apparent to Croce even in the very first critical essay which he published in *La critica*, the one on Carducci (1903). In it he gave a description of the poet's style by means of a series of epithets: "robust, sculpturesque, concentrated, rapid . . . . these and similar descriptions serve at best to recall the physiognomy of Carducci's art to those who are acquainted with it, and not to define it, since it is impossible to detach form from matter and reduce form to a string of adjectives" (*Critica*, I, 30). For the purpose of describing Carducci's poetic motif or emotional content, Croce then hit upon the formula "the impassioned poet of history," which he held to and developed further in the much fuller study of Carducci written in 1909 (LNI, II, 5–110).

This formula may serve as an example of what Croce means

by characterization and will bring out both its function and its limitations. "The poet of history" may mean little or nothing, or may mean something very different from Croce's meaning, to a reader for whom "history" means little or nothing, or something very different from what it meant both to Carducci and to Croce. A whole century of devoted and at the same time critical investigation into the rich and complex past of Italy, of which Croce was later to write a full account (ss), stands behind that formula. There is a connection between the intellectual process of historical investigation and the emotional world of the poet Carducci—a connection not unfamiliar to the great post-Romantic age of historical thinking and nation-building in nineteenth-century Europe. This emotional world is expressed in the brilliant visions of the heroic past which are built up in Carducci's verse and prose. So once its bearing is understood, this formula of the "impassioned poet of history" serves to exclude the rival definitions of Carducci as the poet of civic virtue, or of moral indignation, or of republican liberty, or of neoclassicism, and so forth, and to direct the attention of the reader to what is central and essential in Carducci's work. Furthermore, since this feeling for the past is linked to the Romantic revival, after Croce's analysis the way was open for the interpretation of Carducci, who in theory was an archclassicist, as instead a genuine son of the Romantic movement, an interpretation which was explicitly worked out by post-Crocean criticism.[25] This provides another instance of the fact that Croce's critical method not only illuminates its subject, but opens the way to further investigation by other critics.

Croce's fullest discussion of characterization is to be found in the book on poetry of 1936 (P, 123–28). This book will be dealt with in Chapter XIII, but we will take up here its discussion of characterization in order to complete that subject. In it he explicitly establishes the point that characterization does not refer to the form of the poem, but to its content (P, 123). Form in poetry is beauty, and "beauty is one, indivisible and identical in all poets"; it is the universal element of all art. Attempted descriptions of poetic form turn out to be mere repetitions of the statement that it is beautiful. Croce had already noted that tendency in the critics of Shakespeare who tried to define the formal quality of Shakespeare's art, and found it in its "individuality," "musicality," "lyricism," "ideality," "objectivity," "totality," etc.; all of which, when scrutinized, turn out to be merely "synonyms or metaphors" of the one universal quality of poetic beauty (*Shak.*, 125).

A more recent attempt at defining the formal element of poetry consists in the so-called stylistic approach, which Croce considers a hybrid of aesthetics and rhetoric, and "like all hybrids entirely sterile": "By breaking up the forms of poetry into words and metaphors, similes and figures, syntactical groups and metrical patterns, and so forth, one does not get at the character of a poem, which can only be re-enacted and contemplated in the total intuition, one only succeeds in heaping up a miserable pile of dead fragments, mere shards" (P, 124).

Setting aside these things, the critic turns to the content of the poem, to the emotion expressed, which is now considered in its individuality. In this scrutiny "everything which has not become the content of the poem and which remains outside it, even though it may be connected in some material way with the work or the person of the poet, is excluded from the inquiry" (P, 124). This formally excludes all the deviations of biographical and historical criticism, and paves the way for the exercise of the critical intelligence: "To characterize a poem means to determine its content or its fundamental theme [*motivo fondamentale*] by referring it to the psychological class or type nearest to it. This is where the critic employs his perspicacity and tests his perceptiveness. In this task he is satisfied only when, reading and re-reading and carefully considering the text of the poem, he finally succeeds in identifying its fundamental trait . . ." (P, 125). In other words, the unity of form and content which was broken by the process of analysis is restored in the final phase of the critical operation, when the critic goes back to the text, "reading it and re-reading it," and checks the formula with the reintegrated poem.

It will be noted that Croce here does not say anything about characterizing the *image* presented by the poem. This remarkable omission in critical theory is probably due to the identification of the image with Form, as noted above in Chapter III. But the analysis of the image was not abandoned in his critical practice; for Croce went on characterizing images in the manner described above, even in criticism written after 1936. For instance, we can take one of his very latest papers, a revaluation of one of D'Annunzio's later lyrics, which we shall consider in Chapter XII.

However carefully fashioned, the critical formula always remains separated from the actual poem by a distance which Croce himself did not hesitate to term "abysmal" (P, 125). Nothing can exhaust the individual quality of the work of art. Hence sooner or later discontent will arise even with the most carefully constructed formula, "even with our own." The reader will turn from it and go back to the living poem, for which no equivalent can be given. And if the reader is also a critic, he will reject the unsatisfactory formula and develop a new one. So at this stage criticism inevitably becomes "criticism of criticism"—a phrase which is sometimes used against critics when their discussion becomes really intense.[26] The new formula is a revision of previous ones. If the question is asked: "Who then is the first critic, and on what does he operate?" the answer will be that the first critic is the author himself, and he may characterize his poem by the title he gives to it (P, 300) or the place he allots it in his collected works, or by some other device (mottoes, dedications, etc.).

Croce's practical criticism did not begin explicitly as "criticism of criticism." But it became more and more openly so, and was so characterized by hostile critics, who charged that Croce did not criticize the poet Pascoli (their favorite) but the critics of the poet. In 1913 Croce acknowledged the truth of this charge, but claimed that his action was both inevitable and advantageous (LNI, IV, 218). Further reflection—including his keener awareness of the historical character of all intellectual effort (SS, II, 133)—made him reach nine years afterwards a still more affirmative position. In the preface to *Poetry and non-poetry* (1923) he observed that literary criticism, to be rigorous, should take up questions and issues from previous criticism, so that "criticism of poetry must be one with the criticism of criticism of poetry" (PNP, 6). And in 1920 the study of Corneille had begun with a chapter frankly entitled "Criticism of criticism" (ASC, 207 ff.; cf. P, 127; G, II, 132).

So the formula that the critic finally achieves "comprises within itself all the long process of interpretation, reconstruction and judgment: even though it is not identical with that process, it is the best instrument for reproducing it without repeating all its labor" (P, 127). The formula also enables the reader to get over that sort of inertia, that condition of not knowing where to begin, which is often felt in the presence of a poem. But Croce never tired of repeating that it is no substitute for the living experience of the poem. The reader will not derive any help from it unless he has read the poem with full participation (P, 127–28)—i.e. by the already described process of "taste" supported by historical knowledge.

So far we have considered the analysis of a single poem or of a single work. But most poets write more than one poem, and most critics attempt the definition of the total production of a writer. Their goal is to determine wherein lies the fundamental artistic talent or bent of the author as manifested in the whole range of his production. This is what Croce calls defining the "poetic personality" (P, 148), which of course is not to be confused with the "practical personality" or personal character of the writer as revealed in his biography (cf. ASC, 12–20, 73–85; CC, V, 82). This definition constitutes the supreme object of literary criticism, and involves some of the most difficult and delicate critical operations. For the critic must endeavor to unify the various moods of the individual poems into a single, underlying, comprehensive mood or state of mind. Such a definition is no easy task. The analysis of the single poems must not be sacrificed to the synthesis, and yet the synthesis must be comprehensive enough to include all the results of the analysis. Here indeed the critic needs those qualities of penetration and flexibility that Croce requires from him, and which no piece of abstract reasoning, however logical, is sufficient to produce.

Of course, most poets have themes and moods which recur with variations in a number of poems, so that the result of the analysis of the individual poems will be usually a small number of basic themes or motifs. The problem of synthesis then concerns those few residual motifs, but it may be no less difficult for that reason. The question will inevitably arise: "can a poet have more than one basic mood or emotion?" Croce had already met with the problem in his critical study of D'Annunzio, a writer who was a very chameleon of themes and moods. Yet Croce insisted that there was an underlying unity in his multifarious production. "There have never been artists who had two or more different psychological contents: when it has seemed so, only one was the real content, the others were adventitious and ephemeral" (LNI, IV, 25). So wrote Croce in 1903. In 1917, in his essay on Ariosto, he still stressed the unity of the content in the variety of forms and attitudes (ASC, 65). In 1936 he considered the problem with the benefit of still greater experience, and pointed out a few instances of great poets who present two or three different psychological contents or moods. One is Dante, who from the early mood of his love poems passed on to that of the *Comedy*, and the other is Goethe, who passed from the mood of *Werther* and of the first *Faust* to that of *Iphigenia*. The various moods may alternate, as Croce thinks they did in Shakespeare, whose idyllic mood first appeared in his early plays and then reappeared with a difference in his latest. In all these cases, the critic's function is the same: "The critic then proceeds to look for a mood that lies still deeper, and which is susceptible of extensive development or even of complete reversal, and so he unifies the various moods in a dynamic scheme" (P, 149).

The study of a poet leads to the discovery of a development or process, the patterns of which are infinitely various. A number of them are instanced in the paper on "The Reform of Literary History" (NSE², 170–71) and many others are presented in Croce's own criticism. A poet may find at first difficulty in expression and succeed only in repeating traditional forms and images, until he finally discovers his own vein and achieves originality. Another writer may appear first in the guise of a man of action, a reformer, a leader, but these attempts will prove futile, and reveal themselves as outbursts of spiritual energy which finds its final consummation in artistic creation. A succession of separate poems may be the expression of a single current of feeling and therefore be in effect a unified composition. Conversely, a single work may resolve itself into a number of independent acts of expression, embodying different themes, as Goethe's *Faust* did for Croce. Prose compositions like novels or plays may prove to be more intensely lyrical than many verses, and verse compositions may turn out to be completely prosaic, the vehicle for ideas or practical programs. And so on and so forth. There are as many patterns of development as there are writers, and no two essays by Croce repeat the same formula.

These formulas can only be appreciated in the full development they receive in the studies on each poet. We have seen some small-scale instances of poetic personalities in the discussion of Renaissance poets in Chapter v. Fuller presentations are those afforded by Croce to Dante, Ariosto, Shakespeare, Corneille and Goethe, which will be discussed in Chapter xii. It is here possible to summarize more adequately the characterization of Maupassant. His "poetic personality" is defined as basically "naive" in the sense of being "devoid of any suspicion of what is known as spirituality and rationality, faith in truth, purity of will, sense of duty, religious feeling, moral struggles and intellectual conflicts" (PNP, 307 ff.). Such absence of ethical ideals, however, is not for Croce immorality or wickedness but pure vitality, a state of mind which can yet develop a feeling of sympathy for human suffering and thus inspire the intensely tragic representations of life which Croce finds in the work of Maupassant. The images created by him are a perfect expression of his poetic personality and the critical judgment is therefore positive: this is an artist, and that is his theme or motif.

To show how Croce's method can lead to a judgment of qualified approval, or even a negative judgment, we can instance the study of Balzac. This begins by explicit criticism of criticism: the current formula for Balzac is that he is "excellent in his characters, poor in his plots, and vicious in his style." But these are three separate judgments, based on the rhetorical distinction of character and plot, style and subject; they should find unity in an analysis that goes down to the root of all his work. Both the qualities and the faults of a writer should be derived from the fundamental characteristics of his mind (*PdE*, 441). For Croce, the trouble with Balzac was that he was misled by fanciful inclination toward the colossal and the overwhelming. This prevented his characters from developing according to their inner nature (i.e. he did not let his images develop according to their own character) but forced them into excesses and exaggerations, so that the action becomes a whirl of melodramatic adventures and sensational catastrophes; "and the style, which is one with these actions and these characters, falls from its vigorous and simple plastic quality and becomes nerveless and slovenly, or suffers a transition to the explanatory and reflective tone. The characters do not attain the harmony of discordant concord, so the actions do not develop with naturalness, and the style is lacking in rhythm" (PNP, 249). In this analysis (which is here quoted as illustrating a method and not as necessarily true) the traditional terms of rhetorical criticism—style, plot and characters—are centered in the definition of an artistic personality, which turns out to be imperfect and unbalanced, and of a work of art which is imperfect in the same way, since poetic personality and work of art are one and the same thing (P, 147).

CROCE'S PROCEDURE of characterizing poetry through the definition of its emotional content was the object of repeated criticism in his own lifetime, a criticism to which he gave several answers.[27] His ultimate argument seems to be the fact that there is no logical alternative. No other content can be assigned to poetry than feeling or emotion, for other suggested contents, such as ideas, concepts, moral principles, ethical ideals, etc., are already pre-empted by other forms of spiritual activity. As for so-called "formal" or stylistic analysis, which was also advanced as an alternative, Croce answered by subjecting it to criticism in a number of discussions, some of which have been already quoted,[28] as well as in the paper on "The Reform of Literary History" which we shall consider in our next chapter. Artistic form is not something that one can take hold of between one's fingers (NPS, I, 180). Form is not something external: it is internal, or "inner form" as we have seen at the end of Chapter II, and it is defined by Croce as the synthesis of image and emotion, as discussed in Chapter III. Of the synthesis, a philosophical definition may be given, as a synthesis a priori;[29] but its constituents may be further analyzed, as we have seen in this chapter.

Sometimes a plea is made in favor of a kind of criticism that is more closely akin to poetic creation, and an artist's criticism of another artist is considered more valuable than that of the analytical critic. As T. S. Eliot once observed: "Probably indeed the larger part of the labor of an author in composing his work is critical labor; the labor of sifting, combining, constructing, expunging, correcting, testing: this frightful toil is as much critical as creative. I maintain even that the criticism employed by a trained and skilled writer on his own work is the most vital, the highest kind of criticism."[30] Arguments of this kind were not unknown to Croce, and he answered that in this case the term "criticism" was used not literally but metaphorically. The control exercised on composition—the "sifting, combining, correcting" etc.—is that of the poetic imagination itself, "which does not accomplish its task without self-government, without an inner check, *sibi imperiosa* (to adopt the Horatian phrase), without accepting and rejecting, trying and trying again, operating *tacito quodam sensu*, until it achieves satisfaction in the image expressed by the sound. Not only poetry, but all human activities are accompanied by a simple and direct consciousness of their own object, which is not the same as having a full-fledged philosophical theory about it" (P, 13).[31] Croce had noted earlier that the activity of intuition was conscious, but not in the sense that it was aware of its own universal essence: "otherwise the artist would be a philosopher of art in the very act of producing his work. But there is a consciousness of the object produced" (*PdE*, 483).

Actually what is often desired by writers who call for "poetic criticism" is help in writing their own poetry, in the shape of some sure-fire, fool-proof technical device that will guarantee poetic success to anyone. Such devices, however speciously formulated, are merely a reincarnation of the old rhetorical rules of composition, and can only produce mediocre imitations not original work (cf. *Letture*, 304). From the doctrine of aesthetics as the science of expression no guidance to artists can be derived, save indirectly: it can clear the artist's mind of cant, as Dr. Johnson put it, and deliver it from the bondage of false philosophies, such as the doctrines of "technique," genres and rules, which might restrict or divert his creative imagination. That is what happened, for instance, to the poet Tasso, when he rewrote his *Jerusalem Delivered*. On the other hand, the possession of a sound aesthetic doctrine does not generate creative ability in a writer who does not possess it already, as may be seen in many instances (e.g. PPPA, 341).

It may perhaps be objected that if formal devices, metrical schemes, structural patterns, etc., are abstractions, so are, on Croce's own showing, the psychological formulas which constitute his "characterizations." [32] There is however in Croce's logic a basic distinction between abstract concepts and empirical generalizations such as those of descriptive psychology.[33] An empirical concept is a generalization from a limited number of individuals; whereas abstract concepts are formed upon a universal concept and are abstractions at the second power, therefore doubly abstract. Now the generalizations about formal patterns are made upon the universal category of artistic form, splitting it up into divisions and subdivisions, and are therefore abstract concepts. Also, they are the instruments of prescriptive and judicial criticism, whereas characterizations in Croce serve only as descriptive terms in the manner explained above.

IN CONCLUSION we may summarize Croce's view of the function of criticism as follows. Criticism in the Crocean sense is, in the first place, the responsible exercise of judgment, the decision "is this a poem or not?" based on the controlled re-enactment of the original act of expression. Secondly, it involves the definition of the poetic quality of the work, by means of a process of exploration and discovery. Exploration, because each work is seen as a new problem, over and beyond traditional classifications by genres, types and trends. Discovery, because it aims at the characterization of the individuality of the work, of the image and the emotion in their unique relationship, and ultimately at the determination of its place in the total development of the artist's poetic personality. Finally, this is not presented as a rejection of all previous criticism, but on the contrary as the systematization and corroboration of what has been the practice of literary critics at all periods of history.

CHAPTER ix

The Province of Literary History

THERE SEEMS TO EXIST TODAY in America a deep cleavage between literary history and literary criticism. The two disciplines are not only conceived as separate, but incompatible and are represented by two groups of men who look upon each other with mutual hostility, which sometimes breaks out in public controversy.[1] Attempts at a reconciliation do not appear to have had much success. The conflict is to be deplored, since the two disciplines have the same object, the study of literature, in which facts and values are both important, and which in the present condition of society is in need of all the support that it can find.

The conflict of course is not new.[2] Ever since there has been a historical approach to literature there have been protests from critics to whom values were as important as facts. Croce himself was at the centre of one of the most intense battles fought between criticism and scholarship, aestheticism and historicism. All his life Croce fought against the abuses of historical scholarship, emerging victorious from the fight, at least in his own country. As a critic for whom poetry was essentially lyrical intuition, he found many of the historical approaches irrelevant and misleading. We have already seen his critique of the approach by genres which is one of the stand-bys of historical scholarship. And in his belief in the creativity of poetry he rejected many attempts by historical scholars to reduce literature to a mere repetition of traditional themes and forms, to rhetorical and other conventions, and to a by-product of the social environment. But he also waged a lifelong battle on another front, against the aesthetes, the impressionists and the decadents of all kinds. So his position is complex and to be fully understood must be approached from various directions. I propose now to apply the historical method to Croce himself as a critic and student of literature, and give an outline of the development of his views on literary history, with specific reference to the background from which they emerge. In the first chapter we saw something of the development of Croce as a philosopher; we will now examine his scholarship from the genetic point of view.

In the nineteenth century the critical study of Italian literature, which is almost as old as Italian literature itself, received new impulse from the introduction of the methods of research developed by German scholarship. This had taken place in Italy by the sixties (German philological methods were introduced in the universities of the United States somewhat later). In 1883 the journal of the Italian school of literary history was founded: the *Giornale storico della letteratura italiana* which is still flourishing today although under different management. In its first issue it published a statement of its aims which were similar to those of the great historical journals that had then been started in Germany (1859) and France (1876), the English *Historical Review* coming only a few years later (1886).[3] In this statement, the *Giornale storico* said: "Our libraries and our archives are brimful of documents which are either ignored or little known; the text of the greater part of our writers requires accurate revision; the relationships of our literatures with the other literatures of Europe, and the manifold connections of letters with politics, science and the arts are hardly known for the periods after the Middle Ages. Innumerable points of biographical history, of language history, and of bibliography require discussion and clarification. In brief, there is an immense material to be sifted and arranged before anyone can approach the terrific task of writing a general history of Italian literature in a manner worthy of science" (quoted in ss, II, 151–52).

The claim is familiar and will be easily recognized. Before anyone can venture an opinion on a writer of the past, masses of bibliographical, biographical, historical, exegetical, thematic, and other research have to be accomplished. "What is needed at present is" more bibliographies, more biographies, more critical editions, more source investigations, and so forth. Only when the harvest of historical research is fully reaped, will it be possible to turn to criticism. One has only to scan some survey of contemporary scholarship, such as the thorough and stimulating one made in 1943 by Miss R. Tuve for the literature of the English Renaissance,[4] to hear the same note struck: we must know all the facts about a period before we can understand an author that belongs to it. And the perspective of the facts to be investigated, and of the investigations to be digested, is enormous. So the critical judgment is in effect postponed to the Greek Calends.

It so happens that Italian literature possessed in the nineteenth century a great literary critic, Francesco De Sanctis, who was also the author of a classic *History of Italian Literature* (1871).[5] De Sanctis' critical outlook was developed from several sources. After a full training in traditional rhetoric, he turned to fresher currents of thought from across the Alps, and assimilated the spirit of both French and German criticism.[6] From the French he derived a lively style, and certain views about the development of the Italian mind which he used in his *History*. From the Germans he learnt about aesthetics and their application to literary criticism. Hegel was particularly influential upon him (as upon other young liberals of Naples), even though Hegel's *Aesthetics* reached him only in a French exposition, that of C. Bénard (1840 ff.). From that book De Sanctis derived certain ideas which he proceeded to work into a flexible method of practical criticism. According to Hegel, a work of art develops through a complex dialectical process, starting with the Idea— not the Idea in the abstract but what Hegel calls the Idea in a determinate "situation" which particularizes it and provides the foundation for poetic composition. The poetic situation then generates within itself conflicts and collisions which bring forth what Hegel calls the "universal forces" or master passions of humanity. These appear in the form of intensely individualized characters who clash with each other and engage in dramatic action, thus generating the epic, the drama and other literary kinds.[7]

De Sanctis' mind was anything but systematic [8] and he followed Hegel's formula rather loosely. He suppressed most of the intermediate dialectical stages and usually began with the "poetic situation," concentrating on the final development, character in action, which for him was the supreme aesthetic Form. Character study became his forte, and the "re-creation" of Dante's great characters is considered his masterpiece.[9] But it would be misleading to call him a "psychological critic," for the emotions that he studies are usually not those of the author but those of the character, and so are strictly part of the poetic image. According to De Sanctis' revision of Hegel, the "idea" of the *Divine Comedy* is "the other world" with all that this implies, particularly in the way of the historical development of the notion of divine justice. Dante's poetic situation is "the other world *as seen from this world*," with all that this implies in the way of human passion, political and personal—the passion that assumes poetic form in powerful creations like Francesca, Farinata and Ulysses.

Actually De Sanctis was guided in his practical criticism by his literary taste and by his exceptional capacity for re-creation. The Hegelian terminology provided him with a scaffolding for the exposition of his own insights.[10] He analyzed a work until he came to its core or generating principle, and then proceeded to show how each detail of the composition—style, metre, diction, structure, imagery, etc.—developed from the central theme. His most detailed analyses are real exercises in close reading, in which every particular is thus illuminated and interpreted.[11]

In the *History* [12] he followed to some extent the same method, showing how each work arose from the spirit of the age and expressed its innermost tendencies, while at the same time he exercised all his dialectical skill in endeavoring to preserve the individuality of every author.[13] We shall see an example of this in his criticism of Ariosto, to be cited in Chapter XII.[14] The foundation of the *History* is a concept of the development of the Italian mind, and its material was drawn from long familiarity with the text of the Italian writers; but De Sanctis was not primarily an historical scholar and did not engage in factual research, although he strongly encouraged it.[15] The main value of his book lies not in new facts but in aesthetic interpretations. For this reason, the historical scholars looked askance at his work. There is unquestionably a contemptuous allusion to it in the paragraph quoted above from the *Giornale storico*, with its reference to the "terrific task of writing a general history of Italian literature in a manner *worthy of science.*" Science—that is, the science of nature—was the idol of the positivists of those days, and the historical scholar looked with pride from the heights of his own factual research, which he felt was "scientific," upon the work of a critic like De Sanctis, who was considered speculative and impressionistic (ss, II, 189–91).

Now this is precisely the point at which Croce emerges in the history of Italian literary scholarship. The *Giornale storico* (1888) appeared six years after Croce's earliest publications, 1882—an astonishing date, when one reflects that Croce was then a youth of 16. Yet in that year he printed four essays on scholarly subjects: the *Virgilian Letters* of the Abbé S. Bettinelli (1757), Bettinelli's criticism of Dante, the Canzone to Fortune by A. Guidi (a once famous seventeenth-century poet), and the episode of Dido in the *Aeneid*. These are unusually learned compositions, even for advanced pupils of the Italian classical *liceo* in which Croce was then a student. They were printed in a short-lived literary periodical which had opened wide its columns to all comers, and the young Croce took this opportunity to contribute some of the papers he had written at school, on subjects selected by himself (ps, I, 415–37).

Even at the age of 16 Croce evinced a capacity, which he never lost, to see the other side of the question and to take the unpopular side in a controversy. Bettinelli was a minor eighteenth-century critic who had dared to criticize Dante adversely, and who thus earned perpetual condemnation in all the textbooks of literature. Croce had the curiosity to look up his long neglected works, and found that he was not as bad as he was painted. So young Croce concluded, with a turn of phrase that is typical of his later thinking: "Not that I do not acknowledge his wrong opinions and his eccentricities; but I also find in his works such fine and bold truths, that rank the 'friar secretary of Virgil' [i.e. Bettinelli] next to Baretti" (PS, I, 240). Croce was to go through life looking at forgotten or despised subjects, scrutinizing them impartially, and finding that they were not so bad after all: "not that he denied accepted opinion," but that he saw beyond it.

It is notable that the first two papers of young Croce related to the history of criticism, while the other two were attempts at critical evaluation exercised on a piece of seventeenth-century verse and on a famous episode of Virgil. In the former, Croce is already taking issue with previous critics, and attacking a much eulogized composition. The *Ode to Fortune* is from beginning to end a kind of "sustained metaphor" built around a traditional personification, Fortune, one of the oldest conventions in Western literature. (Critics who believe in the value of "conventions" and in the power of the seventeenth-century mind, prior to the famed "dissociation of sensibility," [16] should see if they can admire this ode upon which Croce cut his critical teeth.) The last paper is the most ambitious, but perhaps the least original, though none the less revealing for that. It shows that Croce had already come under the spell of Francesco De Sanctis, whom he was to look upon as his master in literary criticism for many years to come.

Other critical writings, published between 1883 and 1886, have been collected and reprinted. The last, "Poetry and non-poetry," is a brilliant destructive analysis of a composition by Mario Rapisardi, a mediocre poet who attracted much attention at that time. The phrase became forty years later the title of a collection of essays of the mature Croce (PNP), translated into English less appropriately as *European Literature in the Nineteenth Century* (1924). But in those years Croce had turned almost completely to historical research. Following a dominant trend of the day, and also his own inclination, he devoted himself to the investigation of little-known historical aspects of the city of Naples and became an habitué of the State Archives of that city. His subject was the history of the old theatres of

Naples, for which there was a vast mass of unpublished documents awaiting the patient explorer. He has related in recent years how he used to walk down the Vomero hill every morning in the early hours, remain in the archives until 4 P.M. without a break—"at that time I was able to go without a meal for eight hours at a stretch"—and then leave the archives, whose doors closed at that time, only to enter the gates of the Brancacciana library where he read the texts of hundreds of old plays involved in that stage history (NPS, I, 365–66).

He collected the results of his labors in *The Theatres of Naples from the Renaissance to the End of the 18th Century* (1891), a large volume containing much unpublished material which gave him at once a reputation as a research scholar. He continued working in this field with other studies in the history and the archaeology of the Kingdom of Naples. Among other things, he became a pioneer in the so-called comparative field, with a volume of studies (1892–94) on the influence of Spain on Italian culture during the Renaissance. He thus established himself as one of the leading scholars in historical research over a definite area of seventeenth-century history. He became an editor, planned series of publications, and started a review, *Napoli Nobilissima* (1892–1905). But at the height of his success he experienced a basic dissatisfaction with his own work. He felt that he was merely scratching the surface and wanted to see deeper into the life of history and of literature (*Au*, 50). As we saw in Chapter 1, he then undertook a methodical study of philosophy with a view to ascertaining the methodology of history. This resulted in the publication of his monographs on history in 1893 and on criticism in 1895.[17]

The latter gives a firm statement of allegiance to De Sanctis, whose reputation was then at its nadir among the historical scholars, and is also an explicit attack on the shortcomings of the historical school. The name of criticism, Croce observed, was now abused by being given to almost anything: to the biography of a writer, to the history and genesis of his work, to the edition of his text and to its exegesis, as well as to the aesthetic judgment which should be its sole and proper field. In 1898 Croce edited two volumes of uncollected works of De Sanctis with an appendix in which he made a detailed and lively answer to positivistic and formalistic critics of De Sanctis.[18] He also edited other works of De Sanctis and in several ways labored to preserve and defend the work of his master, as he considered him.[19] It may be said that most of Croce's later theories on poetry and on criticism have in De Sanctis either their logical premise or their historical antecedent. In the field of aesthetics, Croce set De Sanctis' concept of organic form within a broader philosophical framework, suggested in part by Vico's doctrine of poetry as elementary cognition.

FINALLY, in the summer of 1899 Croce began writing what was to become his first *Aesthetic,* in the manner that we have already seen in our first chapter. It is here that we find Croce's solution to the conflict between history and criticism of literature approaching the form which it has kept since. To those who had followed only Croce's historical research, it might have seemed likely that Croce would side with the historians. He had proved himself a skilled practitioner in all the historical techniques. He had searched archives, unearthed documents, established facts, exploded legends, composed biographies, edited texts, and at all times taken pains to rely only on first-hand evidence and original sources.

So Croce was an expert historical scholar. But, as we have noted, he had always shown a capacity to see the other side of the question. In matters of criticism, he had early declared his allegiance to De Sanctis, and that was to contradict the historical school in one of its basic assumptions. For Croce there *was* such a thing as the aesthetic judgment of a writer, and it was *not* the same thing as writing his biography, publishing his manuscripts, investigating his sources, his ideas, his models and his influences. It was, instead, to do what De Sanctis had done for literature: show its life and color, its beauty and its vigor, as a work of creative imagination. But it was not sufficient to point at De Sanctis' work and hold it up as a model. It was necessary to justify its method against the strictures of the historical school. And this led Croce to go more deeply into the question of method. In what way were the various scholarly techniques practiced by historians conducive to the goal of literary history?

In Chapter vii we have seen how Croce defined their function. They are aids to the exact reproduction of the original expression. Most of them are essentially preservative processes. They are therefore indispensable, for without them we would not possess the work of art or the poem; but they are not the appreciation or the evaluation of the work. They look after the records of the poetic process: they preserve and emend the text of poems, they collect all the information that is necessary to understand the language in which a poem is written and the topical references it may contain. But all this is subsidiary and instrumental: the goal is the living work, and the work does not live if it is not read as poetry.

In the modern world, when works of art of all kinds have been multiplying and accumulating for centuries, the processes of preservation and restoration have reached vast proportions. A number of complex and specialized disciplines have been developed, not only for the plastic arts and music, but also for literature. All processes that assume large proportions tend to make exaggerated claims for themselves, and this has happened to the historical study of literature. The subsidiary disciplines sometimes claim that they are the principal or the only scholarly study of literature. Critical judgment is brushed aside as impressionism or at best as private opinion with no scientific value, and the life of some scholars is spent in editing elaborate critical texts which nobody reads, save other scholars in order to edit other critical texts.

A first step in the clarification of the issue would be the establishing of a noncontroversial name for the disciplines employed in the preservation of literature, to mark them off clearly but not unfavorably from the exercise of the aesthetic judgment. Such a name lies at hand in the traditional and highly respected name of "philology," which is still the official designation used in titles of academic journals. Now that linguistics has absorbed in itself what was once known as "comparative philology," there is no danger of exclusive identification of philology with the study of language.[20] "Philology" could therefore be, as it is for Croce, the recognized designation for the historical study of literature—textual criticism, bibliography, biography, sources and influences, themes and models, relations with political and other histories, etc. These studies are useful for the writing of literary history but they are not that history itself. For literary history makes use of the data supplied by these disciplines in order to perform its own function, which is to single out the works of the past in which writing rises to the level of art, and to give an account of their literary quality. Otherwise it is not a history of literature, but of something else: possibly of those books that Charles Lamb called *biblia a-biblia*, books which are not really books.

As a practitioner of all the historical techniques, Croce knew very well the intellectual effort and the practical labor they required, and had often tested for himself the usefulness of their results; but for the same reason he also was well aware of their limitations. Indeed, few critics have unleashed such frequent and such caustic attacks on these limitations as Croce did throughout his career. A typical instance may be given from Croce's lecture on the "Defence of Poetry," written for delivery at the University of Oxford in 1933, in which Croce speaks of the enjoyment of poetry: "The place where it is hardest to find it is precisely among the professional students of poetry and of its historical achievements. They seem gifted with a strange immunity, which allows them all their life to handle the books of poets, edit and annotate them, discuss their various interpretations, investigate their sources, furnish them with biographical introductions, and all without ever suffering so much contagion as to experience in their own persons the poetic fever" (US, 75–76). Many similar passages might be quoted.[21] The asperity of such strictures is softened by a remark in Croce's autobiographical essay, in which he relates that quite often the type of the obtuse historical scholar whom he satirized in his writings was drawn from self-observation: "the real type was my old self . . . when I was working as a pure antiquarian and collector of *anecdota*" (*Au*, 84).

But while criticizing the aberrations of pedantry, Croce always recognized the use of historical knowledge for the re-creation of the expressive act of the poet. It is, as we have seen, an essential part of the process of "taste." Croce therefore firmly rejected impressionistic criticism, as well as "evocative" and "suggestive" criticism. All these critical aberrations come under the general category that Croce designates "aestheticism" and which he discussed in two papers of 1905, which are practically unknown in America where he has enjoyed the reputation of being an impressionist himself (*PdE*, 33–41 and 46–50). "Aestheticism" is the view that rejects the help of historical knowledge for the understanding of poetry: "Aestheticism, by refusing in principle and as a general thesis those philosophical and scholarly aids, those personal and social experiences through which the historical conditions of artistic creation are restored, makes it impossible to explain the process through which the work of art is received in the mind of the observer. So it must either appeal to some miraculous intuition, different from that with which we are acquainted in our self-consciousness, or give itself up to a kind of hedonism, maintaining that the important thing is, not to understand the work of art in its genuine features, but to luxuriate, anyhow, in a picture, a statue, a wave of sound or of verse, even if it results in a work of art different from the one which was in the mind of the author . . . producing a private reverie instead of an artistic understanding" (*PdE*, 38).

On the other hand, the historical disciplines of philology not only help to preserve the work of art in its genuine form and meaning, but even call for the exercise of the imagination, in the form of "taste." An instance from Shakespeare will illustrate this. From a crux in *Hamlet* we can see how history is used for the understanding and for the emendation of a poetic text, and how the crowning effort of restoration calls for the use of imagination. Hamlet, while awaiting the appearance of the ghost, makes some general reflections on human nature, and observes that a good man may be ruined by a single short-coming. The speech ends with this passage, which is a famous textual crux, and is here quoted as it appears in the original text, the Second Quarto:

> . . . the dram of eale
> Doth all the noble substance of a doubt
> To his own scandle.

Now these lines are a part of a characteristic speech by one of Shakespeare's most famous heroes, and the observation has a bearing upon the problem of Hamlet's own character, which to many critics is the central problem of the play. So the lines are of decided critical interest, but as they stand their meaning is not clear.

To make sense out of them, it is necessary to have recourse to almost all the resources of philology. The passage requires the exercise of a) textual emendation, b) linguistic history, and c) historical information. It requires emendation because it is impossible to make sense out of it without correcting at least one word, and many suggestions have been made to this purpose. Emendation in turn requires recognition of obsolete forms of language, beginning with obvious changes in spelling, such as "scandal" for *scandle*, and ending with what is now the accepted emendation of *eale* into "evil," via the obsolete contraction (attested in Shakespeare) *ev'l*. Obsolete English is also involved in the use of *his* for "its," and in the other emendation: *doubt* corrected to "dout," a contraction of "do out," meaning "put out, extinguish, destroy." Acquaintance with Elizabethan spelling is involved in the correlative emendation of *of a* to "often." Historical information of another kind is involved in the suggested emendation "dram of eels" (a poisonous concoction). But the whole passage is cleared by the discovery of the metaphor involved in the *noble substance*. The *noble substance* in alchemy refers to gold, which was only too often spoilt in the alchemist's crucible by the infiltration of some baser element. This identification was made in the *New Cambridge Edition* (1934) by J. Dover Wilson. It, too, involves history (knowledge of alchemy).

But the metaphorical extension of alchemical lore to the moral situation is an exercise of the imagination, repeating the process of the poet's own mind, i.e. "taste." The words of the text, which had been separated for the convenience of philology, are now unified in a total image. Dover Wilson's emendation (if accepted) makes the passage read:

> . . . the dram of evil
> Doth all the noble substance often doubt
> To his own scandal.

Thus all the varied and complex techniques of philology may fulfill their task when handled by a scholar with a fine sense for the particular. But only too often the philologist is content to accumulate information without focusing on the particular, and to build up huge heaps of historical facts with only the vaguest relation to the problem studied. Sometimes it is even required of the historical scholar that he simply know everything that is to be known about a period or an author and study "the totality of all possible influences." But Croce had a strictly functional view of the amount of historical information required for the aesthetic judgment. "What are the historical facts of which the critic must take cognizance?" he asked in 1904. Is it the poet's native country, his environment, his private life, his relations with other artists, his religious and political ideas, etc.? "Which of these sets of facts? or all of them together? The answer must not consist in saying, as usual, that all of those categories are indispensable; nor that some are indispensable, and others not. The correct answer is: all sets of facts may be indispensable, and none of them is so by necessity. . . . The facts that the critic must keep in mind are only those which have actually gone into the make-up of the work of art which he is considering, and which are indispensable for the solution of the critical problem which he set himself: the problem, different in each case, receives in each case a different solution" (*PdE*, 43–44).[22]

As regards the connection between the poet and his age, Croce said in 1922: "It is not true that I deny the connections of art with the life of history. I only say that the connections are there, but are as it were transcended. If one opens my book *Ariosto, Shakespeare and Corneille*, one will find that for each of them I show the historical connection: for Ariosto, pp. 31–32; for Shakespeare, pp. 100–102; for Corneille, pp. 243–45; if one opens my book on the *Poetry of Dante*, the same is done for the *Comedy*, pp. 50–52." [23]

By showing the limitations of impressionistic aestheticism and of the narrow historical approach, Croce steered away from both extremes and turned toward a balanced conception of literary history. This conception necessarily implies an idea of what history in general is, its function and purpose. Such an inquiry should commend itself to the historical scholars, but most of them are so much absorbed in the collection of facts that they are unaware of the general orientation in scholarly thinking that impels them to make such a collection. How many literary scholars, for instance, have ever looked into, I will not say Croce, but Fueter's *History of Modern Historiography* or some work of similar scope? Unless we fall back upon thoughtless conformity or blind dogmatism, we should have some idea of the nature of historical inquiry and of the development of historical studies in modern times, up to our own day. It is symptomatic that, although there are histories of scholarship in specialized areas, there is no general history of the historical study of literature from its beginnings to the present.[24] No wonder that its assumptions and implications are not always clear to its own practitioners.

WE WILL NOW SEE BRIEFLY what Croce's idea of history is and how it helps to define the province of literary history. In Chapter I we saw that for Croce the intellectual process involved in all historical reconstruction was a judgment, or the referring of a particular fact to the universal category to which it belongs. Since the category is the concept of an activity, such as the practical activity or the theoretical activity, this judgment involves the re-enactment of the specific act which resulted in the particular event. Such a re-creation to be historical must of course be performed strictly on the basis of available evidence, of documents and records critically sifted, and not merely in the imagination or the emotions: it holds true for Croce as for all historians that without documents there is no history (TSS, 6 and TPS, II, 112).

From this point of view the history of poetry, or of creative literature in general, can only be the re-enactment of the expressive process of the poet. The historian of poetry begins like all historians with the document, which for him is the text of the poem.[25] This document may have to be critically sifted, i.e. edited or emended, dated or attributed; hence the function of textual criticism, of chronological determination, and studies of the authorship of a work. The document is also related to its place and period, in order to adjust the interpretative process to those conditions. All this, as we have seen, is philology, and not yet history. Then the document is interpreted: the text is read as poetry and the expressive process is re-enacted. At the end of the re-enactment, the historian is in a position to say: "at a certain time, and in a certain place, an historical event, which is characterized as a poetic creation, took place." This is the historical judgment (cf. P, 129). But this judgment is merely a verbal variant of the following: "this work, composed at a certain time and in a certain place, is a work of poetry"—which as we have seen in the previous chapter, is the critical judgment. And the critical judgment is preceded by the re-enactment of the expressive process, just as the historical judgment is. So we come to the following conclusion, which may startle at first: the history of literature and the criticism of literature are essentially one and the same process.

This is in effect Croce's final answer to the problem of the relation between criticism and history: when properly understood, there is no essential difference between them. The historian, to be a true historian, must be a critic, and the critic, to be a good critic, must be a historian.[26] In practice, the two are often, too often, separated, and we get the conflict mentioned at the beginning of this chapter. But the historian who refuses to pronounce critical judgment on poetry is not an historian, but at best a philologist, and the critic who refuses the assistance of historical knowledge is not a critic, but an aesthete or an impressionist.[27] So the conflict can only arise between philology claiming to be history and aestheticism claiming to be criticism, but not between genuine history and genuine criticism.

Croce's identification of history and criticism may seem an extreme simplification of a complex relationship. But he was not speaking of things with which he had only recently become acquainted and to which he was not to give a second thought later. As we have seen, history and criticism had been his main business ever since he awoke to intellectual life and right up to the last day of his long career. Nor did he leave that identification as a witty paradox set down for passing entertainment; he carefully worked it out, considering all the problems of history and criticism in relation to it, and discussing its implications and consequences in a series of considered analyses. Furthermore, he made it his guide in his own work and directed his own activity in those fields in the light of his principle and with explicit reference to it. He also repeatedly discussed the objections made against it.

First of all, this principle of the identity of literary history and criticism goes against a mistaken ideal of "scholarly objectivity" and "scientific impartiality," according to which the historian deals with facts only and must avoid judgments of value—especially of aesthetic value, since the latter are purely "subjective." This is the old positivistic view of history as the science of facts which Croce found before him and fought all his life. For him, history in all its branches—the history of politics as well as the history of knowledge, of economics as well as of literature—involves evaluation, a point of view, a problem, a principle of logical continuity among the facts considered.[28]

The factual history of literature under positivist influence often took the form of an account of the handing down of devices, forms, genres, metres, themes, cycles, plots, etc., from one writer to another, and of the succession of schools, trends, fashions, currents, etc. through the ages. The concept of evolution was applied to this process [29] and literary genres were considered the species of which the historian traced the origin, growth, maturity and decline. Works of literature were seen merely as stages in this continuous evolutionary process. Humanistic scholars prided themselves upon having at least attained a "scientific approach" and fancied that they were rivalling the triumphs of the biological sciences. The prize fallacy of this approach was the idea that masterpieces were produced by automatic accretion of a number of mediocre works. This was considered a parallel to the formation of large coral banks from the accretion of innumerable small organisms. So dangerous it is to take the natural sciences as a guide to the humanities.

One of the concepts by which the factual school established a link between different works and eventually built up a continuity is that of the literary source, and source-hunting (though possibly less in favor today) has long been one of the resources of the historical scholars. The more obscure and mediocre the sources, the greater the "scientific" triumph of resolving a famous masterpiece into its raw material. Croce's view on this can be gathered from a discussion arising out of the studies on contemporary literature which he conducted in the early years of his journal. Among the material collected by Croce and others was a number of source references. Croce prefixed to the collection a typical warning (1909): "A work of literature is such, because it possesses a new and original quality of its own. To go and study it in its sources, in its antecedents, in its material, is to look for it *where it is not*." "When there *is* a work, it is not resolvable into its sources; and when it is resolvable, the work is not." It may be answered that the source hunter is looking not for the work itself but for the material of the work, which the poet has fashioned into a new form. But even this does not lead to conclusive results, for "the material of a work of literature, taken out of the individual form that it has assumed, is—the whole universe, considered in the abstract. Only form gives it determination." Then what is the purpose and the use of source hunting? The purpose is "To call attention to certain antecedents of certain parts of a work, which have been roughly distinguished in it"—a very qualified definition. The use is "to contribute to the exegesis of a work by explaining the precise meaning of some expression or showing by contrast the transformation that a thought, an image or an expression have received in the work in question" (*PdE*, 489–91).

Another concept which is used to link works of literature together is the concept of tradition. We have already seen in Chapter III that Croce recognizes tradition as a factor in literature, but not as a creative factor. It is a fact that expressions arise upon previous expressions and incorporate them making the old part of the new, but that fact is not what makes an expression beautiful. We have called this the principle of Integration. What was once form descends to matter, according to a process which was known both to Aristotle and to Hegel (P, 196). A history of tradition in literature would be an account of form turning back into matter, not a history of form generating new forms. It would depend for continuity on the content of literature, and not upon what makes poetry an art. It would (and often does, for it has been frequently attempted) turn into something that Croce calls "the history of culture" (CC, I, 223–24).

"History of culture" is a concept of which Croce makes frequent use, referring to it many things which are usually included in the history of literature. It is of course derived from the German term *Kulturgeschichte*, upon which young Croce wrote a critical discussion (CC, I, 200–224). After reaching his theory that history is based upon the system of categories, Croce gave to history of culture a specialized meaning. It is the history of the practical activities that promote theoretical activities. It is not the history of learning and the arts themselves, because that is cared for by the histories of the intellectual and aesthetic activities. But these theoretical activities are accompanied by a variety of practical actions, such as the preservation and propagation of works of art, the economic promotion and support of their authors, the organization of this preservation and promotion into groups and associations of all kinds: academies, schools, societies, institutions, publications, theatrical productions, symposia, exhibitions, cliques and coteries, etc. etc. (cf. *PdE*, 94–102, 420–21). All these according to Croce are practical activities directed to the promotion of theoretical activities, and deserve a history of their own, which he called the history of culture. For Croce a literary school is essentially a practical phenomenon, art being always individual, and what unites a group of artists is a common interest in propagating their work or a personal sympathy, which are all practical matters. Works which are excluded from the history of literature as art because they are really efforts at propagating some idea or promoting some practical measure may also be included in the history of culture (cc, III, 74–78).

It might perhaps be objected that the history of culture seems to be a sort of historical rubbish heap upon which Croce casts anything that does not fit strictly into his notion of aesthetic purity. It should therefore be reaffirmed that to exclude some piece of writing or some composition from the history of art is not for Croce to discard it as rubbish, but to assert that it has its proper place in some other sphere of activity. Furthermore, it is a part of Croce's philosophical view of the negative element in the world that there is no absolute evil; if something exists, it must have some positive function (*Pratica*, 126–31). In this again Croce differs from the pure aesthete, for whom the denial of aesthetic value to something is its total rejection. Croce will agree with the aesthete in excluding the nonaesthetic firmly from the sphere of art, but he will consider it his critical duty to find some other sphere for it.

In the case of the history of culture, Croce was so far from considering it a sort of outer darkness to which undesirable elements were to be banished, that he himself made several contributions to it. Much of his early work on influences, the history of the theatre, the "fortune" of types and characters in the drama, is included in what he later categorized as the history of culture. Nor did he repudiate this early research, but he pruned it and condensed it and otherwise perfected it, including it in the final collection of his works. Even after the formulation of the *Aesthetic*, Croce continued to make contributions to the history of culture, while strictly labeling them as such and not passing them off as histories of literature or of poetry. For instance, in the fourth volume of the *Literature of Modern Italy* there is a long paper dedicated to "Literary Life in Naples from 1860 to 1900" (IV, 233–319). In it Croce gives a general picture of what was going on in literature and in scholarship, in philosophical and historical studies, in the universities and in the theatres, during those years in the city of Naples. It is a lively and interesting picture, full of penetrating judgments and amusing anecdotes, and some people would consider it a good example of what a history of literature should be. But for Croce, as he warns the reader in a footnote to the title, it is "history of culture." The importance he assigned to such studies is shown by the fact that he planned for his journal a whole series of them, each dealing with the culture of a different region of Italy, to follow his critical survey of national literature during the period 1860–1900. They were written by various contributors and constitute one of the things that still make Croce's review a useful reference work. So if Croce finally rejected traditional literary history, this was not due to any temperamental aversion to it or intellectual incapacity for it, but to a reasoned conviction about the nature of poetry.

ONE OF THE MAIN AREAS of traditional literary history is the history of genres, and that we have already discussed in Chapter v. Another area is the history of literary periods or ages. Contemporary theorists of literature urge the necessity of periodization and the importance of the problems connected with it.[30] Croce was fully aware of the value of periodization for general history. His history of aesthetics made use of the traditional periodization of the history of philosophy, which is even more sharply defined in his subsequent history of historiography (1917). This, in turn, is inspired by Fueter's *History of Modern Historiography* (1915), which is also very clearly periodized. In Croce's "history of history" we find first the ancient period, then the Medieval, the Renaissance, the Enlightenment, Romanticism, Positivism, and a final chapter on the New History. Each period is first clearly characterized as a whole and then particularized.

In more recent times Croce came to the conclusion that characterizations of periods are what he terms "functional concepts" built around the fundamental categories of the spirit.[31] The basis for characterization is the category which is found to be most active in the period—or, more simply, its prevalent tendency. Being a concept of prevalence it is only approximate and cannot be made to cover all and every event occurring in the period. On the other hand, it cannot, for the same reason, be refuted by quoting some isolated instance of an entirely different tendency from within the period. The relevance of this argument especially to discussions about the "essence" of the Renaissance and its connection with the Middle Ages is obvious.[32]

But for Croce periodization is never the primary task of history. It is always secondary and instrumental, relative to the particular historical problem investigated, and possessed of no absolute and "objective" validity. The historian does not investigate epochs, but problems, for the solution of which he may set up delimitations of phases and stages, or epochs and periods, which are labels for practical convenience and do not correspond to independent entities. Hence the futility of many of the protracted and laborious discussions about the character and essence of the Renaissance and other historical periods, considered absolutely. In the case of poetry and art, periodization is particularly ineffectual, since works of art are individual creations, each of which is "an epoch to itself." The so-called periods of literary history, when carefully scrutinized, turn out frequently to be descriptions of intellectual and social trends, and not literary at all. This point was made by Croce in one of his most important untranslated essays, "The Reform of Literary and Art History" (1917, NSE², 156–80). Here he notes that usually in the history of art or of literature periodization is effected through the definition of the so-called "general character" of the period, and by a description of the dominant trends in matter or style, of its prevailing forms, patterns, and conventions.

Croce believed that literary history owed its origin to the great critics of the pre-Romantic and Romantic age, to "Vico and Herder, Winckelmann and Schiller, Chateaubriand and Mme. de Staël, Schlegel and Hegel" (NSE[2], 162). In this paper he gives a penetrating analysis of their merits and their shortcomings, of their achievements and their influence. In their hands works of art and of poetry became, almost for the first time, "living spiritual values." Criticism gave up its rigid judicial attitude and narrowly pedantic habits, and became sympathetic to the works it criticized, concentrating on their beauty and showing indulgence towards their shortcomings. In this way criticism ceased to be dogmatic and arbitrary, and became really historical, "positive and affirmative like all histories" (NSE[2], 163). However, these critics, progressive as they were, tended to fall into a critical error. They thought that "literature is the expression of society" (a theory already discussed by Croce in *PdE*, 56–60), whereas literature is the expression of the individual intuition.

Croce then took note of the idea, which at that time (1917) was being advanced by Wölfflin and his school, of a history of art that should make connections drawn not from intellectual or social trends, but from art itself. The traits would be common to a number of individuals, but they would be purely artistic. The aim of this school is "a general history of painting as pure painting, with purely pictorial values, abstracting from its material content, i.e. its images and expressions; and hence a history of artistic or stylistic procedures, of which, for instance, one painter set the problem, another carried it towards a solution, a third let it pass by without noticing it, a fourth pushed it further along, a fifth took it up again and solved it, and a sixth, alas, lost it again." From painting Croce turns to poetry: "On this pattern others now propose to write a history of pure poetry, in which the actors are no longer the souls of the poets but rhythms, modulations, inflexions, elevations, pauses, and such-like aesthetic quintessences. But the truth is that from a series of works of art no other general traits can be abstracted save those relating to their matter, hence not artistic but intellectual and practical, because the act of abstraction dissolves and destroys the individuality of the work, i.e. dissolves and destroys it as art.[33] The general aesthetic characters that are alleged are either nothing at all, or things which taken by themselves are material and extraneous to art" (NSE², 166, cf. 261, 274 and NPS, I, 180).

It is essential to see that this argument applies to all common elements that may be abstracted from works of literature, whether relating to its content or to its supposed form. Some of them admittedly refer to content: the subject matter, the cycle of stories to which its plot may belong, the ideas that may be traced in it, the general trends of contemporary feeling or taste that are discernible in it, etc. But others refer to what is often known as its form: linguistic traits, stylistic characteristics, metrical patterns, its literary genre or "form," the narrative or dramatic devices used in it, etc. However all common elements result from a dissection of the work that destroys it as a work of art, so they cannot be aesthetic factors or determinants of its artistic quality. They belong to the class of empirical concepts that we have seen in Chapter IV, which are not anterior to the aesthetic judgment but posterior to it, for the dissection is performed upon a work which has already been judged a work of art. Since for Croce the aesthetic judgment is in effect identical with the historical judgment, the true history of art is anterior to, and independent of, the dissection which results in norms or common traits.

For Croce the true history of literature is the history of poetic personalities, each of which is an individual complete in himself, presented in an individual study. The alternative is to make the personalities of the single writers fit into some developmental scheme by cutting them down to suit it. The writer ceases to be an individual artist and becomes only a phase in a process. Many protests, says Croce, have been made by writers and men of taste against this view, and he quotes one from Tolstoy: "Do not speak to me of the evolution of the novel; do not tell me that Stendhal explains Balzac, and Balzac in turn explains Flaubert. These are critical fantasies . . . Geniuses do not proceed one from the other: genius is always independent" (NSE², 168).

On the other hand, the history of literature as Croce understands it presents a real process of development, continuous and concrete, in the history of the growth and expansion of the individual artist. All links between artistic personalities having been shown one after the other to be irrelevant: the national link [34] as well as the chronological link, the patterns of genres and of trends, of schools and of tendencies, there is no justification for a continuous history of art or literature. This step was taken in the cited paper on "The Reform of Literary and Art History": "the true logical form of literary and art history is the characterization of the single artist and of his work, and the corresponding expository form is the essay or the monograph" (NSE, 173). Croce pointed out that this was no sudden break with the past: the trend away from the general history and towards the critical monograph was already in full swing when Croce was writing, and it has certainly not subsided since. To this principle, consistently maintained, we owe the fact that Croce never wrote a history of Italian literature, although he covered practically all of its territory in his long series of critical and historical studies. He was in consequence often asked by friends to write a history of Italian literature, but he constantly refused.[35]

This does not mean that histories of literature do not serve a useful purpose. But according to Croce it is a purely practical purpose. They are convenient works of reference, not genuine histories with a continuous development. They may even be collections of excellent critical essays on individual authors, held together by a thin framework of general or cultural history. As R. Wellek points out, most English histories of literature belong to this type.[36] Croce declared that he had no intention of denying a right of existence to "surveys, panoramas, outlines and encyclopaedias of which everyone makes use, either to find a piece of information that one needs or to obtain a bird's eye view of the historical territory in which he intends to move." But "the other function that is usually ascribed to them, viz. to offer a complete and faithful reproduction or copy of facts, is entirely imaginary" (NSE², 179).

What about De Sanctis' *History of Italian Literature*, which presents a clear-cut line of development, and which Croce had so long defended against the historical critics? This is the point at which Croce, logically following his principle to its consequences, parts company with De Sanctis. In his critical work Croce found himself disagreeing more and more with De Sanctis' grouping of writers into periods and with the links which he traced between writer and writer. From a disciple Croce gradually turned into a critic of De Sanctis, certainly a friendly and admiring critic who still shared many convictions with him but on the whole had gone beyond him.[37] In Chapter XII we shall see two instances—Dante and Ariosto—of the manner in which Croce revises De Sanctis.

In the very last years of his life Croce took note of a period of Italian literature to which he had not yet dedicated a comprehensive study: the eighteenth century. So he wrote a book on this period, published in 1949, but it is a collection of separate essays, like all his other volumes of criticism. In the same years, he dedicated three rich volumes to the poets and writers of the full and late Renaissance (*Poeti e scrittori del pieno e del tardo Rinascimento*, published 1945–52). The third volume of the series is the last volume of criticism he was to publish; it appeared in the year of his death. But these, too, are collections of essays and papers.[38]

There is one apparent exception to this rule: the book on the seventeenth century, *Storia dell'età barocca in Italia* (1929). This book, as Croce himself claimed, "is really what would have been traditionally called a History of Italian Literature in the 17th Century, for it comprises the same subjects that are usually included in the so-called literary histories, viz. poetry, eloquence, miscellaneous treatises, historiography, discussion of the predominant taste, connections with social life," etc. But in this book, he claimed, they were "critically analyzed and assigned to their proper place": the history of thought, in which Croce found several valuable contributions (cf. US, 35), was separated from the history of literature and both were separated from what Croce called the "history of moral life" in the period, i.e. what is traditionally considered the decadence of Italy after the glory of the Renaissance. About half the book is dedicated to a critical discrimination of the poetry and the literature of the period, in which the various tones and levels of poetry are discussed in separate chapters: e.g. "the silence of great poetry," "the pseudo-poetry of the baroque," "the literary pseudo-poetry," "sensuous poetry," "comic poetry," etc. So the works of the writers of this period are included in a general framework, which is very clearly and firmly constructed and articulated.

It would seem that Croce has here succumbed to the idea of the general history, and it would be all the more significant that this happened in the case of the seventeenth century, because that period was Croce's first and last love, the period of Italian literature which he perhaps knew best. But the truth is that Croce here is not writing a history of poetry but rather the history of an artistic aberration, the *baroque*.[39] For him this term has always preserved its original negative meaning, as the designation of a poetic defect or shortcoming, and he has steadfastly refused throughout his life to join the modern trend which in various ways attempts to give it a positive content as the designation of an art style or art form.[40] And, as may be seen from the quoted chapter headings, even in this book, which represents his fullest and most mature treatment of the problem, he could not find great poetry in the seventeenth-century period of Italian literature. What he did find, and carefully analyzed, are various forms and grades of predominant bad taste, of the baroque aberration, only slightly qualified and tempered by some minor attempts at genuine poetry, which are duly noted and characterized but are not so conspicuous as to invalidate the general framework. So even in this book Croce cannot be said to have violated his principles.

But the baroque is not the only concept of this kind that Croce has met with as a practicing literary critic or historian. He also gave considerable attention to Romanticism. We have already seen Croce's discussion of this concept as a general aesthetic category. In the context of the *Aesthetic* "romantic" was a general term with no definite content. Later, "romantic" was made to stand for the emotional content of poetry and "classic" for the formal element. But what about Romanticism as an historical trend or school of writing? Early in the century attempts were still made by literery historians to give a single definition of it. Well before Lovejoy's famous dissection of Romanticism into a plurality of meanings (1923), Croce in 1906 argued that it was impossible to give a single and unitary definition, and split it into several factors (*PdE*, 287–94). There are three distinct and separate movements which may be called Romantic: 1) Emotional Romanticism or the *mal du siècle*, the Romantic malady or emotional disequilibrium in all its varieties and manifestations. 2) Romantic philosophy, by which Croce means any system which stresses intuition and imagination at the expense of the intellect. Such are the systems of Schelling and of Hegel. Since Croce accepts the idealists' critique of rationalism, these systems for him contain important truths; they have a positive value and must be sharply distinguished from emotional Romanticism, which is purely pathological. 3) Aesthetic Romanticism means art in which the emotional element predominates over form; it is therefore a type of bad art. So there is no positive category of "Romantic art"; that term may be strictly defined as a type of bad art (*Storia*, 131–32). If a writer of the Romantic group produces good art, this art according to Croce is not defined Romantic but classic, since "classic" for Croce has become a synonym for good art (NSE, 136).

But this does not mean that Croce has adopted a classicistic or neoclassical attitude. If "classic" means good, "classicism" as an *-ism* or school of writing or slogan is bad: as we have seen in Chapter III, it stands for the predominance of the formal element over the emotional in frigid and conventional writing. It is therefore the opposite excess to Romanticism (CC, III, 110; US, 75; *Storia*, 131–32). The golden medium is the perfect balance of form and content, the image perfectly expressing the emotion. This is the quality of being "classic" or, as it can be termed in

Italian, *"classicità"* (cc, iii, 125–26). Therefore "classic" for Croce are both Sophocles and Shakespeare, both Racine and Goethe, even the Goethe of the first *Faust*. Classic are also Dante and the other medieval poets, as well as Villon, Baudelaire and Maupassant in their best work (tps, ii, 6).

In 1932 Croce made a detailed analysis of Romanticism in his *History of Europe in the* xixth *Century*. He begins by reiterating his distinction between Romanticism as an emotional disturbance and Romanticism as a positive philosophy: "two things which are different and even opposite" (p. 47). Romanticism as a positive philosophy is the revolt against the forms of art and thought which had prevailed in the Age of Enlightenment, viz. "literary academicism and philosophic intellectualism." It was a reawakening of the feeling for genuine and great poetry, for which it gave the doctrine in the new science of the imagination, or Aesthetic, and made corresponding progress in the other fields of philosophy and history (pp. 47–48).[41] But emotional Romanticism is a purely morbid phenomenon, and if it is asked how an age which was provided with such a brilliant philosophy could sink to such emotional misery, Croce's answer is that the Romantic malady followed closely upon the religious crisis caused by the advent of the new philosophy. The loss of traditional religion produced a deep emotional disturbance in the more sensitive minds, generating world-weariness and despair, together with the hysterical search for new cults to replace the old, such as the cult of passion or of mystical union. The need for a religion survived the loss of faith, and the incapacity to accept a rational view of the world let loose the chaotic forces of emotionalism. The *History* is available in translation, and the reader is referred to it for a complete exposition of this view.[42]

Naturalism, in its Italian variety or *verismo*, was discussed by Croce in his study of contemporary Italian literature. In his essay upon the novelist Giovanni Verga, who belonged to this school, Croce begins by disposing of the pseudo-concept. Like classicism, romanticism, idealism, symbolism and the like, Naturalism is rejected by aesthetics. "Every genuine work of art is at the same time naturalistic and symbolistic, idealistic, Classical and Romantic, etc., because it is a synthesis of matter and form, of the real and the ideal" (LNI, III, II). But a term which stands for a pseudo-concept in aesthetics may have a specific meaning in history. In the history of literature naturalism "is a summary word, a label, to denote a great historical movement, specifically in the history of fancy, which developed in the second half of the 19th century, concurrently with the development of the natural sciences, of psychology and of sociology. The art which preceded it dealt by preference with the ideals of humanity; the art of the second half of the 19th century preferred to look at the facts which may be called brutal or material: to man and men in so far as they do not rise to, and almost have no inkling for, what in man is ideal; in so far as they are not actually, or not any longer, men. Previous art looked in passion for what is intellectual and ethical in it, or at least exquisite and rare; naturalism instead for what is sordid, selfish, common, stupid and mechanical" (LNI, III, 13).

Here Croce was actually considering common elements that may be abstracted from a number of works of art—a procedure which as we have seen he later argued to be inapplicable to literary criticism. But in the description of naturalism he was not engaged in literary criticism, nor was he pronouncing judgment. He did not argue that the writers of the naturalistic school were any better, or any worse, than the earlier writers, nor that their ideas determined the artistic quality of their work. He was then operating as an historian of ideas, describing the beliefs that were common to a group of writers in a certain period. He is led to these ideas by the allegiance to them professed by the writer under discussion, hence he examines them to see what exactly they might mean to him. At the most, naturalism is said to be a trend in the history of "fancy" and not of the imagination, since Croce as we have seen in Chapter III holds to that traditional dichotomy in his own terms.

Croce believed that it was necessary for the literary critic and historian to take cognizance of literary trends, fashions and currents active during the times of the writer under discussion, in order to know what exactly he was up against: the trends may account for his difficulties and for his shortcomings (NSE², 132–33). In the case of Verga, however, naturalism exercised a beneficial effect: it helped him to gain a better knowledge of himself. As we shall see in the next chapter, when we will consider the case of Verga in detail, he became aware of a whole world of images existing in his mind which had not found an outlet in the sensational novels of his early manner. At best, naturalism for Croce was a factor in the development of an individual artist, but Verga was not an episode in the history of "naturalism." The formula does not generate but "merely recognizes and assists the expressions which are already being formed" (E, 58–59; A, 52). Croce's *aperçu* of the content of naturalism, with its plain but carefully considered wording, may serve as an example for similar definitions of other movements still badly in need of such definition. But they should not be hypostatized into aesthetic categories.

THERE IS FINALLY another branch of literary history which may here be considered, comparative literature. In its meaning as a field of research, it was first discussed by Croce in 1902 (*PdE*, 73–78) on the double occasion of the revival of the chair of that subject in the University of Naples, which had once been De Sanctis' and was now assigned to F. Torraca (a disciple of De Sanctis), and on the publication of the older American *Journal of Comparative Literature* edited by G. E. Woodberry, J. F. Fletcher and J. E. Spingarn and to which Croce himself contributed a paper on the history of the concept of "humor" (*PdE*, 275–84).

Comparative Literature, Croce notes, is sometimes intended to designate *Stoffgeschichte* or the history of literary themes, which Croce does not consider literary history, and the study of the influences of one literature upon another, which again is something different from the study of the creative element in literature. The best meaning that can be assigned to the term is the total study of literature, or the study of literature in all its relationships, connections and implications—with political and intellectual history as well as with the history of the arts and of society. And this for Croce is genuine literary history, in its fullest acceptance (*PdE*, 77).

Croce showed the limitations of *Stoffgeschichte* in a series of later reviews: identity of theme does not establish a connection between different works, for the real subject-matter of poetry is emotion, which is different in every poet.[43] In the study of influences, Croce took the stand that the influence of a writer on another literature belongs to the history of the latter and not of the former.[44] The influence of Shakespeare on the mind of Germany, as brilliantly traced by Gundolf, is part of the history of Germany, and has little to do with Shakespeare, who becomes merely "a symbol of the development of the German mind" (*Critica*, xxvii, 244). But perhaps the most important pronouncement that Croce made in this field was in 1927 in his discussion of the influence of Spanish literature on the rest of Europe.[45] Croce here argued that it is only philosophy, and not poetry, that can operate as an influence from one national culture to another. Poetry is essentially form, and form alone cannot influence culture. But the material of poetry, detached from its form, may operate as an influence; it is then no longer art, but emotion or ideas. And ideas may circulate from one country to another without losing their substance. This leads to the practical conclusion that research in comparative literature as a study of influences can only be research in the history of ideas, and this in turn is for Croce essentially the history of philosophy.

To SUM UP. Croce's solution to the problem of the relation between literary history and criticism is that, properly understood, they are one and the same process. The real history of literature consists in the evaluation of the single works of literature, i.e. in criticism. On the other hand criticism deals with poetry, which is an historical reality no less than politics or economics or philosophy; and a genuine criticism of a work is the assertion of an historical proposition: "a work of poetry appeared in the world at this particular time," so criticism is history. Croce here presents more explicitly and logically a truth which is acknowledged and acted upon by scholars of other countries: e.g. in England, where there are historians who are not ashamed to be critics (and vice versa), as H. J. C. Grierson and C. H. Herford were earlier in this century.

Since practically all the links which are usually introduced by historians between different works of literature are artificial, general histories by periods, nations, schools, genres, themes, etc. are to be replaced by the critical monograph, or become part of the history of culture. So that, in the last resort, for Croce it is criticism that absorbs history within itself, as the critical essay and the monograph replace the general narrative.[46]

CHAPTER *X*

Croce's Earlier Criticism

IT IS TYPICAL of Croce's close union of theory with practice that no sooner had he defined his theoretical views in the *Aesthetic*, than he turned to practical criticism for systematic verification and large-scale illustration (LNI, IV, 226; *Au*, 70). Croce decided to conduct a periodical as a vehicle for this literary criticism, for the exposition of his other theories, and to keep in touch with contemporary thought. He named it *La critica:* "a review of literature, history and philosophy." It was preceded in November 1902 by a preliminary statement of its aims and began to appear in January 1903 as a bi-monthly. It continued regularly for 42 years, appearing punctually on the 20th of each alternate month, even during two world wars, and carrying its store of philosophy, history, literary criticism and lively polemics throughout Italy and later also abroad. It was one of Croce's most ambitious and successful projects and was largely instrumental in propagating his views and establishing his influence.

The review was written almost entirely by Croce, but a small number of associates appeared over the years. In the beginning Croce was assisted by Giovanni Gentile, then a struggling young philosopher of brilliant promise, with whom Croce formed an intellectual partnership which lasted for a quarter of a century. This partnership was finally broken up by Fascism, but in the early years of the century the two men fought side by side against common enemies, such as positivism, clericalism, the glib formulas of Italian freemasonry, etc., and worked together on behalf of a stricter historical scholarship and of a systematic philosophical credo rooted deeply in history. Later, A. Omodeo and G. de Ruggiero became important contributors.[1]

The program of *La critica*, which was issued in a prospectus and then reprinted in its first issue, is really the program of Croce's own intellectual life.[2] It begins with showing the need for a new review to deal with questions that cut across several fields and with general problems of scholarship, which found no place in specialized journals. The fact that a whole review was dedicated to such problems undoubtedly helped to focus attention on them and made scholars and critics more aware of the general implications of their own work and of the existence of allied disciplines. Croce then noted as a shortcoming of other reviews "the absence of stable standards and of an organic system of ideas." "Editors give hospitality in their journals to ideas which are disparate and discordant," and "no thought is given to the ultimate end, i.e. to the effect made on the mind of the reader." "Freedom is better served by offering a clear target to opponents, than mixing with them in an insincere fraternization that benefits nobody." He then quoted Bacon: "truth emerges sooner from error than from confusion."

Croce proceeded to specify the principles on which the review was founded. First of all, the method of inquiry was the historical method—no novelty, since it was already well established in Italian universities. "But," he added immediately, "the editor also believes no less firmly that this method is not sufficient for the requirements of thought, and therefore it is necessary to promote a general revival of the philosophical spirit." Then comes Croce's philosophical commitment: "Since philosophy can only be idealism, the editor is a follower of idealism"; but of a cautious and critical idealism which advances gradually and "gives an account of every step taken," and may be therefore designated as "antimetaphysical idealism" or even as "realistic idealism." Nor would "social and political ideas" be ignored, because "it is impossible to abstract from them when discussing books on history and on social and political controversies." What

his attitude might be in these matters, Croce indicates epigram-
matically by "declaring summarily that he abhors all attempts to
'put the world into knickers' and induce adults to become children again." [3] There followed a statement of critical principles,
which will be quoted later in this chapter, when we come to
discuss Croce's critical contributions. Finally, Croce declared
his hostility to a number of undesirable tendencies: first of all,
against dilettantism in scholarly matters; then against positivism,
"scientism," and other trends.[4]

Needless to say, such an ambitious program gave Croce a
full-time occupation for many years. But he had the means and
the leisure to dedicate to it, and he found a young publisher,
Giovanni Laterza of Bari, who made Croce his principal adviser
and produced not only the review, but also Croce's many other
publications, including his own books, works which he spon-
sored and whole series and collections of scholarly editions such
as the *Classics of Philosophy* (a series of translations and critical
texts), the *Writers of Italy* (a standard edition of Italian
classics), etc. Croce's review soon earned a reputation for high
intellectual standards, a clear-cut stand on most questions, and
a forthright criticism of opposing views. With its successor,
Quaderni della Critica (1945–51) it covers a full half-century
of European culture and remains an indispensable source book
for the history of ideas and intellectual trends of this period.[5]

A characteristic feature was that the place of honor in the
review was occupied by long series of articles in specific areas,
carefully planned and written years in advance. The first twelve
volumes of the review contained a critical survey of Italian
philosophy and Italian literature of the past thirty years, or
since Italian unification in 1870. Gentile undertook the survey
of philosophy, composing what became a four-volume history,
while Croce analyzed the literature of the period in a series of
critical studies. He thus took up the systematic study of contemporary literature, a most unacademic choice. Then, as now,
academic scholars were reluctant to commit themselves on the
moderns. Croce wrote an attack on this tendency in what might
be called a preliminary skirmish to his critical engagement (PS,

1, 103 ff.). There is, however, an essential difference between Croce's attitude and that of the militant "modernist." Croce's attitude was always critical, and he did not take sides with any school of writing or -ism. The militant modernist, on the other hand, values contemporary literature simply because it is modern, and usually belongs to a school or trend extolling all writers who belong to this school while despising all others. But for Croce "to look for modernity in art is to look for modernity and not for art" (NSE², 191) as he was to put it later. And Croce's attitude to -isms was clearly defined in the program of *La critica:* "As far as the formulas of aesthetic criticism are concerned, the editor of this review believes in avoiding them all as a matter of course. Writers may capriciously name themselves realists, symbolists, mystics, psychologists, neoclassicists, 'Alexandrines,' 'Byzantines,' worshippers of pure beauty or mouthpieces of social revolt. But the critic should smile at all these formulas and take notice only of what a writer actually accomplishes in the sphere of art, which is one of the most liberal and yet most exacting of realms."

One may see here already the rejection of the "Intentional Fallacy": a writer is to be judged by his actual achievement and not by the formulas or patterns he intended to follow. This eliminates all the manifestoes, school slogans and avant-gardism on the one side, and the historical scholars' faith in the production of poetry according to intentional poetics on the other. It is a typical Crocean attack on opposite extremes of critical theory.

CROCE'S IMPARTIALITY and critical acumen are amply attested in this series of critical essays which he dedicated to contemporary writers, and which later became the first four volumes of *The Literature of Modern Italy* (1914). Each author was evaluated on his merits and not according to his affiliations, literary, political or philosophical (cf. CC, V, 165–67). In his "Memoirs of a critic" Croce later told how his aim was to be a positive critic who singles out what is good in each writer rather than a negative critic who sees only faults, but he soon found that the bad was often intermingled with the good and sometimes very difficult to separate from it. However he persisted in his aim, bringing out insofar as possible what was good in the production of each writer and then defining its characteristics (*Aneddoti*, IV, 413–61; cf. PS, II, 177–80).

For twelve years (1903–14) his review presented regularly a fresh essay in the series, until he had written some eighty critical portraits and covered the larger part of the field. In the course of this survey a number of bubbles was pricked; on the other hand some writers who had gone out of fashion were brought back to notice.[6] Croce also called attention to some new writers who had not yet received critical recognition, such as the poet Francesco Gaeta. Alfredo Oriani, an imaginative and philosophical writer of novels and histories, with prophetic attitudes that make him something like an Italian Carlyle, was brought back to prominence by Croce, and later was to suffer the posthumous indignity of becoming one of the patron saints of Fascism. The main literary lights of the time, like Carducci and D'Annunzio, received objective appraisal. In the study of Carducci,[7] Croce rescued the poet from the critics who saw in him mainly a political and national figure, and in the essay on D'Annunzio he defended that writer from the attacks of the moralists, who saw in him only a corrupt influence. Carducci was defined as "the impassioned poet of history" in the manner we have already seen, and D'Annunzio was defined as "a dilettante of sensations." Many other estimates were also formulated and defended.

G. Castellano, who was for a while something of a Boswell to Croce, says that at this point Croce went about his critical task "listening only to the dictates of his good taste, abandoning himself to his genuine impressions in the manner that De Sanctis had recommended so strongly, and as if he had never written an aesthetic, discerning the poetic from the unpoetic on the strength of these impressions."[8] So Croce found himself judging unfavorably a writer like Luigi Capuana, who happened to be a disciple of De Sanctis and a critic with whose ideas Croce was in sympathy, but who lacked power in his artistic work. On the other hand, Croce found himself drawn with strong admiration to the work of Giovanni Verga, whose artistic slogan was that "naturalism" (*verismo* in Italian) which Croce had refuted as an aesthetic principle, but who was a great writer. Verga's reputation, at that time still in doubt, was firmly placed by Croce on the pedestal which it has never left since.

We have already seen Croce's analysis of naturalism. After showing that it was a European movement that appeared first in France and England and only later in Italy, Croce considered Verga's own pronouncements on it. Verga held that the artist should be an empirical observer of human nature, as impersonal as a scientist. "These ideas are obviously wrong," Croce comments: "Art is always personal" (LNI, III, 18). But erroneous as they were, these ideas helped Verga to get out of the rut of his early writing. His early work consists of sensational novels of crime and passion, set in the world of luxury and of fashion in great cities, with *femmes fatales* who drive their unfortunate lovers to crime or suicide, and similar paraphernalia of morbid romanticism. With the advent of naturalism, an entirely different world was presented as the subject-matter of literature: the world of the humble and of the oppressed, of laborers and of peasants. Now this world happened to correspond to the world of Verga's early experiences in his native Sicily: "Underneath the dead crust of the manners and passions of high life in great cities, there lived in Verga the impressions and memories, vivid, direct, immediate, of his native town, of his childhood and of his youth. A motley crowd of countrymen and country women, of poor folk, of tormentors and tormented, figured in pitiful or tragic episodes of sudden and violent passions, or of passions long smouldering and finally emerging in violent explosions, of sufferings and privations, of anguish and misery of all kinds. And these images possessed a strength and a substance greater than the earlier ones" (LNI, III, 14).

So the poetic image arises from the concurrence of personal experience with an external stimulus, and the critical analysis of a writer becomes the history of his development. Croce follows this development in detail, from the first *Little Novels of Sicily*

to the great novels of Verga's maturity in which the image finds
its fullest realization. And this image expresses a deep human
emotion: sympathy for human suffering and love for ethical
values. It does this by being a very particular and individualized
image, presenting the life of peasants and laborers in nineteenth-
century Sicily, with all their local color, their dialect and their
costume. In its realization this image appears under many names:
Nedda and padron 'Ntoni, Mastro Don Gesualdo and Rosso
Malpelo, Jeli and the Wolf-Woman, Santuzza and Zio Crocifisso,
names that are colorful and characteristic. The setting, the homes
of the characters and the towns they live in, the landscapes and
the seascapes, are an integral part of these images, of their
particularity and definiteness. And so the feeling of anguish—
anguish caused by sheer adversity or by social oppression, and
the correlative longing for justice—becomes a special and determinate feeling, the Verga feeling, which is not identical with
any similar feeling observable in other writers. To grasp this
feeling in its individuality, in its complete fusion with the image,
there is only one way: to read the novels themselves. What the
critic can do is to point out the theme, the leading motif, the
lyrical tone of the images and call the reader's attention to it,
turning it away from distracting side issues, such as the historical or sociological truth of the picture or the "technical devices
of narrative." It will then be seen that the total picture is both
of yesterday and of today, both Sicilian and universally human.

Since the works of Verga are available in translation, they
provide an example upon which the reader may test Croce's
critical method. After reading Verga's work, is it more satisfactory to view it as a bundle of technical devices, or of literary
norms, or of psychological complexes, or of sociological patterns, or to see it with Croce as the expression of a deep human
feeling?

We have thus seen that Croce's doctrine of the lyrical image
is fully capable of accounting for the evolution of a novelist,
even of a naturalistic novelist. It provides a basis for discriminating between the stronger and weaker productions of an artist,
and for a general characterization of his achievement. Croce's

critical method is a working method, and the proof is that other critics can work with it.[9] The history of Verga criticism is an instance. Croce's study is a turning point in the evaluation of Verga. Before Croce, the great problem apparently was whether Verga's language was sufficiently pure, sufficiently "standard Italian," for the admission of the Sicilian Verga to national Italian literature. Croce of course rejected this problem and not only established Verga's standing, but also stimulated further and more detailed analysis of his work.[10]

Following the road opened up by Croce, critics have developed still more precise definitions of the theme or mood of Verga's poetic creation. Croce's definition was pregnant but brief: melancholy and ethical values (*bontà e melanconia*, LNI, III, 28). Fuller definitions and analyses have been given by critics like Luigi Russo and Attilio Momigliano, to name only two outstanding post-Croceans. In 1923 Russo observed that "the objective methods of Verga are not due to extrinsic aims and literary technique, but proceed from an essential problem of humanity: the impersonality of Verga is the very humility and impersonality of human destiny." [11] This is already a step beyond Croce: Verga's ideal of impersonality is seen to be, not just an erroneous artistic belief, but an integral part of Verga's poetic vision, the anonymous face of human destiny in the action of his stories.

In Momigliano's *History of Italian Literature* (1937) Verga's poetic theme or lyrical emotion is defined as "the feeling for that heavy and painful travail which is life." "The theme of Verga's mature art is the representation of the daily struggle, which has no sudden reversals, no dramatic situations, no magnificent scenes, but is consumed in silent and unrelieved anguish: a theme both stoical and melancholy." [12] The reader is referred to Momigliano's book for the full development of this formula. But perhaps enough has been quoted to show that these critics start from the positions reached by Croce and proceed further along the same road.[13]

In the essays on *The Literature of Modern Italy* there is no introductory chapter providing a general framework, chronological or thematic, and writers are not grouped by -isms or trends, genres or geographical areas, but follow each other in roughly chronological order. Occasionally there is a paper on some general topic, such as "The historical criticism of literature and its opponents" (III, 373–91) and "On a certain attitude in contemporary writing" (IV, 179–96), the latter a remarkable ethical analysis of certain national weaknesses which were to contribute shortly afterwards to the success of Fascism. This is only one of a long series of analyses and admonitions which Croce has addressed to his own countrymen, and which make him, in addition to everything else, one of the great moral teachers of Italy. And there are other warnings and exhortations scattered throughout this work. But the only general picture of the literary scene is the already referred to survey of literary life in Naples in 1860–1900 (IV, 233–319), and it is printed as an appendix, not as literary history but as history of culture. For the reasons why no attempt was made at a general picture of the age, the reader is referred to the "Envoy" (IV, 223–26) and to Croce's theory of literary history, expounded in the preceding chapter.

On the other hand, general trends are discussed whenever they arise in connection with a single writer. Realism, as we have seen, was discussed in connection with Verga, decadentism in connection with D'Annunzio (IV, 10–13), romanticism in connection with Boito (I, 259–60), and the ideal of "impersonal art" in connection with Capuana (III, 104–5). In the last essay Croce concluded with a statement which admirably sums up his general attitude: "The artist does not analyze documents, which is the function of the investigator of reality as a whole; does not describe types, for that is the function of the naturalist; does not proceed, as we have said, from the outer to the inner, but from the inner to the outer, and is therefore an artist" (III, 105).

Similar discussions are given to the problem of the writer as a reformer in the case of Sbarbaro (III, 104–5), of the nineteenth-century conflict between science and faith in the case of Zanella (I, 299–300), of the status of dialect literature in the case of

Di Giacomo (III, 98–100), of the disequilibrium between form and content in the case of Nievo (I, 123), and so forth. All these general discussions are kept well within bounds in each essay, where they are strictly functional to the portrayal of the individual writer. And yet they are articulations of Croce's aesthetic doctrine: the example illustrates the theory and the theory explains the example.

It is safe to affirm that no other aesthetic doctrine has ever received such an extensive and particularized "empirical" (or, as Croce would say, historical) verification. Croce's study of the literature of "modern Italy" is the fullest that he has given to any period of literature. It also shows how according to this theory one should deal not only with poets, dramatists and novelists, but with the prose of historians, critics and philosophers. But since it deals with writers unfamiliar outside Italy we will not go into it any further.

AFTER PUBLISHING *The Literature of Modern Italy* in four volumes in 1914–15 (to which two more were added in 1939–40), Croce's next critical engagement was with European literature of the nineteenth century. This also began as a series in the *Critica* (1917). It extended to 25 essays and included German and French writers such as Schiller and Heine, Stendhal and Balzac, Flaubert and Maupassant, Baudelaire and Zola. Also covered were one English author, Sir Walter Scott, one Scandinavian, Ibsen, and one Spaniard, Fernan Caballero, besides eight Italians. The selection, as Croce acknowledged in the preface to the collected edition, is purely casual, and Croce never expanded the series to cover all the writers of the period. It was therefore published under a title which had no reference to chronological or historical limitations, viz. *Poetry and non-poetry* (1923), the same title that Croce had used for one of his earliest critical essays. In the preface Croce also explained that he had been diverted by other studies from extending the discussion to the whole century. The "other studies" referred to include the work on Goethe (of which publication began in

1918), Croce's fullest study of any poet, and the essays on Ariosto (1918), Shakespeare (1919), Corneille (1920) and Dante (1921), the studies on aesthetic problems which were to go into the *New Essays on Aesthetics* (1920), and work in other fields, such as the resumption on a large scale of his studies on the history of the Kingdom of Naples, of which publication began in 1923.

What the book on *Poetry and non-poetry* aims at giving, as the title implies, is a discussion of critical problems in connection with a group of nineteenth-century writers, selected more or less at random. The discussions do not aim at a detailed analysis of the whole production of each author, but rather at taking up the problems that criticism had raised in connection with these authors, and offering new solutions, "clearing up points that were still doubtful and opening the way for new investigations" (p. 6). As Croce was aware, this was likely to be called "criticism of criticism," but by this time (the preface is dated March 1922) he was convinced that this was an essential part of criticism, as we have seen in Chapter VIII.

The result is that this series of spare and tightly-knit papers will not satisfy the reader who may be looking for a conventional history of a literary period by means of genres and sub-genres, schools and regional groups: i.e. the conventional view of literary history, as described by Croce himself in the postscript to his previous work (LNI, IV², 255). Nor was it to be another variety of literary history, "which proceeds as a drama of ideas or ideals in conflict, struggling and overpowering each other, in which every writer and every work takes its place among the *dramatis personae* or among the choruses, who also participate in the battle." And the reason for it not being so is that "a history of this kind can and should be written, but it is a philosophical or social history, and not a history of art" (*ibid.*). It is therefore unfortunate that the book should have been translated into English with the title *European Literature of the Nineteenth Century*, as it was by D. Ainslie in 1924, for the title arouses expectations that are likely to be disappointed.

To some of these essays reference has already been made in

Chapter VIII (i.e. Balzac and Maupassant). In Flaubert and Baudelaire, Croce found a similarity of temperament: both were deeply afflicted with the romantic malady, the *mal de siècle*, and both overcame it by turning it into material for great art. Of the two, the essay on Flaubert was more positively accented than the one on Baudelaire; but Croce was to make full amends for that in later writings on the poet of the *Fleurs du Mal*.[14] He was also to correct, in the very last year of his life, the somewhat qualified recognition of Manzoni in this volume.[15] But to give an adequate account of Croce's essays one would have to take up each critical problem afresh, go through the various solutions proposed by critics, and compare them with Croce's. Such a task would require several volumes. This book can only provide a general introduction to Croce's criticism by explaining his main assumptions and clarifying his leading terms. In *Poetry and non-poetry*, as in all Croce's books, theory and practice go hand in hand and illuminate each other; but the reader is expected to come to the book with previous knowledge of the author under discussion and of the critical problem discussed.

CHAPTER *XI*

The Cosmic Intuition

IN AN ESSAY PUBLISHED IN 1918, "The Character of Totality of Artistic Expression," Croce added another concept to his aesthetic: the "cosmic" or universal character of art. This was designated by Croce himself as an important step. In the already quoted preface to the fifth edition of the *Aesthetic* (1922) Croce said: "the two principal developments that I have given to it are 1) the demonstration of the lyrical character of pure intuition (1908), and 2) the demonstration of its universal or cosmic character (1918)" (p. vii).

With this development, Croce introduced the universal into his concept of art in a way that, taken literally, reverses the main direction of his earlier doctrine, which was entirely oriented towards the individuality of art and its cognition of the particular. In this way he met the wishes of some of his most enthusiastic admirers. J. E. Spingarn had noted the absence of the universal as the only serious deficiency of Croce's first *Aesthetic*. In his review of it, he concluded: "the universalizing power of art is, therefore, not fully felt, nor is it vitally connected with the highest strivings of the human mind."[1] However, Croce's reversal was not complete and unqualified. Had it been, Croce would henceforth have maintained an intellectualistic aesthetic and looked in poetry for truth and logic, which he certainly refrained from doing. Instead, he maintained from then on a position which combined univeralistic statements along with the main body of his previous doctrine. Had he hit upon a new formula which reconciled these opposites? Let us

see what the new doctrine involved and whether it was possible
to reconcile it with his earlier views.

During the years 1917–20, as we have seen, Croce turned
to the greater poets of Western literature, and engaged upon
studies of Ariosto and of Goethe, later passing on to Shakespeare, Corneille and Dante. He found in Ariosto not so much
the expression of an individual mood, as of a feeling for life as
a whole. This he was to describe as "an inclination, an affection
for, and sympathy with, Life itself, for the very life of Reality,
not as truth or as beauty or as anything else specific, but as a
simple living motion, a contemplation of life as a spectacle,
an enjoyment of Being in its perpetual contrasts and its perpetually re-established harmony" (NSE², 293–94). So the emotional content of poetry is found to involve a universal concept,
or something very like it: Life, Being, Cosmic Harmony. (Indeed, Croce's description of Ariosto has been wittily defined
by a critic as that of "a poetic Hegel." ²) This discovery was
made after Croce expanded his aesthetic theory so as to include
these universalistic feelings, which he did in the paper on "The
character of Totality." The Italian original appeared in *La
critica* of mid-1918, and an English translation appeared simultaneously in *The English Review* of June 1918. It now forms
the core of the *New Essays on Aesthetics*, first published in
1920.³

In his endeavor to connect the individual with the universal
in art, Croce found immediate support in various philosophical
doctrines which he had developed in other fields. In logic, he had
found that the particular could not be separated from the universal (*Logica*, 140–51). In ethics, he had asked himself the
question: "what is the individual?" and had answered "the individual is the historical situation of the universal at every moment of time" (*Pratica*, 154). So he now found himself in agreement with the statement made by other critics, to which he
refers at the beginning of this essay: "artistic representation,
even in its form, which is supremely individual, embraces the
Whole, and reflects the cosmos in itself" (NSE, 119). More
specifically, this means that: "every genuine artistic representa-

tion is itself and the universe, the universe in that individual form, and that individual form as the universe. In every poetic accent, in every imaginative creation, there lies all human destiny —all the hopes, the illusions, the sorrows and the joys, the greatness and the wretchedness of humanity, the entire drama of Reality, that grows and develops perpetually upon itself, suffering and enjoying. It is therefore unthinkable that artistic representation may ever affirm the mere particular, the abstract individual, the finite in its finiteness" (NSE, 126). Does this mean that art becomes the sphere of universality? Apparently it does, for Croce goes on to say: "to confer *artistic* form upon an emotional content is to confer upon it at the same time the imprint of *totality*, the cosmic afflatus; and in this sense universality and artistic form are not two but one" (NSE, 128).

German critics of the Romantic age have often predicated the totality and universality of art. But it is apparently from Wilhelm von Humboldt that Croce received the impulse for his universalistic theory. Croce refers explicitly to Humboldt's essay of 1797–98 upon Goethe's *Hermann und Dorothea* (NSE², 121), which Croce must have read for his study of Goethe. The influence which Humboldt's essay exercised upon Croce is understandable when one sees how close Humboldt's aesthetic theory was to Croce's. Humboldt has a fully developed theory of the poetic imagination: "to transform the real into an image is the most general task of all art, to which all others may be reduced more or less directly. . . . Every poetic figure (*Gestalt*) is stamped with the imprint of individuality, and this individuality consists in its form, which can only be grasped by intuition (*Anschauen*), never by a concept." The sections of the essay which Croce cites are iv–x. There we find such statements as "totality is the necessary consequence of the complete prevalence of the imagination," "absolute totality must also be the distinctive character of the Ideal, as the exact contrary of it is the distinctive character of reality," "the task of the artist is to place the reader in a central point from which rays are directed on all sides towards the infinite." [4]

Now there is more than one way in which the universality

of art could be affirmed even within the limits of Croce's earlier doctrine. The process of intuition, being an act of the Spirit, is universal. If art were not the exercise of a universal activity common to all men it could not be taken in and re-enacted by other men, as Croce argues. But this activity has for its object a particular: "the universal artistic activity, which is all contracted and concentrated in the representation of a single state of mind," said Croce in the *Breviary* (NSE, 49; EA, 57).

If not only the activity of intuition, but also its object, becomes universal, then there is a serious conflict with the previous doctrine, and it becomes impossible to distinguish any longer intuitions from ratiocinations.[5] But Croce in this paper continues to affirm categorically the distinction between intuition and ratiocination, the image and the judgment: "art is pure intuition or pure expression, not an intellectual intuition *à la* Schelling, or panlogism *à la* Hegel, not judgment as in historical thinking, but an intuition entirely devoid of concept and judgment, the initial form of knowledge, without which it is impossible to understand the ulterior and more complex forms" (NSE, 124). He then proceeds to a detailed refutation of another view, to which he does not assign an author (possibly Gentile?), that art is a *conceptual* representation, the perpetual formation of a logical judgment embodying the universal concept. Croce reaffirms that such a theory identifies art with historical knowledge, which for him consists in the characterization of a particular fact by means of a universal category (NSE, 124).

Therefore, even at this stage, the universal for Croce is not the object of artistic intuition. Can it be that universality is now predicated of the content of the work of art, of its emotional subject-matter? This content has been so far described as being individual or particular, the desires, longings, or dreams of the practical man in his particularity. But now it is asserted that man, even as a practical agent, is the actualization of a universal, the specification of the world-mind in a particular situation, so his feelings are "both individual and universal, as all forms of reality" (NSE, 127).

It may be thought that Croce is here trying to express a very

familiar idea, *"homo sum et nihil humani a me alienum puto."*
In Croce's essay on Verga we saw that Verga's supposedly
"naturalistic" world of Sicilian peasants was the expression of a
feeling of deep sympathy with the sufferings of humanity. This
feeling was born in the heart of a particular individual, Giovanni
Verga, and it assumed a markedly individual form in his writing. But his feeling is rooted in common humanity, and may be
shared by other men, who are neither Naturalists or Sicilians, nor
born in the nineteenth century. But in this paper Croce affirms
that it is the *form* which universalizes while individualizing:
"artistic form, individualizing, harmonizes individuality with universality, and by so doing universalizes" (NSE, 128). This sounds
very much like a definition of the function of the logical judgment according to Croce's earlier theory. We seem to have
reached an impasse: for Croce, art now is something like judgment, and yet it still is not judgment.[6]

This paper is certainly one of Croce's most difficult and per-
plexing statements. Critics saw their opportunity and proclaimed
that Croce here contradicted himself, or at least renounced his
previous doctrine. When the paper was first published, it was
immediately noted by Gentile as a new departure in Croce. In a
comment published in the same year, 1918, Gentile wrote:
"here we are faced by a new aspect of the Crocean doctrine
. . . a concept which comes unexpectedly to any one who has
followed the development of Crocean thought."[7] Even more
emphatically G. A. Borgese, who for a time was a follower of
Croce but later turned against him, affirmed that in this and
similar statements of Croce "the new wine has burst the old
bottles."[8] And A. Tilgher, a critic who followed a somewhat
similar evolution, spoke of Croce's "three aesthetics," separating
one from the other as different doctrines, and observing that
with the doctrine of totality "we are in any case a long way
from the conception of art as knowledge of individuals."[9]

And yet for Croce, even in this paper, art is not the cognition of universals, but something else. What this something
may be, is hinted at in the following statement: "pure intuition or artistic representation abhors whole-heartedly from ab-

straction; or rather, it does not even abhor from it, because it ignores it, just because of its naive cognitive character, which we have called auroral" (NSE, 126). The full development of this idea is to be found in a later essay on the function of the concept of individuality (1928). There Croce makes it clear that the difference between intuition and ratiocination is as follows. Logical thought is the conscious distinction and unification of universal and particular, whereas poetry is this unity grasped in an undifferentiated stage and not yet logically distinguished: "poetry is thus conceived as the indistinction of individual and universal, which is in turn mediated by thought, that is, distinguished and unified at the same time, converting the world of imagination and poetry in the world of philosophy and history" (US, 370; anticipated in TSS, 49). The change from the previous point of view is also made explicit in a statement of 1936: "the only correction introduced by me in my first Aesthetic on this side has been to clarify that what I at first considered, following Vico and De Sanctis, as the moment of individuality, was really the intuitive and poetic moment of the immediate union of the individual and the universal, which only thought opposes and mediates" (PS, III, 50).

It seems that here Croce has used once too often a logical formula which had stood him in good stead once or twice before, viz. the formula of indifference or neutrality. In Chapter II we have seen how he had defined in his first *Aesthetic* the position of the intuition in relation to the concepts of reality and possibility: intuition was "the undifferentiated unity of the perception of the real and of the simple image of the possible" (E, 6; A, 4). In the *Breviary* he had used a somewhat similar formula: "Intuition is the indistinction of real and unreal" (NSE, 16; EA, 16). In the *Pratica* he had in effect, although not in so many words, defined the feeling that becomes the content of poetry as the indistinction of action and desire (*Pratica*, 169–75). Now it becomes the indistinction of particular and universal. But in the previous formulas there was a positive category beyond the neutrality or indistinction, and this category was the particular. Now the particular itself is merged in an immediate and undifferentiated unity with the universal, and there is nothing positive to take its place as the object of the intuition. Intuition is now defined as knowledge of the "indistinction of the particular and the universal," and it is hard to see what that thing can be except a confused blur.

Therefore this final formula seems not only a departure from the earlier (which of course Croce was entitled to do, if he saw fit), but also to lack the critical value of the previous view. From that, a whole system of criticism was developed by Croce; not very much develops from the later doctrine.[10] It does of course appear in Croce's later criticism; we have seen that it is connected with his interpretation of Ariosto and of Goethe, and it also enters into other essays. For instance, there is an interesting shift in the interpretation of Don Quijote. In the *Aesthetic,* Don Quijote was simply "a type of himself" (E, 39; A, 34)—a phrase which recalls De Sanctis on Francesca da Rimini: she "is ideal, but she is not the ideal of something else; she is the ideal of herself." [11] In 1939 Don Quijote becomes a type of mankind, and represents all men in their capacity for self-delusion: "we are all the Don Quijotes of one thing or another, and deluded like him" (PAM, 251).

But substantially Croce's method in his later criticism remains the definition of the individual mood and the particular character; it remains on the whole consistent with his earlier doctrine and does not shift to his later.[12] It may therefore be affirmed that Croce employed the concept of universality in aesthetics in a manner which (whatever function that concept may have in metaphysics, or logic, or ethics) causes confusion in the sphere of aesthetics. Croce himself acknowledged shortly afterwards, in a passage which we shall quote in full, that the concept of the universal in aesthetics was "ambiguous" and liable to misunderstanding. However, we shall find that it may be interpreted in a positive way, not as a general theory of poetry but as the characterization of the emotional content of certain poems. It helped Croce to understand the motifs of Ariosto and of Goethe on one hand, and to define his attitude to contemporary literature on the other.

In the mature work of the great German poet, Croce found that "Goethe never ceases to feel emotions and to express them, but he feels and expresses also his spiritual harmony, which is the motif into which all his other partial ones merge" (G, I, 14). Croce was discovering in the work of a great poet a state of mind which resulted from the merging together of many moods into a complex whole that could be described by a critical metaphor as a "cosmic" or "universal" harmony. However in his final evaluation Croce expressed a preference, though a slight one, for the earlier work of Goethe, in which spiritual harmony was not yet achieved. It was in Ariosto's masterpiece that Croce found a perfect embodiment of the feeling for total harmony, as shown in the paper quoted at the beginning of this chapter. But in the same paper Croce clearly limited the attribution of this universal quality to the poetry of Ariosto, as its particular theme or motif. "Cosmic harmony" is thus only the content of a special "inclination or affection" of Ariosto's, an individual trait. As he put it explicitly in this essay, "that love for harmony is itself one of the many particular affections" of poets (ASC, 27). And we have already seen Croce's warning (given in the same paper from which we have been quoting) not to make out of the characteristic more than an instrument for a particular situation: "instruments are instruments, and not philosophical doctrines and judgments, and must be used only for the end to which they were fashioned" which is "to direct attention towards the particular and the individual" (NSE, 292). This paper, "The extra-aesthetic concept of the Beautiful and its use in criticism," is dated 1919, later than the essay on Totality, and represents an afterthought, which explicitly qualifies some of the more universalistic statements found in the previous essay.

Croce issued a still more definite warning in 1922 in a paper added to the second edition of the *New Essays* (1926), viz. "A Return to Old Thoughts." This paper reasserts the condemnation of writing that is mere effusion of emotion. Against this kind of writing, Croce says that poetry has been rightly affirmed to be something which possesses "ideality, serenity, harmony, totality, universality, infinitude." "But," he adds, "one must not let the recognition of these characteristics of art, rightly asserted by means of terms that may be ambiguous (universal, ideal, harmony, etc.), lead us deviously back into the abandoned theory of poetry as philosophy" (NSE², 306–7). With this, Croce admitted that the term "universal" as applied to poetry was ambiguous and could lead to misunderstanding, and endeavored to avoid it by rejecting once again the intellectualistic solution.

The condemnation of raw emotionalism was the other application to practical criticism that was evidently in the mind of Croce when he wrote the essay on Totality. It was directed especially against the particular variety of emotional romanticism which characterizes so much writing of the nineteenth and twentieth centuries. This may be considered another step in that turning away from the contemporary which was to become more evident in later years, and to which we will later devote a chapter. As Croce put it in the essay on Totality: "modern literature, that is the literature of the past one hundred and fifty years, is assuming more and more the general air of a great confession, and its fountainhead is precisely the book of *Confessions* by the Genevan philosopher. This often-noted character of a confession designates the frequency in it of personal motives, of particular, practical, autobiographical motives, of what I have called 'effusion' [*sfogo*] distinguishing it from 'expression,' and exhibits a correlative weakness in its relation to integral truth, and therefore weakness in, or absence of, what is usually known as *style*" (NSE, 133–34).

According to Croce, another sign of weakness in modern writing is the large number of women that participate in it. If this judgment seems ungallant, or in conflict with modern feeling on the equality of the sexes, let us compare it with the description of a group of women writers at the beginning of the century (i.e. when Croce began his study of modern literature) by an urbane and gallant historian of modern French letters, Henri Clouard: "Une chevauchée d'amazones, qui firent penser à des centauresses, a débouché soudain derrière le cap séculaire, déchaînant un grand souffle d'audace, de sensuelle avidité, de perversité pathétique, de verbe surabondant. . . . Les puissances de sentir ayant été rassemblées, aiguisées, dopées par le Romanticisme d'abord, puis par un certain Symbolisme . . . un groupe de femmes bien douées, qui en d'autres temps se fussent diverties aux aventures de voyage, du monde, de l'intrigue, se sont jetées dans une expédition poétique où le moment littéraire leur promettait le maximum de satisfaction, de joie, d'orgueil et de triomphe. Quels poètes pouvaient donc mieux qu'elles courir leur chance de bacchanale, de fureur panique et de déchaînement individuel?" [13]

Croce used the same metaphor of Maenad rites: "Women hold Bacchantic revels in modern literature because men themselves have become aesthetically somewhat effeminate; and a sign of this effeminacy is the lack of shame with which men exhibit all their miseries and weaknesses, and that frenzy for sincerity (which as a frenzy is insincere, but a more or less clever simulation), which endeavors to gain credit for itself by means of cynicism, according to the example that was first given by Rousseau. And as the sick, the seriously ill, often resort to remedies which instead of alleviating their sickness only aggravate it, so there have been during the whole of the nineteenth century and in our own day numerous attempts to effect a restoration of form and style, the impassivity, the dignity, the serenity of art and of pure beauty: these things, sought for their own sake, provided fresh evidence of the deficiency that was felt but which was not therefore made good" (NSE, 134).

The last sentence should show clearly that Croce, although like Babbitt denouncing Rousseau as the fountainhead of emotionalism, did not fall into the camp of doctrinaire neoclassicism. Nor did he fall then into moralism, for he compared moralistic art with pornography, to detriment of the former: "obscenity in art, which is the object of scandal among Puritans, is only one instance of immorality in art, nor is it necessarily the worst, for the foolish exhibition of virtue, which makes virtue herself look foolish, seems to me almost worse" (NSE, 131–32). The particular type of bad writing which according to Croce predominated in his own age—an age of late romanticism or *bas-*

romantisme—was characterized by emotion overpowering form and using it as instrument for its gratification. The emotion is not then crystallized in a poetic image, but previously existing images are broken up and distorted to gratify the emotion, and aesthetic contemplation is replaced by a very practical form of action (NSE², 304–6; cf. NSE, 67; EA, 78).

So far Croce's stand on emotionalism is in keeping with his previous aesthetic doctrine. But as Croce extended his exploration of the literature of the immediate past, and as the pressures of the postwar conflicts in Western Europe began to mount, Croce stiffened into an attitude which comes very close to moralism. He reached the conclusion that poetry is grounded in the moral conscience. This is how he argued it in the *Aesthetica in nuce* (1928): "The foundation of all poetry is the moral personality, and since human personality finds its completion in morality, the moral conscience is the foundation of all poetry" (US, 10).[14] By this Croce means that the possession of a moral personality is a condition *sine qua non* for art; in 1932 he said in so many words: "poetry is not possible without a moral personality in the artist" (CC, V, 84–85). In the *Aesthetica in nuce* he acknowledged that morality alone is not sufficient to create art (US, 11), but he came to believe that the lack of a moral personality was sufficient to prevent a man from being a poet. In the revised estimate of D'Annunzio made in the middle thirties, Croce found him deficient in poetry *because* he was deficient in "humanity" (LNI, VI, 259–63). In the essay on Renaissance comedy referred to in Chapter V above, Grazzini was judged an inferior poet because he was deficient "in intellectual and moral depth" (PPPA, 270–71). And there are other instances in his later criticism which will be surveyed in Chapter XII.

This is at complete variance with Croce's earlier proposition which maintained that there is no possible transition from the quality of the content to the quality of form (E, 19; A, 16). From that it follows that nothing can be inferred as to the aesthetic quality of the form from the moral quality of the content (if the content can be so qualified). Indeed, as we have seen in Chapter III, morality was explicitly excluded as a requirement for poetry in the first theoretical formulation of the doctrine of lyricism, the Heidelberg lecture: "a personality of any kind, *the strictly moral being in this case excluded:* a soul, cheerful or sad, enthusiastic or melancholy, sentimental or sarcastic, *benevolent or malevolent:* but a soul" (italics supplied; *PdE*, 18; A¹, 389).

In his earlier criticism Croce often recognized the fact that a healthy aesthetic form may express what he described as a morbid content, and indeed such could happen to writers even of the highest rank. In *Poetry and non-poetry*, as we have seen in the preceding chapter, this was seen to be the case with writers that Croce ranked very high, such as Flaubert and Baudelaire, to whom he added also Leopardi. He then described this case as "art dominating sensual morbidity by means of purity of form" (PNP, 267). But in 1922 he seemed to extol Carducci's poetry for the sanity of its emotional content—as being superior to poetry which possessed a morbid content, like Leopardi's, even though the latter was sublimated by the beauty of its form into "universal humanity" (PNP, 325). In 1943, analyzing what he considered the intellectual and moral weaknesses of Rilke, Croce could still deny that these weaknesses prevented him from being a poet (*Letture*, 201-2). But in 1950 he maintained that the unity of form and content in poetry implied that the poet had to possess a "moral soul," without which it was impossible to write poetry, "since a soul that is fragmentary, unbalanced, disjointed, inhuman, that is to say nonexistent as a soul, cannot rise to the creation of beauty" (*Letture*, 265).

How was it that Croce, who in his earlier years as a critic had battled so long and so valiantly for the independence of art from morality (compare the 1885 polemic in PS, I, 452–61 and the 1905 polemic in CC, I, 34–39), came to modify his views so profoundly? Two reasons, one connected with the history of philosophical thought and the other with the history of political action, may be suggested. First, the philosophical reason. One of the oldest and strongest traditions in philosophy is the stress laid on universality. Plato maintained that knowledge dealt only with universals, the eternal archetypes, such as the Ideas of the

Good and of the True and of the Beautiful; particulars could not
be the object of knowledge because they were in a state of perpetual flux. Aristotle, on the other hand, believed in the primary
reality of individuals, but he agreed with Plato that knowledge
dealt only with universals and that there could be no knowledge
of particulars. So it appears that he was led into the dilemma
of believing that what was real (the individual) could not be
known, while what was known (the universal) was not substantially real. This logical dilemma remained to plague philosophical thought for centuries afterwards. The problem of universals was variously debated by the great schools of medieval
philosophy, nominalists and realists. Modern empiricism in the
seventeenth century solved the problem like the nominalists,
denying the universal and affirming that the particular known
through sensation was the only source of knowledge. The universal regained ground in the philosophies of the rationalistic
school, and was eventually raised again by Hegel to the rank of
the supreme form of knowledge and reality.

But in Vico Croce had found the theory that there are two
forms of knowledge, one of the universal and one of the
particular, and that both are concrete and legitimate, each in
its own sphere. This solved the age-long antithesis between the
universal and the particular by acknowledging the existence of
both, and as such was incorporated by Croce into his own
system of philosophy. But it also inevitably raises other problems, in struggling with which Croce came more and more to
lean toward the universalistic side. This appears most clearly in
the paper on "The Concept of Individuality in the History of
Philosophy" of 1928 (US, 368–72), from which we have quoted
the formula of poetry as "the indistinction of the universal and
the particular." Now, in Croce's system, ethical action is defined
as action directed toward the universal. Accordingly, a universalistic aesthetic turns logically into moralism. This connection Croce made explicitly in 1949.[15]

The other reason that impelled Croce gradually toward a
moralistic aesthetic has been already hinted at in the phrase "the
pressure of post-war conflicts." The breaking up of the liberal

community of Western European nations in the war of 1914, the depression of human values that followed that war, the rise of totalitarianism, the suppression of political freedom in Croce's own country, combined with the cynicism and opportunism of many men of letters, made him feel the paramount importance of rationality and ideality. This in turn led him to emphasize the morality of the poetic content. Such a revulsion is not unprecedented: "Great is the struggle between good and evil, greater than you think: nothing, not even poetry itself, is worthy to make us careless of justice and the other virtues" (*Republic*, 608 B). The thoughts of Plato seem to have risen again in the mind of Croce as he witnessed the triumph of Fascism in Italy and Germany and saw the culture of liberal Europe, indeed the principles of humanity itself, stamped underfoot in the "racist delirium." Decadentism, with its stress upon the irrational and amoral tendencies of human nature, seemed to Croce the natural ally of totalitarianism (*Discorsi*, II, 85). It was at least its forerunner, the "softener-up" for it. (To decadentism we shall return in Chapter XIV.) In opposition to irrationalism and decadentism, Croce asserted more and more vigorously the supreme values: the Good, the True and the Beautiful, to which he added the Useful. Originally conceived as the categories of mind and forms of universal activity, they became to him as "eternal and immutable" as the Platonic archetypes. In this Platonizing trend, the Beautiful once again became identified with the Good.

Through this doctrine of the ethical or universal character of art, Croce came to limit the content of art to a very special kind of emotion: the cosmic emotion, or feeling for totality.[16] This turned Croce's aesthetic into a content-theory, or to use the term that Croce himself used, and probably introduced, "*contenutistica*." [17] Once started on this road, it was inevitable that the definition of the content should be subjected to further clarifications, and indeed Croce in his later work proceeded to make alterations in this definition. Two of these seem to be minor variations on the theme of universality and consequently of secondary interest.[18] There is also a third definition, toward which

Croce was obviously working his way but which was only formulated after his death by his disciple, A. Parente: poetic emotion is not a single emotion, but the concurrence of several opposite emotions, each qualifying the other, and all together forming a cosmic whole.[19] There are approximations to this view in Romantic aesthetics, especially Coleridge's definition of the Imagination as the unity of opposites.[20]

It would seem that Croce presented a better explanation of the intellectual and ethical elements in art in a paper of 1904 on the questions of dramatic criticism. One of these questions was that of "problem plays" or *pièces à thèse*, then being hotly debated. Since poetry may take up any topic for its subject-matter, provided it is lyrically inspired, it may also take up ideas and moral judgments, provided they become "lyrical motifs" (*PdE*, 118). Here one should note the distinction between the subject-matter and the content of poetry; according to Croce the subject-matter consists of the cultural elements from which the poet has derived this or that particular of his image and which are absorbed and transformed in it, while the content is the state of mind or the emotion which is expressed by the total image (cf. ASC, 30–31; *Discorsi*, II, 69). Ideas and concepts, moral and political judgments have already lost their original form when they are swept on the current of a powerful emotion, and this in turn is subject to a still greater transformation when it becomes the object of artistic contemplation or the content of a poetic image. As we have seen in the passage from *Pratica*, 181–82, cited in Chapter III, the emotion becomes an indefinite tendency, a vibration of the soul without conative urges, a "state of mind" or lyrical mood.

To sum up the discussion of this issue, it would seem that the "character of Totality" can be asserted within the framework of Croce's earlier doctrines only with the following qualifications: 1) universality is predicated of the act of intuition, but not of its object, which is individual and particular; 2) to affirm that the individual is inseparable from the universal, is true of the individual *as known by reflective thought*, but not of the individual as known by the intuition, which is the individual as such; 3) certain poets come to express moods which are a merging or harmony of many separate moods or emotions: this harmony may be metaphorically called "universal," "total," or "cosmic," but it remains in the last analysis the particular "inclination or affection" of an individual poet. To say, as Croce did in his later statements, that in art the universal is "indistinctly" united with the particular is to substitute a purely negative statement for what was previously a positive theory of art and of criticism. Finally, the requirement of morality as an indispensable condition for artistic creation is a complete deviation from earlier theory, which affirmed that morality can enter art only by becoming an emotion absorbed into poetry as part of its lyrical content.

CHAPTER Xii

Croce's Later Criticism

THE MOST IMPORTANT critical studies of Croce's maturity are those on the great poets: Dante, Ariosto, Shakespeare, Corneille and Goethe. We have already seen the connection between the aesthetic of totality and the studies of Ariosto and Goethe. The study of Dante came shortly afterwards but will be considered first since it is the study least affected by the doctrine of totality. Croce here speaks only of his "concept of art as lyricism or lyrical intuition," without mentioning the cosmic intuition. He finds in Dante the expression of "a feeling for the world, grounded on a firm faith and sure judgment, and animated by a strong will"; [1] in other words an individual feeling which is still further particularized in the description that follows. Indeed all of these critical studies tend to particularize even when they pay homage to the cosmic theory, and none of them falls back into the reduction of poetry to general concepts or the fallacy of intellectualism.

This is especially notable in the case of Dante, upon whom the intellectualist tradition has lain heavily. However, Italian criticism since the Renaissance has tended more and more to study what is purely poetical in the work of Dante.[2] This tendency is manifest in Vico, who saw in Dante a second Homer—i.e. the poet of a new barbaric age whose leading traits were strong passion and powerful imagination rather than speculative or analytical thought. Vico went to the length of deploring Dante's acceptance of scholastic theology as contrary to the poet's native genius. In the nineteenth century, aesthetic criticism rejected allegory as frigid and unpoetic and directed attention to Dante's dramatic power and his creation of great characters. This was the main theme of De Sanctis' criticism of Dante. He excluded allegory from poetry as an impossible attempt to unite images with concepts and philosophy with poetry, and he established a fundamental distinction between Dante's intentions, didactic and pragmatic as they were, and the poetry he actually produced. Dante's "intentional world" was undoubtedly theological and political, but his "actual world" was purely imaginative and poetic, culminating in great figures like Francesca and Farinata, Ulysses and Ugolino. De Sanctis gave a detailed critical analysis of this "actual world" of the *Comedy* in his essays and in his history.

But after De Sanctis, as we have seen, the historical school prevailed, and attention was turned to the problems of biography, chronology and philology, and to the connections with contemporary intellectual and political trends. Needless to say, and as De Sanctis was the first to acknowledge, the historical school accomplished many essential tasks and opened up several avenues of important research. But in Italy it also led indirectly to the growth of a form of scholarly deviation, which degraded the otherwise honorable name of *Dantista*. The degenerate *Dantista* devoted himself wholly to solving the enigmas which may still be found in the *Comedy*, and which are really not many or vital. To begin with, he attached himself to the allegorical interpretation, not only in its general outline but also in every detail of the poem, particularly those symbols of which no satisfactory explanation has ever been found: such as the prophetic hound that appears in the first canto of the poem, the mysterious number Five Hundred and Ten and Five which occurs in the last canto of Purgatory, and some others.

The other favorite topic of the *Dantista* is what has been called the "moral geography" of the poem, the distribution of the souls in the various sections of the other world according to their sins or their virtues, and the implicit system of arrangement of which Dante occasionally gives some explicit account. But this account is never complete to the last detail, and almost every section presents problems in this area. There are also problems connected with the physical topography of the other world as Dante imagined but never completely defined it. What Dante did not say the *Dantisti* rushed in to expound. But it has become clear by now that it is practically impossible to build up a completely consistent system (using Dante's own partial statements and piecing them out with bits of medieval lore) that will account for every particular of the structure of Hell, Purgatory and Paradise as Dante imagined them, just as it is impossible to devise an allegorical interpretation that fits every single thing in the poem.

But the degenerate *Dantisti* seemed to delight in impossibilities and resorted to ever more subtle, sophistical and extravagant conjectures. It is one of the beneficial effects of Croce's teaching that this type of *Dantista*—the "noiosissimi Dantisti del tempo nostro" (LNI, IV, 251)—has now disappeared from the scene of Italian culture (*Discorsi*, II, 44 and *Letture*, 3–7) and that the study of Dante is now generally directed into more useful channels, both critical and philological. Serious Dante scholarship was of course aware of the insolubility of the riddles upon which the *Dantista* thrived, and abandoned them for positive research into textual and historical problems. But Croce's vigorous championship of the aesthetic approach in matters of poetry and his relentless attacks on the perversions of historical scholarship contributed to deprive the *Dantisti* of their main claim to public notice: viz. that they were "revealing" the "secrets" of Dante.

In his study Croce furthermore challenged the opinion that Dante's poetry requires a different approach and must be judged by a different standard from all other poetry because of its theological, philosophical, and political references. According to Croce all poets possess some such references to a greater or a smaller degree. Admittedly in Dante the doctrinal element assumes larger proportions, and it can well be studied for its own sake. This is done by relating it to the appropriate branches of intellectual and social history, even though according to

Croce its originality and importance are not as great as some-times claimed (D, 14–15).[3] For this area of Dante interpreta-tion, concerned as it is with matters other than poetry, Croce suggested a name: he called it "allotria" or heterogeneous (D, 10; cf. Wellek and Warren's [4] "extrinsic approach").

As for the aesthetic interpretation of Dante, Croce claimed that it had equal rights with the historical or extrinsic, being itself an historical interpretation. Croce here refers to the prin-ciple that we have seen in Chapter ix, that all aesthetic judg-ments are essentially historical. It is therefore absurd to charge Croce with brushing aside, or even depreciating, the historical interpretation in favor of the aesthetic. Both are legitimate in their own sphere, but like water and oil they do not mix. What Croce denies is that the extrinsic interpretation of the *Comedy* is the "condition and foundation" of the aesthetic interpretation (D, 16). Of course historical information is necessary for the understanding of the text, but Croce would limit this information to the pure *explanatio verborum,* "the explanation of the mean-ing of words, broadly understood." "Philosophical propositions, names of persons, references to historical events, moral and po-litical judgments, etc. are, in poetry, nothing more than words, substantially identical with other words, and are to be interpreted within that limitation" (D, 23–24; DE, 24). Accordingly, in *La poesia* we find Croce quoting a number of passages of the *Comedy* to the understanding of which the explanation of words, historically conducted, provides indispensable help (P, 258–59).

In a later paper Croce gave an instance of "the wrong way of handling the historical interpretation" (*Discorsi*, II, 45–47). A German scholar who made a study of Dante's astronomy observed that "between ourselves and Dante there intercedes a spiritual revolution that shook Christianity to its foundations: the collapse of the Ptolemaic universe." Croce replies that this is irrelevant and even misleading: "the essential point is ob-scured that to understand Dante's poetry we must rely, not on his astronomy, but on his poetry. Reference to medieval astronomy is useful only to save us from getting entangled in difficulties which are extrinsic to poetry." As an instance Croce quotes the beginning of Canto xx of *Paradise*. In Longfellow's translation:

> When he who all the world illuminates
> Out of our hemisphere so far descends
> That on all sides the daylight is consumed,
>
> The heaven, that erst by him alone was kindled,
> Doth suddenly reveal himself again
> By many lights, wherein is one resplendent.

"It is useful," notes Croce, "to know that the notion implied in these lines—the sun that illuminates everything, even the fixed stars,—though differing from the science that we learnt at school, was not a personal shortcoming or an eccentricity of Dante, but a doctrine of medieval astronomy. If we did not know or learn that, we might remain perplexed, and wonder about the strangeness of that statement, and might never go beyond it into the realm of poetry." Then Croce himself "crosses the threshold of poetry": "in those lines the sun is not the medieval sun or the modern one, but 'He', a sublime being or power, mighty and beneficent, that lights up the whole world. When He descends to the other hemisphere, leaving our side in darkness, He is at the same time careful to provide us with other light, and the sky by him abandoned 'doth suddenly reveal itself again' and shine with the many stars in which the sun infuses his light. This is a poetic drama, and like all poetic dramas, even those involving natural beings ('a landscape is a state of mind'), it is a human drama, of parting and regret and then again comfort and happiness."

So we see that in Croce's aesthetic criticism everything is referred to the work of the imagination, and all historical material is considered the vehicle for the poet's lyrical expression. Some critics reject this interpretation on the grounds that it does not agree with medieval poetics and in particular with Dante's own views on poetry. But this is a fact of which Croce was well aware, as was De Sanctis before him. "To say, as is often said and as I read again in an American book,[5] that Dante would burn with indignation against his greatest admirers and critics of today, such as De Sanctis and Symonds, who are attracted only by the sensuous and poetic beauty of his work, is not so much an argument against criticism as in its favor, showing that since the days of Dante criticism has gone a long way." In a word, "Dante's poetry is to be interpreted not according to Dante but according to truth" (D, 28; DE, 32–33).

Croce carries the rejection of intellectualism to the point that he denies that the poetic subject of the *Comedy* is, as commonly formulated, a picture of the other world. The substance of this picture, with its attendant cosmography and chronology, its division into three realms and its subdivision of each according to ethical and theological concepts, is a contrivance or construction of the fancy in the service of certain ideas and dogmas, or as Croce calls it "a theological romance" (D, 60; DE, 84). This contrivance or artifact, which has given rise to such a mass of commentary and interpretation, is an intellectual structure completely extraneous to the essence of poetry, but necessary to reconcile Dante's rigid conscience to the exercise of the poetic faculty. So Dante's poetry wells up all round and all over this structure without ever identifying itself with it, but pouring itself out freely in the various episodes of the poem. Every episode is thus "a lyric by itself" (D, 64; DE, 92), and the *Comedy* is a collection of such lyrics, arranged by their author in three separate volumes "according to their affinity" (D, 71, in a passage omitted by the translator).[6]

This conclusion provoked a chorus of shocked amazement and outright indignation from the *Dantisti*. Croce appeared to deny the poetic unity of the *Comedy*, and if there is a poem which impresses the reader with its solid unity it is the *Comedy*. A long and lively discussion then followed among critics and scholars (such as K. Vossler, M. Barbi, L. Russo, U. Cosmo, V. Arangio-Ruiz, M. Rossi, etc.), which it is not possible to summarize here.[7] For the present purpose it may suffice to note that Croce's position was that the two elements, "structure and poetry, theological romance and lyricism, cannot be separated in the work of Dante, just as one cannot separate the parts of the soul of Dante, of which one is conditioned by the other and therefore flows into the other; and in this dialectical sense the *Comedy* is certainly a unity." [8] In other words, the two constituents are to be found in varying proportions at every point of the poem, which therefore cannot be broken up into poetic and unpoetic sections. So Croce has never proposed to split the *Comedy* into an anthology of "beauties" or poetic fragments (cf. D, 68; DE, 97). His own discussion of the poem proceeds by taking up each *cantica* in succession and going right through it from beginning to end, in regular order (see Chapters IV–VI of the book on Dante). Furthermore, when Croce speaks of the *Comedy* as a "collection of lyrics" it should be remembered that for him a collection of lyrics may present a compact aesthetic unity and be treated by the critic as a single act of expression, as Croce has done more than once in his own criticism. Nor can there be any doubt as to Croce's admiration and love for the poem. It is shown in his happy interpretations of many episodes and passages (including some that had not been so fully appreciated before him). Among other things, Croce revaluates the *Paradiso*, rejecting the Romantic glorification of the *Inferno* as the only poetic section of the poem (D, 146; DE, 216).[9]

Croce found poetry even in Dante's theological passages: "The poetry of Dante, when it can do nothing else, vivifies the argumentative and informative and technical parts of the narrative, even the not infrequently labored conceits of the erudite historian, and invests all with its own accent, emotional and sublime" (D, 67; DE, 96). And this is not because, as De Sanctis argued, the theology of the *Paradiso* is itself poetic: "if the doctrinal sections of the *Comedy* possess poetic afflatus, as they almost always do, they cannot originate from a matter that is poetic itself, as we have shown above, nor can they be restricted to decorative insertions of poetic images into intellectual disquisitions which, if they are intellectual, will remain such; but they must originate from a living emotion" (*Discorsi*, II, 50).

Hence we may consider Croce's argument on the theological structure of the poem as a *reductio ad absurdum* of the intellectualist interpretation of Dante. If the unity of the *Comedy* is to be found in its intellectual structure, then Croce argues that the *Comedy* has no *poetic* unity. But if we believe that the *Comedy* does possess poetic unity, then we must look for it elsewhere than in the intellectual structure. Some critics are still reluctant to follow this argument, not realizing that to seek the poetic unity of the *Comedy* in its theological framework is to commit oneself to the aesthetics of intellectualism. This of course leads to the impossible position that the poetic quality of a poem depends upon the ideas or concepts that may be found in it—which would make the *Metaphysics* of Aristotle a great poem, and the *Iliad* a very poor one. Now the poetic quality of the *Comedy* cannot depend on those things which it may have in common with the *Metaphysics* (viz. concepts or general ideas, which furthermore are never presented pure in poetry), but must depend on those which it has in common with the *Iliad* (viz. characters, situations, descriptions, or more simply images). This assumption is not so different from the attitude of Dante himself, who ranged himself in the company of Homer and the other poets, and not in that of Aristotle and the philosophers (*Inferno*, canto IV).

If we declare that a great poem must possess metrical form and rhetorical ornaments superimposed on doctrinal content and allegorical fiction, then why is the *Quadriregio* of Federigo Frezzi not a great poem? For this obscure composition, known only to medievalists, possesses all these features. Yet it is Dante who is the great poet, and not Frezzi—nor Francesco Stabili, nor Fazio degli Uberti who are authors of somewhat similar didactic poems. Why not? The answer is clear: Dante possessed a poetic imagination and Frezzi did not. Dante created vivid pictures in which concreteness of texture is united with the expression of lyrical emotion. The critic of Dante should therefore direct his attention to the lyrical and imaginative values of the poem, and not to the theological structure and other intellectual elements, save as materials which are absorbed and transcended. The setting up of a classification of sins or of virtues is an act of the generalizing intellect; the assignment of individual cases to the classes thus set up is an act of the classifying intellect; only the creation of an individual character or situation is poetic, and it is the creation of such characters and situations that makes Dante a poet. In this creation concepts lose their general meaning and become details of an individual picture, vehicles for the expression of Dante's individual emotions. Croce's argument therefore seems to lead the way toward a view that asserts firmly the poetic unity of the *Comedy*, but seeks it in a lyrical motif and not in a theological romance. The poem will then appear not, as in Croce's more paradoxical statements, a collection of lyrics, but as a single lyric, as Leopardi saw it (D, 187; DE, 278)—a single, continuous lyric, modulated in a wide variety of tones and with several levels of intensity, continually transcending an intellectual element which only occasionally clogs it.

As for the allegory, according to Croce it is even more alien to poetry than the intellectual structure. Croce however differs from his Romantic predecessors in his definition of allegory. For Croce, allegory is essentially a kind of cryptography or writing in code. By an act that is purely arbitrary, and therefore belongs to the sphere of the practical will and not that of the imagination, a writer decides that a certain sign shall stand for a certain thing with which it is not usually connected. For instance, Dante himself says in the *Convivio:* I will make the word "heaven" stand for science and "eyes" for demonstrations, and so forth (D, 13; DE, 6). In this manner a cipher may be constructed which will be completely unintelligible unless the writer himself provides the key. When Dante omits to do this, it is hopeless to attempt the recovery of his hidden meaning.

A writer who deliberately plans an allegory is thus making a purely practical decision. To claim that a poem must be judged in conformity with the intentions of its author is a form of the intentional fallacy, which Croce has always rejected. Suppose such an allegorical scheme has been set up, as is admittedly the case with some parts of the *Comedy*. If the writer happens to be a poet, when he passes from his abstract intention to actual composition his imagination will take over and produce concrete images, not abstractions. These images will then develop according to their own law, which is intuitive and not logical, and turn into rich and complex poetic patterns which have little or nothing to do with the original scheme. In this way Dante's characters emerge out of his intentional Hell in all the heroic grandeur of the passions with which his imagination has endowed them, regardless of the eternal infamy to which the framework of the poem condemns them, or of the concealed meaning which they may have been intended to convey. In like manner Beatrice, poetically considered, is "simply a woman once loved and now happy and glorious, and yet benevolent and helpful to her former lover." Poetically, Matelda in Purgatory is just "a young woman who goes gathering flowers in a grove in the cool of the morning, something like a nymph or a fairy of the spring" (D, 22; DE, 21–22). Cato in Purgatory is substantially a creature of Dante's imagination, incorporating some details from Dante's not too exact recollections of ancient history (D, 18; DE, 15). In cases like these the allegory is set aside and poetry achieves a victory over intellectual abstractions. But what happens if in spite of everything the allegorical intention persists even during composition? Then it can only interrupt the poetic process, and distort or mutilate the images upon which it was working. This can happen occasionally even to Dante, though usually with him things go the other way round, and poetry is achieved in spite of the allegorical intention (D, 22–23; DE, 21–22).

In sum, either there is an allegory, and then there is no poetry; or there is poetry, and then there is no allegory. One can never have them both together "Because of the contradiction that does not consent it," to use a line of Dante (*Inferno*, 27, 120).[10] This conclusion goes against a tendency of some contemporary critics to consider allegory as a "mode of expression" or "poetic medium" or "convention," according to various formulations of what is essentially a rhetorical concept, belonging to the doctrine of "technique" which we have discussed in Chapter IV. One ingenious attempt in this direction was made (apparently in complete ignorance of the critical tradition of Vico and De Sanctis) by T. S. Eliot, who argued in his essay on Dante that allegory helps poetry because it tends to produce "clear visual images." [11] There are of course many such images in Dante, but whether they are due to allegory is another matter. Can a poet see something concrete just when he is trying to conceive something abstract? As Croce observed, "it is impossible to see together two things, one of which appears only when the other disappears" (D, 21; DE, 20).

Since Croce's essay, allegory was defended in Italy by some traditionalist scholars like L. Pietrobono, but also by some critics who accepted Croce's main theses. Among the latter there is F. Flora in his *History of Italian literature* (1940). Flora accepts Croce's definition of allegory as essentially a code, a practical device, but finds in Dante some allegorical passages which nevertheless are poetic. This happens because their function is to convey an emotion—specifically, a feeling of religious awe. In other words, because they are lyrical (in Croce's meaning) rather than allegorical. Beyond the sensuous representation of the allegorical mystery "there is nothing to be sought, because in it the poet has said all that he wished to convey." [12]

Croce worked out the critical principles, here formulated in general terms, in a detailed analysis of the whole *Comedy*, canticle by canticle. A still more detailed commentary to the poem has been supplied by Attilio Momigliano (1947), on aesthetic principles which obviously owe much to Croce. Indeed such a close reading as Momigliano's has not yet been attempted in English for any great poem. There is nothing like it for Shakespeare or for Milton. In 1948 Croce could look back with satisfaction on the effects of his Dante criticism during the succeeding quarter of a century, even though his distinction of poetry and structure was not universally accepted (*Letture,* 7).

THE POEM OF ARIOSTO no longer enjoys such an international reputation as it did in the age of the Renaissance. But in its own country it still remains firmly established as a classic, one of the great poems of Italian literature. The reasons for this admiration are of course no longer those advanced by critics of the Renaissance, working with the ideas of the period. In the nineteenth century the rise of modern critical theory and literary history provided fresh points of view, new problems and new formulations. German critics and thinkers like Hegel gave Ariosto a philosophical interpretation and a broader setting in their systems of aesthetics. But the most important critical interpretation was that of De Sanctis. He saw the poem as a perfect embodiment of the Renaissance cult of formal beauty, an artistic masterpiece with no other inspiration save the intense love for aesthetic form itself. De Sanctis saw the Italian Renaissance as an age in which all the religious and patriotic ideals that inspired the Middle Ages were dead, and the only ideal that obtained universal allegiance was that of art, of formal beauty. Ariosto was for him the supreme artist of Renaissance literature. Ariosto's plastic imagination was exercised upon the material of the chivalrous epic without much sympathy either for chivalry or for epic ideals, merely for the sake of the free play of the imagination. Hence Ariosto's detachment from his subject, and his frequent ironization of it. Hence also the limitations of his work: he was a great artist, but not a great poet—a great poet, like Dante, being one who unites perfection of form to richness of content, and gives imaginative shape to broadly human emotions. This interpretation is both historical and aesthetic: it places Ariosto in his age and also provides a formula for the aesthetic analysis which De Sanctis performed in his *History*.

Croce took up the discussion from this point. He did not find De Sanctis' formula satisfactory. He showed that there is instead a rich and varied emotional content in the poem: not only humor but also pathos, a feeling for the tragic side of life, and even for the epic qualities of loyalty and self-sacrifice, for generosity and constancy. There are some moving tragic episodes, tales of star-crossed lovers, as well as stories of gay and sensuous passion. Love is the most frequent theme, but Ariosto never allows any single emotion to become predominant: he brings it up to a certain point of intensity, and then effects a quick change of subject, involving a different emotion. The poetic theme of the *Orlando* is therefore for Croce not a single emotion or passion—not even that for pure art, as De Sanctis thought—but a passing from one to the other in order to produce an artistic effect which can only be described by the word "harmony." Ariosto is the poet of harmony: the harmony of all human passions and emotions, felt with a depth and an intensity which make it universal or "cosmic." Here, as we have seen in Chapter XI, Croce finds an example of the "cosmic intuition" of which he was then formulating the theory. Therefore Ariosto becomes for him one of the great cosmic poets, along with Shakespeare and Goethe.

It may be perhaps difficult for critics outside the Italian tradition to accept such a high estimate of Ariosto. For outside Italy his reputation has been steadily dwindling since the Renaissance. His finer artistic effects are so inseparably bound to his language and rhythm that they can only be appreciated in the original. Furthermore, he wrote a long poem in an epic tradition now dead. Modern people do not have the time or patience to read an epic in 46 cantos. It is therefore difficult to do justice to Croce's finely shaded and detailed discussion, to the manner in which he works out and adjusts his formula so as to account for the principal aspects of Ariosto's poem, the characters, the episodes, the similes, the tone, the metre, and so forth. However, to give a specimen of Croce's discussion, I will quote one critical remark, the interpretation of a single stanza, which shows Croce at work on a very particular point.

Croce praises eloquently the metre of the poem. Ariosto's stanza, the *ottava rima*, is judged "a marvel, a thing that seems to live a life of its own," "a manifestation of a life that is both unfettered and harmonious, energetic and balanced, pulsating in its richly-blooded veins and lulled by this unceasing pulsation" (ASC, 46). Croce then quotes the stanza (x, 18) describing how "Olympia, after many vicissitudes, including a long and stormy sea voyage, lands with her lover in a wild and desert island." The quality that Croce finds in this stanza can be seen best, or only, in the original; but for the benefit of the English-speaking reader a rough translation will be given first. It is based upon Rose's, but rhymes have been sacrificed in an attempt to get closer to the swing of the original:

> The travail of sea-voyage and the fear
> That had for some days long kept her awake;
> The knowledge that she is now safe ashore
> Removed from noise, and sheltered by the glade,
> And that no further thought, no further care,
> Since she is with her lover, now can hurt;
> Were reasons that Olympia slept more sound
> Than bear or dormouse sunk in sleep profound.

Here is the original:

> Il travaglio del mare e la paura
> che tenuta alcun dì l'aveano desta;
> il ritrovarsi al lito ora sicura,
> lontana da rumor, ne la foresta,
> e che nessun pensier, nessuna cura,
> poi che 'l suo amante ha seco, la molesta;
> fur cagion ch'ebbe Olympia sì gran sonno,
> che gli orsi e i ghiri aver maggior nol ponno.

And here is Croce's comment: "There is here a complete analysis of the reasons for the deep slumber into which Olympia falls, all precisely observed; but all this clearly subordinated to the inward feeling expressed by the *ottava*, which seems to take pleasure in itself, and indeed takes pleasure in the resolution of a motion, of a becoming, which reaches completion" (ASC, 47). No analysis of "structural function," of "viewpoint of the narrator," of "epic technique," of "episodic value," but a definition of the inner movement of the stanza as a poetic image that develops from a certain point and finds completion in another. Croce extends this method to a number of stanzas and episodes, finding in all of them the expression of this fundamental mood of harmony, the harmony of all human passions and emotions seen as parts of a cosmic whole.

Croce's study gave a new impetus to Ariosto criticism in Italy. While scholarly work continued on the historical and philological levels, several critics took up Croce's formula and introduced variations or corrections in it, at the same time engaging in a more complete analysis of the text. Ariosto criticism is today richer by a number of books, like A. Momigliano's

(1928), based on an aesthetic method of interpretation that owes much to Croce while differing from him in their particular conclusions. There is a full and complex discussion of all these interpretations in a continuing series of monographs and papers. The subject is too large to be taken up here, but the reader is referred to recent accounts of Ariosto criticism, of which there is more than one.[13] These accounts also follow a Crocean precedent, for Croce in 1910 had given an outline history of Ariosto criticism to show how such an investigation should be conducted (*PdE*, 438–42).

EVEN LESS than for Ariosto is it possible to go into the many problems of criticism and methodology that cluster around Shakespeare, to whom Croce devoted in 1919 a study of no less penetration and significance. Croce himself told me that as historical groundwork for his study he made a complete digest of the 50-odd volumes of the *Shakespeare-Jahrbuch*, which provided a fairly complete and accurate survey of Shakespearean scholarship in all countries at the time. It may seem, however, that in the interval of nearly forty years modern scholarship has made great progress in Shakespearean studies. The validity of Croce's study has also been challenged by Italian scholars who have alleged his imperfect knowledge of English.[14] But the fundamental problems of criticism do not change very much and it is there that Croce's strength lies. In 1947 I prepared an annotated edition of the Italian original of Croce's essay in which I attempted to show the relevance of Croce's critical arguments to contemporary Shakespeare studies, and the reader is referred to it for a number of points that will not be repeated here.[15]

Today it is perhaps easier to find support for Croce's main contention: that Shakespeare should be studied primarily as a poet. When Croce wrote in 1919, the tide of nonpoetic interpretation of Shakespeare was rising rapidly in England and in America and was to reach unparallelled heights in the years that followed. In 1922 one of the leading English exponents of the biographical approach to Shakespeare, Sir Sidney Lee, proudly observed: "It is interesting to note the signs of a growing reaction against the purely aesthetic appreciation which has long held the place of honour, and the substitution of an historic method which seeks to determine the degree in which Shakespeare's works reflect the conventions of the Elizabethan theatre and the taste of Shakespeare's audience."[16] Thus the concept of "convention" was recognized as a cornerstone of the historical method. By the time the hunters for "conventions" were through, Shakespeare had been brought down from his eminence as one of the world's great poets and reduced to a manufacturer of miscellaneous scripts to a catch-penny company performing for an audience of illiterates and half-wits.[17] This miserable conclusion was hailed as one of the great achievements of modern scholarship, the triumph of "realistic" criticism, while all previous analysis of Shakespeare's works in terms of imaginative power were brushed aside as romantic nonsense.

Such an attitude was typical of the age of positivistic scholarship, or "philologism," to which Croce had already given decent burial in Italy. For instance, similar to this attitude in Shakespearean scholarship was the famous remark of a great romance philologist, Pio Rajna, who concluded his exhaustive investigation of the sources of the *Orlando Furioso* with the solemn critical judgment that "Ariosto's crown of glory would be richer by more than one leaf of laurel if he had invented himself the many things that he obtained from others." This opinion was smartly dealt with by Croce in his critique of Italian philologism (LNI, III, 383–84) and has not raised its head since.

When Croce came to similar misconceptions which beset Shakespeare, and were then gaining authority from research into the history of Elizabethan literature and dramatic methods, he was able to deal with them no less firmly and decisively. The fifth chapter of his study is dedicated to Shakespearean criticism and remains a classic analysis of critical aberrations (ASC, 193–209). From it and from the previous chapter on Shakespeare's art, where other critics are discussed, one may also learn of the historical antecedents of modern realistic or "skeptical" criticism in the work of the nineteenth-century German critic Gustav

Rümelin.[18] Rümelin argued in detail that there was a contrast between Shakespeare's characters and the actions which the poet as-
cribes to them, the characters being vivid individuals while the
actions are inconsistent, or absurd and theatrical (p. 59 ff.). He
also derived characteristic features of Shakespeare's plays from
the tastes of his audience, analyzed according to class composition
(p. 41 ff.). Similar theses were developed at length by twentieth-
century scholars such as L. Schücking and E. E. Stoll [19] not to
speak of Robert Bridges in England, and the answer that Croce
gave to Rümelin applies to them as well. Croce concluded his
rebuttal with the affirmation that "in Shakespeare there is a
single poetic current, the waves of which cannot be either distinguished or opposed to each other as characters and action,
speeches and dialogue, and such" (ASC, 185).

    This point also affords a critique of another modern trend,
that of studying Shakespeare's images out of their context, as independent units of meaning to be analyzed and rearranged according to some abstract scheme of classification. Shakespeare's
poetic images consist of human characters, emotions, feelings and
actions, in an integrated whole, and should be studied as such.[20]
They are not the similes and metaphors, antithesis or hyperboles
or what not, that may be extracted from the texture of his verse
and set apart. As we have already seen, these will be merely
"a heap of dead fragments" (P, 124). On the other hand, the
study of characters should avoid the pitfall of earlier "objectivistic" criticism, as Croce calls it, i.e. the analysis of Shakespeare's
characters as if they were real people (ASC, 200–205), the latest
development of which is the psychoanalytic study of Hamlet.
How far Croce is from all forms of such "objectivism" in the
analysis of Hamlet, may be seen by the fact that Hamlet for him
is simply the expression of a mood (ASC, 160–62).

    Croce's first chapter is a reasoned rejection of another critical
heresy, the biographical interpretation, and should be read by
any who still believe that Croce's aesthetic of expression favors
what is known as "self-expression" in English, i.e. the expression
or effusion of the practical personality of the poet.[21] Croce's
doctrine aims instead, as is made abundantly clear in this essay,

at the definition of the poet's imaginative creation as an objective world which can be studied in its individual structure and articulation. This Croce does in the central chapters of the book, in which he defines the Shakespearean poetic vision and its ideal moments or phases. As already mentioned, it is defined by Croce as the vision of the central conflicts of human life in their unresolved contrast: good against evil, joy against sorrow, will against passion, virtue against vice, loyalty against deceit, decision against irresolution, and so forth (ASC, 93). In each of these pairs the positive is always felt as positive by the poet, as right against wrong, light against darkness. But the conflict has no resolution; it is eternal, deeply rooted in the nature of things, and the triumph of the positive power in this world is never assured but always in doubt. So human life is ultimately a tragic mystery (ASC, 92–98).

This vision of conflict is not in Shakespeare a concept, a doctrine intellectually formulated and held, but a feeling (*sentimento*, ASC, 96), a mood which becomes the lyrical content of Shakespeare's plastic images of characters and situations. These plastic images may be grouped in six clusters which do not necessarily correspond with the chronological development of Shakespeare's art although they approximate it. They are: love as a comedy, romance as a play of the fancy, interest in practical action, the tragedy of good and evil, the tragedy of will, and finally justice and forgiveness. As an instance of what Croce can do with these groupings, it may be seen how the romantic quality of some of Shakespeare's plots, especially in the comedies, with their sometimes abrupt changes and summary psychological portrayal, of which much is made by the "realistic critics," is shown by Croce to be mainly the play of Shakespeare's fancy around the material provided by contemporary literature, according to the second of the motifs listed above: "even in the play of fancy he takes lively interest: interest in amazing coincidences, in sudden meetings, in the *romanesque* [*romanzesco*], in the idyllic or pastoral: he loves all these things, he composes them in order to enjoy them, he caresses them with the magic of his style" (ASC, 125).

So one of the main blemishes of Shakespeare according to the realists is seen as a positive manifestation of his artistic fancy. Croce's organic and flexible definition of Shakespeare's poetic motifs still awaits application and verification in a detailed analysis of the texts. "Historical" criticism busied itself instead with the reduction of Shakespeare's mind to that of the typical or "average Elizabethan," with all its limitations and prejudices, superstitions and credulities. These were carefully excavated from second-rate compilations and textbooks of the period, and then fashioned into a sort of dunce cap placed on the head of the poet. Much was made of the fact that Shakespeare's contemporaries still saw the world in the framework of Ptolemaic astronomy and believed in the order and harmony of the spheres.[22] Echoes of this "Elizabethan world view" in the text of the poet have been made the grounds for an intellectualistic interpretation, in restricted historical terms, of the poetic world of Shakespeare. But on this question it is sufficient to refer to Croce's discussion of Ptolemaic astronomy in Dante, a poet who really had definite intellectual interests.

Today one hears more frequently the judgment that Shakespeare was primarily a poet and that his work must be studied as poetry.[23] However in some instances this turns out to mean only that Shakespeare was a writer of verse and used language and rhetorical figures to construct artifacts of a sort. So he must be studied as a manipulator of those "media," preferably according to Elizabethan notions of rhetoric. In this way what is granted with one hand is taken away with the other. Others who stress that Shakespeare was a poet mean that his art is to be found only in his metrical sections, and not in character or plot at all, as if drama were not poetry. Since Shakespeare's work took the form of plays, it is in these compositions, considered as wholes—i.e. as unified lyrical images—that his poetic power must be sought.

This point of view has been gaining ground lately against the strictures and the pedantry of traditional dramaturgy and genre criticism.[24] But it has never been affirmed by any critic as firmly and clearly as by Croce in his study of 1919, which still offers a promising foundation for a genuine aesthetic criticism, in detail, of the poet. Instead of the trite didactic aim which the historical critics still persist in attributing to poets, Croce found in Shakespeare a vision of life deeper and more complex than that of any other poet before him, a vision which gives a meaningful unity to the rich variety of Shakespeare's poetic creations.

CROCE'S STUDY of Corneille appeared originally in 1920, shortly after the studies of Goethe, Ariosto and Shakespeare, and was published in a volume together with the last two in the same year (ASC). The work of the great French dramatist was a clear challenge to Croce's principles, since he could obviously not accept the neoclassical theory of tragedy, with its rules and unities, its principles of verisimilitude and decorum or the imitation of nature, and the concept of tragedy itself as a literary genre. It must be added that in his youth Croce had shared in the Romantic lack of sympathy with Corneille (PS, I, 472). But in his mature study Croce, while rejecting the doctrines of neoclassicism, makes out Corneille to have been a genuine poet.

Croce begins with the masterful chapter frankly entitled "Criticism of criticism," in which he clears the ground of many unsatisfactory interpretations of Corneille: not only the neoclassical, but also several later and more subtle eulogies of Corneille as a great tragedian. He thus paves the way toward his own interpretation, that of Corneille as essentially a lyrical poet in the Crocean sense. Corneille has an individual theme or motif, an emotion which he felt deeply and which is the soul of his poetry. This emotion Croce describes as devotion to the ideal of "the deliberative will," the free will of man in the act of weighing different choices and deciding in one way or another. This ideal is not a logical concept, such as a philosopher might have, but a mental picture which Corneille loves to compose and to contemplate (cf. CC, v, 138–41). So there is a lyrical theme in Corneille and he is a poet, not because he wrote plays according to a certain dramatic structure, but because through them he expressed this unique and individual feeling.

This is enough to revise the traditional judgment of Corneille as a great dramatist, but Croce does not stop here. He points out that in Corneille this ideal of the deliberative will is cut off, as it were, from all other emotions and contemplated in itself, in isolation. Hence the poet, when he proceeds to bring together a set of actions and events and to build up the plot of a play, is forced to find connections between his isolated ideal and other human passions. Since these are not generated directly by his ideal, they tend to be forced and artificial: hence the mechanical quality of many of Corneille's plots and actions, characters and speeches. Here the conclusions of the Romantic critics of Corneille are reaffirmed, but with a different foundation, and subordinated to a thesis which nevertheless acknowledges that there is poetry in Corneille.

This is what Croce's vindication amounts to: there are genuine passages of poetry in Corneille, to be found between stretches of conventional and artificial writing. But it should be obvious that this critical conclusion has nothing in common with the rhetorical critic's selections of the "beauties" of an author, extracted from the body of his work and collected in anthologies. For the "beauties" that rhetorical criticism finds in a writer are determined by the principle of the separation of form and content, diction and style, figures of speech and thought, action and character, prose and verse; whereas in Croce the discrimination of poetry and nonpoetry is based upon the principle of the unity of form and content, which is realized in pure poetry but disturbed and diverted by the intervention of other spiritual activities.

Croce also rejected another critical commonplace, the supposed decadence of Corneille as a poet after he had written his four greatest plays. For Croce there is just as much poetry to be found in episodes and speeches of the later plays as there is to be found in the central plays, the famous "quadrilateral." Corneille as a writer was uniform: having found his pattern of composition, he did not deviate from it either to rise or to sink too much.

Croce's re-evaluation of Corneille is one of his subtlest and most ingenius pieces of criticism, and must be read in full to be appreciated in all its logic. He does not subvert tradition, like the extreme Romantics who denied all poetic value to Corneille, but on the other hand he does not praise Corneille for the traditional reasons. He rejects all dramatic systems: these "systems either do not concern poetry or are patterns abstracted from single poems" (ASC, 233).

No less vigorously he rejects the conception of Corneille as representative of the French mind, French rationalism, and so forth: "What is one to think of 'rationalistic poetry', of the 'poetry of the intellect' or 'of logic', or 'non-lyrical' poetry? Just this: that it simply does not exist. And of French poetry? Just the same: that it does not exist; because what is poetry in France is, of course, neither intellectualistic nor essentially French, but simply poetry, identical to all other true poetry that blossoms in 'our earthly gardens'. And if today this belated Romantic glorification of nationality, which requires that all art, all thought and everything else should be national, arises again in French nationalists under the guise of anti-Romanticism and Neo-classicism, that is only a confirmation of the spiritual confusion and mental weakness of those nationalists" (ASC, 229).

This was written in the early twenties, when the world was about to witness the disastrous effects of nationalism in Italy and other European countries. The storm was coming and Croce felt it.

To GOETHE Croce dedicated the fullest and most detailed study that he has given to any poet, a fact which is sufficiently indicative of his love and admiration for the great German poet. Croce says that he "re-read the works of Goethe during the dark days of the world war [i.e., 1917] and obtained comfort and serenity from them, such as I could not have received perhaps from any other poet: and that stimulated me to write down some critical concepts which had spontaneously arisen in me and which had always helped me to understand those works rightly" (G, I, vii–viii).

The criticism was accompanied by a rather unusual supplement, a series of verse translations from the poet studied. Croce modestly presented them as the result of his desire "to caress poetry that has given me pleasure: to caress it with the sounds of my native tongue" (G, I, ix). The attempt was also useful to his critical understanding, since he was able through it to scrutinize more closely "the inner structure of Goethe's poetry"; but he reaffirmed his previous thesis as to the ultimate untranslatability of poetry. In effect Croce's verse translations may be an aid to interpretation for Italian readers, but on the whole they are not poetic.

Croce's critical study is a deliberate turning away from the biographical approach to Goethe which was prevalent in German criticism. Croce acknowledged the intrinsic interest of Goethe's unique personality and of his "wisdom of life," and indeed gave a brilliant account of them in the first chapters of his book, but maintained that nevertheless Goethe's work must be judged by purely aesthetic standards. Goethe's gradual unfolding and development, his ripening from a preromantic rebel and "Titanist" to cosmic wisdom and serenity is declared admirable, but belonging to the ethical sphere and not to the poetic. The aesthetic analysis concludes inversely that the poems inspired by Goethe's early rebelliousness are superior to those inspired by his mature wisdom (G, I, 12).

But even the first part of *Faust*, the masterpiece of this early period, is considered by Croce to be devoid of poetic unity. He finds in it three different poetic organisms, mechanically joined together (G, I, 52) and proceeds to distinguish them, characterizing the poetic theme of each. We have already referred in Chapter VIII to Croce's delightful portrayal of the figure of the pedant Wagner, which is the first poetic organism that Croce analyzes in *Faust*. The other two are the early presentation of Faust the Titanist, and the tragedy of Margaret. The general scheme by which Goethe later tried to expand *Faust* and give it a second part is shown to be intellectual and not poetical: the notion of a poem that provides an answer to the question as to the meaning and goal of human life. This complete breaking down of the external unity of Goethe's masterpiece and the rejection of its didactic framework has caused almost as great an outcry against Croce from traditional criticism as his rejection of the external unity of the *Divine Comedy*. It may be a manifestation of the tendency which we noted in the earliest critical writings of Croce to see the other side of a question, that inclines Croce to see variety where traditional opinion sees unity, viz. in the *Comedy* and *Faust*, and on the other side to stress the unity underlying the variety of Shakespeare's productions.

In later years Croce twice resumed his study of Goethe, once in the dark years of the Fascist dictatorship and then again in the dark days of the second world war, when the Nazi armies committed barbarous atrocities and destructions in Croce's own city (G, I, xi). How can you read a German poet under these circumstances?—Croce was asked. He answered that he himself did not share the blindness of the barbarians; besides, "the language in which Goethe's works are written is not the German language, but is the language of Wolfgang Goethe" (*ibid.*). Poetry is supranational.

These new essays on Goethe either discuss further some of the works he had already analyzed, in the light of some new critical study or of some critic of the past, or take up some of the many other works of Goethe which had not been discussed in the earlier book. The new essays make up an entire volume, so that now the study of Goethe in Croce's collected works consists of two volumes, of which only the first has been translated into English. But it is not necessary to go any further into them, since they have been the object of a recent study in English by Lienhard Bergel.[25]

THE SEVENTEENTH CENTURY of Italian literature was the subject of a volume entitled *History of the Baroque Age in Italy* (1929), which contains much criticism of secondary works, and the main aspects of which we have considered in Chapter IX. In the thirties Croce turned to the Italian writers of the great age from the fourteenth to sixteenth centuries and wrote the studies collected in 1933 under the title *Popular Poetry and Art Poetry* (PPPA). The title essay is a discussion of the often-debated problem of folk poetry. Is folk poetry a special kind of poetry, to be judged differently from the poetry of conscious art, or can they both be placed over a common denominator? After a thorough sifting of the previous solutions proposed by critics and scholars, Croce presents his own. Folk poetry is not essentially different from the poetry of art; it is only poetry which "portrays simple feelings in correspondingly simple forms" (PPPA, 5), whether composed by a known or unknown poet or transmitted orally or set down in writing for publication. This volume also contains the essays on Renaissance comedy and tragedy, lyric poetry and fiction etc., which we have already referred to in Chapter v.

Croce finally published in 1938 and 1940 volumes v and vi of his *Literature of Modern Italy* (LNI). Here Croce deals with writers like Pirandello [26] who had come into prominence since 1913, besides a number of minor figures whom he had not discussed in the first four volumes. He added a recantation of his originally favorable judgment on D'Annunzio and brought up to date his discussion of Pascoli, Fogazzaro, Oriani, Ada Negri and Gaeta without altering substantially his earlier conclusions on these writers. These essays complete the literary gallery initiated in the earlier volumes, but on the whole they are not as pioneering and seminal as the earlier group. The three volumes dedicated later to *Poets and Writers of the Late and the Full Renaissance* (1945 and 1952), like the volume dedicated to the eighteenth century in 1949, are, as Croce said in the introduction to the latter volume, mainly "gleanings"—i.e. discussions of lesser known writers and works—and do not aim at a thorough analysis of writers such as Ariosto and Tasso, Machiavelli and Aretino, most of whom Croce had already studied. The volumes on the Renaissance in particular are full of interesting studies on out-of-the-way subjects. To some of them we have had occasion to refer in other chapters.

While these volumes are dedicated to Italian literature, Croce turned to foreign literature in the two volumes entitled *Poetry*

Ancient and Modern (1941) and *Readings of Poets and Reflections on the Theory of Poetry* (1950). The first contains a series of essays on a wide-ranging selection of poets, from Homer and Virgil to Baudelaire and Gerard Manley Hopkins, including an episode from the Gospels, the *Dies Irae*, Walter von der Vogelweide and Bertran de Born, Dante and Petrarch, *La Celestina* and Lazarillo de Tormes, Ronsard and Cervantes, Lope and Gongora, Racine and Molière, Diderot and Beaumarchais, Burns and Chénier, Foscolo and Leopardi, Hugo and Carducci. It is observable that the proportion of foreign and classical authors to Italian is here overwhelmingly greater than in *Poetry and non-poetry* (1923), and the chronological range is correspondingly wider. For this extrinsic reason, and for the intrinsic value of the criticism they contain, these essays are indispensable to any evaluation of Croce's status as a critic of world literature. The essays on Baudelaire give a much more positive and enthusiastic evaluation than Croce's first essay on him in *Poetry and non-poetry*. As time went on, Croce's opinion of Baudelaire both as a poet and as a critic and aesthetician continued to rise, and he returns to him again and again in his later volumes as one of the few Frenchmen with clear vision in matters of art and poetry.[27] This, of course, is an appreciation always in terms of Croce's own views, and not from the standpoint of the more fanatical Baudelairians of today who extol his very weaknesses and failings. Baudelaire for Croce is a creator of intensely lyrical images and a critic who grasped the autonomy of the poetic imagination.

In his last volume of critical essays, *Readings of Poets*, Croce returns to Dante and to Spanish poetry of the Golden Age (Calderón, Tirso de Molina, Cervantes), takes an unexpected excursion through the work of Rétif de la Bretonne, and then comes to the nineteenth century. Here he compares a lyric by Goethe with one of Carducci's, takes up Benjamin Constant, and discusses two works of Manzoni and two modern German poets: Mörike and Rilke. After a reminiscent look at the *Dame aux camélias* and the French theatre of the nineteenth century, he plunges into a critique of the great lights of modern French poetry, Mallarmé and Verlaine, which will be examined in a successive chapter on Croce's attitude to contemporary writing.

These essays, published by Croce in his 84th year, are of an amazing vigor and vitality. They show that Croce never lost his ability to see the particular and to portray the individual. Whatever may be thought of some of their judgments (and the ones on contemporary literature are the more controversial), to the last he certainly lived up to his aim of judging poetry on its own merits, as individual works of art expressing individual moods. One of the most striking instances is contained in a paper that is included in the second part of the book, "Reflections on the theory and criticism of poetry" (which comprises among other things a vindication of Poe as a critic against Yvor Winters). Answering the charge of "fragmentism" or fragmentization made against his literary criticism, Croce returns to D'Annunzio and notes that, even though on the whole a decadent poet, he was capable of producing a poem of pure beauty. With extraordinary memory and perceptivity, Croce recalls a lyric from old volume of D'Annunzio, *Isaotta Guttadauro* of 1886, and shows its original quality and imaginative power.[28] It is the story of a love affair, a mere episode; morality has little to do with it, but neither has D'Annunzio's imperialism and other manias. While still rejecting the latter, Croce, the lover of poetry, brings back to notice this exquisite little poem, in which there is a vision of the sunset among the ruins of the Forum, a Roman afternoon crystallized in all its splendor. The "indistinction of universal and particular," the "moral personality" and the other concepts of Croce's universalistic phase seem to have vanished, and on the critical horizon there only remains the poetic image, unique, individual, concrete, and rich in lyrical emotion.

CHAPTER Xiii

"*La Poesia*"

I N 1936 at the age of 70 Croce published a book entitled *La poesia*, or *Poetry: an Introduction to the Criticism and to the History of Poetry and of Literature*. This book presents the final stage in the development of his doctrine of poetry. It marks considerable progress over the *Breviary of Aesthetics* of 24 years before, the latest work of Croce's known to most English-speaking students. *La poesia* incorporates all the later developments in doctrine, such as the theory of the cosmic character of art, as well as the fruit of Croce's mature literary criticism, such as the studies on Dante, Shakespeare and Goethe. It then proceeds to break into new ground, introducing the doctrine of "literature" which is now distinguished from poetry and assigned a sphere of its own. The new doctrines are connected with the old in a single systematic exposition, composed in a more elaborate manner than in any preceding work. Its style is obviously carefully studied, as befits a work which expounds the civilizing function of good writing. Croce also provides an unprecedented wealth of illustration and practical criticism in a series of short *postille* or postscripts, which take up the whole second half of the book and bring in quotations from poets and critics, discussions of special points, and brief characterizations of scores of writers and works.[1] Of all the untranslated critical works of Croce, *La poesia* is the one of which an English version is most urgently needed.

Croce begins by expounding his doctrine of poetry in the terms of the universal character of art: e.g. the image transcends the emotion which it expresses as the universal transcends the particular (P, 8). In a postscript he explains that he is deliberately abstaining from the use of his old terminology, such as the "pure intuition" or the "lyrical intuition," in order to avoid the tedium of repetition and "the superstition of words." But he adds that " 'pure intuition' implies 'non-conceptual' and 'non-historical,' and this can only be 'lyrical' intuition, i.e. emotion transformed into contemplation [*teóresi*]" (P, 210). So the poetic image is still, as ever, the contemplation or sublimation of emotion. And although the universal or total character of poetry is constantly affirmed, yet the individuality of expression still remains the foundation of the argument: language is individual (P, 79), the poetic image is unique and untranslatable (P, 100), and the genres and other classifications are still considered "abstractions formed from single works" (P, 117).

Individuality emerges explicitly in the doctrine of the "individual personality" (P, 103) as the substance of the work of poetry and as the object of critical attention: "criticism adheres to the individual quality of the work" (P, 123). The whole doctrine of critical characterization, which we saw already in Chapter VII, turns on the concept of individuality (P, 123 ff.).[2] Poetry is to be dealt with not in general histories but in monographs "with reference always to the concreteness of the individual work" (P, 134). Finally, the term "intuition" itself re-emerges in the later portions of the work, where poetry is again defined as the union of "feeling with intuition" (P, 117–18; cf. 124). The critical judgment is still defined as "the identification of the intuition and the category" (P, 122). And all the attendant corollaries are also maintained: viz. the rejection of all resolutions of poetry into ideas, conventions or trends (P, 136 ff.), of evolutionary schemes (P, 140 ff.), of source-hunting (P, 163), of philologism (P, 61–62) and of the histories of genres (P, 174 ff.).

But it will be well to take up a question which may arise now in the mind of the reader. Here is Croce writing a whole book on Poetry by itself, i.e. on one of the arts in separation from the others. But did he not reject the existence of separate arts and affirm the sole validity of the science of Aesthetics to deal with all problems relating to art? Does he now acknowledge the separation of poetry from the other arts, and the validity of Poetics? Croce was well aware of this possible objection and he made it quite clear that he had not given up the doctrine of the unity of the arts nor the validity of Aesthetics as the science of art (P, 182–83). At the same time, however, the terms used in the discussion of certain groups of works differ from those used in the discussion of others. This difference may arise from exclusive or excessive attention to the extrinsic circumstances of externalization and preservation, and should be corrected by a discussion of those terms to show their identity with the terms used for other groups. For instance, in the so-called plastic arts much use has been made of the terms "illustration" and "decoration" (e.g. by B. Berenson); a similar distinction exists also for poetry, such as "fable" and "lyric," or "structure" and "poetry" (P, 185). Similarily questions which center around the conception of "pure painting" are essentially the same as those which center around the concepts of "pure poetry," (P, 185–86). Croce concludes that there is a place for books that discuss the problems connected with each "separate art" or the group of works so labelled, in order to analyze the concepts involved and bring them back to the unity of all art (P, 187).

This book also contains a full discussion of the process of taste or the re-enactment of aesthetic expressions (P, 65–78). The function of historical knowledge in exegesis is pointed out again, and the aesthetes or dilettanti are again castigated for their reluctance to undertake the labors of research (P, 69). The preparation and training of the poet also receive a full discussion (P, 161–74). Traditional rhetoric is given here the most favorable treatment it had yet received from Croce. The poet should certainly read books on rhetoric and composition, on language and prosody: "What will he learn from them? He will receive the suggestion to take notice of this or that form of expression historically existing, in connection with the work that he is engaged in. In order to duplicate those forms? Certainly not; mere aping, which certainly does occur, does not enter the present discussion. To allow them to operate on his mind and incline it in a certain direction? Yes, indeed. The lack of such a habit and such a discipline is clearly observable in the shortcomings of certain writers" (P, 171). On all previously discussed questions Croce here makes new observations, introduces new arguments and brings in fresh illustrations, so that this book is indispensable for a full understanding of Croce's mature position, and reference has continually been made to it in the previous chapters of this book.

A new departure in *La poesia* is the introduction of the concept of "structure" or to be more correct of "structural parts" of poetry. In general, poetic structure for Croce can only mean poetic form, or the individualizing intuition, so every poem has a structure which is different from all others. This obviously rules out the traditional concept of structure deriving from a genre: the "epic structure," the "tragic structure," etc. are no less pseudo-concepts than the genres to which they relate. But in *La poesia* Croce takes note of the fact that a good poem is not usually perfect in all its parts, but includes some that are not poetic or not perfectly executed. These Croce divides into two kinds: genuine imperfections and "structural" parts. The first could be conceivably corrected or eliminated; they are real defects or blemishes that should not be in the poem and that the poet has left in it because he was either too lazy or too hurried to eliminate them. But structural parts cannot be eliminated without breaking up the whole poem. They contribute to its unity and yet are not poetical; they are mere links or connections inserted by the poet to keep together groups or clusters of images. The unity thus effected is not genuinely poetic, and yet it is hard to conceive of a different way of bringing those images together.

It should be noted that Croce here is frankly being empirical or descriptive, not philosophical or categorical. Structural parts are something actually found in poems, but not an essential feature of poetry in general, so there is no need for their presence in any particular poem. But it is a fact of experience that such parts sometimes occur in poems, so they should be accounted for, as Croce endeavors to do here. Some critics, who consider Croce the sworn foe of all empiricism, may be surprised at seeing him assume such a frankly empirical attitude. But thanks to his conception of the distinct spheres of mental activity, Croce has always been able to recognize the practical use of empirical classifications, while excluding them from the sphere of speculative and normative concepts. Even in his first *Aesthetic* Croce acknowledged an "empirical sense of the rhetorical categories" which he excluded from the philosophy of art.[3] In 1927, as we have seen in Chapter v, he even suggested a new Poetics, meaning a new classification of genres, on an empirical basis. He repeats this suggestion in the book on Poetry, and adds: "A work of sound empiricism is, in a certain sense, more difficult and more complicated than a purely philosophical work or the specific criticism and history of poetry, since it presupposes both the latter and the former, and not in the brains of others, but active through exercise and experience in one's own. It is not only a work of conceptual creation and intellectual acumen, but of practical equilibrium and of wisdom—the kind of wisdom that does not always immediately follow strenuous intellectual efforts" (P, 159).

In the empirical classification of "structural parts," the first instance given involves the sacrifice of a detail of the poem, a word or a phrase, to the harmony of the whole; that detail is deliberately left imperfect in order to achieve unity. This is most common in rhyming. An imperfectly expressive word may be used "for the sake of the rhyme." This is a blemish, but it serves the purpose of preserving the total harmony of the composition. It may be objected that this is a harmony of mere sound; but this sound "is itself an image, answering to the poetic motif" (P, 91).

Secondly, there is a certain kind of "padding" (*zeppe* or *chevilles*) which is used to connect two verse passages or two clusters of images, e.g. transitional passages in longer poems, not excluding the *Divine Comedy* which provides Croce with some interesting instances. They are not poetic in themselves and yet cannot be eliminated, for they help the author to pass from one climax of poetic inspiration to another. This is an explicit answer to Poe's famous criticism of long poems (P, 276–77). A. C. Bradley had also noted the existence of these connective passages in long poems, but he thought that poets like Virgil and Milton transformed them entirely into poetry.[4]

Of the same kind are the expository parts of plays, poems and novels, and many similar connectives or commentaries which occur in literature, such as the reflections of the chorus in Greek tragedy, "psychological explanations in the novel," and particularly the introduction of characters and episodes to carry on the action of the plot. All these parts are secondary and subordinate and should not be allowed to rise too high. If they did, they would upset the balance of the whole. It should be carefully noted that Croce does *not* argue that these are necessary or essential parts of all poems or novels, but only that they occur in some instances and call therefore for evaluation of their function. They may be designated as aesthetically neutral, neither beautiful nor ugly, but mere links between points of beauty (P, 95).

However, the aesthetic critic is specially bound to take notice of them since they have become one of the main props of historical criticism: "Hence the praise that is extended to Corneille, to Calderón, to Apostolo Zeno, and similarly to others, for having provided French tragedy, Spanish *comedia*, Italian melodrama and other genres with a structure and a contrivance which they transmit to their successors, whether they are poets or not; the extolling of Aeschylus as the inventor of the second actor in Greek tragedy, and the merit attributed to the inventor of the sonnet or of *ottava rima* and to those who introduced them to other nations" (P, 95–96). Croce concludes the paragraph with a remark which is of particular relevance to contemporary criticism: "The consequence is that the misunderstanding of the nature of the structural element causes poetry to be considered a sequence of conventions and artifices, and those who invent that kind of thing are considered poets; and the inventions and devices, one would almost say the tricks and artful dodges, employed by them, form the subjects of special investigations, full of wonder and admiration for such things" (P, 96).

This unintelligent admiration for the nonpoetic parts of a poem has inevitably produced a reaction to the other extreme. This is the doctrine of "pure poetry" which will not allow in a poem anything which is not 100 per cent poetic. The doctrine takes two forms: one affirms that only short poems can be poetic, and the other that poetry can only exist in "fragments" or fulgurations and that it should be composed that way. Croce here makes a formal refutation of the first doctrine, which is of course Poe's, by introducing a point which also applies to other problems, i.e. the irrelevance of the time element: "it (Poe's theory) commits the serious fallacy of introducing a time element into an ideal process, as if the composition of the poem and the reading of it, whether it lasts a minute of the clock or several years, did not follow an ideal rhythm which takes hold of the poet and the reader and carries them out of time. This theory is also refuted by experience, for the poetry of poems, plays and novels which are genuinely inspired does not consist of single parts only, but circulates throughout the whole composition, from which no piece may be extracted and placed in an anthology as a thing of beauty, and yet one feels poetry diffused throughout the whole of it. This observation will also refute the second form of the theory" (P, 97).

In his practical criticism Croce had occasion to point out that certain poems not of the first rank were redeemed by a flash of inspiration, a successful image, occurring in the midst of otherwise uninspired stretches. From this some hasty critics had jumped to the conclusion that all the rest of the poem was to be discarded, and adopted the theory of "fragmentism," which Croce in 1915 had immediately rejected, as we have seen above in Chapter III.

A third use of structural parts occurs when a poet takes up a traditional tale or subject and uses it "as a kind of warp upon which he weaves his own poetry, sometimes covering up the warp entirely and concealing it from sight, and in effect abolishing it, but at other times leaving it visible to a larger or smaller extent. In this case again the attitude of the poetic interpreter must be that of indifference to the warp and of sole attention to what is woven upon it. But unintelligent readers confuse the warp with the embroidery and appraise it as substantial poetry or poetic motif; hence all the dissertations printed on the manner in which a theme should be handled according to its essence and to the various ways in which various authors have treated such themes as Prometheus and Orestes, Lucretia and Sophonisba, Faust and Don Juan, and so forth."

And here comes a pointed reference to Shakespeare criticism: "Since tales treated in that manner are to be found also in Shakespeare, who more than once rose to high flights stepping lightly from legends and fairy tales, a persistent criticism has been directed to the contradictions and incongruities and puerilities of Shakespeare; and one of the most recent of such critics was Leo Tolstoy, who mistook the warp, or plot, of *King Lear* with the poetry of *King Lear*" (P, 97–98). Tolstoy was by no means the last critic of that persuasion. Much modern Shakespearean criticism of the historical school has followed that lead, including Schücking's much lauded "discovery" of the naive and rudimental character of Shakespeare's characters.

As a last instance of structural parts, Croce cites the philosophical and doctrinal sections of such poems as the *Divine Comedy* and *Faust;* those parts are definitely not poetry, yet they were indispensable to the poet, because he, Dante or Goethe, happened to be also a philosopher and would not have allowed himself to indulge in a purely poetic composition if he had not been able to bring into it his philosophical views. In this case the structural part is not something indifferent to the poet, like the warp in the previous case; it is instead a vital part of his mind, both conjoined to and distinct from his poetry. "Nor can it be indifferent to us in our effort to understand the spirit of the poet and the character of his poetry, but indifferent it must remain as all other structures, in the sense that his poetry is not to be found precisely in it" (P, 99).

In this book Croce also reiterates his rejection of the validity

of intentions for the criticism of poetry. This refers to the so-
called "Intentional Heresy" and since we have not discussed it
before, we will consider it now. That expression cannot be produced by a mere act of will, was already argued in the *Aesthetic*
(E, 57; A, 51). Croce formally denied the relevance of intentions to criticism in a paper written as early as 1905, entitled
"The Aims of the Poets" (*PdE*, 61–64). The professed intentions of the poets—to edify, to amuse, to satirize an opponent, to
support a party or a religious dogma, etc.—are practical de-
cisions which precede composition and have no necessary connection with it. This point goes a long way back. Already in
1894 Croce noted that De Sanctis had based his own criticism
on that principle and quoted him briefly: "the poet sets out with
the poetics, the forms, the ideas, the preoccupations of his own
time; the less of an artist he is, the more exactly he renders his
intentional world [*mondo intenzionale*]." [5] So this is an old
theory in Italian criticism (cf. NPS, I, 201).

For Croce, the meaning of the work is to be found within
the work; no judgment of intention is relevant unless corroborated by the work itself, in which case it is superfluous
(*PdE*, 63). There are poets who believe themselves animated by
high moral ideals and are really decadent or morbid. Others consider themselves ruthless realists, but are actually inspired by
deeply-felt sympathy for the oppressed and by indignation for
social wrongs (Croce was here probably thinking of D'Annunzio and Verga, respectively). "The man is sometimes superior, sometimes inferior, to the state of mind portrayed by
the artist." Historical scholarship has made a great point of ascertaining the intentions of an author and interpreting his work
accordingly. But in aesthetic criticism "the crude seeking for
the aims of poets" is replaced by the investigation of the state
of mind expressed by the work of art, which is a much more
delicate operation. It is far easier, but irrelevant, "to allege aims,
quoted from some extra-aesthetic document, or introduced arbitrarily into the work of art" (*PdE*, 63).

In the paper on Totality, discussed in Chapter XI, Croce
argued that a poet may start with the intention of gratifying

some passion of hate or lust, but during the course of composition he can be carried away by his creative imagination and rise to pure art (NSE², 127). In the book on Poetry of 1936 Croce took up again the question and reaffirmed his belief that even the poets who have special aims and formal beliefs set them aside when engaging in the creative act, or preserve them only as particular tones of emotion in the harmony of the whole. Hence, he says, "it is an illusion to see the idea of Fate in Greek tragedy or the idea of Providence in the work of a Christian poet, because Fate and Providence are concepts and therefore the objects of thought and not of representation. What is actually represented will be, always and only, under the name of Fate, a feeling of terror and of resignation, and under the name of Providence, a feeling of confidence and of hope: lights and shadows, and not concepts" (P, 86).[6] Spingarn, it should be acknowledged, had clearly and vigorously made this point: "The poet's real 'intention' is to be found, not in one or another of the various ambitions that flit through his mind, but in the actual work of art which he creates. His poem is this 'intention.' In any other sense, 'intention' is outside the aesthetic field—a mere matter of the poet's literary theory or his power of will— and so matter for the biographer of the man rather than for the critic of the poem." [7]

This Intentional Heresy that Croce denounces (although not using that name which it is the merit of Wimsatt to have coined) [8] is involved in several questions. Its relevance to Dante has already been shown in Chapter XII above (see also CC, III, 194; V, 104–5). It also arises frequently in connection with the literature of an age like the Renaissance, when didactic theories prevailed in criticism and were at times professed by the poets themselves. But all such professions, such as Spenser's famous intent "to fashion a gentleman," are irrelevant to the artistic composition. This also applies to drama. It has been laboriously argued by the historical critics that because Shakespeare wrote for the stage, and therefore aimed at pleasing his audience, he could not have written great poetry but only scripts for the entertainment of the London populace. The whole school of "realists" with E. E. Stoll at their head had poured scorn on the critics of the Romantic age who had found great poetry in Shakespeare's plays. Such is the strength of the Intentional Heresy.

A related question, of less critical moment, concerns the intentional referring of a poem to a particular set of circumstances, sentimental or otherwise extrapoetic, which go beyond the lyrical emotion expressed in the poem and may be an object of personal interest. This may be done by the poet himself after he has completed the poem, or by a reader who may take pleasure in referring the image of the poem to some concern of his own. This is an operation to which Croce in his later years showed himself more indulgent than previously (NSE[2], 130), dedicating to it a number of papers and arguing that it is an innocent transference as long as it does not claim to be either poetical or critical (*Discorsi*, II, 62–80; TPS, I, 74; *Letture*, 220–21). Even philosophers do it when they use a quotation from a poet to illustrate a point in philosophical theory (*Discorsi*, II, 67). "The poetic image," says Croce, "is . . . so rich that it contains within itself the infinite particular situations of reality and of life" (*ibid.*, 65).

A curious case of the kind is that of a sonnet which occurs in Bruno's *Eroici Furori* and which was long admired (even by De Sanctis) as a beautiful expression of the philosopher's longing towards the Absolute. It turned out to have been written originally by the poet Luigi Tansillo to convey a rather different emotion: the lover's passion for a lady who happened to be stationed above him in rank. Croce at first saw in this case the exceptional coexistence of two different poems in the same set of words, or rather in words that were apparently the same, identical in sound but not in meaning: a kind of colossal pun (*PdE*, 136–39). In 1944 he revised this opinion in the light of his new theory of emotional reference (*Discorsi*, II, 71–72). The sonnet is now seen as a single poem expressing an indeterminate feeling, a "state of mind," which Tansillo intentionally referred to his own love affair, while Bruno intentionally referred it to his own philosophic efforts. Both intentions are declared to be extrapoetic; the poetry lies in the indeterminate, depersonalized emotion expressed by the image.

PERHAPS THE MOST IMPORTANT NOVELTY in *La poesia* is Croce's definition of literature as distinct from poetry.[9] This definition has also made critics charge that Croce was radically changing his views or backsliding to traditional positions. Actually this doctrine is no new departure but had been developing for years. Although it reaches here a form and prominence that had never been given it before by its author, yet it deals with one of Croce's oldest preoccupations, viz. what to do with pseudo and quasi art.[10] Since Croce had never thought that all verse is poetry, nor that all literature is creative, he was faced with the problem of defining what was not poetry in literature, and assigning it a function in the system of the spirit. In *La poesia* he gave his final answer to this problem by proposing to limit the term "literature" to all compositions that are not poetry, or achieved expression, but have only the semblance of poetry, while actually exercising another function, which Croce here defines as "civilization" in a broad sense. At the same time he brings together in a systematic classification a number of other categories of pseudo art which he had formulated in the course of his long career as critic and historian of literature, such as the category of "oratory," "pure poetry," etc.

     This led him to extend the number of meanings of the term "expression." Besides aesthetic expression, which for Croce remains the only real expression, he had acknowledged in the *Aesthetic* two other things which are commonly called expressions: "naturalistic expression" and the expression of thought (concepts) in "prose." The first designates the outward signs of emotion, which are not expressions of it but actually part or symptoms of it, as we saw in Chapter III. They therefore remain outside the domain of art. (This was recognized also by Dewey in a striking passage.[11]) The second is what Croce calls "prose" or the expression of reflective thought (concepts), which is not so much expression as symbolization, or representation by means of a sign, the image converted to the uses of thought; in this case the image and the concept remain separate and distinct, as we saw in Chapter III.

These theses constitute in effect Croce's theory of meaning. Meaning for Croce is an act that differs according to the function it performs. The meaning of a poetic text is an expressive act; the meaning of a philosophical text is an act of conceptual thinking; the meaning of an historical proposition is an act of judgment or the referring of a particular event to a universal category. In the first of these acts, the poetic, words and meaning are one and the same; in the other two, words symbolize the thought: they can be translated or represented by other signs, while poetry cannot.

The next form of nonaesthetic expression that Croce now enumerates is "oratory." This important concept seems to have emerged for the first time in 1915, in a paper entitled "Poetry, prose and oratory: value of this triple distinction for literary criticism" (CC, I, 58–63). "Oratory" is not to be identified with the art of speech. It designates all compositions which are primarily addressed to the emotions. It makes use of images already produced by the expressive activity, taking them out of their context, breaking them up and rearranging them in a manner that may arouse the emotions and hence direct the reader towards some form of action. Oratory always implies an audience to be influenced and directed, whereas poetry does not. Oratory seems to coincide with the whole function assigned to poetry by some modern critics, such as Kenneth Burke, but for Croce it is something quite different. For him it belongs to the category of practical action. It is therefore subject to all the regulations, restrictions and controls which society may place upon action, while art is free. From the historian's point of view, it belongs to the history of action and therefore must be related to history of politics, of economics, or of other social activities, while poetry as we have seen rises above them.

Here we find in Croce a doctrine of semantics. Long before the modern semanticists, Croce was aware that words were not only a vehicle for thought but could also be used as purveyors of stimuli. Oratorical expressions are not susceptible of being analyzed aesthetically or logically: they may have the form of words and sentences, but they have neither logical meaning nor aesthetic value. It is therefore futile to try to extract at all costs a logical meaning from all linguistic expressions, or aesthetic value from didactic and political verse. So a considerable amount of the territory of literature is given up as unpoetic, and surrendered to the history of manners, politics, religion or culture.

Another kind of emotional arousal is the function of the literature of entertainment which is distinct from "oratory." The literature of entertainment makes use of previously formed images for the purpose of arousing not one definite emotion, but a succession of emotions of all kinds, emotions simply for the sake of emotion. Hence it arouses not only the pleasurable emotions, which are gratified also in wishful thinking and in the so-called "pleasures of the imagination" (another subdivision of this area), but also painful or restrictive emotions, since the aim of "entertainment" is to excite, to thrill, to keep in suspense, to give one "a good cry," etc.: anything to keep the emotions alive.

We have according to Croce four nonaesthetic forms of so-called expression: natural emotions, prose, oratory and entertainment. They all make use of words for their purposes, i.e. they use already formed aesthetic expressions. This use may be crude or skilful, clumsy or graceful. Grace is achieved in so far as they approximate to aesthetic expression. Supposing they actually pass the borderline and turn into art, then they lose their original practical or intellectual tendency and become pure contemplation. But short of that there is still a wide range of territory that they can cover, and that for Croce is the domain of "literature" as distinct from poetry. Literature may now be defined as the handling of nonaesthetic expressions in such a way that they resemble poetry while still falling short of it. Croce considers literature, so defined, one of the great forces of civilization: a continuous approximation to beauty, brought into the sphere of practical action, thus reminding it of the

existence of that sphere of contemplation which rises above its
stir and tumult. While being itself practical and not theoretical,
it effects a sort of "harmony" between different spheres of activity. But strictly speaking, it is "a practical device to satisfy
two different requirements" (P, 34; cf. 48). So it is not a new
form of spiritual activity, to be added to the four already recognized by Croce; it is merely a special product of one of these
activities, the practical, operating upon the products of another
form, the aesthetic. This is one of Croce's most elaborate
formulas of interaction among his four basic activities, and it
is not a philosophical or logical definition, but empirical. "Literature" may be described as an historical phenomenon, circum-
scribed in time and place, even though the time may be centuries and the space continents.

This concept of literature has given rise to much discussion
and variant evaluations. Croce himself said that the concept
was a delicate one, to be handled lightly and not to be pressed
too far. In any case, it is clear that literature for Croce is not
poetry, and what he says about it does not affect his aesthetic
theory. In poetry it is not possible to distinguish genres or types.
The contrary is true of literature. Furthermore in poetry form
cannot be separated from content. But in "literature" they may
legitimately be judged in separation or in conjunction.[12] We may
approve, or disapprove, of the content of a work of entertainment, i.e. of the emotions aroused, or we may praise its formal
structure—its plot, rising action, falling action, catastrophe,
tension, suspense, etc.—apart from the emotions aroused. But we
cannot do this with works of real poetry. The heresies of aesthetics thus become the truths of pseudo art—which is not so
surprising.

"Literature" according to this doctrine possesses four genres,
corresponding to the four forms of nonaesthetic expression already enumerated: sentimental or effusive, didactic or expository, oratorical and entertaining. In each of these, "literature"
operates so that the unpoetic expression is not too divergent
from poetic expression. The effusion of feeling, or release of
emotions, is a common phenomenon; literature sees to it that it

uses words and forms which belong to the realm of good writing, and assume an appearance of comeliness and dignity. To this class of writing belong the typical effusions of Romantic sentimentalism to be found in Byron, Lamartine, Musset, etc. In the second class Croce includes the skilfully constructed prose of such great writers as Plato and Cicero, Thucydides and Livy, and in later times the Latin prose of Petrarch and Erasmus, or the still later vernacular prose of Galileo and Voltaire. In the third class, literature adjusts the various forms of persuasion so that they, too, present a decorous aspect and a certain resemblance to real art. Hence political poetry, novels, plays like Voltaire's *Mahomet* and Schiller's *William Tell*, are all reduced to the same class as *Uncle Tom's Cabin*. In the fourth class works of mere entertainment are worked over and polished so as to have some semblance of art (P, 40–48).

Being a spiritual act, "literature" is susceptible of evaluation, positive or negative. There is good "literature" and there is bad "literature," according to the measure of success with which its object is achieved. For instance, says Croce, there is no reason to be ashamed of enjoying such a work of pure entertainment as *The Three Musketeers*; in its way it is a well-composed piece of writing, and Croce frankly states his (nonaesthetic) enjoyment of it (P, 60). For if "literature" is nonpoetic, it is not for Croce to be identified with the antipoetic or the ugly. No offence is given to poetry by the existence of works of "literature." Ugliness and the antipoetic are now defined as the intervention of the practical will within the imaginative process, to interrupt or divert it (P, 60). But "literature" is different. It might be described as homage paid to beauty by the nonbeautiful, somewhat like (but this simile is not Croce's) hypocrisy is said to be homage paid to virtue by vice.[13]

Since the effect on an audience, which is not necessary to pure art, is essential in the case of "literature" (P, 36), it is possible to make a positive evaluation of writers like Dryden and Pope, attacked by Romantic critics as writers of prose in verse. Their social virtues as writers of the Court or of Society are now acknowledged as something positive and valuable, as well as the

civilizing function of urbane wit in the style that they cultivated. Such writers may now be recognized as great masters
of "literature"—but Croce still excludes them from poetry
(P, 239).

To the discussion of these forms Croce also adds an analysis
of what he calls "art for art's sake" (P, 48–54), which is the
kind of imitative writing cultivated by lovers of poetry who
do not achieve original expression but continue to fondle and
manipulate the forms of previously achieved art simply out of
love for it. This is not "literature" in Croce's meaning, for it
has no "extra-aesthetic object" (P, 50).

Croce also devotes a section to the discussion of the modern idea of "pure poetry" or the doctrine of symbolism, which
we shall quote more fully since that doctrine is the basis of much
modern criticism. "So-called 'pure poetry' is usually prefaced
by a solemn formulation of doctrine, which alone concerns us
here. The practical realization of that doctrine, in so far as it
results in anything individual and original, is entirely outside the
sphere of theory and contemplation. This theoretical formulation begins by rejecting all conceptions of poetry as sentimental
effusion, or as the expression of a conceptual, oratorical or
emotion-arousing content. In other words, it is a protest against
the confusion of poetry with what in this book we have called
mere literature" (P, 54).

This protest, according to Croce, is justified as far as it
goes, but it lacks a foundation in a complete theory of art and
in the history of critical doctrines. "That in itself would not be
so bad, as the fact that these theorists persist in interpreting
genuine poetry—actually, all the poetry that has been composed from Homer to Goethe or to Ibsen and Tolstoy, all the
poetry which historically exists—as a mere literary vesture
which may clothe an emotional, practical or conceptual content" (P, 55).

"So the poetry of which they speak, and which is supposed
to begin with them, does not aim at being mere literature. But
it is not poetry either. By poetry I mean unity of form and
content, expression of complete humanity, vision of the partic-

ular in the universal, as expounded at the beginning of this book.

" 'Pure poetry' is instead the negation of poetry as expression. The idea of expression is replaced by the idea of 'suggestion.' Suggestion is produced by means of articulate sounds which mean nothing, or nothing in particular (which is the same), but stimulate the reader to understand them as he may like, and invite him to make up for himself images that please him and correspond to his way of feeling.

"Now all the things that surround us are at all moments stimulating and occasioning images and thoughts in our minds, and even impulses and actions: so they all 'suggest' things to us. Hence the perfect futility of the concept of 'suggestion,' which is supposed to define the operation of pure poetry" (P, 56).

This argument is a complete refutation of the much-touted concept of "suggestion" in modern poetics. Furthermore, the practical realization of this program, when it is consistent, results in a kind of vapid writing that Croce describes as "an effort of spasmodic and industrious energy, not leading to expression, this operation does not belong to poetic inspiration or to any contemplative or cognitive process, but to the practical will. Through reflection and calculation the will forges sounds and rhythms and builds up an object in which its author finds pleasure, but which does not offer to the reader anything more, as we have seen, than a blind and casual stimulation, accidental in its effects.

"In the construction of this artifact a certain diversion is to be obtained, either for oneself alone or for propagation outside oneself. The word 'diversion' has in effect been uttered by some of these theorists and encouraged the strangest practices and programs of pure poetry" (P, 56; cf. the essay on Mallarmé quoted in the next chapter).

This is a shrewd if destructive analysis of much modern verse deliberately composed to fit the symbolist formula. Croce also notes the curious alliance between pure poetry and certain forms of mysticism. His description of the pure poet that participates in this alliance is enlivened by gentle irony: "The pure poet assumes a serious and solemn air as he presents himself to his audience: his person is enveloped in mystery, his head is surrounded by a halo, his words sound as a promise, made through obscure hints or skilfully distributed silences, of wonderful changes in the world, of a new way of feeling life and of facing it. Mallarmé was considered by his faithful almost as the priest of an inaccessible divinity, and when one reads what his disciples say of Stefan George, one ends by not knowing whether they speak of a poet or of the founder of a religion. . . . Even Arthur Rimbaud is supposed to have been in his way a seer, who tried to attain a new vision of the world and a new ethic, by repudiating logic and morality, giving himself up to a wild and disorderly orgy of all the senses and realizing the perfect urchin [*voyou*] or the perfect criminal, so as to reach, through an experience of that kind, the ultimate foundations of reality" (P, 57–58).

So for Croce the literal realization of the program of pure poetry lies outside poetry, in the sphere of action—and of futile action at that. "What does not belong to it are the single lines, single stanzas, and some small compositions that in Mallarmé, in George, in Valéry and their like, can be understood and can be felt, and are admired, liked and learned by heart. These do not belong to "pure poetry" or to its theories, but to the hidden operation of the old expressive and 'impure' poetry, or rather to poetry without adjectives, which gathers up the finite into the infinite" (P, 58). The very last phrase belongs of course to the universalistic theory discussed in Chapter XI.

Since this indictment of modernism is likely to bring up countercharges of insensibility in the critic, let us see how Croce interpreted one of the lines most admired by the theorists of pure poetry. It is the line of Racine:

La fille de Minos et de Pasiphaé.

This is one of the lines of classical poetry which those critics exempt from their blanket condemnation of all poetry written before their time. It is recognized as poetry because it is thought to be absolutely meaningless and to depend for its intense beauty on its sound alone. Croce remarks: "It is certainly beautiful, but not in virtue of the physical combination of sounds. One might make infinite other combinations of such sounds without producing any effect of beauty. It is beautiful because these sounds, these syllables and accents, bring before us, in an instantaneous imaginative fusion, all that was mysterious and sinister, all that was divine and fiendish, all that was majestic and perverted, both in the person and in the parentage of Phaedra. And this is expressed by two epic names, that of the royal Cretan legislator and that of his incestuous wife, at whose side rises in our imagination the brutal figure of the bull" (us, 73).[14]

In this way Croce proves he can account for what is actually beautiful in "pure poetry" without resorting to its theories of "suggestion" and sound magic. So much for "pure poetry," which Croce added to his enumeration of the nonaesthetic expressions. This multiplication of divisions and subdivisions of "literature," "art for art's sake," "pure poetry" etc., reveals a capacity for minute classification that Croce had formerly been able to keep well within bounds, if not to suppress altogether, at the cost of being called a killjoy by the admirers of traditional classifications (PdE, 245; TPS, II, 185) and even (as we have seen) of being charged with "theoretical paralysis." Now admittedly not all of these classifications of Croce's are firmly established. But some of his classes of the unpoetic, such as oratory (which corresponds to what Collingwood was later to call Magical Art[15]) are genuine additions to the critical vocabulary and of considerable use in practical criticism.[16] It is good that critics and historians of literature should be relieved of the impossible task of evaluating as poetry many works of persuasion and edification which encumber the highways of literary history, and should have no longer to cudgel their brains for finespun and sophistical reasons therefor, relying on such pseudo concepts as "conventions," "techniques," "myths," etc., to justify their recognition of those works as poetry. It is well to have a class for great writers who are not genuine poets, such as Pindar and Juvenal, Lucretius and Rabelais, Montaigne and Voltaire, Pope and Swift. For it is no degradation to classify a work as "literature" when it has been premised that literature is a highly civilizing process, indeed a great institution. Poetry itself remains the unscheduled, unprogrammatical, spontaneous creation of genius.

Finally Croce has written in this book one of his richest and most packed critical passages, in which general theory is united with specific judgment over a wide area of world literature. It follows upon Croce's repeated warning not to be misled by the label of genres, and is here translated in part: "Suppose the label is 'a didactic poem.' What could be more poetically discredited than a didactic poem? and yet it could be the *Georgics* of Virgil, which is poetry. A comedy: how does a comedy come to differ from prose? lacking [as Horace says] a 'lively spirit and power' in words and things, is it not a mere prose discourse, a *sermo merus*, even when it is in metre? and yet that comedy may be *The Marriage of Figaro*, which is poetry, or full of poetry. A fable exemplifies a moral or prudential maxim: but the fables of La Fontaine go beyond Aesop and Phaedrus, and are little plays, each perfect in itself, or witty notations, feelings and reflections of the author. A *terzina* of the *Paradiso*, scholastic and theological in content, may rise to sublimity, and a *Spruch* by Goethe may charm us by its smiling grace. On the other hand, epics in swift and elegant stanzas, such as the *Lusiads*, are merely a political panegyric of a nation and of its history. . . . Novels that wear the mask of creative literature are found to be in reality books on history or historical popularizations, essays in the portrayal of social types, burning exhortations to action, magic lanterns for entertainment, confessions of tortured souls or exercises in artistic prose" (p, 112).

After publishing *La poesia* (1936), Croce continued for 16 more years to write papers on aesthetics and on general problems of literary criticism. They were collected in the two volumes of *Discourses on Various Philosophical Subjects* (1945), in the *Readings of Poetry* (1950) and in the *Investigations on Hegel* (1952). To these should be added a preceding volume provisionally entitled (Croce being then sixty-eight) *Last essays* (1935). Then there are Croce's minor writings, collected in the three series of *Pagine sparse*, etc. Each paper discusses some critical problem and brings some new argument or new illustration to the doctrine. Several of these papers have been already referred to in the text or the notes of this book. To one special topic we will devote the next chapter.

CHAPTER XIV

Croce and "Decadentism"

C ROCE'S ATTITUDE towards modern literature underwent a marked change during the 50 years of his career as a critic. As we saw in Chapter x, contemporary literature
was the subject of his first major critical engagement. Croce
then affirmed that an interest in contemporary writing was a
healthy thing for a critic and attacked historical scholars for
their indifference to the moderns. He even went to the length
of suggesting that all students of the classics should spend a
period of "military service" in the study of contemporary
writers, "in order to free themselves from pedantry, to acquire a
feeling for what is alive, and to prepare themselves to treat
ancient literature as if it were contemporary" (*PdE*, 114). All
this goes to support the contention of Luigi Russo that Croce
was the critic who conferred dignity upon the study of the
moderns and made it a serious discipline.[1]

During Croce's lifetime the leading groups of writers in
Italy were successively the school of Carducci, the aesthetes of
the D'Annunzio school, the Naturalists, the Futurists, and the
followers of French trends like symbolism and pure poetry.
Whatever the slogan of the group, Croce's critical approach
made him feel very little sympathy with -*isms*, and we find him
constantly engaged in argument against the doctrines (or the ra-
tionalizations) of one or other of these schools. In a remarkable
and almost prophetic paper of 1907, "On a tendency of the
most recent Italian literature" (LNI, IV, 179–96), Croce denounced the general insincerity and pretentiousness which he

275

found in contemporary trends like the aestheticism of D'Annunzio, the erotic mysticism of certain Catholic writers, and the sentimentalism of the Pascoli school. The D'Annunzio group was tending more and more towards a bellicose nationalism with imperialistic ambitions and antidemocratic overtones, thus paving the way for what later was to become Fascism. Croce condemned in strong terms this tendency, branding it as ethically corrupt and politically reactionary, especially in its hostility to socialism. In those years Italian socialism was still in its heroic age; it was raising the standard of living of Italian workers and giving them a new hope—a hope with which, it may be recalled, Croce had sympathized towards the turn of the century. And even in 1907, speaking of these proto-Fascists, Croce declared roundly that anyone who undertook to fight socialism "in its idea" was fighting civilization itself (LNI, IV, 195).

Another remarkable statement of sympathy with social reform occurs unexpectedly in a discussion of the independence of art from morality in 1905. There Croce described "a poor peasant eking out a living for his large family on a small field of a quarter of an hectare which is not sufficient to nourish him, while near him a whole estate extends for hundreds of hectares for the enjoyment of a single idle proprietor." For this unfair situation we should blame "the social institutions that cause these inequalities" (CC, I, 38).

But both the cause of social reform and civilization itself suffered a serious setback in 1914 with the outbreak of the World War, which put an end to the peaceful world of international cooperation and intellectual activity in which Croce had grown to manhood.[2] In this crisis Croce did not withdraw into an ivory tower or proclaim himself *au dessus de la mêlée*, like some other intellectuals, but took sides in the political debate and engaged himself without reservation, as is related in more detail in the biographical appendix to this book. It was during the last years of that war that Croce developed the aesthetics of Totality and denounced the literature of effusion and of emotionalism in all its forms, as we have seen in Chapter XI. In 1918 the cult of certain French writers elicited from him a succession of sharp attacks on what he then called "Enthusiasms of the pre-war period," viz. Barrès, Claudel and Rimbaud.[3] The essay on Barrès is a devastating piece of criticism, exposing the intellectual and moral weakness of Barrès' pretentious literary edifice. Claudel is shown to be merely a "neuro-pathological phenomenon." Rimbaud's doctrines and ideals were also subjected to destructive criticism (a summary of it is in the paragraph quoted in the last Chapter from P, 58), although one cannot say that Croce really came to grips with his poetry.

During the postwar period the stature of Mallarmé upon the literary horizons of France and Italy grew continually taller, and Croce, always sensitive to contemporary trends, took notice repeatedly of his doctrines and his accomplishment. There was a formal essay on him in 1933 (included in the later editions of PNP, 314–25), and another discussion in 1941 (PS, III, 286–87). In 1947 Croce reviewed a number of books on Mallarmé (NPS, II, 113–15) and another book gave him occasion for an essay of 1949 on "The secret of Mallarmé" (*Letture*, 158–67). Finally in 1950 he made a typically paradoxical parallel between Mallarmé and a poet of the Cinquecento: "The 'Après-Midi d'un Faune' in Mallarmé and in Pietro Bembo" (*Letture*, 168–73).[4]

The fame of Mallarmé is associated with the concept of "pure poetry," or the symbolist doctrine which was propagated by his group and which Croce criticized in the manner that we have seen in the previous chapter. To it he dedicated another paper in 1945, "On 'pure poetry'" (*Letture*, 259–72). Croce's objection to this doctrine is not only that it substitutes the vague concept of "suggestion" to the precise concept of expression, but that it claims to produce a new kind of poetry, different from all previous poetry ever written. This is at bottom a Romantic fallacy, indeed it might be called *the* Romantic fallacy *par excellence*, the fallacy first propounded by Friedrich Schlegel in his famous Fragment 116 of the *Athenäum*. There Schlegel proclaimed that there are two kinds of poetry, the poetry of the past and the poetry of the future: the former tied down to set forms and fixed patterns, the latter soaring unrestrained in the regions of pure whim. This dichotomy, which

itself owes something to Schiller's distinction of naive and sentimental poetry, was reincarnated in a variety of forms throughout the nineteenth century: as Classic and Romantic, Apollonian
and Dionysian, Naturalistic and Abstract, etc., until it reached
its present form.[5] In the twentieth century it also took the form
of "Futurism versus *Passatismo*." Croce had always rejected the
Romantic fallacy of the partition of poetry, and consequently
rejected also its later incarnations, however artfully disguised.
He himself was to become a prime target of the Futurist movement, one of its most celebrated pronouncements being a speech
made in Rome by a writer who was then one of its leaders,
Giovanni Papini, "Against Rome and Benedetto Croce"—or, as
Croce himself put it, "against the eternal city and this transitory
individual" (CVM, 269). And this although Croce had generously
encouraged some of the Futurists, like Papini, in their earlier and
more intelligent efforts. But he expected them to settle down
and work, like himself; and this they were not inclined to do.[6]

Croce saw in the contemporary movement other tendencies,
no less pernicious. He discerned a wide-spread irrationalism, or
the abandonment of reason for blind instinct or some other nonrational force, with the result that man's faith in freedom was
sapped and the way was open for the advent of totalitarianism.
He identified Fascist doctrine (in so far as there was such a
thing) with this irrationalistic trend, designated as "anti-historicism" or the rejection of historical thinking, in a paper of
1930 which made a deep impression at the time.[7] Irrationalism
was denounced again in a lecture of 1933, delivered at Oxford
when an honorary degree was conferred upon him, and entitled
"The Defence of Poetry." [8] He came to the attack again in
1940,[9] and in 1944 he took Proust as a representative of what he
called a decadent view of historical thinking.[10]

It is worth noting that Croce saw a connection between
these degenerate forms of literature and social conditions, particularly modern industrialism. In the *Breviary* he had observed
that "our own age is, or was, naturalistic in its culture and in-
dustrial in its practice; and artistic and philosophic greatness
will be unanimously denied to it" (NSE, 70; EA, 81). In 1928 he

said about decadentism: "the connection between this movement in its modern form and industrialism and the psychology that industrialism favours and fosters, is evident. Practical life, as it is lived today, is something entirely different from art; and modern art, instead of being the expression and hence the transcending of this life in the infinitude and universality of contemplation, aims at being the shouting, gesticulating and chromatic section of that life itself" (us, 27).

Irrationalism and aestheticism, the lack of positive ideals and the cult of morbid sensations are the main constituents of what Croce came to call "decadentism" and to define as the leading characteristic of this age. He included in it such writers as Verlaine, Valéry, Proust, Gide and George, and dedicated a series of discussions to them in his later work.[11] To this trend belongs an essay on Rilke, more favorably accented, but also remarkable for providing in the excellent quotations it makes from that poet the evidence for a somewhat higher evaluation of him than Croce himself gave (*Letture*, 188–208).

Finally in 1945 Croce discussed the "Aversion to Contemporary Literature" which he then frankly acknowledged (*Letture*, 324–29). He condemned the chicanery, the logrolling and the factionalism of the cliques of modern writers, and reaffirmed his rejection of "pure poetry" as a mere toy.[12] But even in this, his most hostile mood, Croce still maintained that there is no justification for indifference to, or neglect of, contemporary writing. On the contrary, he recommended it again to the student of the earlier periods of literature, because "the world of art is essentially one" (*Letture*, 328). The critic, he said, should avoid a consistently hostile attitude and stress the good things he is able to find, preferably passing the other things by in silence. This is presumably the reason why Croce the critic never wrote a study of the work of F. T. Marinetti or of G. Papini, or of any of the writers of poetry and of criticism prominent in Italy in the late thirties and forties.

In his attacks on "decadentism" Croce exposed many of the fallacies that are extolled as "the modern point of view" or "modern thought" or "modern poetics." This critique especially concerns the writer who aspires to be "modern" in everything, and who often combines the adoption of some contemporary literary -*ism* with a liberal attitude in political and social questions (for to be modern one must be a liberal). He may be a novelist who follows the naturalistic school in some of its more recent varieties, or he may be a poet and follow some symbolistic or postsymbolistic trend. He often combines these tendencies with a belief in psychoanalysis as the most advanced school of modern psychology, and yet cherishes ideals of political and social progress. But if man is under the irresistible domination of his instincts or complexes, if all his thinking is mere flow of consciousness, if man in a word is only an animal or a mechanism, how can he be expected to control his impulses and build society upon rational principles? Croce did not believe in the eighteenth-century idea of Reason nor in automatic progress, but he believed in the reason of history and in the spirituality of man. This means that for him history was a perpetual struggle for the realization of an ideal which can never be finally achieved but must always be fought for again. Hence for him irrationalism and decadentism were the forerunners of totalitarianism and were "softening up" society for it. Certainly Croce's own resistance to irrationalistic totalitarianism was prophetic and makes him one of the great moral teachers of our age.

But if Croce's criticism is valid against these ideologies, the general attitude of condemnation of contemporary writing which he approached cannot be maintained, on his own showing. His aesthetics has always taught that no blanket generalizations are possible in the realm of art, and that the program or the intention of the poet does not determine the character of the poem. Hence no general judgment of contemporary writing (that slippery chronological designation) is really permissible, but only studies of individual authors, each on his own merits, "*caso per caso.*" So Croce's critical principles still provide a basis for a more positive evaluation of modern writing than he himself gave to it. This is confirmed by the fact that "decadentism" has been studied by critics who worked under his influence and dealt with it so affirmatively that the term lost its negative meaning, and is now currently used in Italy as a noncontroversial name for modern trends.[13]

Croce's lack of appreciation for the poetry of some of the great names of the modern Parnassus, such as Mallarmé and George, may be due to a shortcoming of his individual sensibility. Every critic, as Croce has acknowledged late and early (NSE², 221; TSS, 130; CC, III, 11), has his limitations and cannot be equally sensitive to all varieties of poetry. But when it came to the charge that he himself was constitutionally incapable of judging modern poetry, Croce demurred, and retorted (as usual) with a witty anecdote (*Letture*, 226). No man can be young twice; and when Croce was young, he gave considerable evidence of sympathy with the literature of his own day, including close association and personal friendship with contemporary poets. He recalled his youthful labors in the very last sentence of the book from which most of these uncomplimentary remarks upon the moderns have been quoted (*Letture*, 329), and that seems sufficient indication how he wanted to be remembered by posterity—not as an enemy of the moderns, but as a positive critic of all periods of literature.

CHAPTER XV

Croce and the History of Criticism

CONCLUSION

AT THIS POINT we shall look briefly at Croce's contributions to the history of literary criticism. If by
criticism we mean general theory, then Croce's main contribution is the history of aesthetics which forms the second part of
his book of 1902. This history is often condemned for being explicitly written from the point of view of the author's doctrine,
so that every other theory is seen either as leading up to it or
away from it. But few, if any, of the critics have seen Croce's
anticipated defence of his own procedure, which was made in a
paper of 1901 referred to in Chapter I (*Primi saggi,* 193–96).
Croce's argument was that the history of a science can only be
written from the point of view of that science itself. If aesthetics,
as Croce argued, is the science of expression, then the history
of aesthetics is the history of the concept of expression. Or to
put it differently: the history of a science, or of a body of truths,
is an account of the manner in which those truths came to be
discovered. And the only way in which we can identify the
truths discovered in the past is to know what is true according
to the science of today, or to the best of our knowledge.

Discussion of recent histories of literary criticism confirms
that it is impossible for the historian not to have a point of view
—i.e. a conception of what literary criticism is, or should be.[1]
The only way out of this dilemma—history referring to general
theory and general theory referring back to history—is to achieve
as comprehensive a theory of aesthetics as possible, i.e. one that

includes and does justice to all the insights obtained on the subject in the past. In the first part of his paper on the lyrical intuition (*PdE*, 3–15), as we have seen in Chapter III, Croce showed how his own theory fulfilled this requirement. However, we saw in Chapter I that Croce renounced his own history of aesthetics when he rejected the notion of the "single problem" of philosophy, and replaced it with the conception of the history of aesthetics as a history of particular problems, each to be evaluated in terms of what preceded it and not of what followed it.[2] But he still depended on his conception of aesthetics for the definition of what an aesthetic problem was, so his defence of his method in 1901 still holds good.

On the other hand, if by literary criticism we mean practical criticism, or the judgment on individual authors and works, then Croce's contributions to its history become too numerous to be discussed in detail. He began, as usual, with the question of method in a series of papers written between 1903 and 1909 (*PdE*, 419–42). The main problem in a history of criticism is the proportion of space to be assigned in it to general theories of aesthetics (*PdE*, 422). Saintsbury wanted to exclude them entirely from the history of criticism. But it is a cardinal principle of Croce that critical practice cannot be divorced from critical theory. Every judgment on a work of art involves a concept of art, and every concept of art arises in connection with individual works of art and pronounces judgment upon them. However, Croce believed that in practice the two could be distinguished, but only practical convenience could dictate in each case how to separate one element from the other. For instance, said Croce, in a history of German literary criticism the names included would be not Leibniz or Kant, but Lessing, Herder and Gervinus, not the first volume of Hegel's aesthetics but the second or third. Writers excluded from the history of criticism may receive a prominent place in the history of aesthetics, and vice versa. Some excellent philosophers of art are poor critics; this happens because they lose touch with their ideas when they face the living work. Some poor philosophers of art are good critics: this happens because when they face the work of art they forget their theories and have resort to different ideas (*PdE*, 422–23).

These discussions of general principles are as usual accompanied by a full measure of exemplification in the shape of a number of contributions to the history of criticism in Italy. They range all the way from the sixteenth century (F. Patrizio) to the end of the nineteenth. Croce contributed also to the history of literary criticism in other national areas (especially German), and reviewed a good number of books on the subject. His critique of Saintsbury's *History* is a classic; just by giving a faithful summary of a section of this book, Croce demonstrated its lack of inner connection. Saintsbury's observations may be true singly, but they do not form any recognizable pattern (CC, II, 280–89).

On the theoretical side, Croce came to stress more and more that the history of aesthetics, or of critical ideas, is grounded upon the history of philosophy in general. "The advance of aesthetic thought from the *mimesis* of Greek philosophy to modern 'lyrical intuition' is the same advance that led from philosophical materialism or dualism to absolute spiritualism" (P, 197; cf. NSE², 100, 211, 319–20; CC, V, 79; *Letture*, 218).

On the practical side, a peculiarly Crocean contribution is the history of the criticism of individual writers. As we have seen in Chapter XII, Croce wrote surveys of Dante and Ariosto criticism which are models of their kind, besides *aperçus* of previous criticism in the studies of Shakespeare, Corneille, Goethe, etc. This has proved particularly beneficial to Italian scholarship, which following Croce's lead has produced a number of such histories. In other countries one usually finds only collections of essays on a writer by various hands, without any intrinsic connection and without concern for the effect on the mind of the reader; they provide material for a history of criticism, but not the history itself. In English there is no general history of Shakespearian criticism to speak of; the only considerable attempt of the kind, by A. Ralli,[3] is little more than a collection of book digests.

Possibly as the result of his experience in writing these histories of criticism, Croce modified in 1925 his previous view of the scope of the history of criticism. While he continued to assign its theoretical content to aesthetics (and therefore to the history of philosophy), he now identified the history of practical criticism with that criticism itself: "the history of criticism in its particularity, as the history of the problems concerning each work of art, coincides with literary criticism itself, which is always a prosecution, discussion and correction of previous criticism, making it broader and deeper" (cc, iii, 69). The opinions of previous critics on a writer should not be cast out on the rubbish heap, but interpreted so as to show how some views, inadequate in themselves, yet point to a fuller and truer view and may be integrated in it. In this manner the neoclassical and romantic interpretations of Corneille are transcended and integrated in Croce's own interpretation of that poet, as we saw in Chapter xii.

But the later developments of Croce's theory of history which we have not mentioned yet, raise certain problems which affect also the history of criticism. At one time (1909) Croce's trend towards a thoroughgoing historicism led him to assert that "even the concept varies" (*Logica*, 147). Now the categories under which we subsume historical facts are concepts, and Croce in later years came to assert more and more firmly their immutability. As we have seen, they came to resemble in this respect the Platonic Ideas.[4] This led Croce to the belief in what may be called the "omnipresence" of the categories: they have all been present to the mind of man at all times and places.[5] So the category of art, which includes poetry, is not only always and eternally the same, but has also always been present as such to man's thought (us, 68) and operated in all the aesthetic judgments ever pronounced (nse, 95; p, 297).

If this is so, how is it that systems of aesthetics and philosophies of the Beautiful differ from each other? At times Croce answers that it is not the categories that change, but our thinking of them (*La storia*, 25; English translation, 35–36).

But are not the categories the organs of our thinking? so how can they be immutable and eternal objects standing over and against our own mutable and transitional thinking? This problem leads us to the heart of Croce's *Logic*, but here we can only indicate it without discussing it further.

At other times Croce gave an answer which is more consonant with his concept of philosophy as the methodology of history. The formulations which the eternal categories receive in different theories vary because of the different historical conditions under which they were formulated, and particularly because of the fresh historical facts (new works of art, new events in political and social history, etc.) which the new philosophy arises to interpret (us, 216). Furthermore, as he says elsewhere (us, 68), there are always new errors and confusions to deal with or new forms of old errors, error being for Croce the result of the interference of the practical activity in the theoretical (*Logica*, 274–77). So the old truth, reaffirmed against a new error, requires a new formulation.

Empiricists of course may smile at Croce's eternal categories. But everybody, including the empiricists, uses categories in thinking about things, and we might as well know what they mean and how they harmonize with each other. This of course has been the problem of philosophy ever since Plato, but there have been few philosophers with a stronger feeling for history than Croce and with a better knowledge of it. He brought the age-old problem of values and universals in close touch with the living problems of historical and critical inquiry and made philosophy more historical and history more philosophical. The two disciplines can never be the same after his discussion of them. We can of course take refuge in skepticism and reject all attempts at philosophy. But as Croce has repeatedly shown, there is no attitude that is more dogmatic and authoritarian than the skeptical: for the skeptic believes that he alone is right and everybody else is wrong, whereas Croce believed that all other philosophers were right, at least in part, and that he himself was right only in so far as he could interpret and integrate the thoughts of other men. That is what he called "historicism."

IT WILL BE by now apparent that when we speak of the doctrines of Croce we must make a distinction between the Croce of 1902 and of 1912, of 1925 and of 1936—not to speak of minor variations, such as between 1893 and 1945 or 1950. We have a series of successive systematizations, as Croce himself called them, rather than a single, rigid system. From these systematizations—which although historically continuous are not always logically consistent—it is possible to pick out certain leading ideas and build up a useful doctrine for literary criticism, such as I have tried to present in this book. I will conclude by summing up these ideas.

Croce's doctrine of lyrical intuition, as exemplified and particularized in Chapters II and III seems his best effort in this direction. The concept of totality, discussed in Chapter XI, appears to be a deviation from this doctrine, which counteracts it and runs the risk of losing the ground gained, unless totality is understood in a very qualified sense or as a mere metaphor. In his earlier doctrine, Croce established a place for the knowledge of individuality which few philosophers before him had ever approached. The doctrine of totality, on the other hand, represents a tendency which can proceed only in the direction of intellectualism, or the denial of knowledge of individuality as an independent form of mental activity. If Croce did not relapse into this, it was because the survival in him of most of his earlier tendencies and aptitudes preserved him from an unequivocal return to intellectualism. But they did not preserve him entirely from assuming a certain kind of moralism, which is covered in Chapter XI.

Thus qualified, Croce's doctrine presents a coherent system of solutions to most of the problems of literary aesthetics and criticism. Poetry, or creative writing in general, is seen as the building up of an individual image, a total picture, a form expressing a deep emotional content, an art which is not an algebra of signs or a meaningless artifact unrelated to the basic impulses of humanity. The concept which I have called the principle of Integration means that the image is a synthesis of previous images, blending them so as to form a new individual. It accounts for the fact that a work of art is not an isolated phenomenon, but presents similarities and affinities with other works, without any need of resorting to classification by genres or to evolutionary schemes of development.

The concept which I have called the principle of Contextuality affirms that poetry is not made up of isolated words, but on the contrary that single words are abstracted from the continuous unit of expression, the sentence or the poem. This principle explains the relation of words to poetry, or of poetry to speech, and accounts for the impossibility of translation and paraphrase of poetry.

These two principles, when brought together and considered in relation to each other, will be found to be only one principle, seen from two different sides: and that is the principle usually known as the organic unity of poetry. For the principle of Integration sees the Multeity in Unity (to use again Coleridge's terms), while that of Contextuality sees the Unity in Multeity. Both see the poem as the synthesis of a multiplicity.

Organic unity is now widely accepted by critics, but few even today have carried it to its ultimate logical consequences as Croce did. This, as we have seen, means the rejection of all doctrines which separate form and content, i.e. all the doctrines of rhetoric, of ornament, of diction, of metre and style as a garment of thought. It also means the rejection of literary genres as aesthetic entities and as standards of criticism. And since form is individual, it means the rejection of literary history as a developmental scheme in favor of critical monographs on individual works or writers.

But at the same time the concept of organic unity is attacked by critics of pragmatistic or positivistic tendencies, who see in it only a delusion, a metaphor taken literally, or the resemblance between a poem and a living body erected into a logical concept.[6] But the metaphor is no more than a metaphor, and the principle itself may be stated without any reference to biological organisms.[7] Its formula is the relation of the parts of a work to the whole as a unity which determines its constituents, or as a form which absorbs and transcends its content. This principle can be called with equal propriety by a name which has no reference to organisms, such as the principle of synthesis, or of integral unity, of total unity, of complex unity, of unity in variety, etc., and still stand as a logical principle.[8]

No doubt every abstract term that we use in a logical discourse implies ultimately a metaphor, since all abstract terms were once concrete; but this only goes to support Croce's theory of the priority of the intuition over the concept. In the same context of logical discourse every metaphor stands for a concept, otherwise the critic's own argument against Croce would be meaningless.

Croce differs from some other upholders of organic unity in conceiving it as a function of the expressive act and not as a static quality of an external object, the artifact. For some modern critics the poem, "as object, is as separate from the poet as a brooch is from a jeweller." [9] This is what a philosopher might call "naive realism." Surely it is not necessary to adopt an idealistic epistemology to see that a poem is the creation of the mind of man, and exists only in the mind of man, whatever may be true of "rocks and stones and trees."

This creation Croce defines as the expression of an emotion through an image, the image and the emotion both coming to be at the same time. We have seen other critics working their way toward this concept of expression, apparently unaware of what Croce did for it. We have also seen that "intuition" is not a peculiarly Crocean term, and that there is good precedent for it in English criticism.

We have seen, too, that for Croce criticism is not only "taste" or the reproduction of a previous expression by an informed observer; it is something more, it is judgment by means of a category or universal concept. Hence Croce rejected critical relativism: the concept of expression, being a universal, is valid at all times and places. Hence also the thesis that criticism does not differ essentially from literary history at its best: criticism must be historical and history must be critical, or they both degenerate and become impressionism and philologism respectively.

Croce's analysis of the method of practical criticism appears to be the most comprehensive and flexible prescription for the evaluation of literature yet developed. The only notable shortcoming we found in Croce's doctrine of criticism was the omission of the characterization of the image. But this omission did not reflect itself in Croce's practice, for he was continually characterizing aesthetic images and estimating their unity and consistency, their quality and vigor. Finally, Croce's dialectic of the various activities of mind affords a method for discriminating nonpoetry from poetry and for assigning the unpoetical in its various forms to its proper sphere in the system of mind and in the field of history.

APPENDICES AND NOTES

Biographical Notes on Croce

THE FOLLOWING NOTES are intended to be only an outline of important events in the life of Croce. There is no attempt here to give a finished portrait of the man or to settle the various controversies about his political and other attitudes. The reader is referred to two other biographical treatments: Cecil Sprigge, *Benedetto Croce, The Man and the Thinker* (London, 1952), which is the best general account of Croce's career in English, and Raffaello Franchini, *Note biografiche di B. Croce* (Turin, 1953). A vivid impression of Croce will be found in Vincent Sheean's introduction to his translation of Croce's *Germany and Europe* (New York, 1944). A recent discussion of Croce's role in the fight against Fascism will be found in Nino Valeri, *Da Giolitti a Mussolini* (Florence, 1956), pp. 197–212. See also F. Nicolini, "Brevi cenni sulla vita" etc., in *Nuova Antologia*. CDLVII (1953), 9–20, 120–53. For further references see the bibliographical Appendix.

Benedetto Croce was born at Pescassèroli in the Abruzzi region of Italy on February 25, 1866. He belonged to a well-to-do family of the upper middle classes, with estates in the Abruzzi and a home in Naples. Croce himself gives an account of his forbears and their background in the papers on Montenerodomo and Pescassèroli reprinted in the Appendix to his *History of the Kingdom of Naples* (1925), pp. 291–394.

The young Croce was given a strict Catholic education (*Au*, 28 ff.). His literary interests bore their first fruit at the age of 16 when (1882) he published his first articles (see above, Chapter IX). In 1883 he published his first book, a school edition of Politian's *Stanze*. In the summer of the same year he lost both his parents and his sister in an earthquake at Casamícciola. He was himself buried under the ruins for the whole night and received lasting physical scars. A younger brother, elsewhere at the time survived.

Croce's spirit was broken by the tragedy and he even contemplated suicide (*Au*, 40). He went to live in Rome with his uncle Silvio Spaventa, a parliamentary leader of what was then the Right and brother of the philosopher Bertrando Spaventa. The latter, who had developed Hegelianism in a subjectivist direction, died early in 1883; Croce had little sympathy or contact with him (*Au*, 87–91). Through Silvio Spaventa, Croce came in contact with the political and social life of the capital, but it did not arouse him out of his lethargy. He attended courses at the Faculty of Law in the University of Rome without much enthusiasm, and left without taking a degree; the only degrees he was to receive were honorary degrees from foreign universities (Oxford, Freiburg, and Marburg). But in Rome he came under the influence of A. Labriola (as related in Chapter 1), who provided a lasting stimulus to his intellectual life.

In 1886 Croce returned to Naples and dedicated himself to historical research, as related in Chapter ix (cf. Franchini's biography, p. 19). He employed his private means to build up a great library and travel across Europe; he visited Germany, Spain, France and England (Franchini, *op. cit.*, p. 20). He was in London in 1891: see the amusing description of Croce at this time made by a friend, the poet S. Di Giacomo (quoted by L. Russo, *Critica letteraria contemporanea*, 2nd ed., 1946, I, 331).

The traditional account of Croce's conversion from pure historical scholarship to philosophy is that one day he read an article by the historian Pasquale Villari on the question: "Is history a science or an art?" (1891). This was supposed to have undermined Croce's faith in history and turned him to philosophy (cf. PS, I, 207; for Croce's opinion on the article by Villari see *Primi saggi*, p. 7, note). Actually Croce had early in his life undergone a religious crisis, as related in Chapter I, then sought around inconclusively for another faith or philosophy (*Au*, 41–44). His early philosophical studies under Labriola belong to this period. But the discussion of the question on history led to a reorientation which resulted in Croce's first philosophical monograph, *History brought under the general concept of art* (1893), followed by a parallel discussion of *Literary criticism* (1894), which aroused a storm of controversy (cf. Franchini, *op. cit.*, pp. 20–21).

In 1895 Labriola introduced Croce to the works of Marx, and

for a while Croce became an enthusiastic student, and even follower, of Marxism. But he thought his way out of Marxism by making, as usual, a thorough study of its doctrines which resulted in a critique, embodied in the book on Marxism published in 1900 (English translation, 1914). Croce then returned to aesthetics, and after a period of intense concentration during the summer of 1899 (*Au*, 63–64) he completed the first sketch of his work, or the *Theses of Aesthetics* printed in 1900, and then worked up into the *Aesthetic* of 1902 (see Chapter IX).

Meanwhile he had met Giovanni Gentile and entered into a close intellectual alliance with him, resulting in their collaboration in the review *La critica*, which started publication in 1903 (see Chapter X). In 1905 he printed the first sketch of his *Logic* and in 1907 a section of his *Filosofia della Pratica*, the final version of both being published in 1909. The study of Hegel appeared in 1907 and of Vico in 1911. In 1908 he gave the lecture on the lyrical intuition at the philosophical congress of Heidelberg (see Chapter III). From now on his publications multiply and no attempt will be made to enumerate them.

In 1904 Croce began his cooperation with the publisher Giovanni Laterza of Bari, operating under the name of "Giuseppe Laterza e Figli," and edited, besides a collected edition of his own works, a series of publications which became an essential part of Italian culture: the collection of Italian classics, *Scrittori d'Italia*, the "Classics of Philosophy," the "Library of Modern Culture," etc. (NPS, I, 7–9). For his services to Italian letters he was made a Senator in 1910, a life appointment in the nomination of the then Prime Minister, Giovanni Giolitti. In 1914 Croce married Adele Rossi, from whom he had four daughters, Elena, Alda, Lidia and Silvia.

During the early period of the war of 1914 Croce took sides with those Italians who, like Giolitti, believed that Italy should remain neutral or at least bide her time. This led to bitter political controversies. Like Giolitti, Croce was accused of being a "Germanophile," an obvious partisan distortion, for Croce, while an admirer of German philosophy and scholarship, had not waited until 1915 to show his dislike of Prussian militarism. On this point see Croce's own account, *Germany and Europe* (English translation cited above), and Sprigge's biography, pp. 16–17 and 49–50. Croce's culture extended beyond Italy and Germany to France and Spain and to a lesser degree England. He never became thoroughly familiar with the English-speaking world, though he used the literature in English on any subject he took up, from economics to aesthetics. Indeed the clarity of his style has been ascribed, by at least one critic, to his study of the English economists (Sprigge, *op. cit.*, p. 28).

When the Italian government, overriding the opposition of the Giolitti group and the Socialists, finally entered the war in May, 1915, Croce as a patriotic citizen accepted the decision and gave his support to the war. But he continued to criticize the excesses of nationalist propaganda and expressed skepticism in the democratic ideals professed by the Allies (see *Pagine sulla guerra*). The aftermath of the war, notwithstanding victory, was a political and economic slump, which saw the rise of communism and a reaction against the war party. Giolitti returned to power for a while and made Croce his Minister of Education (1920–21). Croce then proposed educational reforms which were supported by Gentile, who had always taken a deep interest in such questions, but the proposals were defeated by Parliament (NPS, I, 47–59). After the fall of Giolitti parliamentary government gradually crumbled, leading to Mussolini's seizure of power in the fall of 1922.

Croce at that time was favorably disposed to Mussolini, who made Gentile Minister of Education and gave him *carte blanche* to reform the whole school system. Gentile easily carried the reforms that Croce had attempted in vain, as well as other measures that also appealed to Croce and which he supported. After the murder of the Socialist opposition leader Matteotti in 1924 things changed. Gentile resigned his portfolio, but remained as a leader in the Fascist party. He fought a losing battle in defence of his educational reforms, which on the whole were more liberal than Fascist (cf. NPS, I, 63). Croce gradually turned to the opposition, joining in October the Liberal Party, or what might be called the old party of his uncle Silvio.

In 1925 Gentile issued a "manifesto of Fascist intellectuals" to which Croce replied with an anti-Fascist manifesto which was signed by a large number of intellectuals and completely eclipsed Gentile's. Croce's manifesto is reprinted in PS, II, 380–83, together with other public statements he made at the time. The rift between Croce and Gentile, who had worked side by side for a generation and become a byword among Italian intellectual youth, was never healed. Fascism became a dictatorship; Croce continued to vote against the government and to make, or to try to make, speeches in the Senate, the last and most important of which was in 1929 against the Treaty and Convention with the Papacy. The speech was shouted down in the Senate by the majority and a wave of arrests of Croce's friends followed its publication. Croce's complete works were placed on the Catholic Index in 1932, following the publication of his *History of Europe in the 19th Century* (TPS, I, 176).

Croce became now a fulcrum of intellectual resistance to Fascism. Anti-Fascists sought his advice and guidance, which he continually gave. I shall quote one instance, drawn from my personal experience, which I do not think has yet been published. When the Fascist regime finally made party membership compulsory for all new teachers, younger men following academic careers were faced with a serious dilemma. Either join the party, which most of them were disinclined to do, or give up their career altogether. In this predicament Catholics turned for guidance to their Church and Communists to their Party. Others who were neither Catholics nor Communists turned to Croce. His answer (by word of mouth, since writing had become dangerous) was as follows. All men who were in a position to give up their jobs should do so, as a protest; the others, who had to to teach for a living, should join the Fascist Party and continue to teach, but at the same time they were to keep in touch with the men who would be ousted by the Fascists, and endeavor to uphold the principles of liberty in their teaching.

On November 2, 1926 Croce's home was raided by a gang of Fascist toughs, and attempts were repeatedly made in the following years to suppress his review and silence his voice. But Croce was both a Senator of the Kingdom of Italy and an international figure, and by skilful defence tactics he and his publisher, G. Laterza, who always stood by him, succeeded in keeping the review going throughout the whole period of Fascism and even through the war years. On this fact see Croce's letters to his publisher and other documents in *Pagine politiche* (Bari, 1945), pp. 119–34, and his account of his relations with the regime in NPS, I, 69–71, and in *Contributo alla critica di me stesso*, 1945 edition, pp. 75–76.

In September 1943, when Allied forces approached Naples and the German army took over in most of Italy, to escape arrest Croce fled with his family to the island of Capri, already in the hands of the Allies. His role in the ensuing political developments, including the King's attempts to form a government with the anti-Fascist parties and Croce's renewed tenure of the Ministry of Education, was related in his diary, published in English by S. Sprigge as *Croce, the King and the Allies* (1950).

Croce celebrated his 80th year by opening a postgraduate school of historical studies in his home, the "Istituto italiano di studi storici in Napoli." His inaugural lecture may be read in *Filosofia e storiografia*, 351–67, and he gave a series of occasional talks to the students, collected in TSP, I, 3–116. *La critica* ended its publications after liberation in 1944, with 42 years of service. But Croce continued to write for and publish a periodical without regular date, called *Quaderni della Critica*, of which 20 issues were published in 1945–51.

Croce suffered a stroke in February, 1950, which greatly impaired his energies. He was still able to read and dictate, however, and went on working to the end, which came on November 20, 1952. See his last message to his friends, TPS, I, 118–20.

Crocean Bibliography

THERE IS NOW a full bibliography of Croce's works: Fausto Nicolini, *L' "editio ne varietur" delle opere di B. Croce*, saggio bibliografico con taluni riassunti o passi testuali e ventinove fuori testo (Napoli, 1960; Biblioteca del "Bollettino" dell'Archivio Storico del Banco di Napoli, vol. V). This gives the date of every collected paper by Croce. It supersedes E. Cione, *Bibliografia crociana* (Turin, 1956), which contains a number of inaccuracies: e.g., it lists as published in 1942 (p. 399) the volume that was being edited for the *Library of Living Philosophers* by P. A. Schilpp as published in 1942 (Nicolini, pp. 201, 438, 479), but which never saw the light. However, Cione can still be used for the literature on Croce. His work incorporates part of the following: G. Castellano, *Introduzione allo studio delle opere di B. Croce* (Bari, 1920); G. Castellano, *B. Croce, il filosofo, il critico, lo storico* (Bari, 1936); Anon., *L'opera critica, storica e filosofica di B. Croce* (Bari, 1942).

CROCE'S COLLECTED WORKS IN ITALIAN

The author classified and arranged his own works which were published by the well-known firm to which he was adviser, Giuseppe Laterza and Sons of Bari. Dates of the first edition and of the latest I have seen are given. It should be remembered that some works were originally published outside this collection with different titles. An asterisk marks the works of which there is an English translation.

1. *Philosophy of Spirit*

*1. *Estetica come scienza dell'espressione e linguistica generale.* 1902. 9th ed., 1950.

*2. *Logica come scienza del concetto puro.* 1909. 8th ed., 1958.

*3. *Filosofia della pratica, economica ed etica.* 1909. 6th ed., 1950.

*4. *Teoria e storia della storiografia.* 1917. 7th ed., 1954.

2. *Philosophical Studies*

1. *Problemi di estetica.* 1910. 4th ed., 1949.

*2. *La filosofia di G. B. Vico.* 1911. 4th ed., 1947.

*3. *Saggio sullo Hegel, seguito da altri scritti di storia della filosofia.* 1913. 4th ed., 1948. (Only the study of Hegel has been translated, and not the other papers included in this volume.)

*4. *Materialismo storico ed economia marxistica.* 1900. 8th ed., 1946.

5. *Nuovi saggi di estetica.* 1920. 3rd. ed., 1948.

*6. *Etica e politica.* 1922. 3rd ed., 1945. (Translated in part as *Politics and Morals,* 1945.)

7. *Ultimi saggi.* 1935. 2nd ed., 1948.

8. *La poesia.* Introduzione alla critica e storia della poesia e della letteratura. 1936. 5th ed., 1953.

*9. *La storia come pensiero e come azione.* 1938. 4th ed., 1943. (Translated as *History as the story of liberty,* 1941.)

10. *Il carattere della filosofia moderna.* 1941. 2nd ed., 1945.

11 & 12. *Discorsi di varia filosofia.* 2 vols., 1945. (Some of these papers are translated in *My Philosophy,* 1949.)

13. *Filosofia e storiografia.* 1949.

14. *Indagini su Hegel e schiarimenti filosofici.* 1952.

3. *On Political and Literary History*

1. *Saggi sulla letteratura italiana del Seicento.* 1911. 3rd ed., 1948.

2. *La rivoluzione napoletana del 1799.* 1897. 5th ed., 1948.

3–6. *La letteratura della nuova Italia.* (4 vols.) 1914–15. 5th ed., 1947–49.

7. *I teatri di Napoli dal Rinascimento alla fine del secolo decimottavo.* 1891. 4th ed., 1947.

8. *La Spagna nella vita italiana durante la Rinascenza.* 1917. 4th ed., 1949.

9 & 10. *Conversazioni critiche.* Serie I e II. (2 vols.) 1918. 3rd ed., 1942.

11. *Storie e leggende napoletane.* 1919. 4th ed., 1948.

*12. *Goethe.* 1919. (The 4th edition, enlarged to 2 vols., 1946, is not available in English.)

13. *Una famiglia di patrioti ed altri saggi storici e critici.* 1919. 3rd ed., 1949.

*14. *Ariosto, Shakespeare e Corneille.* 1920. 4th ed., 1950.

15 & 16. *Storia della storiografia italiana nel secolo XIX.* (2 vols.) 1921. 3rd ed., 1947.

*17. *La poesia di Dante.* 1921. 6th ed., 1948.

*18. *Poesia e non poesia.* 1923. 5th ed., 1950.

19. *Storia del regno di Napoli.* 1925. 3rd ed., 1944.

20 & 21. *Uomini e cose della vecchia Italia.* (2 vols.) 1927. 2nd ed., 1943.

*22. *Storia d'Italia dal 1871 al 1915.* 1928. 9th ed., 1947.

23. *Storia dell'età barocca in Italia.* 1929. 2nd ed., 1946.

24. *Nuovi saggi sulla letteratura italiana del Seicento.* 1931. 2nd ed., 1949.

25 & 26. *Conversazioni critiche.* Serie III e IV. (2 vols.) 1932. 2nd ed., 1951.

*27. *Storia d'Europa nel secolo decimonono.* 1932. 7th ed., 1947.

28. *Poesia popolare e poesia d'arte.* 1933. 2nd. ed., 1946.

29. *Varietà di storia letteraria e civile.* Serie I. 1935. 2nd ed., 1949.

30. *Vite di avventure, di fede e di passione.* 1936. 2nd ed., 1947.

31. *La letteratura della nuova Italia.* Vol. 5. 1939. 3rd ed., 1950.

32. *Conversazioni critiche.* Serie V. 1939. 2nd ed., 1951.

33. *La letteratura della nuova Italia.* Vol. 6. 1940 3rd ed., 1950.

34. *Poesia antica e moderna.* 1941. 2nd ed., 1943.

35 & 36. *Poeti e scrittori del pieno e tardo Rinascimento.* (2 vols.) 1945.

37. *La letteratura italiana del Settecento.* Note critiche. 1949.

38. *Varietà di storia letteraria e civile.* Serie II. 1950.

39. *Letture di poeti e riflessioni sulla teoria e la critica della poesia.* 1950.

40. *Poeti e scrittori del pieno e del tardo Rinascimento.* Vol. III, 1952.

41–44. *Aneddoti di varia letteratura.* 2nd ed. (4 vols.), 1953.

4. Miscellaneous ("Scritti vari")

1. *Primi saggi.* 1919. 2nd ed., 1927.
2. *Cultura e vita morale.* 1914. 2nd ed., 1926.
3. *Pagine sulla guerra.* 1919. 3rd ed., 1950 (with the title *L'Italia dal 1914 al 1918: Pagine sulla guerra*).
4–8. Still to be published. (Presumably PS and NPS, now in following section.)
9–10. *Terze pagine sparse.* 2 vols. 1955.

PUBLICATIONS IN ITALIAN
OUTSIDE THE COLLECTED WORKS

5. More Miscellanies

Some miscellaneous writings were gathered in the following volumes published by R. Ricciardi of Naples. They were not numbered by the publisher, but are here numbered for convenience:

1. *Curiosità storiche.* 1919.
2. *Nuove curiosità storiche.* 1922.
3. *Aneddoti di varia letteratura.* 3 vols., 1941. Collects the material included in the two preceding volumes and adds considerably to it. The 2nd ed. was included in the Collected Works, as above, section 3, vols. 41–44.
4. *Pagine sparse, raccolte da G. Castellano.* Serie I–IV. 1919–27. 2nd ed. in 3 vols., 1943.
5. *Nuove pagine sparse.* 2 vols. 1948.
6. *Bibliografia vichiana*, accresciuta e rielaborata da F. Nicolini. 2 vols. 1948.

To these must be added some volumes published by Laterza outside the collected edition, including *Gli scritti di F. de Santis e la loro varia fortuna, Saggio bibliografico*, 1917, and *Storiografia e idealità morale*, 1950, which contains two philosophical papers (pp. 133–38) not reprinted elsewhere.

6. Letters

Carteggio Croce-Vossler 1899–1949. Bari, 1951. With an introductory note by Vittorio de Caprariis. Croce himself published occasionally in *La critica* selections from his vast correspondence: e.g. with George Sorel in 1927–30. The latter is fully discussed in Serge

Hughes' unpublished dissertation, "The role of French culture in the development of Croce's thought" (Princeton, 1955).

7. *Reviews*

Croce edited more than one review in his lifetime, but the most important is *La critica*, published by Laterza in 42 volumes, 1903–44. An index to the first 12 vols. was published in vol. XII (1914), 453–70. This journal was followed by *Quaderni della Critica*, 20 issues, 1945–51.

8. *Selections*

Filosofia, poesia, storia. Pagine tratte da tutte le opere, a cura dell'autore (Milano-Napoli: Ricciardi, 1951). Selected by Croce, with a short account of his work by himself (pp. 1177–82) and a chronology of his works (pp. 1182–87). Notwithstanding the sub-title, there is no selection from the *Aesthetic* or the *Breviary*. The full index, prepared by R. Gerbi, pp. 1191–1237, is the only available subject-index to any portion of Croce's work. The *Estetica* had a subject-index in its first two editions, but it was suppressed in the third. However, the English translation has a subject-index.

9. *Political Writings*

Also outside the Collected Works are some volumes published immediately after the end of World War II, containing miscellaneous political writings. Most of them were published by Laterza:

Per la nuova vita dell'Italia. 1944.
Pagine politiche. 1945.
Pensiero politico e politica attuale. 1946.
Due anni di vita politica italiana. 1948.
**Quando l'Italia era tagliata in due*. 1948.

The last item contains extracts from Croce's diary and was translated by Sylvia Sprigge as *Croce, the King and the Allies*, 1950. See below, section 12.

10. *Works Edited or Translated by Croce*

These make a long list, which will be found in the bibliographies listed above. Croce edited several books, contributed introductions and prefaces to others, and translated among other things Hegel's *Encyclopaedia of Philosophical Sciences* (1907, 2nd ed. 1922). From the Neapolitan dialect of the 17th century he translated into Italian a collection of fairy tales, *G. B. Basile's *Cunto de li cunti,* and added an introduction and commentary (1925). It was translated into English by N. M. Penzer, 1932, as *The Pentamerone* (2 vols.).

11. *Autobiography*

Croce's autobiographical essay, entitled *A contribution to the criticism of myself,* was originally written in 1915 and published separately. It is now included in the Collected Works, in the second and later editions of 2.6, *Etica e politica,* with later additions to the narrative. The original essay was ably translated by R. G. Collingwood with a preface by J. A. Smith as B. Croce, *An Autobiography,* Oxford, 1927.

12. *Manuscripts*

As may be seen from the above list of publications, there is not much that Croce left unpublished. In the later additions to his autobiography he refers to certain memoirs ("ricordi") of his on the Fascist era which he left to be published posthumously: see *Contributo alla critica di me stesso,* Nuova edizione con un'appendice inedita (Bari, 1945), p. 72 note. There is also his diary, in which he kept a daily record of his work and of which extracts from July 1943 to July 1944 have been published and translated: see Nicolini, p. 439. His large correspondence is now being collected with a view to publication: see Nicolini, pp. 423–38.

For the appearance of a Croce manuscript, the reader is referred to a photo of the first page of the book on Vico in C. Antoni (and others), *Omaggio a B.C.* (Torino, 1953), facing p. 4. See also Nicolini, facing p. 297.

TRANSLATIONS OF CROCE'S WORKS
ON AESTHETICS AND CRITICISM

Douglas Ainslie's translations of Croce are notoriously faulty: cf. C. J. Ducasse, *The Philosophy of Art* (New York, 1929), p. 42, and E. Roditi, "The Growth and Structure of Croce's Philosophy," JAAC, I, (1942), 17. The later translators (Carritt, Collingwood, etc.) are much better, and Arthur Livingston was almost perfect. In the preface to his translation of *The Conduct of Life* (New York, 1924;

the original is now included in 2.6), pp. ix–xi, he outlined the principles which he followed. References by numbers below are to the sections and volumes of the above list.

Aesthetics

Aesthetic as Science of Expression and General Linguistic, transl. by D. Ainslie (London, 1909). The appendix gives a translation of the Heidelberg lecture, pp. 371–403. Part II of the *Aesthetic* is very poorly summarized. A revised translation by Ainslie, with the Part II given complete but the Heidelberg lecture omitted, was published in London by Macmillan in 1922 and reprinted as a paperback by the Noonday Press, New York, 1953 (3rd impression 1956).

The Breviary of Aesthetic, transl. by D. Ainslie (in *The Book of the Opening of the Rice Institute*, Houston, Texas, 1912), II, 450–517.

The Essence of Aesthetic, transl. by D. Ainslie (London: Heinemann, 1921). A badly needed revision of the translation of the *Breviary* with a new title but still some of the old errors.

The original of the *Breviary* is included in the *Nuovi saggi di estetica* (above, 2.5), together with a number of other papers, of which only the following have been translated: "The Character of Totality of Artistic Expression," *The English Review*, June 1918; "Literary Criticism as Philosophy," *Contemporary Review*, October 1920; "Nationalism in Literature," the *Menorah Journal*, x (1925), 428–35; "On the Nature of Allegory," *The Criterion*, III (April 1925), 405–12.

Of the *Problemi di estetica* (1910, 2.1 above) complete translations have only been made of the following papers: the Heidelberg lecture, in the 1st edition of the English translation of the *Aesthetic*, as above;

"The Nature of Architecture," transl. by D. Ainslie, *Architecture*, XVI (1923), 273–78.

"Aesthetics" was translated by R. G. Collingwood for the *Encyclopaedia Britannica*, 14th ed., 1929. The original is printed in *Ultimi saggi* (1935, 2.7 above) with the title "Aesthetica in nuce."

"Aesthetic Education" appeared in *Pitman's Encyclopaedia of Education*, London, ca. 1915. The original is in cc, I, 79–86.

The Defence of Poetry, transl. by E. F. Carritt (Oxford, 1933), was reprinted in J. H. Smith and E. W. Sparks, *The Great Critics*, an *Anthology of Literary Criticism* (3rd ed., New York, 1951), pp. 695–709. The original is in us, 59–78.

"Introduction to xviiith Century Aesthetics," transl. by R. G. Collingwood, *Philosohy*, ix (1934), 157–67. The original is in us, 106–23.

"On the Aesthetics of Dewey," transl. by K. Gilbert, *Journal of Aesthetics and Art Criticism*, vi (1948), 203–7. The original is in 2.12.

"Dewey's Aesthetics and Theory of Knowledge," transl. by F. S. Simoni, *ibid.*, xi (1952), 1–6. The original is in 2.14.

My Philosophy, and Other Essays on the Moral and Political Problems of Our Time, selected by R. Klibansky and transl. by E. F. Carritt (London, 1949). A selection of essays from 2.7, 2.11 & 12, and 2.13, including a few on aesthetics.

"The Condition of Criticism in Italy," transl. by F. J. Thompson, *Johns Hopkins University: Lectures in Criticism* (New York, 1949), pp. 171–86. The original is in nps, i, 165–72.

"Poetry (Selections)," transl. by A. H. Gilbert, in G. W. Allen and H. H. Clark, *Literary Criticism from Pope to Croce* (New York, 1941), pp. 628–45.

Critical Essays

Ariosto, Shakespeare and Corneille, transl. by D. Ainslie (London, 1920); 3.14 above.

The Poetry of Dante, transl. by D. Ainslie (London, 1922); 3.17 above.

Goethe, with an Introduction by D. Ainslie and a portrait (London, 1923); 3.12 above (only vol. i translated). The translation is by Miss Emily Anderson.

European Literature in the Nineteenth Century, transl. by D. Ainslie (London, 1924); 3.18 above.

The essays in this volume on Balzac, G. Sand, Flaubert, Ibsen and Scott, were originally published in various periodicals in English translations.

"The Poetry of Racine," *The Dial*, lxxxiv (1928), 483–88; the original is included in later editions of asc; "Commedia dell'arte," transl. by P. D. Bury, *Theatre Arts Monthly*, xvii (1933), 929–39; the original is in 3.28, 503–14; "Goethe and Germany" in *Goethe: Homage*, published by unesco (New York, 1950), pp. 41–47; the original in tps, i, 219–23.

AIDS TO THE STUDY OF CROCE'S PHILOSOPHY

As a help to the study of Croce's thought, the following is a rough classification of his works on philosophy. The basic works are the four volumes of the Philosophy of the Spirit, i.e. (following the numeration adopted above) 1.1 *Aesthetic, 1902; 1.2 *Logic, 1909; 1.3 *Philosophy of the Practical, 1909; 1.4 *Theory and History of Historiography, 1917 (translated and published in the United States as *History, Its Theory and Practice,* 1921).

Two parts of the system, Aesthetics and Historiography, were followed by whole volumes of developments and revisions. The *Aesthetic was followed by 2.1 *Problems of Aesthetics,* 1910; 2.5 *New Essays on Aesthetics,* 1920; and 2.8 *Poetry,* 1936, all of which are fully discussed in the present volume. The *Theory of Historiography* received an important development in 2.9 *History as Thought and as Action,* 1938 (translated as *History as the Story of Liberty,* 1941, reprinted by Meridian Books, 1955).

After the latter work, Croce did not compose any other single book on philosophy, but continued to write short papers. He collected a large number in a series of volumes entitled as follows: 2.7 *Last Essays,* 1935, so called because Croce was then 68; but they are not, and were not intended to be, his last work; 2.10 *The Character of Modern Philosophy,* 1941; essentially a continuation of the 1938 volume on *History;* 2.11 & 12 *Discourses of Various Philosophy,* 1945, 2 vols.; 2.13 *Philosophy and Historiography,* 1949; 2.14 *Investigations on Hegel and Philosophical Clarifications,* 1952. All these volumes contain occasional papers on aesthetics. The selection and translation from them with the title *My Philosophy* (1949) is useful, but not to those who are unfamiliar with the foundations of Croce's thought. Croce's main contributions to the history of philosophy are his studies of *Vico (2.2, 1911) and of Hegel, the latter a famous essay of 1907, *What is dead and what is alive in the philosophy of Hegel* (English translation, 1915), which was reprinted in volume 2.3 (1913) of the Works, together with a number of papers on the history of philosophy. Other papers on this subject are scattered in the volumes of essays listed above.

Croce's doctrines on ethics and politics were developed in a volume entitled 2.6. *Ethics and Politics* and were applied in the writings on war and Fascism in 4.3 and in the uncollected writings. A few of the more topical were translated as *Germany and Europe:*

A Spiritual Dissension, with a lively introduction by Vincent Sheean (1944). The miscellaneous essays on ethical questions that Croce entitled *Fragments of Ethics* (earlier title of 2.6) were brilliantly translated by A. Livingston as *The Conduct of Life* (1926).

Croce was very active in reviewing books and answering critics, and the many short pieces which he wrote in this vein are collected in several volumes. Croce himself edited his reviews and minor writings in the five series of *Critical Conversations* (3.9, 10, 25, 26, and 32). In this collection he arranged them topically and often revised them, sometimes introducing significant alterations (especially in the earlier texts). The original texts in *La critica* and elsewhere should be consulted by anyone interested in tracing in detail the development of Croce's thought, as has been occasionally attempted in this volume. Still more material of the same kind, including many of his lively *Postille* in his review, is collected as *Pagine sparse* (*Scattered Pages*). Of the latter, there are three series, comprising a total of seven volumes: 5.4 *Pagine sparse,* 2nd edition, 1948; 5.5 *Nuove pagine sparse,* 1949; and 4.9 & 10, *Terze pagine sparse,* posthumous, 1955. A fourth series is forecast in Nicolini's bibliography, pp. 283–369.

The incunabula of Croce's philosophical thinking—the essays on *History* of 1893 and on *Literary Criticism* of 1894—were reprinted by Croce, together with other writings of the same period, in a volume entitled 4.1 *Primi saggi,* 1919 (*First Essays*). Still earlier efforts will be found in the appendices to the *Pagine sparse,* vol. 1, and to the *Nuove pagine sparse,* vol. 2.

For the history of Croce's thought, the successive Introductions to the various volumes are particularly useful. The Introduction to *Primi saggi* reviews his earliest efforts, and there is an important "Note" in the *Logica,* pp. 226–27. And of course there is the *Autobiography,* now much more extensive than the original version which was translated into English by Collingwood in 1927.

A SHORT SUBJECT-INDEX TO
CROCE'S CRITICAL ESSAYS

This index includes all completed critical essays on literary figures or works and adds briefer references in a few cases of special interest. In particular, *La poesia* contains critical *aperçus* on a large number of writers, ancient and modern, which are in the main too brief to be listed here. The index is arranged by national literatures, authors being listed in approximate chronological order under each literature. References are to the sections and volumes of Croce's collected works. Works of which there is an English translation are marked by an asterisk.

Greek Literature

Homer 3.34, 31–38. The Homeric Question 2.3, 269–89, and 2.10, 184–92. Aristophanes 2.1, 94–102, and 2.8, 251–52. Sophocles' *Antigone* 2.8, 251–52.

Latin Literature

Lucretius 3.34, 39–47 (with the *Georgics*). Virgil 3.34, 48–54 with Lucretius, and on Dido 3.34, 55–64. Terence 3.34, 1–30. Catullus 3.34, 65–71. Propertius 3.34, 72–96. Horace 3.34, 97–101; cf. 2.28, 245–57. Juvenal 3.34, 102–7. Martial 3.34, 108–15. Suetonius *Quaderni della Critica*, XIV, 10–17.

Biblical and Medieval Literature

On the Gospel narrative of Jesus and the adulteress 3.34, 116–22. The *Dies Irae* 3.34, 123–30. The *Quid, tyranne, quid miraris?* 3.34, 131–37. Bertran de Born 3.34, 143–47. Shorter discussion of medieval epics (*Cid, Nibelungenlied*, etc.) 2.28, 285–86, 384–85.

French Literature

Ronsard 3.34, 257–64; cf. 2.8, 272–73. Du Bartas 3.24, 195–209. *Corneille 3.14. Racine 3.14, 2nd ed. 267–74 and 3.34, 305–17 and 3.42, 33–36. Molière 3.34, 318–23; cf. 2.8, 290–91. Mme de la Fayette *Quaderni della Critica*, XIX–XX (1951), 144–46. Saint-Évremond 3.42, 206–10. Diderot 3.34, 333–39. Beaumarchais 3.34, 340–49. Chénier 3.34, 358–65. Rétif de la Bretonne 3.39, 89–96. P. L. Courier, 3.43, 394–98. Hugo 3.34, 383–94. *De Vigny 3.18, 120–32. *Stendhal 3.18, 90–102. Constant 3.39, 104–13. *George Sand 3.18, 186–206. *Balzac 3.18, 240–51. *Musset 3.18, 226–39. Baudelaire 3.18, 252–65; see also 3.34, 395–411 and 3.39, 268–69; 5.5, II, 107–10. *Flaubert 3.18, 266–78. *Zola 3.18, 279–91. *Daudet 3.18, 287–90. Mallarmé 3.18, 320–32 (added to 2nd ed.); "The Secret of M." 3.39, 158–67; "The *Après-midi* of a faun in M. and in Pietro Bembo" 3.39, 169–73. "The *Dame aux Camélias* and French Drama of the later 19th century" 3.39, 138–57. *Maupassant 3.18, 307–19. Becque 3.25, 282–95. Huysmans 3.38, 298–312. Verlaine 3.39, 174–87. Rimbaud 4.3, 200–207. Barrès 4.3, 185–93. Claudel 4.3, 193–200. *Proust 2.12, 138–45 (English translation in *My Philosophy*, listed above.)

Notes on Paul Valéry and Goethe 4.10, 172–73; on Pierre Louÿs and Chateaubriand 3.44, 494–99; and on Gide's anthology of French verse 4.9, 235–38. For a list of references to other French writers, see Anon. *L'opera* cit., p. 309, n. 23, and O. Ruggiero, *La letteratura francese nella critica de B. Croce.*

English Literature

Shakespeare: Croce's essay appeared in *La critica* in 1919, in a special double issue entirely dedicated to Shakespeare. In addition to the critical essay, pp. 129–222, it included a review of two books on Shakespeare's influence in Italy by L. Collison-Morley (1916) and S. A. Nulli (1918), to which was appended a full bibliography of Italian studies on Shakespeare 1880–1919 (pp. 244–53). The bibliography was brought up to date and reprinted by Croce in *Nuove curiosità storiche* (Naples, 1922), pp. 228–37. The Shakespeare issue included also the text of De Sanctis' lectures on Shakespeare, pp. 223–43 (reprinted in F. De Sanctis, *Teoria e storia della letteratura,* ed. B. Croce, Bari, 1926, II, 196–231), and a note on "Shakespeare, Naples and the Neapolitan *Commedia dell'arte*" (pp. 254–63), reprinted in 3.24, 269–83. The critical essay was included in 3.14* and edited with introduction and notes by N. Orsini, Bari, 1948 (a new edition, 1960, is in the press); the introduction contains references to later Shakespearian discussions by Croce.

Burns 3.34, 350–57. *Scott 3.18, 65–76. G. M. Hopkins 3.34, 419–46. D. H. Lawrence ps, III, 7.

German Literature

Walter von der Vogelweide 3.34, 143–42. Gessner *Quaderni della Critica,* XVII–XVIII (1950), 118–25. *Goethe 3.12. On a ballad by Goethe and a sonnet by Pistoia 3.34, 200–208; on two lyrics by Goethe and by Carducci 3.39, 97–103; on a lyric by Goethe 3.34, 326–28. *Schiller 3.18, 31–44; cf. 2.1, 458–61. Hölderlin 2.11, 54–72. *Kleist 3.18, 52–59. *Werner (Z). 3.18, 45–51. *Chamisso 3.18, 60–64. *Heine 3.18, 172–85. Mörike 3.39, 132–37. Rilke 3.39, 188–208. George NPS, II, 114–16.

Scandinavian Literature

*Ibsen 3.18, 291–306. Oehlenschläger 3.29, 302–19.

Spanish Literature

Romances 3.34, 185–99. *La Celestina* 3.34, 209–22. Torres Naharro *Quaderni della Critica*, xv (1949), 79–87. *Lazarillo de Tormes* 3.34, 223–31. Cervantes, *Don Quijote* 3.34, 247–56; *Viaje del Parnaso* 3.1, 121–54; *Persiles y Sigismunda* 3.39, 52–62. Spanish Preachers and Fray Gerundio 3.1, 155–81. Diego Duque de Estrada 3.30, 321–59. Lope de Vega 3.34, 265–84; *Dorotea* 3.32, 128–34. Calderón 3.39, 21–42. Tirso de Molina, *Condenado por desconfiado* 2.12, 56–62; *El burlador de Sevilla* 3.39, 43–51. Góngora 3.34, 285–304. *Fernán Caballero 3.18, 207–25.

Italian Literature

Dante: 3:17, *The Poetry of Dante* (1922), is entirely dedicated to the aesthetic criticism of Dante. On *Paradiso*, XXXIII, see 3.34, pp. 151–61. On *"The Nature of Allegory," with special reference to the *Comedy*, see 2.5, 2nd ed., pp. 329–38. Later discussions in 3.39, pp. 1–20, "On the poetic reading of D.," and on *Paradiso* 2.12, pp. 41–56. *On Dante's political theories, see Croce's article in the *Encyclopaedia of Social Sciences*, 1931, IV; 708–9 (the original is in *Pagine sparse*, II, 225–27). On Dante's meaning for the modern world, an answer to a questionnaire, *New York Evening Post*, September 1921, in *Pagine sparse*, II, 257–61. Several monographs on Dante are discussed in *Conversazioni critiche*, s. II, 3.10, 209–14; s. III, 3.25, 187–215; s. V, 3.32, 96–105.

14th and 15th centuries 3.28. *Ariosto 3.14. Tasso 3.23, 236–39, and 3.24, 232–46. 16th century 3.28, 3.35–36, 3.40. 17th century 3.1, 3.23–24. 18th century 3.37. 19th century 3.18, 3.3–6. 20th century 3.31, 3.33.

Croce has in effect covered in these volumes the whole field of Italian literature: all major and several minor writers. For the reason why he did not collect them into a history of Italian literature, see Chapter IX, note 35. A more detailed listing of Italian literature subjects will be found in the Italian bibliographies quoted above. There is a generous selection of the essays themselves edited by Mario Sansone in B. Croce, *La Letteratura italiana per saggi storicamente disposti*, Bari, 1956, 3 vols.

Notes

INTRODUCTION

1. See John Crowe Ransom's "Poetry: a Note in Ontology" in *The World's Body* (New York, 1928), pp. 111–42, and his "Wanted: an Ontological Critic" in *The New Criticism* (Norfolk, Conn., 1941), pp. 279–336. Recently Ransom has been assaying the aesthetics of Kant and of Hegel in "The Concrete Universal: Observations on the Understanding of Poetry," *Kenyon Review*, XVI (1954), 554–64, and XVII (1955), 382–407. Sir Herbert Read's *The True Voice of Feeling* (New York, 1953) prints as an appendix the famous address by Schelling on the relation of the arts to nature.

2. Cf. L. Bergel, "Croce as a Critic of Goethe," *Comparative Literature*, I (1949), 349 ff. See also R. Wellek, "B. Croce, Literary Critic and Historian," *ibid.*, V (1953), 75–82, apparently the forerunner of a chapter in Wellek's masterly *History of Modern Criticism*. The chapter on Croce in W. K. Wimsatt Jr. and C. Brooks, *Literary Criticism: A Short History* (New York, 1957), is the best account of Croce available in any general history in English.

3. Aestheticians of the German school are often critical of Croce for treating aesthetics as the theory of art, and not as the theory of the Beautiful. See for instance H. Kuhn in D. Runes and H. G. Strickel (eds.), *Encyclopaedia of the Arts* (New York, 1946), pp. 741 and 746. Croce was well acquainted with this conception of aesthetics, having started from it himself, as we shall see in Chapter I. But the concept of the Beautiful was subjected to criticism in the *Aesthetic* in Chapters X and XI (E, 87–95; A, 78–86). It was taken up again in "The extra-aesthetic concept of the Beautiful and its use in criticism," NSE, 285–93 (cf. US, 123). E. Utitz' distinction between the two conceptions of aesthetics was discussed by Croce in CC, I, 20–21. Dessoir's analogous distinction was discussed in *La critica*, VII (1909), 122–33, by A. Gargiulo.

As instanced above, references will be given throughout both to the pages of the Italian original (E) and to the pages of the

English translation (A) of the *Aesthetic,* even though the translation given in this book is usually revised. The same has been done for the *Essence of Aesthetic* (EA) and for its original, the "Breviario di Estetica," in the *New Essays on Aesthetics* (NSE). For an explanation of the symbols used and the editions referred to, see the List of Abbreviations, page ix. A full list of Croce's works is given in the Bibliographical Appendix.

4. Ortensia Ruggiero, *La letteratura francese nella critica di B. Croce* (Napoli, 1955).

5. Statements by Croce on the phases of his aesthetics are to be found in the preface to the 5th (1921) and subsequent editions of the *Aesthetic* (E, vii–viii), not translated into English, the English translation (A) being based on the 4th edition, 1912; and also in *PdE*[4], 30, note 1; NSE[2], 127; US, vii–viii; P, 210–11; CC, V, 84–85.

6. J. E. Spingarn, *Creative Criticism and Other Essays,* new and enlarged edition (New York, 1931), p. 176. Spingarn's own contribution to the expounding of Croce will be discussed in Chapter VIII.

7. Reprinted in *Primi saggi,* 1919, p. 28 and note.

8. A number of instances of this failure to contact will be cited in the course of this book. But it may be noted here that the valuable bibliography appended to N. Foerster (ed.), *Literary Scholarship, Its Aims and Methods* (Chapel Hill, 1941), pp. 239–55, does not list a single book by Croce, although it includes continental critics and covers the years 1904–41 in which Croce was most active.

9. Spingarn, *Creative Criticism . . . ,* p. 175.

10. R. Piccoli, *B. Croce: An Introduction to his Philosophy* (New York, 1922).

11. Cf. "Il superamento" (1910), CVM, 116–19 and 206; "I superatori" (1914), PS, I, 377–79; "Considerazioni sul superamento" (1928), CC, IV, 71–72; TPS, I, 79. On some of the earlier controversies that prompted these remarks, see G. Castellano, *Ragazzate letterarie. Appunti storici sulle polemiche intorno a B. Croce* (Napoli, 1919).

12. For Croce's impact on the U.S. in general, see F. S. Simoni, "B. Croce: A Case of International Misunderstanding," *Journal of Aesthetics and Art Criticism* [JAAC], XI (1952), 7–14, and my article, "Note sul Croce e sulla cultura americana," in F. Flora (ed.), *B. Croce* (Milan, 1953), pp. 361–66, together with L. Bergel's observations on the two preceding papers, "Croce in America," *Lo Spettatore Italiano,* VI (1953), 503–4. For the impact of Croce's critique of poetic genres on American scholarship, and the attacks

of the New Humanists on Croce, cf. Irvin Ehrenpreis, *The "Types Approach" to Literature* (New York, 1945), pp. 43-49.

Other recent American discussions of Croce's aesthetics are: Guido Errante, "Croce's Aesthetics as Related to the Whole of His Philosophical Thought," in the volume by various authors, *Italian Culture in the Twentieth Century* (New York, 1952), pp. 29-43. The same volume also contains a paper by A. W. Salomone, "The 'New Sciences' of History in Italian Thought: Machiavelli, Vico and Croce." For A. R. Caponigri's book see Chapter I, note 37. A. A. De Gennaro, "The Drama of the Aesthetics of B. Croce," JAAC, XV (1956), 117-21; by the same author, "Croce e Ortega y Gasset," *Italica*, XXXI (1954), 237-43, and "B. Croce e Ch. A. Beard," *ibid.*, XXXV (1958), 112-18. M. C. Nahm, "The Philosophy of Artistic Expression: The Crocean Hypothesis," JAAC, XIII (1955), 300-313. M. Krieger, "B. Croce and the Recent Poetics of Organicism," *Comparative Literature*, VII (1955), 252-58. L. Bergel, "B. Croce (1866-1952)," *Books Abroad*, XXXI (1957), 349-52. P. A. Bertocci, "Croce's Aesthetic in Context," *The Personalist*, XXXVIII (1957), 248-59. Further references will be given in the body of this book. I have not been able to see the unpublished dissertation of Gaetano Nardo, "The Aesthetic of B. Croce, a Critical Evaluation of its Terminology and Internal Consistency," New York, 1957.

The publication of my paper in the JAAC for 1955 was followed by a discussion in vol. XIV (1956), 318-23, 387-88 and XV (1956), 257-58. See also A. Scaglione, "Croce's Definition of Literary Criticism," *ibid.*, XVII (1959), 447-56; and E. Wasiolek, "Croce and Contextualist Criticism," *Modern Philology*, LVII (1959), 44-54.

13. Calvin G. Seerveld, *Benedetto Croce's Earlier Aesthetic Theories and Literary Criticism: A Critical Philosophical Look at the Development During His Rationalistic Years* (Kampen, Netherlands, 1958).

CHAPTER *i*

1. For Italian Positivism cf. cvm, 41–46; ss, ii, 107 ff., ii, 193; lni, iv, 179 ff.; *Storia d'Italia dal 1870 al 1915*, 1928, 2nd ed., pp. 133–51. For reactions against Positivism from other quarters, see R. Wellek, "The Revolt Against Positivism in Recent European Literary Scholarship" in W. S. Knickerbocker (ed.), *Twentieth Century English* (New York, 1946), pp. 67–89.

2. Among the works recommended by Labriola was R. Zimmermann's *History of Aesthetics* (a Herbartian book). See M. Corsi, *Le origini del pensiero di B. Croce* (Florence, 1951), p. 180. Corsi's book is a detailed account of this early period, with previously unpublished material.

3. For Croce's mature opinion of Herbart see the paper on him (1908) in *Saggio sullo Hegel* etc., 1913, pp. 352–62, and his "Farewell to Herbart" (1943) in *Discorsi*, i, 97–106. See also the references in the essay on Hegel, the *Aesthetic*, the *Logic* etc. It is not possible to give a complete index to Croce in these notes; only the more important references will be cited, together with some of the others. For instance, on Herbart see also tps, i, 123–24.

4. For Croce's attendance at the lectures of Tari, which "were one of the regular sights" of the University of Naples (a, 384), see tps, i, 6; *Letture*, 265. For Croce's mature judgment on Tari, see e, 428–32, a, 383–87; lni, i, 407–13; ps, i, 226.

5. The Tari review is reprinted in ps, i, 478–80.

6. *Primi saggi*, 1919, pp. 65 and 163.

7. *Ibid.*, pp. 8–12 and 35. Similar conclusions were reached 65 years later by J. A. Passmore in *Philosophy*, 33 (1958), 97–111.

8. Cf. Croce's *Materialismo storico ed economia marxistica*, 1921, 4th ed., p. xiv. In the papers of this period there is a keen appreciation of Hegel's concept of the Idea (*ibid.*, p. 5) as well as a defence of Kant's ethic against Marxist critics (*ibid.*, p. 31; *Au*, 92). For the substance of Croce's critique of Marxism, see the summary in Seerveld, *op. cit.*, pp. 9–10.

9. Much to the disgust of Labriola; see ps, iii, 46. On Labriola's influence on Croce cf. cc, iv, 73–76, and the paper on "Marxist Theory in Italy (1895–1900)" in *La critica* of 1938, reprinted in the 6th edition of *Materialismo storico* etc., 1941. See also ss, i, 185–87; tps, i, 124.

10. The *Theses of Aesthetics* were reprinted by A. Attisani, *La*

prima forma della Estetica e della Logica, Memorie accademiche del 1900 e del 1904 (Messina-Roma, 1924).

11. Reprinted in *Primi saggi,* 1919, pp. 193–99.

12. For a list of philosophical theses which Croce held in common with Gentile and in which Gentile's influence may well be paramount, see cc, II, 67–68. But the claims of wholesale derivation of Croce's aesthetic from Gentile, made by Gentile himself in 1913 in controversy with Croce, and still later by Gentile's disciple Ugo Spirito (for these claims see Spirito, "Gentile e Croce," *Giornale critico della filosofia italiana,* gennaio-marzo 1950) are preposterous. While Gentile did influence Croce in 1899 on some particular doctrines of aesthetics (see below, Chapter III, note 30, and Chapter VII, note 2; cf. Croce's own acknowledgment, *PdE,* 339, note 4), the foundations of Croce's aesthetics, and indeed of his system, had already been laid in 1893, as shown above in the text. Spirito's claims of abundant acknowledgments made by Croce in unpublished early letters to Gentile can refer, at the earliest, to the year 1896 (Spirito's own date, pages 5, 7 and 10 of the offprint). From the formulation of 1893 Croce's system developed into a dialectic of "distinct" forms of spiritual activity, in contrast to the dialectic of opposites in Hegel and in Gentile. Cf. Croce's own rebuttal of Spirito, TPS, II, 86–91.

13. For Croce's method being both inductive and deductive, see E, 48; A, 42; both a priori and a posteriori, *Logica,* 140–44. See also the paper "Against the concept of the a priori in philosophy," *Discorsi,* II, 12–14.

14. Croce's theory of the concept and of the pseudo-concepts will be referred to in Chapter V on literary genres.

15. For an answer to the question: "is there such a universal element in man's mind?" see the *Logica,* 3–13. For the ulterior question (which of course is metaphysical, even if Croce does not call it so) "can we identify spirit with reality in general?" see *Pratica,* 168–70. A complete answer is given only by the whole system.

16. As noted by E. Troeltsch: see *L'opera filosofica, storica e letteraria di B. Croce* (Bari, 1942), p. 167. Cf. "the real job of philosophy is understanding facts, i.e. the world we live in," CVM, 239, and also US, 217. On the positive contributions of positivism cf. Croce's *Teoria e storia della storiografia,* 1920, 2nd ed., p. 138.

17. Cf. "Are we Hegelians?" answered in the negative, CVM, 47–52, and *Au,* 87–101.

18. Against metaphysics see *Logica*, 169–70, 192–94, 352–57; *Teoria e storia*, cit., 136–48; NSE, 304–8; US, 213–21, 264–65; *Carattere della filosofia moderna*, 1–22; *Discorsi*, II, 28–35.

19. Cf. *Logica*, 15–27, 384–88; *Saggio sullo Hegel* etc., 146; NPS, II, 145–46 (review of a book by M. Planck) and 146–47.

20. See CC, I, 142–47; *Discorsi*, II, 16; *Indagini su Hegel*, 136; and particularly PS, I, 186–87. The last reference belongs to a discussion with Professor F. De Sarlo (1907), a very bitter but also very illuminating controversy. The personal breach with De Sarlo was healed years later when Croce took the initiative of inviting him to the International Congress of Philosophy at Oxford in 1930.

21. As already noted, especially by D. Pesce, "Platonismo e monadismo nella filosofia di B. Croce," *Giornale critico della filosofia italiana*, 1955, p. 71. This paper is one of the best short philosophical discussions of the basic principles of Croce.

22. A general exposition of the dialectic of "distincts" is in EA, chap. III; NSE^2, 52–69.

23. *Logica*, 54; *Saggio sullo Hegel*, 58–60, 165–66. For early statements of the distinction see the cited volume, *Materialismo storico* etc., 1921, 4th ed., pp. 101, 128, 232–33, 241–44.

24. E, 84; A, 75; *Pratica*, 15–21. This point is of course debated by critics of Croce. For general references to criticism of Croce see the bibliography included in the appendices.

25. The relation of the forms was first defined as circular apparently in 1908: see *Pratica*, 205. For an account of the various stages of development of the theory of circularity, see A. Bruno, "La formulazione crociana dei distinti" etc., in F. Flora (ed.), *B. Croce* (Milan, 1953), pp. 107–28.

26. The introduction of the form-matter relationship in the dialectic of "distincts" (e.g., *Indagini su Hegel*, 268) is discussed by D. Pesce, *op. cit.*, p. 75, and by C. Antoni, *Commento a Croce* (Venice, 1955), p. 165. The Aristotelian dyad of form and matter is cardinal in Croce, who applies it to the most varied problems of aesthetics (e.g., *PdE*, 442), of logic (*Logica*, 157), of ethics (*Discorsi*, I, 160–61), of political theory (PS, III, 13), of theory of historiography (*Storia*, 7), etc. But he never gave an *ex professo* discussion of it, though well aware of its historical connections with Aristotle and with Hegel (P, 196).

27. Against "aesthetic primitivism" or the identification of poetry and art with an early stage of human development, see Croce's re-

peated criticism of Vico (E, 256–57; A, 232–33, etc.), and cf. NSE², 303 and P, 297–98. The problems of origins must never be confused, according to Croce, with the problem of essence: e.g., E, 145; A, 132; PdE⁴, 201; CC, I, 55, etc. See also "Il primitivo," CC, V, 62–65.

28. The problem of the relation between the opposites and the "distincts" is one of the most critical points in Croce. In the *Saggio sullo Hegel,* pp. 55–68, the opposites were, so to speak, subordinated to the "distincts." But in 1909 Croce went further and argued that the opposites were produced by the "distincts": *Logica,* 68; cf. *Saggio sullo Hegel,* 165 (a passage which is dated 1912); US, 341–43 (1924); *Filosofia e storiografia,* 1949, pp. 16, 60–61; and *Indagini su Hegel,* 1952, pp. 51–52.

D. Faucci's closely analytical book, *Storicismo e metafisica nel pensiero crociano* (Florence, 1950), is largely concerned with this problem; cf. Croce's comment on it, TPS, I, 123–25. See also L. Scaravelli, *Critica del capire* (Florence, 1942), pp. 77–96 (also noted by Croce, *Discorsi,* II, 13 n.); C. Antoni, *op. cit.,* pp. 48–65; and R. Franchini, *Esperienza dello storicismo* (Naples, 1953), pp. 204–10.

29. "Provisional systematizations" appears in the preface to the third edition (1917) of the *Logica:* see the 8th ed., 1958, p. vi; and again in *Filosofia e storiografia,* p. 58.

30. For the rejection of the single fundamental problem of philosophy see TSS, 139–41 (1917). This theory was taken by I. Babbitt to mean that "there is no permanent problem in philosophy" ("Croce and the Philosophy of Flux," *Spanish Character and Other Essays,* Boston, 1940, p. 67). But what Croce maintained was that there was no permanently *unsolved* problem of philosophy. If, as Babbitt believed, there was a permanent problem (Babbitt's problem of the One and the Many) and it has not been solved yet, then according to Croce it must be a poorly formulated problem, or else philosophy is little more than a "sublime inconclusiveness" (US, 353–59).

31. Croce acknowledged that this approach to the history of philosophy was seriously criticized by A. Labriola (E, viii) and others (NSE², vii).

32. The problem of the history of aesthetics will be taken up again in Chapter xv.

33. On the "nondefinitive" character of philosophy see *Logica,* 338; *Pratica,* 390; NSE, 5–6; EA, 3–4; CC, I, 256; *Filosofia e storiografia,* 177–82. For its application to the history of aesthetics, see

the paper "The beginning, the periods and the character of the history of aesthetics" (1916), NSE, 93–120; US, vii–viii; *Discorsi*, II, 102–3; *Letture*, 218.

34. Croce's answer to this objection is in CVM, 201–9 and CC, V, 265–66.

35. For a penetrating and fully documented study of the way in which the concept of a "nondefinitive" philosophy alternated in Croce with the concept of immutable truth, see S. Zeppi, *Studi crociani* (Trieste, 1956), pp. 105–41, although I do not feel that the terms he uses in his conclusions (e.g. *"umanistico"* and *"teologico,"* pp. 113, 122 etc.) are appropriate to Croce's problems. See also below, Chapter xv.

36. For the abandonment of "idealism" see CC, V, 372 and *Discorsi*, II, 15–18. For "historicism" see *Carattere della filosofia moderna*, p. 22, etc. Cf. Franchini, *op. cit.*, pp. 34–39. Discussions of Croce's later views are also in R. Franchini, *Metafisica e storia* (Naples, 1958); F. Battaglia, *Il valore nella storia* (Bologna, 1948), and D. Pesce, *Saggio sulla metafisica* (Florence, 1957).

37. For "ethico-political history" see the essay of 1924 in *Etica e politica*, 3rd ed., pp. 271–83 and *Storia, passim*. The translation of the latter as *History as the Story of Liberty* by S. Sprigge (1941) was reprinted as a "Meridian Book," New York, 1955. A fully documented discussion of Croce's own contributions to "ethico-political history" is available in A. R. Caponigri, *History and Liberty; the Historical Writings of B. Croce* (Chicago, 1955). Caponigri is also the author of *Time and Idea, the Theory of History in G. B. Vico* (London, 1953).

38. Besides his critical essays, to be referred to in later chapters, and his historical writings (on his study of the Neapolitan revolution of 1799 see especially Caponigri, *History and Liberty*, p. 19 ff.), see Croce's biographical studies, collected in *Storie e leggende napoletane* (1919), *Una famiglia di patrioti*, etc. (1919), *Uomini e cose della vecchia Italia* (1927), *Varietà di storia letteraria e civile* (I, 1935; II, 1949), *Vite di azione, di fede e di passione* (1936), and *Aneddoti di varia letteratura* (2nd ed., 1953).

CHAPTER *ii*

1. Cf. C. Day Lewis, *The Poetic Image* (London, 1947), p. 18.
2. I. Kant, *Critique of Pure Reason*, transl. N. K. Smith (New

York, 1933, reprint of 1950), p. 272. Cf. A. C. Ewing, *A Short Commentary on Kant's Critique of P. R.* (London, 1938, reprint of 1950), p. 193. For a fuller discussion of this particular transition in Croce, see Seerveld, *Croce's Earlier Aesthetic Theories and Literary Criticism . . .* , p. 18–22.

This is a passage in which D. Ainslie makes Croce say the opposite of what he meant. After the words quoted in the text Croce goes on to contrast sensation with intuition, and Ainslie translates: "These are not two acts of ours, opposed one to another; but the one is outside and assaults us and sweeps us off our feet, while the other inside us tends to absorb and *identify itself with that which is outside*" (A, 6). Instead of the words which I have italicized, Croce says: "make that which is outside identical with itself" (*a farlo suo*, E, 8; same reading in earlier editions). Croce says that the *external* is *internalized*, and not vice versa.

3. On the "ideal" character of art see E, 32; A, 28; *PdE*, 485; NSE², 16; *Discorsi*, II, 77; PS, III, 263; *Uomini e cose della vecchia Italia*, I, 298.

4. For Croce's use of the term "impression" and its implications, cf. E. F. Carritt, "Croce and His Aesthetic," *Mind*, LXII (1953), 454: Croce "like Hume, uses the word 'impression,' though, as Hume more explicitly says, with no implication of any external cause." Hume's words are: "By the term of impression I would not be understood to express the manner, in which our lively perceptions are produced in the soul, but merely the perceptions themselves; for which there is no particular name either in the English or in any other language that I know of"; *Treatise of Human Nature*, I, i, I (ed. T. H. Greene and T. H. Grose, London, 1878, I, 312 n.). Hume, looking within his mind, found there "impressions" and made them the object of his inquiry. Croce, also looking within his mind, found there both intuitions and concepts and made them the subject of his inquiry.

5. Cf. A. Lalande, *Vocabulaire technique et critique de la philosophie*, 5th edition (Paris, 1947), pp. 522 ff.

6. Cf. W. T. Stace, *The Meaning of Beauty: A Theory of Aesthetics* (London, 1929), p. 242. Croce reviewed Stace and answered his other objections, CC, III, 15–19, but apparently did not take the trouble to answer this one. Cf. his replies to later critics: "Against the request to define one's terms" in *Discorsi*, II, 7–11, and "Intuition and the a priori synthesis" in *Storiografia e idealità morale*,

1950, p. 133: "I have been accused of not having said what intuition exactly is" and his answer, which is obviously charged with irony. See also TPS, II, 72.

7. Based on the definition of *Anschauung* in R. Eisler, *Wörterbuch der philosophischen Begriffe*, 2nd ed. (Berlin, 1904), I, 41. Cf. *Trübners deutsches Wörterbuch*, ed. A. Götze (Berlin, 1939), I, 96.

8. Lalande, *op. cit.*, p. 526.

9. John Dewey, *Psychology*, 3rd ed. (New York, 1891), p. 237.

10. S. T. Coleridge, *Biographia Literaria*, ed. J. Shawcross (Oxford, 1907), II, 230.

11. Sir W. Hamilton, *Lectures on Logic* (Boston, 1873), pp. 90–91. Cf. Hamilton's edition of Reid (Edinburgh, 1846), p. 987.

12. A. C. Ewing, *A Short Commentary on Kant's Critique of Pure Reason* (Chicago, 1950), p. 18, defines it as "the awareness of individual entities." Cf. C. J. Friederich, *The Philosophy of Kant* (Modern Library No. 266, 1944), pp. xxx–xxxi.

13. For a medieval antecedent see E. Panofsky, *Gothic Architecture and Scholasticism* (1951, reprinted New York, 1957), pp. 13–15. For nontechnical meanings of *Anschauung* in modern German see R. B. Farrell, *A Dictionary of German Synonyms* (Cambridge, England, 1953), p. 250. For critical usage cf. M. Schütze, *Academic Illusions in the Field of Letters and the Arts* (Chicago, 1934), pp. 117–24.

14. P. Carus suggested the translation *atsight* (from "at sight"): see his "Croce's Use of the Word Intuition," *The Monist*, XXVI (1916), 313.

15. E. Roditi, "The Growth and Structure of Croce's Philosophy," *The Journal of Aesthetics and Art Criticism*, I (1941), no. 5, p. 20.

16. See *Saggio sullo Hegel* etc., 1913, pp. 59–60. Also *Pratica*, 6, 108–9; CC, I, 106 and PS, III, 397.

17. W. A. Hammond, *Aristotle's Psychology* (London, 1902), p. lvii. For Kant see the above cited discussion by C. J. Friederich. For *Anschauung* used in German for both the activity and the result, see J. Hoffmeister, *Wörterbuch der philosophischen Begriffe* (Hamburg, 1955), p. 49. A similar observation for *intuition* in Lalande, *op. cit.*, p. 525. For Coleridge, see *Biographia Literaria*, ed. cit., I, 109.

18. I. A. Richards, *How to read a page* (New York, 1942), p. 132.

19. H. Weyl, *Mind and Nature* (Philadelphia, 1934), p. 30.

20. Sir Philip Sidney, *An Apologie for Poetrie*, ed. E. S. Schuckburgh (Cambridge, 1896), p. 38.

21. S. Alexander, *Beauty and other Forms of Value* (London, 1933), pp. 38–39; M. Baring, *An Outline of Russian Literature* (London, 1914), pp. 203–4.

22. G. Santayana, *The Sense of Beauty* (1896; edition of New York, 1936), p. 135.

23. See Croce's critique of this doctrine in *Carattere della filosofia moderna*, 2nd ed., 1945, p. 72. Cf. what will be said on the self-regulation of the imagination in Chapter VIII.

24. Dante, *Convivio*, Canzone I, 55–61, and II, xi, 4–5. However, see Croce, *La poesia di Dante*, 176 (English translation, p. 260).

25. This famous identification was formulated in the very first chapter of the *Aesthetic*, then in *The Essence of Aesthetic* (NSE, 36–39; EA, 41–44) and in *Aesthetica in nuce* (the *Encyclopaedia Britannica* article; see US, 15–16). Cf. also P, 221. Other references will be given in the course of the present and the following chapter.

This identification, though it still meets with considerable resistance from some traditionalist critics, is far from new. It may even be traced back to *rem tene, verba sequentur*: cf. A. Rostagni's commentary to Horace's *Ars Poetica*, line 311 (Turin, 1930, p. 90). Even closer to Croce is the formulation it received from a commentator on Horace in the eighteenth century, Richard Hurd. For Hurd begins by stressing the poetic quality of particular images (in Croce's term, the intuition). The use of particular images "is one of the surest characteristics of real genius. . . . having these bright and determinate conceptions in his own mind, he finds it no difficulty to convey the liveliest ideas of them to others." Whereas "the shapes and appearances of things are apprehended, only in the gross, by dull minds. They think they *see*, but it is as through a mist . . ." This is a close parallel to E, 12–13, A, 9–10. See Q. Horatii Flacci *Epistola ad Augustum*, with an English Commentary and Notes (London, 1751), pp. 121–22. Hurd, happy man, found "no difficulty" in what to some moderns appears to be an almost impossible task.

However, here is a modern English critic (and poet) who seems to have learnt something from Croce: "The image, the shaped and concrete *thing*—this is what poetry deals in; the abstract of thought and the intangibles of fantasy, poetry translates into forms, into vividly actual definition—what Shakespeare, practising his theory while he enounces it, calls 'a local habitation and a name.'" See Lascelles Abercrombie, *The Theory of Poetry* (New York, 1926), p. 15.

26. Cf. *Carattere della filosofia moderna,* p. 78; *Indagini su Hegel,* p. 52.

27. A. W. Schlegel, *Lectures on Dramatic Art and Literature,* translated by J. Black (London, 1846), p. 340. This is the passage of which Coleridge made such good use: see *Coleridge's Shakespearean Criticism,* ed. T. M. Raysor (Cambridge, 1930), I, 224.

28. I. A. Richards, C. K. Ogden, J. Wood, *The Foundations of Aesthetics* (New York, 1925), p. 43.

29. C. Brooks observes that "one of the critical discoveries of our time—perhaps it is not only a discovery but a recovery—is that the parts of a poem have an organic relation to each other," in "Irony and Ironic Poetry," *College English,* IX (1948), p. 231–32. Brooks' suspicion that the concept is not a modern one was more than justified. It has a very long history behind it. The principle of organic unity is to be found in ancient (i.e. Greek) criticism formulated as the relationship between the parts and the whole, whereas, broadly speaking, it appears in modern criticism (i.e. Romantic) as the relation between form and content; see note 27 above. In American criticism the principle of organic form was also formulated during the Romantic period: see W. Van O'Connor, *Age of Criticism 1900–1950* (Chicago, 1952), p. 57 ff., and with more detail H. H. Clark, "The Organic, 1800–1840" and R. H. Fogle, "Organic Form in American Criticism, 1840–1870" in F. Stovall (ed.), *Development of American Literary Criticism* (Chapel Hill, 1955), pp. 71–73 and 75–111 respectively. Of course the Romantic critics did not carry the principle into a full and systematic discussion of all issues, as Croce does. The principle now finds a place, at least in part, even in textbooks: see C. Brooks' own book (with R. P. Warren), *Modern Rhetoric, with Readings* (New York, 1949), pp. 499–503: "The Inseparability of Form and Content."

30. J. C. Ransom, paper cited, *The New Criticism,* p. 300.

31. Wimsatt and Brooks, *Literary Criticism* . . . , p. 753.

32. W. Pater, *Appreciations* (London, 1889; reprint of 1924), p. 6. There is a grudging and ungracious recognition of this anticipation by Pater in I. A. Richards, who quotes the cited sentence of Pater and adds: "It would be difficult, outside Croce, to find a more

unmistakable confusion between value and communicative efficacy" (*Principles of Literary Criticism*, London, 1924, reprint of 1934, p. 255). The confusion is in Richards himself: Croce has always carefully distinguished between aesthetic value and communication. See below, Chapter IV, on externalization, and cf. CC, I, 13–14, III, 26; US, 17; and the paper by A. B. Walkley, "Art as Liberation," in *More Prejudice* (London, 1923).

33. Pater, *op. cit.*, p. 27. Note the remarkable fact that here and elsewhere Pater, who is relativist when it comes to philosophical truth, is an absolutist in aesthetics; he discovers his absolute in the act of aesthetic expression.

34. "Inner Form" is a concept much discussed by recent German students of the history of Aesthetics, who trace it to the *endon eidos* of Aristotle via Plotinus. See O. Walzel, *Vom Geistesleben alter und neuer Zeit* (Leipzig, 1922), pp. 1–57; H. A. Korff, *Geist der Goethezeit*, II (1923), 151 ff.; R. Schwinger, *Innere Form, ein Beitrag zur Definition des Begriffes auf Grund seiner Geschichte von Shaftesbury bis W. von Humboldt* (München, 1935); P. van Tieghem, *Pré-romantisme* (Paris, 1948), I, 46.

For the actual phrase *"forma interna"* in Croce see PNP, 277; TPS, II, 157: "un atto spirituale, la 'forma interna,' con la quale la poesia nasce nello spirito del poeta"; *Letture*, 128: "forma interiore." In E, 365 and A, 327–28, it is Humboldt's "inner Form" of language.

35. Cf. A. W. Schlegel, *op. cit.*, p. 343.

CHAPTER *iii*

1. This is the account of the transition to lyrical intuition given by Croce himself, *Saggio sullo Hegel*, 1912, pp. 404–5 note. Further details are in the authorized account by G. Castellano, *B. Croce, . . . ,* 1936, 2nd ed., pp. 33–34. The theory certainly emerges before 1907. In an article of 1904, reprinted in 1905, Croce already speaks of "motivi lirici" and "personalità," which are key terms of the lyrical theory (*PdE*, 116–18). The principle was clearly formulated in the first draft of the *Logica* (1905): "every work of art, be it a tragedy or a novel, a piece of sculpture or of architecture, is lyrical" (A. Attisani, *op. cit.* in Chapter I, note 10, p. 141), as noted by G. Gentile, *Frammenti di estetica e di letteratura* (Lanciano, 1920), p. 171 note.

2. See the paper "Intuizione, sentimento e liricità," PS, I, 160–63.

This pleasant episode of cooperation between two critics regrettably turned in later years into an acrimonious controversy: see PS, III, 81–85 and (from Croce's point of view) C. Sgroi, *B.C., Svolgimento della sua estetica* (Messina, 1947), pp. 108–9.

3. For Croce's protests in 1915 see PS, I, 368–69 (on "lyricism") and 386–90 (on "fragmentism" or the cult of the fragment). For the Futurist Ardengo Soffici's use of the aphorism quoted in the text, cf. CC, III, 109. See Croce's summing up of this controversy in historical perspective, *Storia d'Italia dal 1871 al 1915*, 1934, 5th ed., p. 258. Croce's reasons for rejecting Futurists and their like are corroborated by the material collected by E. Garin, *Cronache di filosofia italiana, 1900–1943* (Bari, 1955), pp. 300–303. As for the general charge that Croce was "the virtuous father of vicious children," see Croce's answer, *Indagini su Hegel*, p. 143.

4. Cf. H. Osborne, *Aesthetics and Criticism* (London, 1955), p. 282: "When an emotional situation is presented the reader does *not* . . . become aware of the emotion by experiencing it . . . He is aware of the emotion imaginally, as he is aware of a presented perceptual situation generally." Since "imaginal" awareness of emotion is substantially Croce's lyrical intuition, one wonders why Osborne rejects Croce so categorically as he does on p. 142.

5. Croce has defined *Classic* and *Romantic* differently in different contexts. They were denied value as theoretical terms in a passage of the *Aesthetic* (E, 78; A, 70) that will be quoted in Chapter IV. In the present chapter two other sets of meanings will be given. Yet one finds recent and otherwise well-informed scholarship lamenting that for Croce "the word 'classical' was meaningless": G. Luck, "Scriptor Classicus," *Comparative Literature*, x (1958), 150 note.

6. I noted this curious reversal of terminology in a paper, "Fantasia e immaginazione nella terminologia estetica europea" in *Lingua nostra* (Florence), January 1943, v, 12–13. I have since found that it had been already noted by O. K. Struckmeyer, *Croce and Literary Criticism* (Cambridge, 1921), p. 25 note, and M. M. Rader, *A Modern Book of Aesthetics* (New York, 1925), p. 169 note. In 1949 it was the subject of a note by Croce himself in *Quaderni della Critica*, xv, 117, reprinted in TPS, II, 164 without correction of the misprints in the English names cited.

7. For Imagination and Fancy in Croce, see also NSE, 23, corresponding to EA, 24–25, where the terms are correctly translated; *Pratica*, 186; CC, III, 30; and NPS, I, 187–88, where again misprints

in English names were not corrected. For the use of the dichotomy by De Sanctis see E, 403–4, corresponding to A, 361, where the terms are correctly rendered. Perhaps the most interesting use of the dichotomy in Croce is in his interpretation of Balzac (PNP, 240–51), for which see Chapter XII.

8. Other references: 1903, *PdE*, 169–70 note; 1904, *PdE*, 231–32; 1908, *Pratica*, 121; 1912, CC, I, 68, NSE, 22, EA, 24; 1918, ASC, 27; 1929, CC, III, 349; 1934, CC, V, 71–73; 1937, *Poesia*, 172–73; and c. 1939, CC, V, 148.

9. See p. 6 of the reprint by Attisani cited in note 10, Chapter I. This point was noted by R. Garbari in his lively little book, *Genesi e svolgimento storico delle prime tesi estetiche di B. Croce (1893–1900)* (Firenze, 1949), p. 74. For the various meanings of *sentimento* in Croce, cf. PS, I, 162–63; of *passione*, NPS, II, 81.

10. See Introduction, note 5, for references.

11. *The Breviary of Aesthetic*, translated by D. Ainslie, in *The Book of the Opening of the Rice Institute* (Houston, c. 1912), II, 430–517. The book contains also an interesting early photo of Croce.

12. B. Croce, *Filosofia, Poesia, Storia*, Pagine tratte da tutte le opere a cura dell'autore (Milano-Napoli, 1951). See the Bibliography for notes on this book.

13. If by "expressionism" we mean the view that poetry is essentially expression of emotion, then expressionism was maintained by a number of English 19th century critics, from J. S. Mill and J. Kemble onwards. See M. H. Abrams, *The Mirror and the Lamp* (New York, 1953), especially pp. 144–54; for its earlier development, see pp. 70–99. In the late years of the century an expressionist aesthetic was constructed by Eugène Véron, *Aesthetics*, translated by W. H. Armstrong (London, 1879); on him see Croce, E, 459, A, 410. For a twentieth-century statement of expressionism, see A. Huxley, "E. Thomas," in *On the Margin* (London, 1923), pp. 149, 152–53. Cf. my article on "Expression" in the forthcoming *Dictionary of Poetics*, ed. by Dr. F. J. Warnke.

14. For "naturalistic expression" see E, 103–4, A, 94–95, where reference is made to Darwin's *Expression of Emotion in Man and Animals* (1872). It is called "immediate" or "natural" in P, 3 and 193–94, and "symptomatic" in *Poesia*⁴, note added to p. 194. Cf. US, 8, and E. F. Carritt, *What is Beauty?* (Oxford, 1932), p. 90: artistic expression "is not a symptom." This term has reappeared recently in Mrs. Langer, who agrees with Croce in holding that

"cries like 'Oh' and 'Ah' " are "not symbols of thought but symptoms of the inner life, like tears and laughter, crooning and profanity"; see S. K. Langer, *Philosophy in a New Key* (Mentor Reprint, 1953), p. 67.

15. R. E. Nettleship, *Philosophical Lectures and Remains* (London, 1897), I, 30. E. F. Carritt called attention to this passage as an anticipation of Croce in his *Theory of Beauty* (London, 1914), p. 264 note, and even included it in his anthology, *Philosophers of Beauty* (Oxford, 1931), pp. 188–89. Cf. a similar statement by B. Bosanquet: "imaginative expression creates the feeling by creating the embodiment," etc.: *Three Lectures on Aesthetics* (London, 1915), p. 34.

16. On the unity of intuition and expression Croce was to say later: "the proposition is purely speculative and is founded on the critique of the abstract distinction, as in the natural sciences, between internal and external, mind and body, and such like" P, 196. For a speculative critique of the distinction of internal and external, see Hegel, *Logic*, Bk. II, Sec. ii, Ch. iii, par. C. Cf. CC, I, 18 (answer to Carritt) and CC, III, 8–9 (answer to Mrs. Dodds).

17. S. Alexander, *Beauty and Other Forms of Value* (London, 1933), p. 59. On the connection between his ideas and Croce's, see p. 132.

18. R. G. Collingwood, *The Principles of Art* (Oxford, 1938), p. 56. Lyrical expression is therefore *not* what is often known as "self-expression": J. E. Spingarn, *Creative Criticism*, new ed. (New York, 1931), p. 171.

19. E. Cassirer, *Essay on Man* (New Haven, 1944), p. 142.

20. See the important chapter on the a priori synthesis, *Logica*, 153–61. Cf. EA, 39; NSE, 34; and "L'intuizione e la sintesi a priori," *Quaderni della Critica*, XVII–XVIII (1950), 9–11, reprinted in *Storiografia e idealità morale* (Bari, 1950), pp. 133–35. See also C. Antoni, *Commento a Croce* (Venice, 1955), p. 160. On this point Gentile anticipated Croce in 1899: *Frammenti di estetica e letteratura* (Lanciano, 1920), p. 40.

21. J. Craig La Drière, "Expression," in J. Shipley, *Dictionary of Literature* (New York, 1943), p. 226. Cf., from a different point of view, J. Hospers, *Proceedings of the Aristotelian Soc.*, LV (1955), 313–44.

22. A. C. Bradley, *Oxford Lectures on Poetry* (London, 1909), pp. 16–17. This is from the famous inaugural lecture "Poetry for

Poetry's Sake," the strongest statement on organicism made by an English critic. Cf. E. F. Carritt's reminiscences of the lecture, in "Croce and His Aesthetic," *Mind*, LXII (1953), 452 ff.

23. "It is indifferent, or a mere matter of terminological convenience, to present art as content or as form, as long as one understands that the content is formed and the form is filled, that the emotion is figured emotion and figure is emotionalized figure" (NSE², 34). Here evidently "form" equals "figure" which equals "image."

24. C. Baudelaire, *Les Fleurs du Mal,* ed. Van Bever (Paris, 1917), p. 27. The original title was "L'artiste inconnu." The poet himself called attention to the fact that the two images were borrowed from Gray and from Longfellow: see R. B. Chérix, *Commentaire des Fleurs du Mal* (Geneva, 1949), p. 64.

25. T. S. Eliot, *Selected Essays 1917–1932* (New York, 1932, reprint of 1938), p. 244.

26. J. C. Ransom, paper cited, *The New Criticism,* p. 178. Neither Eliot nor Ransom noted the transformation of the image in Poe's admirer, Baudelaire.

27. Brooks and Warren, *Modern Rhetoric,* pp. 451–53.

28. É. Souriau, "L'esthétique de B. C.," *Revue internationale de Philosophie,* VII (1953), 287, note 5.

29. Sir H. Read, *The True Voice of Feeling* (New York, 1953), p. 21. Also, Sir Herbert sometimes speaks as if organic form in poetry and the doctrine of organic form in criticism were the same, and the former, as well as the latter, appeared only with Romanticism. If the concept of organic form is valid, it applies to poetry of all times.

30. Cf. the *Breviary:* "Certainly art is symbol . . . but symbol of what?" EA, 28; NSE², 25. In a late paper "On the Use and the Abuse of the Term 'Symbol,'" *Letture,* 216–26, Croce said that it is impossible to define "the symbol in itself, as if it were an independent mental activity possessed of its own theoretical rights, whereas, if it is so defined, it becomes immediately identified with undesired [*deprecata*] allegory. If this identification is rejected, one cannot define it for the good reason that it is not a new and original act additional to that of poetic creation, but is a synonym of poetry itself, which is always 'symbolic,' i.e. always (the tautology is here inevitable) *poetic*" (p. 217). As E. F. Carritt observed, "many people speak of the symbolism of art and really mean its expressive-

ness, as for instance Mr. W. B. Yeats in his *Ideas of Good and Evil,*" *What is Beauty?* (Oxford, 1932), p. 91. Yeats' "emotional symbol" anticipates the "lyrical image," cf. "The Symbolism of Poetry" (1900) in *Ideas of Good and Evil* (New York, 1903), pp. 241–44.

31. W. Weidlé, *Les abeilles d'Ariste* (Paris, 1954), p. 297. On Croce's death, Weidlé wrote a very appreciative obituary, but it does not show a very extensive knowledge of his works. See "Grandeur de B. Croce," *Pensées,* II, cahier Déc. 1952, pp. 3–5.

32. C. Brooks, *The Well-Wrought Urn* (New York, 1947), pp. 68–69. As Wellek notes, an influence of Croce on modern American criticism "is not clearly traceable," but he believes that the *Aesthetic* "must be assumed as background"—"Literary Scholarship" in M. Curti (ed.), *American Scholarship in the Twentieth Century* (Cambridge, Mass., 1953), p. 122. Cf. Wasiolek, cit. note 12 to p. 9.

33. And not only to poetry, but also to painting. For an instance, see J. P. Sartre, *What is Literature?* (New York, 1949), pp. 9–11; cf. C. Rau, "The Aesthetic Views of J. P. Sartre," JAAC, IX (1950), 139–47. Alfred Stern's claims of Sartre's derivation from Croce (see his *Sartre, His Philosophy and Psychoanalysis,* New York, 1953, pp. 75–78) are based upon a misunderstanding.

CHAPTER *iv*

1. T. E. Hulme, *Speculations,* ed. H. Read (London, 1924), p. 180: intensive manifolds are "finite beings whose parts interpenetrated in such a manner that they could not be separated or analysed out." This point has been foreshadowed in Chapter II.

2. Bergson's theory of conceptual "labels" is adopted by Croce in E, 12, A, 10; see the historical part, E, 476, A, 416–17. Bergson's views were also expounded by T. E. Hulme, *op. cit.,* pp. 143–69, in a brilliant essay but with no awareness of their convergence with Romantic thought (Romanticism being anathema to Hulme). For Bergson's convergence with Hegel see Croce, *Indagini su Hegel,* p. 78, which relates a conversation between Croce and Bergson. On the two in general, see M. Ciardo, "Croce e Bergson nel pensiero contemporaneo," in F. Flora (ed.), *B. Croce,* pp. 383–95.

3. Croce's papers on language will be cited in the course of this section: see also *PdE,* 144–219; CC, I, 87–113, III, 95–106; *Discorsi,* I, 235–50; *Letture,* 254–58; PS, III, 112; NPS, II, 81–83; TPS, II, 15–18 and 165–68. For linguistics, see below, note 11. For critical dis-

cussions of Croce's views by linguists, cf. G. Nencioni, *Idealismo e realismo nella scienza del linguaggio* (Firenze, 1946). After this chapter was written, there appeared S. Cavaciuti, *La teoria linguistica di B. Croce* (Milan, 1959), superseding in comprehensiveness all previous discussions of the subject, although weak on the philosophical side.

4. Hence Croce's theory is not open to the objection recently raised by W. Sutton against critics who believe in a cognitive theory of art but conceive cognition as reference to an external object; see his "The Contextualist Dilemma,—or Fallacy?" *Journal of Aesthetics and Art Criticism*, XVII (1958), 219–29.

5. Cf. the statement of a linguist: "We never repeat the same phrase twice; we never use the same word twice with the same value; there never are two absolutely identical linguistic facts." J. Vendryes (1922), quoted by C. K. Ogden and I. A. Richards, *The Meaning of Meaning* (London, reprint of 1947), pp. 152–53.

6. Through neglect of this important saving clause, Wimsatt is led to exemplify Croce's theory of language with the sentence "Peteriswalkinginacountryroad" (*Literary Criticism*, p. 513, note 6). But this is an artificial sentence, devised by Wimsatt, such as those constructed in grammars as examples of rules. A genuine sentence for Croce would be the whole of the *Divine Comedy*, beginning with the first line and ending with the last, as Croce himself says, CC, II, 181.

7. Cf. A. Rosetti, *Le mot. Esquisse d'une théorie générale* (Bucharest, 1947, 2e éd. revue et augmentée), pp. 20 and 38; S. Ullman, *The Principles of Semantics* (Oxford, 1957), pp. 43–65; M. R. Cohen, *A Preface to Logic* (New York, 1944; reprint of 1956), pp. 60–62.

8. H. Werner, *Comparative Psychology of Mental Development* (Chicago, 1948, revised ed.), pp. 279–80. I owe this and other references on this topic to the kindness of Prof. R. Wells of Yale.

9. R. Blackmur, *Language as Gesture, Essays on Poetry* (New York, 1952), p. 22. This statement (in which the italics are the author's) is not given as representative of Blackmur, but only as a passing reference which affords an interesting contrast to Croce. On Croce Blackmur read a paper at the Modern Language Association Meeting of December 27, 1954 ("Croce's Estate: A Selective Inventory") which I regret not being able to trace in print.

10. I. A. Richards, *The Philosophy of Rhetoric* (New York,

1936), pp. 54 and 55. For criticism of Richards' atomism, cf. S. Ullman, *Principles of Semantics*, p. 60: "Since 'interinanimation,' echoing Bergson's 'interpénetration' [see Richards, p. 70], presupposes two or more entities interpenetrating one another, it implies *ipso facto* the independent existence of such elements." Cf. also Richards' later paper "The Interaction of Words" in A. Tate (ed.), *The Language of Poetry* (Princeton, 1942), pp. 65–87.

11. This would seem to lead to a radical empiricism which rejects any kind of analysis of language whatsoever and which would make a science of language, or linguistics, impossible. Through discussions with linguists Croce reached a more positive attitude towards their discipline. He then developed the theory that the function of linguistics is ultimately to contribute to the "History of Culture" in the special meaning that Croce gives to that term (see Chapter IX). See his review of the book by K. Vossler in CC, I, 93–95; cf. P, 307–8 and *Discorsi*, I, 241–43. In 1922 Croce looked upon etymology as concrete history, the investigation of an individual problem, parallel to the history of art that investigates an individual work of art (*PdE*[4], 205–10). But in 1944 he judged that etymology was "abstract history" because "the single word is an abstraction" (*Discorsi*, II, 81). A remarkable shift occurred in 1946. In his review of a book by an Italian linguist, G. Nencioni, cited in note 3 above, Croce raised the question: if there is no such thing as a separate word, what are the words which are the objects of etymological investigation? The question was all the more pertinent since Croce himself had investigated some etymologies: see *La Spagna nella vita italiana durante la Rinascenza*, 1917, pp. 190–91, and *PdE*[4], 209 note. Croce's answer now was that the single words investigated by etymology are "signs" which stand for "things or facts" and which are made out of "naturalistic expressions," i.e. sounds used by volition for practical purposes and not expressions produced by intuition for aesthetic enjoyment (*Letture*, 248–49). This conflicts with Croce's earlier theory that all signs are originally aesthetic expressions. The revised view seems to be referred to also in the 1948 paper on "Definitions of linguistics," NPS, I, 197–98. In 1949 however Croce made the statement (TPS, II, 164) with which I shall conclude this section of Chapter IV; so he apparently reverted to his earlier view which was also affirmed in *Discorsi*, I, 236, and TPS, II, 158.

12. M. Krieger, *The New Apologists for Poetry* (Minneapolis,

1956), p. 68 note. For a statement on the "resistance of language" by a linguist sympathetic to Croce's views, see K. Vossler, *Positivismo e idealismo nella scienza del linguaggio* (Bari, 1903), pp. 114 ff.

13. I. A. Richards, *Philosophy of Rhetoric*, p. 51. The doctrine of good usage is of course much older than the 18th century. In the Western tradition it is nearly as old as grammar: e.g. the Alexandrians and their ideal of "Atticism."

14. Richards, *Philosophy of Rhetoric*, pp. 12–13. All that Richards himself provides in the way of positive doctrine is to fall back in the last resort upon the "inexplicable" and the "mysterious" (p. 35), as all positivists tend to, according to Croce (*Logica*, 287).

15. Richards, *Philosophy of Rhetoric*, pp. 69–70.

16. Cf. E. Wilson, *Axel's Castle* (New York, 1931), pp. 21–22.

17. B. A. Morrissette, *Les aspects fondamentaux de l'esthétique symboliste* (Clermont-Ferrand, 1933); cf. P, 249.

18. This proof is given in the first draft of the *Logica*, 1904–5: see *La prima forma dell'Estetica e della Logica*, ed. A. Attisani, pp. 158–59. It was however omitted in the final version of the *Logica*, 1909. It may seem strange, too, that the theory of language as a sign or symbol of the concept does not appear in the sections of the *Logica* of 1909 dedicated to the relation between thought and language, i.e., *Logica*, 4–5, 75–82 and 407–21. There is only a hint of it in another section: "the same truth, or the same concept, may assume infinite verbal or expressive forms" (p. 89). But in the *Logica* of 1909 the doctrine that prevails is that of the total identity of the concept with verbal expression, e.g., p. 75. This is due to Croce's tendency in 1909 to identify all intellectual processes into one. Croce however returned to the symbol theory in later writings: CC, I, 60 ff.; P, 16; *Discorsi*, I, 236. It is also referred to in his *Saggio sullo Hegel*, 1913, p. 62. For his shifts of position on this question see the penetrating discussion by S. Zeppi, *Studi crociani*, pp. 153–59 and 161–62.

19. According to C. J. Ducasse, *The Philosophy of Art* (New York, 1929), p. 43, Croce should have endeavored "to formulate definitions of the term [expression] that would fit these solid language facts," the "solid language facts" being "the various meanings that the term expression actually has in the language." Croce had anticipated this: "One can well imagine what sort of scientific results would be attained by allowing oneself to be led astray by

verbal usage and classing together facts widely different" (E, 104; A, 95). Further objections of Croce to this point of view are in *Primi saggi*, p. 198 and TPS, II, 183. It is not surprising therefore that Croce should be one of the targets of the contemporary "analytical" school of philosophy, as may be seen in W. Elton (ed.), *Aesthetics and Language* (Oxford, 1954), pp. 6–7 and 100–107. These critics have been answered by J. Hospers, "The Croce-Collingwood Theory of Art," *Philosophy*, XXXI (1956), 291–300 and by A. Donagan, "The Croce-Collingwood Theory of Art," *ibid.*, XXXIII (1958), 162–67.

20. R. Wellek and A. Warren, *Theory of Literature* (New York, 1940), pp. 205–13.

21. Cf. I. A. Richards' critique of the theory that metaphor is "a grace or adornment or *added* power of language, not its constitutive form," *Philosophy of Rhetoric*, p. 90. This is practically Vico: cf. E, 248, A, 225–26. But Richards makes no reference either to Vico or to Croce.

22. Cf. H. Levin, "The Revival of Rhetoric," in "Criticism in Crisis," *Comparative Literature*, VII (1955), 153–54; A. Tate, *The Man of Letters in the Modern World* (New York, 1955), p. 165; and the remarkable list of "Examples of Rhetorical Form in Aeolus" in S. Gilbert, *James Joyce's Ulysses* (New York, 1955), pp. 194–98.

23. H. W. Fowler, *Dictionary of Modern English Usage* (Oxford, 1926), p. 134.

24. For an interesting example of inevitable "inversion" cf. Vernon Lee (Violet Paget), *The Poet's Eye* (London, 1926), p. 18.

25. R. Puttenham, *Arte of English Poesie*, eds. G. D. Willcock and A. Walker (Cambridge, 1926), p. lxxx.

26. Sister Miriam Joseph, *Shakespeare's Use of the Arts of Language* (New York, 1947).

27. *Ibid.*, p. 145.

28. W. G. Rutherford, *Scholia Aristophanea* (London, 1905), III, 294. Cf. Croce, *Indagini su Hegel*, p. 230.

29. Croce, *Aneddoti di varia letteratura*, 2nd ed., 1954, II, 16 and 14.

30. Croce gave a different account of metaphor in his universalistic phase. See below, Chapter XI, note 10.

31. E. Roditi, paper cited, JAAC, I, 21: "If, therefore, figures of speech must be used literally [?], he has no right to use synecdoche"—referring to E, 27, A, 23.

32. For stylistics see E, 79, A, 71, and for the history of the classification of styles, E, 521, A, 463. Later discussions: *PdE*, 147–48; CC, I, 12, II, 180–81, and III, 64–65; on Strich's application of Wölfflin's methods to literature, P, 4th ed., p. 309. In recent years Croce tended to connect stylistics with what he called "decadentism": cf. "La cosiddetta critica stilistica," *Letture*, 284–94; "La critica stilistica," *Indagini su Hegel*, pp. 248–51; NPS, I, 219–21; TPS, II, 40.

33. Cf. N. Friedman, "Point of View in Fiction: The Development of a Critical Concept," PMLA, LXX (1955), 1160–84.

34. P. Lubbock, *The Craft of Fiction* (London, 1921), p. 251.

35. TPS, II, 61–63; cf. LNI, VI, 138 on the ideal of "the well-made novel" and PNP, 241–43.

36. Reprinted in J. W. Aldridge (ed.), *Critiques and Essays in Modern Fiction, 1920–51* (New York, 1952), pp. 67–82.

37. Cf. Schorer, *op. cit.*: "technique alone objectifies the materials of art" (p. 71), technique introduces "order" into "experience" (p. 77), technique "masters" the emotions (p. 75), etc. For Inner Form, see above, Chapter II, note 34. See also my article on "Form" in the forthcoming *Dictionary of Poetics*, ed. by F. J. Warnke. Schorer also connects "technique" with T. S. Eliot's "convention," upon which see my paper, "T. S. Eliot and the Doctrine of Dramatic Conventions," in the *Transactions of the Wisconsin Academy of Sciences, Arts and Letters*, 43 (1954), 189–200. This paper (which presents a critical analysis of the concept) seems to have escaped the otherwise comprehensive survey by R. M. Browne, *Theories of Convention in Contemporary American Criticism* (Washington, 1956).

38. "*Character*—like *plot, rhythm, construction* and all other critical counters—is merely an abstraction from the total response in the mind of the reader or spectator." L. C. Knights, *Explorations* (London, 1946), p. 4. The fact that abstractions such as "viewpoint" have little to do with art is shown by the way that they can be employed just as effectively in discussing such forms of entertainment as detective fiction. See Dorothy Sayers' analysis of the shift of viewpoint in the detective story, in an essay reprinted by H. Haycraft (ed.), *The Art of the Mystery Story, A Collection of Critical Essays* (New York, 1946), pp. 98–101. This analysis, being originally published in 1928, makes Miss Sayers a pioneer of modern "technical" criticism of the novel, and should entitle her to inclusion in Mr. Friedman's learned survey of the field, where she is absent.

39. J. E. Spingarn, *Creative Criticism*, Essays on the Unity of Genius and Taste (New York, 1925), p. 107.

40. The line from Shakespeare quoted by Spingarn, *ibid.*, p. 106, "In his study of imagination," is incorrect. It comes from *Much Ado About Nothing*, IV, i, 227, and should read "Into his study of imagination," which of course makes the line more regular. Spingarn may have been misled by a review by K. Vossler in *La critica*, IV (1906), 55, where the line is quoted as Spingarn prints it, together with the Milton line that Spingarn also quotes: "Rocks, caves, lakes, fens, bogs, dens, and shades of death."

41. *Ibid.*, pp. 113 and 109. On rhyme see also Croce, P, 275: "A poem can be judged . . . only by comparing it to itself through the evaluation of the consistency of the forms in which it develops and realizes itself. Only then it is possible to discriminate the instances in which it sounds perfectly harmonious from those in which verse and rhyme are forced . . ."

42. Cf. *La poesia di Dante*, pp. 164–65; ASC, 46 ff. For Pascoli, P, 336.

43. The main discussion of externalization is in the *Aesthetic*, Part I, Chapter xv. Cf. *PdE*, 229 ff.; CC, III, 26, 47, 170; US, 17; PS, III, 52, and the references in note 45 below.

44. See Hospers' cited paper, *Philosophy*, XXXI (1956), 295 note.

45. See the historical part of the *Aesthetic*, Chapter xix, section 3: "The theory of the limits of the arts." Cf. on the same question *PdE*, 226–64; NSE, 46–51; EA, 53–59; NSE, 255–61, a discussion of Wölfflin; US, 18–21; TPS, II, 30–35. Croce's view was defended by S. Zink, "Intuition and Externalization in Croce's Aesthetic," *Journal of Philosophy*, XLVII (1950), 210–16. See also the able discussion by Hospers cited in the previous note.

46. O. O. Walzel, *Vom Geistesleben alter und neuer Zeit* (Leipzig, 1922), p. 38. For Croce on Plotinus, see E, 181–83, A, 166–68, and *Discorsi*, II, 37–39. Some Renaissance antecedents to Croce's doctrine of the inwardness of art are suggested by G. Morpurgo Tagliabue, *Il concetto dello stile* (Torino, 1951), p. 181. For a fully documented and philosophically articulated history of this trend of thought from ancient times to the 17th century see E. Panofsky, *Idea, ein Beitrag zur Begriffsgeschichte der älteren Kunsttheorie* (Berlin, 1924).

47. J. P. Sartre, *The Psychology of the Imagination* (a translation of *L'imaginaire*, 1940, published in New York, 1948), pp. 274–75.

48. B. Bosanquet, *Three Lectures on Aesthetic* (London, 1915),

pp. 69 and 71. Far from refuting Croce, as claimed in the *Journal of Aesthetics and Art Criticism*, XII (1958), 281, Bosanquet misunderstood him. Bosanquet is included in the historical section of the *Aesthetic* (E, 469; A, 418), cf. US, 147–60. For Croce's personal relations with him, see *Aneddoti*, IV, 403–12.

49. *The Times Literary Supplement*, June 3, 1915, translated in G. Castellano, *Introduzione . . .* , pp. 95–100. When Bosanquet criticized the doctrine again in the *Proceedings of the British Academy*, IX (1919), Walkley replied with "A Point of Croce's"; see his *Pastiche and Prejudice* (London, 1921), pp. 194–99. In "Art as Liberation," *More Prejudice* (New York, 1923), pp. 144–48, he defended the theory of expression against that of communication. In "Croce at Oxford," *Still More Prejudice* (London, 1925), pp. 49–53, he gave an account of J. A. Smith's pamphlet on behalf of Croce, *The Nature of Art* (Oxford, 1924). Bosanquet's criticism was also rebutted in Castellano, *Introduzione . . .* , p. 204. Cf. CC, I, 19.

50. S. Alexander, *Beauty and other Forms of Value* (London, 1933), pp. 57 and 72. For Croce's personal relations with Alexander, see PS, III, 88–89.

51. See Croce's review of A. E. Powell (Mrs. E. Dodds), *The Romantic Theory of Poetry, An Examination in the Light of Croce's Aesthetic* (London, 1926), in CC, III, 7–13. All these English critics—including L. A. Reid, *A Study in Aesthetics* (New York, 1921), pp. 166–70—fail to make the distinction that Hospers perceptively makes between *physical medium*, "the paint on the canvas," and *conceived medium*, color as thought by the artist; see the paper cited above, *Philosophy*, XXXI (1956), 297. Nor is externalization "the exact copy of the intuition," as N. Porter believed ("An Interpretation of Croce's Aesthetic," *Australasian Journal of Psychology and Philosophy*, VII [1929], 19–36).

52. E. Cassirer, *Essay on Man* (New Haven, 1944), pp. 141–42. (On Cassirer, cf. *Discorsi*, II, 255–56.) For still another instance of this misapprehension, see A. H. Warren, Jr., *English Poetic Theory 1825–1865* (Princeton, 1950), p. 49, where it is assumed that for Croce feeling is poetical before it ever assumes literary style and metrical form. And cf. Hospers' shrewd remarks on "mute inglorious Miltons," *Philosophy*, XXXI (1956), 298.

53. Cf. A. Isenberg, "The Technical Factor in Art," *Journal of Philosophy*, XLIII (1946), p. 1 of reprint: "But the question is, what becomes of the artist's *training* . . . ?" Isenberg was unaware that

Croce had answered the question on the artist's training. Isenberg also believed that to affirm that "the 'internal' factor is already bodily action" was "irreconcilable with Croce" (p. 19). But Croce had affirmed as much in the cited passages from the *Aesthetic*, Part I, Chapter XIII, etc. A refutation of art as technique is also in R. G. Collingwood (*op. cit.*, pp. 15–29), referred to in the cited papers by Hospers and Donagan, *Philosophy*, XXXI and XXXIII.

54. See his early monograph on the "Concept of History" (1893), reprinted in *Primi saggi*, p. 28.

55. M. C. Nahm, *Aesthetic Experience and Its Presuppositions* (New York, 1946), p. 95.

56. Cf. *PdE*, 118. In this manner even moral judgments may enter into a work of art and become part of it.

CHAPTER *V*

1. These arguments were formulated somewhat differently at different stages of Croce's thinking, as may be seen from the quotations from the *Aesthetic*, the *Breviary* and *La poesia* given in the body of this chapter. Indeed Croce's earliest reference to genres in 1885 is in support of their critical value (PS, I, 471). Ten years later he took his stand against it (*Primi saggi*, p. 139), an attitude which he maintained consistently ever after. In addition to the references in the text, see *Poeti e scrittori del . . . rinascimento*, II, 262–63; PS, III, 53–54; *Indagini su Hegel*, 140–42; and cf. my article on "Genres" in the forthcoming *Dictionary of Poetics*, ed. F. J. Warnke.

2. In Croce's terminology, they are empirical pseudo-concepts and not concrete universals (cf. NSE², 321). But art is a concrete universal. For the logical theory implied, see the second chapter of the *Logica*.

3. E. A. Poe, "Hawthorne's Twice-Told Tales" (1842) in *Representative Selections*, eds. M. Allerton and H. Craig (New York, 1935), p. 360.

4. W. P. Ker, *Form and Style in Poetry*, Lectures and Notes, ed. R. W. Chambers (London, 1928), p. 104.

5. U. von Wilamowitz, cited in L. Cooper (ed.), *The Greek Genius and Its Influence* (New Haven, 1913), p. 164.

6. E. K. Chambers, *W. Shakespeare*, A Study of Facts and Problems (Oxford, 1930), I, 294, 348, 368, 408, 442. *Lear* was actually called a "Chronicle History," I, 463.

7. A. W. Schlegel, *Lectures on Dramatic Art and Literature*, transl. J. Black (London, 1846), p. 379. In contrast, see N. H. Pearson, "Literary Forms and Types, or a Defense of Polonius," *English Institute Annual, 1940* (New York, 1941), pp. 61–72. Note how Pearson on p. 66 slips without warning from the concept of aesthetic "form" —which being an essential principle is one and individual—to "forms" in the sense of genres, which are insuperably multiple and disparate.

8. I. Behrens, *Die Lehre von der Einteilung der Dichtkunst, vornehmlich vom 16. bis 19. Jahrhundert* (Halle, 1940; Beihefte zur Zeitschrift für romanische Philologie, No. 92). For the ancient period, cf. H. Färber, *Die Lyrik in der Kunstlehre der Antike* (Munich, 1936); and J. J. Donohue, *The Theory of Literary Kinds* (2 vols., Dubuque, 1943 and 1949). For the theory of tragedy, cf. L. W. Elder, *A Criticism of Some Attempts to Rationalize Tragedy* (University of Pennsylvania Diss., 1915) and K. Jaspers, *Tragedy is not Enough* (Boston, 1952).

9. Cf. E. Ermatinger (ed.), *Philosophie der Literaturwissenschaft* (Berlin, 1930); J. Petersen, *Die Wissenschaft von der Dichtung. System und Methodenlehre der Literaturwissenschaft*, Band 1: *Werk und Dichter* (Berlin, 1939); H. Oppel, *Morphologie der Literaturwissenschaft* (Mainz, 1947); W. Kayser, *Das Sprachliche Kunstwerk. Eine Einführung in die Literaturwissenschaft* (Bern, 1948). Cf. also the treatment of genres by R. Petsch, *Wesen und Forme der Erzählkunst* (Halle, 1934) and *Wesen und Formen des Dramas. Allgemeine Dramaturgie* (Halle, 1945). R. Wellek and A. Warren's *Theory of Literature* (New York, 1943, and later editions) seems to represent this trend in America. For more speculative attempts to reformulate the genre theory, cf. E. Staiger, *Grundbegriffe der Poetik* (Zurich, 1946).

10. This review was much fuller in its original form in *La critica*, II (1904), 163–67, which should be read for a complete history of this controversy. By making additions to the bibliography of the Italian novels of the 17th century (which may now be seen in *Nuovi saggi sulla letteratura del Seicento*, 1931, pp. 43–45), Croce showed that he knew more about the history of the genre than its historian. His denial of genres is therefore not due to ignorance of facts or to any impressionistic disinclination to the labor of scholarly research, but to critical principle.

11. Elementary presentations of the genres and their subdivisions for educational purposes are called by Croce "istituzioni di lettera-

tura" (e.g., NSE², 49), a term which may puzzle English readers unfamiliar with Italian academic terminology.

12. For Croce's support and encouragement of the study of Renaissance Poetics, see also *PdE*, 204, and Croce's introduction to the Italian translation (1905) of J. E. Spingarn's book on Renaissance criticism, CC, II, 286–87. Croce himself made some contributions to it. On F. Patrizio, see *PdE*, 297–308; on other critics, *Poeti e scrittori del . . . Rinascimento*, II, 74 ff.; on Fracastoro, *ibid.*, III, 93–100, and also CC, III, 36–39.

13. Mario Fubini, *Critica e Poesia* (Bari, 1956), pp. 306–7. Another instance might be cited: the characterization of Pulci's *Morgante* as a sort of "picaresque novel," ASC, 64.

14. The reader is referred to Croce's dissociation of these writers from their genres as a particularly cogent presentation of his critique of genres: PPPA, 239–40, 290, 303–8, 353–54, 500–502. It is supported by recent scholarship on the *novella*: see *Rassegna della letteratura italiana*, VII (1958), 437.

15. Croce made some later additions to his discussion of Renaissance comedy writers in his *Poeti e scrittori del . . . Rinascimento*, I and II (1945) and III (1952). He also edited some of these plays, such as Sforza Oddi's *Erofilomachia* (Naples, 1946) and the anonymous *Farsa dell'uomo che non vuole aver pensieri* (Florence, 1951). The collection *Scrittori d'Italia*, under his sponsorship, published two volumes of *Comedies of the Renaissance*, edited by I. Sanesi. Croce's services to the study of the *Commedia dell'arte* are too extensive to be summarized here. For the reaction of the historical scholars to Croce's essay on the comedies, see PS, III, 65. For more recent studies of the comedies by other scholars, see L. Russo, *Commedie fiorentine del Cinquecento, Mandragola, Clizia, Calandria* (Florence, 1939), and the series of articles begun by G. Pullino in *Lettere italiane* (1955 ff.), M. Barotti in *Belfagor* (1952), etc. But no attempt is made, either in this note or elsewhere in this book, to give a full bibliography of recent studies on subjects discussed by Croce.

16. C. Sprigge, *B. Croce*, p. 47, *à propos* of the expulsion of the Absolute from Croce's system. For a reasoned defence of the genre theory see J. Craig La Drière ("Classifications of Literature" in J. Shipley [ed.], *Dictionary of Literature*, New and Revised Edition [New York, 1953], pp. 62–64) who however does not take into account the logical and historical grounds of Croce's argument.

17. The denial of genres as categories is supported by W. T.

Stace, *The Meaning of Beauty*, p. 85, as well as by J. Dewey, *Art as Experience* (New York, 1934), pp. 225–26, and by W. K. Wimsatt Jr., *The Verbal Icon* (Lexington, 1954), p. 53. Croce's view was adopted by R. K. Hack, "The Doctrine of Literary Forms," *Harvard Studies in Classical Philology*, XXVII (1916), 1–65, who believed that it was originated by Sir H. Newbolt in his *New Study of English Poetry* (London, 1919), not noticing Newbolt's acknowledgments to Croce, p. 8. Cf. my cited paper in *Journal of Aesthetics and Art Criticism*, XIII, 308. For another aspect of Newbolt's relations with Croce, see PS, I, 390–91.

CHAPTER *vi*

1. M. C. Nahm, *The Artist as Creator: An Essay of Human Freedom* (Baltimore, 1956), pp. 265–67.

2. A somewhat similar misunderstanding is that of an English critic, J. Smith, who believed that for Croce all critical judgments were tautological, or of the type "A is A." His prize example, a passage from Croce's *Logic*, turns out to be a mistranslation. Croce is made to say that naming the *Divine Comedy* is to criticize it: "to say that a thing is the fact that we call the *Divine Comedy* is to say what its value is, and so to criticize it." This is from Ainslie's translation of the *Logic*, 1917, p. 294 (J. Smith, "Croce," *Scrutiny*, II, 1933, p. 44). But Croce never said that. What he did say was something quite different: "to say *what* thing is that fact that is called the *Divine Comedy*, is to say what its value is, and so to criticize it" (italics mine; "dire che cosa è quel fatto che si chiama la *Divina Commedia*, è dirne quale ne sia il valore, e, cioè, farne la critica," *Logica*, 205). To say *what* a thing is is to define its quality, its essence, its *ti estí*, and not merely to repeat its name. So much can a philosopher suffer from the mistranslation of a single, small word.

3. NSE², 301. Cf. *Logica*, 22, and L. Venturi, *History of Art Criticism*, translated by C. Marriott (New York, 1936), p. 271. Venturi's introduction, as we shall see again in Chapter VIII, is largely an exposition of Croce's views on criticism.

4. *Comedy*, ed. W. Sypher (Anchor Books, 1956), pp. 157 ff., 164–65. For a fuller discussion of Bergson's aesthetics, from a point of view not far from Croce's, see A. Tilgher, *Le Voci del Tempo* (Rome, 1923), pp. 190–202. Croce referred briefly to Bergson's *Le rire* only to note that he had been anticipated by Taine: CC, I, 75–78.

5. Classification by kinds and species is the mainstay of empirical aesthetics. For Croce's discussion of empirical aesthetics, see E, 119–20 and 433–45, A, 108–9 and 388–98; A¹, 371 ff. corresponding to *PdE*, 3 ff.; PS, I, 154–58; TPS, II, 27–30.

6. *Letture*, 149–53; PS, III, 71.

7. Cf. also PPPA, 484 ff., the reference to Grotius' praise of civil and religious liberty: "Where could one hear in Italy a voice like that of Hugh Grotius . . . ?" Against nationalism in the history of literature see his critique of A. Bartels, NSE, 185–95, and against the "national character" of poetry see also P, 312–13; ASC, 229.

8. I have translated "cooperation with the authors," but the Italian text says *altri*, "others," which might be a misprint for *gli autori*, "the authors."

9. This last sentence has been translated rather freely for the sake of clarity. The original reads: "in questa seconda considerazione rientra nei singoli ordini a cui quei fatti appartengono nelle varie storie."

10. See my paper, "Stato attuale degli studi shakespeariani," *Paideia*, VIII (1953), 172.

11. J. E. Spingarn, "A Note on Dramatic Criticism," *Essays and Studies by Members of the English Association*, IV (1913), 7–28; reprinted in *Creative Criticism*. The controversy aroused by Spingarn's views on this subject is also referred to by R. C. Flickinger, *The Greek Theatre and Its Drama* (Chicago, 1918), pp. xi–xvii.

12. Included in the new edition of Spingarn's *Creative Criticism*, 1931, pp. 162–78.

13. See *The Times*, March 20, 1911, page 12.

CHAPTER *vii*

1. *Primi saggi*, pp. 103–8; cf. *Estetica*, 2nd ed., 1904, p. 502.

2. Discussions of aesthetic relativism are to be found also in the Heidelberg lecture; *PdE*, 27; *A¹*, 399; CC, I, 106–7 and V, 78–79; P, 65–106 and 262–63; PNP, 186 ff.; *Aneddoti*, III, 100–103; PS, III, 56–57; and in other places cited later in this chapter. For Gentile's aesthetic subjectivism, see CC, IV, 304–9, and the reply to G. De Ruggiero, PS, III, 391–415. (Cf. P, 74.) However, Gentile in 1899 had anticipated Croce's theory of re-creation: see the cited *Frammenti di estetica*, pp. 43–45.

3. *Storia dell'età barocca*, 2nd ed., 1946, pp. 165–71 and US, 35.

Cf. my article on "Taste" in the forthcoming *Dictionary of Poetics,* ed. F. J. Warnke.

4. Croce's discussion of historical skepticism is here relevant: see *Logica,* 201 ff.; TSS, 23–24, 41–45; *Storia,* 268–73, Engl. transl. (Meridian Book, 1955), pp. 266–72; *Discorsi,* II, 26; TPS, I, 18 and 22.

5. Croce identified criticism with "taste" in Chapter XVI of the *Aesthetic,* Part I, and in Chapter XVII (E, 144; A, 131) he acknowledged that there was a logical judgment on art, or the application of the category to the reproduced intuition, but considered it the function of the history of art, and not of art criticism. Hence in the proposition on taste, designated as No. 2 at the beginning of this chapter, he speaks of the identity of the reproduction with the "judgment" on art (not the mere enjoyment). The revised doctrine made its first appearance in 1908, *Pratica,* 62: cf. Seerveld, *Croce's Earlier . . . Theories and . . . Criticism,* pp. 61–62.

6. See the following chapter for further discussion and other references.

7. Cf. my article "Croce e la critica shakespeariana (1709–1809)," *Rivista di letterature moderne,* IV (1953), 146–48.

8. I. A. Richards, *Principles of Literary Criticism* (London, 1952 edition), p. 176.

9. I. A. Richards, *Science and Poetry* (New York, 1926), p. 76 n.

10. T. S. Eliot, *Selected Essays* (London, 1950, new edition), pp. 229–31.

11. See the paper entitled "A judgment of Macaulay on Vincenzo da Filicaia," *Nuovi saggi sulla letteratura del Seicento,* 1931, pp. 315–22.

12. "Angelo di Costanzo poeta e storico," *Uomini e cose della vecchia Italia,* I, 1927, pp. 87–88. Other references to this form of historical relativism: 1934, in CC, V, 121–22; 1936, P, 297, "On the different idea of poetry according to various times and nations"; 1939, PS, III, 261–62; 1949, *Letture,* 244.

13. *Varietà di storia letteraria,* II, 59.

14. For a qualification to the principle of assuming the point of view of the poet, see, in the case of Dante, CC, V, 14 note, and in general, NPS, I, 200–201. Assuming the "point of view" of the poet does not mean accepting the intentions of the poet, prior to composition, as a standard of judgment. That is the Intentional Heresy, which Croce has always rejected. See below, Chapter XIII.

CHAPTER *viii*

1. Croce himself does not give the above formula in so many words. But this formula is based on his aesthetic theory as we have seen it in Chapters II and III and is borne out by his critical practice, as exemplified in this and other chapters. A similar formula is given for Croce's earlier criticism by M. Sansone in his selection from Croce's essays on Italian literature (1956, see Bibliography), I, xl–xli, where "evidenza" belongs to the image, "sincerità" to the emotion and "coerenza formale dell'espressione" to the synthesis. For some of Croce's own accounts of his critical method see note 19 below, and LNI, II, 34; CC, III, 82–83, IV, 304; NSE², 283–84.

2. For Croce's approval of empirical distinctions when they are used descriptively and without critical implications, see above, Chapter V, on the use of genre concepts, and also *Logica*, 249; NSE², 285, 295 and 321; *Poesia*, 159; *Letture*, 274–75.

3. The early essay on Matilde Serao (1903) is mainly an exposition of the characters, plots and setting of her stories, within the framework of a general critical assessment (LNI, III, 33–71). But in the first essay on Baudelaire—which came later (1919)—the main problem is the definition of the poet's emotional content in its seriousness and sincerity; little is said of individual poems (PNP, 252–65). Some of these were taken up in his later studies on Baudelaire: PAM, 395–411.

4. Since the concept of individuality in art still meets with resistance from persons who think it somehow irreconcilable with the "English tradition in criticism," some formulations of it by English critics may here be given. It was Addison who said that a good critic will discern "not only the general beauties and imperfections of an author, but discover the several ways of thinking and expressing himself which diversify him from all other authors, with the several foreign infusions of thought and language, and the particular authors from whom they were borrowed" (*Spectator*, No. 409). Lamb recognized in the artist "that individualizing faculty, which should keep the subject so treated distinct in feature from any other subject, however similar, and from common apprehensions almost identical" ("On the Barrenness of the Imaginative Faculty" etc., *Works*, ed. C. Kent, London, 1876, p. 522). "The function of the aesthetic critic is to distinguish, to analyse, and separate from its adjuncts, the virtue by

which a picture, a landscape, a fair personality in a life or a book, produces this special impression of beauty or pleasure" (W. Pater, *The Renaissance*, London, reprint of 1922, p. xi). "No writer is self-supporting, but every writer is individual in his work, and each of his works is individual if it is of any value at all" (W. P. Ker, *Form and Style in Poetry*, London, 1928, p. 145). That "individuality" is "the soul of poetry" may even be found in such an orthodox work as the *Cambridge History of English Literature:* see C. E. Vaughan on *Coleridge*, XI, 119.

5. For observations on style, see LNI, IV, 42 (D'Annunzio); PNP, 102 (Stendhal), 113 and 118–19, (Leopardi), and 122 (de Vigny). For observations on vocabulary and diction, see LNI, III, 10 (Verga), 67 (Serao); IV, 50–51 (D'Annunzio), 132 (Fogazzaro); on structure in the novel, IV, 135–36 (Fogazzaro). On the artistic error of choosing the wrong narrator in a novel, I, 131–37 (Nievo).

6. For the first opinion, cf. I. Babbitt, "Genius and Taste" (1918), reprinted in J. C. Bowman, *Contemporary American Criticism* (New York, 1926), p. 97: "The whole business of the critic is to receive so keen an impression from the resulting expression that when passed through his temperament it issues forth as fresh expression." This is given as Croce's view. Of course Croce does not speak of "temperament" in this connection: the word has been polemically injected by Babbitt. For Babbitt's influence on later American opinion, cf. my paper "Il caso Spingarn e il crocianesimo in America" in *Criterio*, I (1957), 521–22. The second opinion is expressed by M. Krieger, *The New Apologists for Poetry*, p. 137: "the critic, if he is to be consistently Crocean, can only stand in speechless admiration before the successful poem."

7. The only passage I can find in Croce that lends any support to this statement is the following: "of the beautiful, in so far as it is beautiful, there is nothing else to say. In its presence the art connoisseur who knows his job not only *obstupescit* [is astonished], but also *obticuit* [is silent]" (NSE², 284). Croce is here rejecting the doctrine of the "modifications of the Beautiful," i.e. the theory that there are several aesthetic categories, the sublime and the pathetic, the picturesque and the idyllic, the primitive and the classic, etc., as well as the beautiful: see Chapter VI. (This is borne out by the repetition of the cited passage in P, 300, referring to P, 116–20, where the "modifications of the Beautiful" are again criticized.) In the same page (NSE², 284) Croce assigns to the critic two operations: 1) the expres-

sion of a critical judgment, and 2) the description of the lyrical theme. So even here the critic is far from being silent in the presence of the perfect poem.

8. For the theory that criticism is judgment, in addition to the paper of 1909 in *PdE* cited in Chapter VII, see NSE, 82–83; EA, 94–95; ASC, 3–4 and 279; CC, II, 269–70, III, 131; P, 107–15, 121–22 and 128–30; US, 28–29; *Discorsi*, I, 271; *Letture*, 231.

9. "Taste must reproduce the work of art within itself in order to understand and judge it; and at that moment aesthetic judgment becomes nothing more nor less than creative art itself." J. E. Spingarn, *Creative Criticism and Other Essays*, 1931 edition, p. 37.

10. *Ibid.*, p. 128.

11. *Ibid.*, p. 170. Further details will be found in my paper cited in note 6 above, pp. 517–23.

12. T. G. Stenberg in his article "Croce and American Literary Criticism," *Sewanee Review*, XXXIII (1925), 222, denied that criticism for Croce was limited to taste, and saw that it involved history and philosophy, but did not give the theory of criticism as judgment. Even J. Smith, a critic who was completely at sea when it came to the a priori synthesis, was aware that Croce defined criticism as judgment: see his cited article in *Scrutiny*, II, 33–34. But Smith had taken the trouble of reading the *Logica* and both *PdE* and NSE. Compare the fixation of American scholarship on the position maintained by Spingarn; e.g. "If, with the Croceans, critical theory inquires solely: 'What has the artist tried to express and how has he expressed it?', taste and judgment tend to become critical tools for re-creating the artist's aim: they become similar to, if not identical with, genius" (B. C. Heyl in J. T. Shipley, *Dictionary of World Literature*, new revised edition, New York, 1953, p. 414).

13. L. Venturi, *History of Art Criticism*, translated from the Italian by C. Marriott (New York, 1936); for criticism as judgment see p. 33. See also the revised version in Italian, *Storia della critica d'arte* (Florence, 1948, p. 30). Venturi's polemical pamphlet, *Art Criticism Now* (Baltimore, 1941), is based in part on Croce, in part on theories which are his own. For Croce's agreement and disagreement with Venturi, see NSE², 276 and 281–85. Venturi's main difference from Croce lies in the special meaning he gives to "taste" (*gusto*): cf. CC, III, 112–15, 124–28, and 131–32, and my article on "Taste" in the forthcoming *Dictionary of Poetics*.

14. Croce noted the branding of Spingarn as an impressionist and

protested against it, NPS, I, 203. For Croce's answers to Babbitt, see CC, III, 13–15, 70 and 379.

15. "Literary Criticism as Philosophy," NSE², 201–15. See also CC, II, 266–70 and *Letture*, 228.

16. For a full list of references to Sainte-Beuve in Croce see O. Ruggiero, *La letteratura francese nella critica de B. Croce*, pp. 58–59. See especially NSE², 208–10 and NPS, I, 250–51.

17. Croce's dissent from Taine is frequently expressed. For full list of references see Ruggiero, *op. cit.*, pp. 63–65. Main discussions of Taine: E, 437–40; A, 392–94; NSE², 209–10; PNP, 240; *Storia*, 187–93; CC, I, 75–78, II, 130–35.

18. On M. Barrès see *L'Italia dal 1914 al 1918*, 3rd ed., 1950, pp. 185–92; *ibid.*, pp. 200–206, on Rimbaud's views on life and art.

19. Cf. NSE², 284; CC, III, 82; US, 69. *Poetry and non-poetry* (1923) is the title of a critical work of Croce (PNP) to be discussed in Chapter XII. For a warning against the abuse of this method see "The deformation of one of my aesthetic theories" (1915), PS, I, 386–90.

20. The first of these (P, 121–28) was translated by A. H. Gilbert in G. W. Allen and H. H. Clark, *Literary Criticism from Pope to Croce* (New York, 1941), pp. 633–40, together with the two preceding and following sections, pp. 628–45. For "characterization" see also *Letture*, 232–36, 275–76. One of the earliest references to it is in the *Carteggio Croce-Vossler*, p. 67.

21. "In literary criticism and history the inquiry turns on two points, or rather may only by abstraction be distinguished into two moments, in the first of which one inquires whether a work is poetry, in the second *what* poetry it is" (NSE², 324; from the essay on "Modern Poetics" already cited in Chapter V). Cf. CC, III, 82–83.

22. "I do not work in the field of psychology but in that of the theory of knowledge and the philosophy of spirit" (PdE, 188). "I observe myself, and I am obliged to make use of myself, since I confess that I am not acquainted with the psychology of others, or of children and of animals, save through my own spirit" (PdE, 484. Cf. *Pratica*, 66 ff. on psychology and "practical description").

23. For Hegel's interpretation of Shakespeare's villain-heroes see my paper "Critica e filologia shakespeariana nell'epoca romantica" in *Rivista di letterature moderne e comparate*, IX (1956), 12. See the same paper for Hegel's interpretation of Hamlet and a similar interpretation in Croce. A convergent view of Hamlet has been conceived

(as it seems) independently, and brilliantly worked out, by G. Wilson Knight, *The Wheel of Fire* (1939; new edition, New York, 1957), pp. 17–42: "Hamlet's disease is mental and spiritual death." Cf. Croce, ASC, 161–62.

24. Only the individual is effable, *solum individuum effabile*, is Croce's principle: see above, p. 38, and *Saggio sullo Hegel*, 1913, p. 86, and CC, III, 103.

25. Cf. the account of Carducci criticism by E. Alpino in W. Binni (ed.), *I classici italiani nella storia della critica* (Firenze, 1955), II, 556 ff.

26. H. L. Mencken's lively essay "Criticism of criticism of criticism" in *Prejudices, 1st Series* (New York, 1919, reprint of 1926), pp. 9–12, although relating to Croce—or rather to Spingarn—does not discuss this point, but comments on Spingarn's argument with his opponents.

27. Cf. EA, 40; NSE², 34; P⁴, 319; CC, V, 44; *Letture*, 304–5; NPS, I, 222–23 and 179–80 ("Interiorità della Forma"); TPS, II, 187–89. Cf. also *Critica*, XXVII (1929), 99 note, reprinted in SS², II, 203 note. See also the penetrating discussion by D. Pesce, "Sulla dottrina crociana dell'incaratterizzabilità della forma artistica" in the review *Carro Minore* (Trento), II (1947), No. 5–6.

28. On stylistics see Chapter IV, note 32. Cf. also NPS, I, 179–80.

29. D. Pesce, cited article in *Carro Minore*, II, p. 4: "qui forma vuol dire: sintesi, attività, creazione."

30. T. S. Eliot, "The Function of Criticism" (1923) in *Selected Essays* (London, 1932), p. 30. Cf. NSE², 70–72; EA, 86–87.

31. *Sibi imperiosa* is a quotation that Croce apparently derived through Shaftesbury. Cf. *Uomini e cose*, I, 298.

32. Cf., as early as 1905, *Carteggio Croce-Vossler*, p. 67; and again, CC, V. 82.

33. Cf. *Logica*, pp. 17–20. Wimsatt, one of the very few American critics who have taken notice of Croce's doctrine of characterization, compares it to an irrational number, which is both against the letter and against the spirit of Croce's doctrine. Cf. *Verbal Icon*, p. 83.

CHAPTER *ix*

1. Cf. the joint symposium on "Literature and the Professors" in the Autumn 1940 issues of the *Kenyon Review*, II, 403–42 and the *Southern Review*, VI, 225–69. Cf. also the controversy between D.

Bush and C. Brooks in the *Sewanee Review*, LX (1952), 363–76 and LXI (1953), 129–35, preceded by a statement of their different points of view in the *Kenyon Review*, XIII (1951), 72–91. For some anecdotes indicating bitterness of feeling see Y. Winters, *The Function of Criticism* (Denver, 1957), pp. 13–14. Cf. also W. Van O'Connor: "It seems strange to find such a decided animus between scholars on the one hand and poets, novelists and critics on the other," in S. J. Kunitz (ed.), *Twentieth Century Authors, First Supplement* (New York, 1955), p. 731.

2. For a nineteenth-century definition of the Historical Fallacy, see M. Arnold, "The Study of Poetry," *Essays in Criticism, Second Series* (London, 1888, reprint of 1898), pp. 6–7.

3. These introductions have recently been made available by F. Stern, *The Varieties of History* (New York, 1956), pp. 170–77.

4. R. Tuve, "A Critical Survey of Scholarship in the Field of the English Literature of the Renaissance," *Studies in Philology*, XL (1943), 236–38.

5. On De Sanctis see, in English, L. A. Breglio, *Life and Criticism of F. De Sanctis* (New York, ca. 1940); J. Rossi, "De Sanctis' Criticism: Its Principles and Method," PMLA, LIV (1939), 526–64, and "Mazzinian Echoes in De Sanctis' Criticism," *Italica*, XXXIII (1956), 264–78; and R. Wellek, "F. De Sanctis," *Italian Quarterly*, I (1957), 5–43. Cf. also J. Rossi, "I critici americani e inglesi del De Sanctis," *Italica*, XV (1938), 5–8.

6. See in his essay on Lamartine (1857) a famous comparison of the French (or psychological) and German (or philosophical) schools of criticism: *Saggi critici*, ed. Arcari (Milan, 1914), II, 9–12.

7. *Cours d'Esthétique par W.-Fr. Hegel, analysé et traduit en partie, par* M. Ch. Bénard (Paris, 1840), I, 73–84. Cf. De Sanctis' exposition of the same passage in his lectures, *Teoria e storia della letteratura*, ed. Croce (Bari, 1926), II, 86–91. Cf. also Hegel, *Aesthetik*, 1842, I, 247–73 and Masson's ed., 1931, 275–301.

8. As he acknowledged in his lecture on Zola's *L'Assommoir*, *Scritti vari inediti e rari*, ed. Croce (Naples, 1898), II, 83.

9. These essays are now available in a lively English translation by J. Rossi and A. Galpin, *De Sanctis on Dante* (Madison, 1957).

10. Cf. Croce, *Primi saggi*, p. 121 note. I therefore do not share the view that the concept of "situation" is central in De Sanctis, a view put forward recently by G. F. Contini and rightly rejected by R. Wellek in the cited paper in the *Italian Quarterly*, I, 13. The pur-

pose of my own paper on this topic ("De Sanctis e la situazione poetica," *Civiltà moderna*, xiv, 1942, 138–40), which Wellek also refers to, was historical: to show the derivation of the term from Hegel.

11. The "close reading" of poetry by De Sanctis has recently been pointed out by Wellek in the cited paper, pp. 34, 35 and 36. This is the more remarkable since it is a common belief that "close reading" is an invention of the twentieth century.

12. F. De Sanctis, *History of Italian Literature*, translated by Joan Redfern (New York, 1931), 2 vols., with an introduction by Croce.

13. Many ideas and interpretations of De Sanctis are accessible to the English reader by being incorporated (without complete acknowledgment) in J. A. Symonds' popular book on *Italian Literature*, part of his larger work on the Renaissance. This was first noted by Spingarn and later shown in detail in my papers, to be cited on p. 359 n. 5.

14. Wellek has given a detailed exposition of De Sanctis' scheme of development of Italian literature in his cited paper, pp. 18–27. Croce's later criticism of this scheme as a whole will be discussed later in this chapter; see below, note 37.

15. See the essay on Settembrini, *Saggi critici* (Milan, 1914), iii, 73–75. The fact that De Sanctis, after working long as an aesthetic critic, could appreciate and even adopt the point of view of the historical critics is typical of his flexibility, which in his last essays made him welcome Zola and naturalism.

16. This famous critical myth propagated by T. S. Eliot seems now discredited: cf. F. Kermode, "Dissociation of Sensibility," *Kenyon Review*, xix (1957), 169–94.

17. Both have been republished by Croce in his *Primi saggi* (1919) with an introduction in which he gives his own account of his early development.

18. *Scritti vari inediti e rari* di F. de Sanctis, ed. B. Croce (Naples, 1898, 2 vols.). Croce's defence of De Sanctis was reprinted in *Una famiglia di patrioti* etc. (1919), together with other papers on him.

19. See Croce, *Gli scritti di F. de Sanctis e la loro varia fortuna, saggio bibliografico* (Bari, 1917), to which additions were made later in F. De Sanctis, *Pagine sparse, contributi alla sua biografia e supplemento alla bibliografia* (Bari, 1934). References to De Sanctis are to

be found *passim* in Croce. The main discussions before 1917 are in *Primi saggi*, pp. 119–33; E, 400–412; A, 358–69; and LNI, I, 359–79. For Croce's later attitude, see note 37 below.

20. An eminent linguist thus abandoned "Philology" to the students of literature: "philology is the study of national cultural values, especially as preserved in the writings of a people, linguistics is the study of man's function of language," L. Bloomfield, *An Introduction to the Study of Language* (New York, ca. 1913), p. 308 n.

21. Other attacks on "philologism" or the abuse of the historical method in literature are to be found in CC, III, 336, V, 32; P, 69–70, 162–63, 325; *Discorsi*, I, 158. A critical survey of historical scholarship which includes a number of sharp remarks is in LNI, III, 373–91. Croce was equally critical of "professors of philosophy" (e.g. PS, I, 170–73, III, 162) and was never popular among Italian academic students of the subject. There never was a "school of Crocean philosophy" to speak of, in Italian philosophical faculties. Croce made adherents among the historians and the literary critics and scholars, and art critics and historians, but most Italian philosophers during his lifetime belonged to other schools. So it is also pointless to speak of a "decline" of Croce's "dominance" over Italian philosophers after his death.

22. For further quotations from this paper in English translation see L. Venturi, *History of Art Criticism*, pp. 24–26.

23. *La critica*, xx (1922), 49 note. This interesting note was omitted in the reprint, CC, III, 22–24.

24. For English literary history a substantial beginning was made by R. Wellek, *The Rise of English Literary History* (Chapel Hill, 1941). Cf. the same author's survey of American literary scholarship in M. Curti (ed.), *American Scholarship in the Twentieth Century* (Cambridge, Mass., 1953), pp. 111–45. And of course there are monographs and papers on several individual historians, topics and problems. But the only attempt to survey the whole of the 19th century seems to be the old sketch by C. M. Gayley, "Literary Studies in the 19th Century," *Proceedings of the St. Louis Congress of the Arts and Sciences*, 1906, III, 332 ff. Taine, Courthope, etc. are also discussed in my *Introduzione allo studio delle letterature inglese e americana* (Milan, 1942), pp. 164–74.

25. According to Croce, the history of art and of literature does not differ from political history in having its objects present to the observer while the facts of political history belong to the past and

exist no longer (cf. R. Wellek and A. Warren, *The Theory of Literature*, p. 266). All history presupposes the presence of the object to be studied in the mind of the inquirer (NSE, 219–21).

26. Croce came to this conclusion in 1909 (*PdE*, 51–55), thus modifying the view of literary history presented in the *Aesthetic*, where literary history, like all history, consists in the application of the existential categories (real and unreal, external and internal) to the intuition (E, 32 and 144; A, 28 and 131). See above, Chapter VII, note 5.

27. R. Wellek also argues in favor of "a history of the art of literature, written with critical insight, according to critical standards," and points out that "surely many of the greatest critics were also literary historians: the Schlegels, Sainte-Beuve, De Sanctis, Taine, Brunetière, Croce," in M. Curti (ed.), *American Scholarship*, p. 124. Wellek refers to Martin Schütze's *Academic Illusions* (p. 119), and in that book we find a similar statement: "true history and criticism are two inseparable organic aspects of a proper understanding of letters," etc. See M. Schütze, *Academic Illusions in the Field of Letters and the Arts: A Survey, a Criticism, a New Approach, and a Comprehensive Plan for Reorganizing the Study of Letters and the Arts* (Chicago, 1934), p. 299.

28. Cf. E, 147; A, 133; *Logica*, 199–204. On the objection that this is "subjectivism," cf. PS, I, 138–42.

29. Cf. R. Tuve, cited article in *Studies in Philology*, XL, 228–29; and see R. Wellek, "The Concept of Evolution in Literary History," Reprinted from *For Roman Jakobson* (The Hague, 1956), pp. 653–61. For Croce's critique of evolutionism, see also CC, II, 192–207, V, 65–66; and TPS, II, 9. In the first *Aesthetic* Croce admitted the possibility of aesthetic development in a cycle like the poems of chivalry (E, 149, A, 136), but soon after rejected it: see E, p. ix, and TPS, II, 9.

30. Wellek and Warren, *Theory of Literature*, pp. 263–84, and Wellek, "The Concept of Romanticism in Literary History," *Comparative Literature*, I (1949), 1–23, 147–72.

31. For "functional concepts" see *PdE*, 292; CC, V, 23, 235; *Storia*, 56–57, 131–33, and the English translation, *History as the Story of Liberty* (Meridian Books, 1955), pp. 67–68, 127–29, which includes also the additional chapter on the subject of "Chronological and Historical Periods" (pp. 296–301) added to the later Italian editions. See also *Discorsi*, II, 152–56 and TPS, I, 48.

32. For Croce's concept of the Renaissance as an historical period,

see TSS, 205-21 and *Storia dell'età barocca in Italia*, pp. 3-19, which are the main statements. Other discussions in *Varietà di storia letteraria* etc., II, 52-53; PS, III, 173-78, 371-72; TPS, I, 144-45, II, 237-38; *Discorsi*, I, 163, II, 152-56; *Storia*, 288-294 (on humanism), English translation, pp. 311-17; CC, IV, 77; US, 43-44; *Poeti e scrittori del . . . rinascimento*, I, 1-16.

33. Cf. De Sanctis: "The common element can never account for the intrinsic value of a work, which consists not in what it has in common with its century, with its school, with its predecessors, but in what is uniquely its own" (*Saggi critici*, ed. Arcari, Milan, 1914, III, 85).

34. For Croce's critique of nationalistic histories of literature see his discussion of A. Bartels, NSE, 185-92; of others, PS, III, 147-49 and *Discorsi*, II, 182-83. Croce's critique of Bartels was translated by A. Livingston, "Nationalism in Literature," *The Menorah Journal*, x (1924), 428-35.

35. For Croce's refusal to write a History of Italian Literature see CC, V, 247; PPPA, pp. ix-xi and *Poeti e scrittori del . . . rinascimento*, II, 87 ff., 251-58; NPS, I, 196-97; TPS, II, 64-65; *Letture*, 68-69.

36. See R. Wellek in N. Foerster et al., *Literary Scholarship*, p. 116.

37. E, p. x (preface to the 5th ed., 1921); PS, III, 409-10, and the bibliography there given on the question of the historical links (*nessi*) in literature; *Au*, 78-85; P, 311. See also the preface to the translation of De Sanctis' *History* into English (1931), reprinted in CC, V, 28-31, and "The Condition of Criticism in Italy" in *Lectures in Criticism*, *The Johns Hopkins University* (New York, 1949), the original of which is in NPS, I, 165-72. Cf. also TPS, I, 193-99 and *Indagini su Hegel*, 216-21. Of the innumerable discussions of the relations of Croce to De Sanctis I will only refer to the one by F. Flora in the miscellaneous volume edited by himself on *Croce* (Milan, 1953), pp. 195-232, and the one by L. Russo in *La critica letteraria contemporanea* (Bari, 1953, 3rd ed.), I, 284-95.

38. This book includes a survey of literature in late 16th century Naples (II, 227-80) which refers to the beginning of the baroque and is conducted from a point of view similar to that of the book on the baroque age, discussed in the next paragraph of the text.

39. A full account and discussion of Croce's book on the baroque age is in A. R. Caponigri, *History and Liberty*, pp. 89-166.

40. The *History of the Baroque Age* is Croce's main discussion

of the baroque. His statements previous to 1939 are listed in R. Wellek's full bibliography of the baroque published in the *Journal of Aesthetics and Art Criticism*, v (1946), 98–103. To this list should be added the following items, presented here in the manner of the Wellek bibliography:

1931. Review of K. Eschweiler, "Die Philosophie der Spanischen Spätscholastik," *Gesammelte Aufsätze zur Kulturgeschichte Spaniens* (1928), in *La critica*, xxix, 63–65; reprinted cc, iv, 26–29.

1932. "Categorismo e psicologismo nella storia della poesia," *La critica*, xxx, 157–60; reprinted us, 373–79.

1936. *La poesia*, pp. 119–21, 298.

1938. "Teorie e fantasie moderne sul barocco," *La critica*, xxxvi, 225–29; a reply to E. D'Ors, reprinted cc, iii, 15–20.

1941. Review of C. Calcaterra, *Il Parnaso in rivolta: barocco e antibarocco nella poesia italiana* (1940), *La critica*, xxxix, 54; reprinted nps, ii, 105–6.

1941. "Contro gli esaltatori del barocco," *ibid.*, xxxix, 387; reprinted ps, iii, 63.

1945. "Il Tebaldeo," *Poeti e scrittori del . . . rinascimento*, i, 51–54.

1946. Review of the Italian translation of E. D'Ors, *Del barocco* (1945), *Quaderni della Critica*, iv, 83–84, and reprinted in nps, ii, 61–63.

1948. "Cervantes, *Persiles y Sigismunda*," *Quad. Critica*, xii, 71–82; *Letture*, 55–57.

Croce's concept of the baroque was used by an Oriental scholar to characterize the style of Arab literature: G. E. von Grunebaum, "The Aesthetic Foundation of Arabic Literature," *Comparative Literature*, iv (1952), 323–40.

41. However, Croce's final view was that Romanticism should not be wholly credited with the theory of the creative Imagination; he recognized several anticipations, even in ancient aesthetics. See "L'intuizione e la sintesi a priori" (1950), *Storiografia e idealità morale* (Bari, 1950), p. 134.

42. For other discussions of Romanticism see *Pagine sulla guerra*, 3rd ed., 1950, pp. 123–26; cc, iii, 64–67; us, 373–77; p, 118–21, 294–96; ps, iii, 278–79; nps, i, 182–84. Against ignorant contempt of Romantic doctrines, see pppa, 20.

43. Cf. Croce's discussion of books on the themes of Sophonisba and of Mary Stuart in *PdE*, 80–93, and of Don Carlos, cc, ii, 189–92.

See also his critique of a history of the Madonna in art, *PdE*, 267–71. For an instance of how such subjects should be properly handled, see his review of E. Della Valle, *Antigone* (1935), CC, V, 95. Contrariwise, CC, V, 86–87.

44. ASC, 211. Cf. B. Munteano, *Revue de littérature comparée*, XXVI (1952), p. 280, and M. Bataillon, *ibid.*, XXX (1956), p. 142: "Ne faudrait-il pas, pour rejoindre la réalité vivante de la littérature, substituer le point de vue de la *littérature réceptrice* à celui du grand écrivain émetteur, influent?" On "influences" see also the review of A. Farinelli, *Dante in Francia* (1908), CC, II, 187–89. Cf. also *PdE*, 75.

45. *Uomini e cose della vecchia Italia*, 1927, II, 217–18.

46. For a more recent statement of this view, see *Poeti e scrittori del . . . rinascimento*, II, 1945, 251–58, and 259–65.

CHAPTER *x*

1. The echo of the enthusiasm produced by this review may still be heard in the words of a private letter of a youth who was to become a leading critic, Renato Serra: "Croce and Gentile, Gentile and Croce. That is their strength: they are themselves. They have become familiar, they are the friends of the man who reads. Every month one expects their opinion on the event, on the book, on the question of the day." The letter is of March 1910, and is cited by A. Parente, *La "Critica" e il tempo della cultura crociana* (Bari, 1953), pp. 17–18. Here it is not possible to go further into the complex and tragic story of the Croce–Gentile quarrel. But reference must be made to Croce's account of how he felt when the news came that Gentile had been shot by the Communists. See his diary for April 17, 1944, in *Quaderni della Critica*, IX (1947), pp. 102–3, and translated in *Croce, the King and the Allies* (New York, 1950), pp. 111–12.

2. The program of *La critica* was reprinted in CC, II, 353–57. Its epilogue—the words with which Croce introduced its 42nd and last volume—is reprinted in NPS, I, 3 ff.

3. For Croce's broader aims in promoting a revival of philosophic idealism in Italy, see his later statements in CVM, 9–40 (1908) and his summing up in *Storia d'Italia dal 1871 al 1915* (1934, 4th ed.), pp. 255–57.

4. On "scientism," cf. the papers cited in note 3 and PS, II, 271–72.

5. An index to vols. I–XII is in XII (1914), 453–70.

6. For more details on these essays see Seerveld, *Croce's Earlier . . . Theories and . . . Criticism*, pp. 32–34 and 65–68.

7. The first essay on Carducci is in *La critica*, I (1903), 7–31.

8. G. Castellano, *B. Croce*, . . . , 1936, 2nd ed., pp. 33–34.

9. The present writer has used it for a study of Tennyson: see G. N. Giordano Orsini, *La poesia di A. Tennyson*, Bari, 1928.

10. Cf. G. Santangelo, "G. Verga," in W. Binni, *I classici italiani*, II, 593 ff.

11. L. Russo, *I narratori* (Roma, 1923), p. 133. A revised edition has appeared with the sub-title "1850–1950" (Bari, 1951). To Verga, Russo dedicated a full-length study in a volume of 1919, which is now in its fifth edition: *G. Verga* (Bari, 1955). To it the reader is referred for a complete aesthetic analysis of Verga.

12. A. Momigliano, *Storia della letteratura italiana* (Milano, 1937), pp. 528–29.

13. For recent evaluations of Verga see M. Schorer, "The Fiction of G. Verga," in R. Richman (ed.), *The Arts at Mid-Century* (New York, 1954), pp. 137–45, and A. J. De Vito, "Roba e miseria motivi dominanti nell'opera di G. Verga," *Italica*, XXXI (1954). A new translation has also appeared: G. Verga, *The She-Wolf and Other Stories*, translated with an Introduction by G. Cecchetti (Berkeley, 1958).

14. For Croce's later judgments on Baudelaire see the essays in PAM, 395–411, and *Letture*, 268–69, as well as the book-reviews in NPS, II, 107–10, and TPS, II, 149–50. A fuller list of references to Baudelaire will be found in the cited book by O. Ruggiero, *La letteratura francese nella critica di B. C.*, pp. 30–33. Ruggiero, however, omits the significant fact that Baudelaire is absent from the earlier versions of the *Aesthetic* (e.g. ed. IV, 1912, and A, the English translation of this edition) but is honorably included (together with Flaubert) in the fifth (1922) and later editions, in Chapter XVIII of the historical section (E, 460, 462).

15. For Croce's change of mind on Manzoni, see TPS, I, 128–30 and 160–61.

CHAPTER *xi*

1. Spingarn's review appeared in *The Nation*, LXXV (1902), 252–53.

2. A. Caracciolo, *L'estetica di B. Croce nel suo svolgimento e nei suoi limiti* (Torino, 1948), p. 66.

3. No date is appended to the article in *La critica*, XVI (1918), 129–40, but it was given as "1917" at the end of the essay as printed in volume form (NSE, 138; NSE², 134). In his unpublished diary (kindly inspected for me by Dr. Alda Croce) Croce states that he completed the essay in July 1917, i.e. five months before he began the Ariosto essay (December 1917, as stated in the same diary).

4. W. von Humboldt, *Gesammelte Werke*, (Berlin, 1843), IV, 17, 22 and 29–31.

5. W. K. Wimsatt Jr. is apparently the only American critic who has taken cognizance of Croce's universalistic concept: see "The Concrete Universal" in his *The Verbal Icon*, p. 283 note. He refers to it as a sort of passing expostulation ("Croce protests that . . .") and concludes: "But the main drift of Croce's aesthetic, being against conceptualization, is radically against the universal." However in Croce the doctrine of totality was more than an occasional outburst, it was a new doctrine, bearing directly on Wimsatt's theme, the connection between particular and universal in literature.

6. In an essay of 1934, "On *intúito* and judgment," Croce identified the logical judgment, which he calls *intúito*, with Lalande's (Kantian) intuition (US, 260 note), thus reversing the theory expounded above in Chapter II.

7. G. Gentile, *Frammenti di estetica*, p. 175. Gentile, however, observed in a note on p. 176 that an anticipation might be found in the *Breviary:* "The emotion or state of mind is not a particular content, but the whole universe viewed *sub specie intuitionis*" (NSE, 38; EA, 40). Cf. the Heidelberg lecture: "the aesthetic image is loosened from the limitations of space and time . . . and belongs not to the world but to the super-world, not to the passing moment but to eternity" (*PdE*, 27; A¹, 399). Cf. also: "the power that Schelling and Schopenhauer found in music to reproduce not the ideas but the ideal rhythm of the universe and to objectify the will itself, belongs equally to all forms of art" (*Pratica*, 188). For Gentile's criticism of Croce's aesthetics see in English the article by G. Gullace, "Gentile versus Croce," *Symposium*, XI (1957), 75–91.

8. G. A. Borgese, *Poetica dell'unità* (Milano, 1934), p. xxiv. On the relations between Croce and Borgese, which became quite bitter in later years, see Croce's polemic in NPS, I, 341–46.

9. A. Tilgher, *Estetica, Teoria generale dell'attività artistica* (Roma, 1931), pp. 18–19. The Italian critics of Croce are quoted on this particular point and not on others, not because other points of

Croce's doctrine were not discussed by them, but because their criticism seems particularly relevant here. Tilgher himself represents a type which has become increasingly frequent in Italy, that of the critic who asserts his independence from Croce by attacking him, and then repeats ideas of Croce's with slight verbal variants.

10. One of the few theoretical developments that Croce made of it was a revision of his theory of metaphor; see the "Note on Metaphor," *PdE*[4], 160–64: "poetry always sings of the world in its unity, the universal rhythm of things," and the vehicle in the metaphor represents the infinite "in the same way that every part of the universe represents the whole." This concept is formulated again in PS, III, 258.

11. F. De Sanctis, *Saggi*, ed. Arcari, II, 189.

12. This point was also noted by A. A. De Gennaro in his cited article, JAAC, XV (1956), p. 171, note 17.

13. Henri Clouard, *Histoire de la littérature française du symbolisme à nos jours* (Paris, 1947), II, 504.

14. Cf. also *Discorsi*, II, 83–90. Statements of this sort might perhaps have allayed the concern of critics like Stuart P. Sherman, who charged Spingarn, Croce's American disciple, with separating "in his super-subtle Italian fashion" beauty from morality; see "The National Genius" (1921) in *Criticism in America: Its Function and Its Status* (New York, 1924), p. 244.

15. "I believe that the said requirement that a writer, in order to possess some literary value, great or small, must be first of all a moral spirit, deserves the stress that it usually does not receive. Moral spirit does not mean the spirit of a moralist, or of a critic and reformer of manners, a profession ill received and often not unjustly suspected of hypocrisy and arrogance; but a spirit so inclined that in it the passion for the universal should prevail over personal passion and tendencies; and in this case, and only in this case, poetry or art in general is, at the same time, moral strength." *La letteratura italiana del settecento*, 1949, p. 352.

16. Cf. A. Caracciolo, *L'estetica di B. Croce . . .*, p. 67: "In all the meanings discussed and clarified, the term 'totality' has appeared to us with the character of content [*con carattere contenutistico*]."

17. The adjective *contenutistico*, as well as the correlative noun *contenutismo*, has no equivalent in English, although its opposite is designated by *formalistic* and the correlative noun *formalism*. In Italian it may have been coined by Croce himself, who did not hesitate to forge terms which horrified the purists, such as *praticistico*.

The epithet *contenutistica* occurs in the historical section of the *Aesthetic:* E, 469. Ainslie uses in his translation (A, 418) the term *contentism*, which certainly has not gained currency. For the currency of *contenutistico*, see an instance in the preceding note. W. K. Wimsatt uses "contentual" in his and C. Brooks' *Literary Criticism*, p. 275.

18. *Filosofia e storiografia*, 1949, p. 79, and *Letture*, p. 219. (See also PAM, 178–79). A penetrating and detailed analysis of this later aesthetic of Croce is in Dario Faucci, "Poesia e verità nella critica estetica crociana," *Rivista di Estetica*, III (1958), 172–205.

19. A. Parente, "La terza scoperta dell'estetica crociana: dialettica di passioni e suo superamento nell'arte" in F. Flora, *B. Croce*, pp. 25–105. Cf. *Aesthetica in nuce:* in poetry "joy and sorrow, pleasure and pain, strength and weakness, seriousness and levity, etc., are linked to each other and pass into each other through shades and transitions" (US, 9). The beginning of this sentence is badly mistranslated in the *Encyclopaedia Britannica:* "Feeling, not crushed [*sic*] but contemplated in the work of poetry, is seen to diffuse itself in widening circles . . ." This should be: "Feeling, not experienced in its travail but contemplated in the act of poetry, is seen to diffuse itself" etc. ("il sentimento, non vissuto nel suo travaglio ma contemplato," US, 8).

20. For the parallel with Coleridge on the cosmic theory cf. M. Krieger, *The New Apologists for Poetry*, p. 34 n.

CHAPTER *xii*

1. D, 31 and 161. The translation by D. Ainslie (*The Poetry of Dante*, London, 1922) will be cited as DE. For the two passages referred to in D, see DE, 38 and 242. On the characterization of Dante's spirit, cf. D, 56; DE, 78.

2. For the history of Dante criticism see Croce's Appendix, D, 173–205; DE, 256–307. Cf. also F. Maggini, "La critica dantesca dal 300 ai nostri giorni," in A. Momigliano (ed.), *Problemi ed orientamenti critici*, III (1949), 123–66, and D. Mattalia in W. Binni (ed.), *I classici italiani*, I, 1–93.

3. Croce's views on Dante's political ideas are also set forth in the *Encyclopaedia of Social Sciences*, 1931, IV, 708–9 (the original in PS, II, 225–27). See also his answers to a questionnaire on Dante in the *Evening Post*, New York, September 1921 (PS, II, 257–61).

4. Wellek and Warren, *Theory of Literature*, pp. 65–66.

5. Croce is evidently referring to A. Mordell, *Dante and other Waning Classics* (Philadelphia, 1915)—a book which he quotes elsewhere in his study (D, 181; DE, 266)—who said: "Can one conceive of Dante's indignation on discovering a fine critic like John Addington Symonds ignoring the weighty philosophical discourses and explanations of the universe in the poem and waxing enthusiastic over a simile?" (p. 44). The fact that Croce joins Symonds to De Sanctis in the quoted passage should not seem an arbitrary conjunction, for Symonds' criticism incorporates many pages of De Sanctis, as noted originally by Spingarn and as traced in detail in two papers of mine, "La Storia del Rinascimento di J. A. Symonds," *La cultura*, VI (1927), 408–13, and "J. A. Symonds e F. De Sanctis," *ibid.*, VII (1928), 358–76. Views similar to those referred to by Croce are to be found in A. La Piana, *Dante's American Pilgrimage, A Historical Survey of Dante Studies in the U.S., 1800–1944* (New Haven, 1948), pp. 250–51 and 258, and in H. Hatzfeld, "Modern Literary Scholarship as Reflected in Dante Criticism," *Comparative Literature*, III (1951), 310–19.

6. Ainslie here omits by mistake ten lines in which Croce clarifies his position: D, 70; DE, 101. Also, Croce does not speak here of Dante's "works" but of his "volume," the *Comedy*, considered as a book.

7. Cf. for references D. Mattalia in W. Binni (ed.), *I classici italiani*, pp. 79–80 and Mario Rossi, *Gusto filologico e gusto poetico, Questioni di critica dantesca* (Bari, 1942), pp. 201–33. See also A. Vallone, *La critica dantesca contemporanea* (Pisa, 1953) and the useful collection by G. De Feo and G. Savarese, *Antologia della critica dantesca* (Messina, 1958). For the last word of Barbi on this matter, see his posthumous *Problemi fondamentali per un nuovo commento della Divina Commedia* (Florence, 1955), pp. 7–19.

8. This statement on the "dialectical unity" of the *Comedy* (D, 67; DE, 96) should be taken with the clarification it received in *Letture*, pp. 10 ff., where Rossi's book, cited in the last note, is discussed. The painstaking study of Dante's thought by C. S. Singleton, *Commedia: Elements of Structure* (Dante Studies, 1; Cambridge, 1954) does not touch upon Croce's concept of the "structure" of the *Comedy*. Neither does J. Mazzeo's fine book on *Structure and Thought in the Paradiso* (Ithaca, 1958).

9. On the last canto of the *Comedy*, PAM, 151–56; on other passages, *Discorsi*, II, 41–65; *Letture*, 3–20; cf. P, 275–78. Discus-

sions of books on Dante will be found in cc, ii, 209-14, iii, 187–215, v, 96–105; ps, ii, 166–68 and 171, iii, 256–59; tps, ii, 36–40. Cf. also the survey of modern Italian studies in *La critica*, xxvii (1929), 89–91, included also in the second ed. of ss, ii, 189–92. But references to Dante are everywhere in Croce's works.

10. Croce discussed allegory more fully in a paper "On the nature of allegory," nse², 329–38, translated in *Criterion*, iii (1925), 405–12. He there distinguished it from figures of speech and from "sustained metaphor" and went more fully into its history in criticism. Allegory was already discussed in nse, 24; ea, 26. See also *Varietà di storia letteraria*, ii, 54–60 and g, ii, 232 ff. For references to the debate on the allegorical interpretation of Dante see D. Mattalia, *La critica dantesca, questioni e correnti* (Firenze, 1950), pp. 89–93. Cf. M. Barbi, *Problemi fondamentali . . .* pp. 115–40.

11. T. S. Eliot, *Dante* (London, 1929), pp. 22–23. Cf. E. Guidubaldi, "T. S. Eliot e Croce, due opposti atteggiamenti critici di fronte a Dante," *Aevum*, 31 (1957), 147–85; an interesting discussion, but the statement that Croce "ignores every possibility of lyrical coloring of what savors of intellectual origin" (p. 163) is refuted by the quotations from Croce above in the text, from d, 67 and *Discorsi*, ii, 50. John V. Falconieri, "Il saggio di T. S. Eliot su Dante," *Italica*, 34 (1957), 75–80, refers to Eliot's observations on allegory but does not particularize them.

12. F. Flora, *Storia della letteratura italiana* (Milan, 1945) 3rd ed., i, 194.

13. W. Binni, *Storia della critica ariostesca* (Lucca, 1951) and R. Ramat, *La critica ariostesca* (Florence, 1954). For other discussions of Ariosto in Croce, see ps, iii, 259–61; nps, ii, 101–4. A lively appreciation of Ariosto is in C. S. Lewis, *The Allegory of Love* (Oxford, 1936), p. 298 ff.

14. M. Praz, "Come Shakespeare è letto in Italia," in *Ricerche anglo-italiane* (Roma, 1944).

15. B. Croce, *Shakespeare*, nuova edizione a cura di N. Orsini (Bari, 1948). A new edition is in the press (1960). See also my "Croce e la critica Shakespeariana (1709–1809)," *Rivista di letterature moderne*, iv (1953), 145–54, and the references therein.

16. *The Year's Work in English Studies for 1922* (Oxford, 1923), p. 61. For a more recent survey, see K. Muir, "Fifty Years of Shakespearian Criticism," in *Shakespeare Survey*, 4 (1951), 1–25.

17. A more balanced view of the audience was presented by

A. Harbage, *Shakespeare's Audience* (New York, 1941). Of one of the pictures presented by the "historical" scholars, Harbage says: "The atmosphere created is suggestive of the Old Stone Age" (p. 150). It remained for M. A. Prior to break down the presumed dependence of the plays on the audience: see his "The Elizabethan Audience and the Plays of Shakespeare," *Modern Philology,* XLIX (1951), 101–23.

18. G. Rümelin, *Shakespeare-Studien* (2nd edition, Stuttgart, 1874). It was originally published in a journal in 1864–65 for the Shakespeare tercentenary (p. vi). Edward Dowden, perhaps the last English Shakespearean critic thoroughly conversant with German Shakespearean scholarship, answered some of Rümelin's criticisms in his *Shakspere's Mind and Art* (1875; see the new edition, New York, 1918, notes on pp. 98 and 189), and also referred to him in his textbooks (e.g. *Introduction to Shakespeare,* New York, 1916, pp. 108–9). Croce refers to him in ASC, 87, 184–85, 198.

19. As noted by T. M. Parrott, *W. Shakespeare, a Textbook* (New York, 1934), p. 223, and before him by R. W. Babcock in *Sewanee Review,* XXXV (1927), 15.

20. For a penetrating critique of this method, see W. R. Keast in R. S. Crane (ed.), *Critics and Criticism, Ancient and Modern* (Chicago, 1951), pp. 108–37.

21. For the confusion between "self-expression" and Croce's aesthetic expression, cf. J. E. Spingarn, *Creative Criticism,* New ed., p. 171.

22. The reconstruction of the "Elizabethan World-View" can also be criticized from a purely historical point of view: see F. Aydelotte's review of Tillyard's *Elizabethan World Picture* in the *American Historical Review,* L (1944), 112–13: "He does less than justice to the seeds of modern philosophy which had already sprouted and were beginning to grow in the fertile minds of Elizabethan thinkers . . . the medieval conception of fixed order and degrees in civil society in England had already been doomed two centuries before by the Black Death."

23. There have been throughout this period some scattered protests against philologism and some affirmations of Shakespeare's poetic power: e.g. Lascelles Abercrombie, *A Plea for the Liberty of Interpreting* (London, 1930); Logan Pearsall Smith, *On Reading Shakespeare* (New York, *ca.* 1933); and of course G. Wilson Knight's powerful and imaginative interpretations, even if his symbolism is

not always convincing. Of *Scrutiny* and Leavis' remarkable contributions I have spoken elsewhere. In more recent times, E. F. Halliday in *Shakespeare and His Critics* (London, 1949) gave the most balanced general survey of Shakespeaean criticism now available, a survey which does not forget German criticism. His *Poetry of Shakespeare's Plays* (London, 1954) interprets poetry often in terms of technique. Cf. also E. Hubler, "The Sunken Aesthete," *English Institute Essays 1950* (New York, 1951), pp. 32–56, and the paper cited in the following note.

24. For an instance see H. T. Price, *Construction in Shakespeare* (Ann Arbor, 1951). Price does justice to German Romantic criticism, but his choice of *Henry VI* as an instance of structural unity is debatable.

25. L. Bergel, "Croce as a Critic of Goethe," *Comparative Literature*, 1 (1949), 349 ff., see also, by the same author, "Croce, Blake and Goethe" in F. Flora (ed.), *B. Croce*, pp. 195–232.

26. Cf. D. Vittorini, "B. Croce e L. Pirandello," in F. Flora, *op. cit.*, pp. 555–66.

27. For Baudelaire cf. *Letture*, 268–69, and above, Chapter X, note 14.

28. *Letture*, 276–78.

CHAPTER *xiii*

1. The third edition has a number of additional postscripts; see preface to 4th ed., 1946, p. viii.

2. As noted in Chapter VIII, note 20, these sections have been translated by A. H. Gilbert.

3. See the marginal note, E, 78; A, 70.

4. A. C. Bradley, *Oxford Lectures on Poetry*, p. 31.

5. De Sanctis quoted by Croce in *Primi saggi*, 1919, p. 24.

6. See also P, 113 and 289, and the addition in the later editions: P^5, 307.

7. J. E. Spingarn, *Creative Criticsm*, new ed., p. 167. A vigorous attack on "intentions" is also to be found in G. Wilson Knight, *The Wheel of Fire* (1930); see Meridian Books ed., 1957, pp. 6–7.

8. "It is surely an act of justice to give Wimsatt the credit he deserves because of the usefulness of his verbal act. By naming the mode of approach that he opposed, he fulfilled a genuine need. Without labels objects tend to lack phenomenological identity,

even if our voyager, like Amerigo Vespucci, comes to a continent that others discovered." E. Vivas, "Mr. Wimsatt on the Theory of Literature," *Comparative Literature*, VII (1955), 346. Wimsatt's concept of Intention is not always identical with Croce's.

9. The only discussion in English is by Domenico Pesce, "A Note on Croce's Distinction between Poetry and Literature," *Journal of Aesthetics and Art Criticism*, XIII (1953), 314–15.

10. There is a discussion of the problem of pseudo art in the very first year of *La critica*, I (1903), 464–65, in a review of a book on the eighteenth-century Italian novel by G. B. Marchesi, reprinted in part in CC, II, 237–38; then see "Poeti, letterati e produttori di letteratura" (1905), *PdE*, 106–14; "La storia della letteratura come arte e la prosa," (1906), *PdE*, 125–30; "Storia della critica e storia della cultura" (1907), *PdE*, 94–105; "Il giornalismo e la storia della letteratura" (1908), *PdE*, 131–35; "Dire la verità" and "I piaceri dell'immaginazione" (1915), *Frammenti di etica*, 1922, pp. 35 and 66 (see the English translation, *The Conduct of Life*, Chapters VIII and XV); "Poesia, prosa e oratoria: valore di questa tripartizione per la critica letteraria" (*ca*. 1915), CC, I, 58–63; "Ironia, satira e poesia" (*ca*. 1918), NSE, 139–43; "Angelo di Costanzo poeta e storico," *Uomini e cose della vecchia Italia* (1927), I, 88–90; "Le condizioni presenti della storiografia in Italia" (1929), SS, 3rd ed., 1947, 194 (on "oratory"). Also NSE, 145.

11. J. Dewey, *Art as Experience*, pp. 61–62.

12. See the paper on "The Duality of Content and Form, extraneous to Aesthetic and belonging to the Theory of Literature," *Discorsi*, I, 251–60.

13. Cf. Fubini's critique: "We had better give up Croce's account of 'literature' as a practical form and conceive it instead as the consciousness of the immanence of poetry in all our life." M. Fubini, *Critica e poesia*, p. 402–3.

14. This piece of criticism is much praised by Wimsatt; see Wimsatt and Brooks, *Literary Criticism*, p. 515. And yet he goes on to say in the same page that Croce's criticism tends in general to follow "a genetic and biographical standard." Just as Croce's analysis of the line of Racine successfully brings out the imaginative and emotional elements that constitute that poetic synthesis, so does Croce's analysis of Shakespeare's work (which Wimsatt does not equally appreciate) bring out the characteristics of the images and the emotions that unite in it.

15. R. G. Collingwood, *Principles of Art,* pp. 69-77.

16. They are adopted even by critics who differ from Croce on other points, such as G. Calogero, *Lezioni di filosofia,* III, *Estetica, Semantica, Istorica* (Torino, 1947), pp. 304-5.

CHAPTER *xiv*

1. L. Russo, *La critica letteraria contemporanea* (2nd ed., Bari, 1946), I, 154.

2. Cf. Croce's diary for March 1, 1944, printed in *Quaderni della Critica,* VIII (1947), 117, and in *Croce, the King and the Allies,* translated by S. Sprigge, 1950, pp. 89-90.

3. These essays, originally published in *La critica* of 1918, were later collected with a slightly different title in *L'Italia dal 1914 al 1918, Pagine sulla guerra* (3rd ed., 1950), pp. 185-206. Croce returned to Claudel in CC, III, 395-97.

4. Other references in O. Ruggiero, *La letteratura francese . . . ,* pp. 50-51. For a discussion of Croce's criticism of Mallarmé see E. Bonora, *Gli ipocriti di Malebolgie e altri saggi* (Napoli, 1953), pp. 112-31.

5. For the connection between Schiller's "naive and sentimental poetry" and Schlegel's "classic-Romantic," see A. O. Lovejoy, *Essays in the History of Ideas* (Baltimore, 1948), pp. 207-27. The later descent of nineteenth-century dyads from Schiller and Schlegel was noted in 1925 by T. Vianu: see *Archiv für Geschichte der Philosophie,* XLI (1932), 282-83. For another incarnation of the dyad —line and color—see CC, V, 59-60. The dichotomy of abstract versus naturalistic art passed from Worringer into T. E. Hulme, who adopted it in ignorance of its Romantic ancestry: cf. L. Bergel, "L'estetica del nichilismo," *Lo Spettatori Italiano,* VI (1953), 71.

6. For Croce's appreciation of the early work of Papini see CC, II, 137-38. This appreciation was accompanied, however, by a frank warning (*ibid.,* 138-42), which later turned into open criticism (*ibid.,* 142-51). Croce at first succeeded in making Papini write a translation of Berkeley for his collection of philosophical classics, a labor the memory of which was evidently intensely painful to Papini, for he was later to call Croce "the beast of burden and of labor": see E. Garin, *Cronache di filosofia . . . ,* p. 301. See also Croce's posthumous judgment on Futurism, "Futurism as something

extraneous to Art," (1918), reprinted in *L'Italia dal 1914 al 1918*, 3rd ed. 1950, pp. 271–74. For Croce's opinion of Papini after the latter's religious conversion, see cc, iv, 242–43 (not 342–43, as erroneously printed in the index); ps, iii, 176, 193, 196, 225, etc.

7. See "Anti-storicismo," us, 246–58, especially p. 253. Cf. *Storia d'Italia dal 1871 al 1915*, 5th ed., 1934, p. 258.

8. *The Defence of Poetry* (Oxford, 1933), English translation by E. F. Carritt. Reprinted in J. H. Smith and E. W. Parks, *The Great Critics*, An Anthology (3rd ed., New York, 1951), pp. 691–709.

9. "Modern Philosophy and Philosophy of the Times," *Carattere della Filosofia Moderna*, pp. 261–66, especially p. 262.

10. *Discorsi*, ii, 138–45, translated in English in *My Philosophy and Other Essays* (London, 1944), pp. 208–13. For a defence of Proust, and of the moderns generally, by a critic who is also a warm admirer of Croce's resistance to Fascism, see Pietro La Via, *Mente e Realtà, Il pensiero di B. Croce nelle meditazioni di un eretico* (Florence, 1947). For other references of Croce to "decadentism," see *Discorsi*, ii, 83–90; pam, 283–84; nps, i, 221–22; tps, ii, 53; *Letture*, 225–26.

11. On Verlaine, *Letture*, 174–87; on Valéry, tps, i, 224–32; on Gide, tps, i, 231–38; on George, nps, ii, 114–16. On Proust see previous note. Cf. also the negative judgment of a poem by Ungaretti in *Letture*, 300–301.

12. Cf. *Letture*, 271. Matters were not improved by the fact that Croce in his old age held up as genuine poetry some compositions in traditional verse by second-rate poets, which can only be called sentimental (e.g., tps, i, 164–65, 177). The best commentary on these judgments was the one that Croce himself pronounced on similar weaknesses in his own master, Francesco De Sanctis: *Aneddoti di varia letteratura*, iv, 174.

13. Cf. A. Momigliano, *Storia della letteratura italiana* (Milan, 1937), pp. 579–609, and Walter Binni, *La poetica del Decadentismo* (2nd ed., Florence, 1949). Modern art was also positively evaluated in Italy by critics of Crocean inspiration: cf. *Letture*, 311–18.

CHAPTER *xv*

1. Cf. M. H. Abrams' review of Wellek's *History of Modern Criticism* in *Yale Review*, 45 (1955), 146–49, and H. Levin's review

of Wimsatt and Brooks in *Modern Language Notes,* 73 (1958), 155–60.

2. See above, Chapter 1. Croce gave examples of a history of aesthetics conducted from his revised point of view in the volume *History of aesthetics in single essays (Storia dell'estetica per saggi,* 1942), which is not his old history in a different form but a new book. It includes essays on the method of this history, on the aesthetics of the Renaissance (Fracastoro), the theory of art in the baroque age, the aesthetics of Vico (from the monograph of 1911), the aesthetic of Baumgarten, an introduction to eighteenth-century aesthetics (see bibliographical appendix for English translation), theories of Hamann and Herder, Schleiermacher, Hegel's theory of the end of art, a theory of G. Capponi, the aesthetic of *Einfühlung,* R. Vischer and the contemplation of nature, the theory of art as pure visibility, nationalistic and modernistic aesthetics in Germany, and the aesthetics of J. Dewey (for translations of the last two see the Appendix). This collection does not comprise all of Croce's later studies in this area. It is interesting to compare the treatment that certain thinkers received in the early history with later evaluations under the new dispensation: e.g. Shaftesbury (E, 227; A, 206), reconsidered in *Uomini e cose della vecchia Italia,* 1927, I, 297–98, and Winckelmann: E, 291–94; A, 262–64, and in *Discorsi,* II, 103–12.

3. A. Ralli, *A History of Shakespearian Criticism* (Oxford, 1932). A less ambitious but more genuinely critical attempt was the book of C. F. Johnson, *Shakespeare and his Critics* (Boston, 1909). The more recent book with the same title by F. E. Halliday (London, 1949) contains an outline history of Shakespeare criticism on pp. 235–66.

4. See the discussions by D. Pesce cited above in Chapter 1, note 21, and by S. Zeppi cited in note 35 of the same chapter.

5. The first mention of "omnipresence" that I have found is in TSS, 246–47. See also NSE, 95, and US, 216.

6. See the discussion of "analogical thinking" in my review of M. H. Abrams, *The Mirror and the Lamp* (1953) in the *Yearbook of Comparative and General Literature,* V (1956), 71.

7. Croce, needless to say, was well aware of the danger of taking metaphors literally—especially the organic metaphor. Cf. *PdE,* 183, and more fully in the cited "Note on Metaphor" (1940), *PdE,* 162: "in the field of science one is always warned against being distracted

or seduced by metaphors and taking them as the expression of the reality of things"; Croce goes on to cite as a warning A. Schäffle's celebrated misuse of the organic analogy in sociology.

8. Here is an instance from Croce: "l'unità sintetica di contenuto e di forma, di sentimento e di intuizione" (*Letture*, 265).

9. R. J. Smith, "Intention in an Organic Theory of Poetry," *Sewanee Review*, LVI (1948), 626.

INDEX

Abercrombie, L., 323, 361
Abrams, M. H., 326, 365, 366
Abruzzi, 293
Absolutism, 22
Abstract art, 150, 278
Abstraction, 25, 27, 99, 214–15
Acting: art of, 119–24
Addison, J., 343
Aeschylus, 25, 47, 115, 137, 258
Aesop, 273
Aestheticism, 148, 154–55, 166–67, 176, 184, 255, 279
Aesthetics: and practical criticism, 3–4, 5, 148, 198, 209, 283; Croce's history of, 22; metaphysical, 104; history of, 185, 282
Agnition, 82
Ainslie, D.: his inaccuracies, 49, 304, 320, 359; translator of Croce, 208
Albalat, A., 67
Alexander, S., 38, 92
Allegory, 81, 227, 234–36
Allotria, 229
Amicis, E. de, 67
Amiel, H. F., 47
Alpino, E., 347
Analytical philosophy: modern, 77
Anderson, E., 306
Anschauen, 212
Anschauung, 33–34
Anti-historicism, 278
Antoni, C., 304, 317, 318, 327
Apodictic, 53
A priori, 316
A priori synthesis, 8, 19, 57–58, 88, 163, 289, 320–21
Arangio-Ruiz, V., 231
Archetypal images, 44
Ardigò, R., 12
Aretino, P., 111
Ariosto: Croce's criticism of, 236–40; mentioned, 41, 89, 101–2, 103, 106, 179, 208, 211, 216, 217, 284
Aristophanes, 81–82
Aristotelianism. See Agnition; Peripety

Aristotle, 34, 37, 58, 98–99, 102, 104, 114, 116, 183, 221, 233, 317, 324
Arnold, M., 348
Art for art's sake, 269
Art: modern, 365. See also Abstract art
Arts: fine, 10, 42–43, 67, 90–95
Aspirazione, 54, 56
Athenäum, 277
Atomistic doctrine of images, 44–45, 56, 71
"Atsight," 321
Atticism, 332
Attisani, A., 315
Audience, 99, 117, 241, 242, 265, 268
Autobiography, 106
Autonomy of poetry, 4
Autotelic character of poetry, 4
Avant-garde, 47
Aydelotte, F., 361

Babbitt, I., 219, 318, 344
Babock, R. W., 361
Bacon, F., 199
Balzac, M. de, 162, 189, 207
Barbi, M., 231, 360
Baretti, G., 171
Baring, M., 39
Baroque, the, 190–91, 249
Barotti, M., 339
Barrès, M., 148, 277
Bartels, A., 352
Basile, G. B., 304
Bataillon, M., 354
Battaglia, F., 319
Baudelaire, C., 41, 59–60, 193, 207, 209, 221, 251, 343
Baumgarten, A. G., 366
Beach, J. W., 85, 110
Beaumarchais, P. A. C. de, 251, 273
Beautiful, the: 5, 217, 312–13; modifications of, 112–17, 344
Behrens, I., 105
Bembo, P., 277

Bénard, C., 168
Beolco, A. *See* Ruzzante
Berenson, B., 255
Bergel, L., 249, 312, 314, 364
Bergson, H., 66, 114, 115–16
Bernhardt, S., 118
Bertocci, P., 314
Bettinelli, S., 170–71
Bibbiena, 111
Bible, 251
Binni, W., 360, 365
Biographical fallacy, 40, 143, 157, 242, 248
Blackmur, R. P., 70, 330
Blake, W., 362
Bloomfield, L., 350
Boiardo, M. M., 119
Boito, A., 206
Bonora, E., 364
Borgese, G. A., 214
Born, B. de, 251
Bosanquet, B., 92, 327
Bradley, A. C., 40, 58, 104, 258
Breglio, L. A., 348
Bridges, R., 242
Brancacciana: library, 171
Bretonne, Rétif de la, 251
Brooks, C., 63, 312, 323, 328, 348
Browne, R. M., 334
Brunetière, F., 147
Bruno, A., 317
Bruno, G., 104, 111, 263–64
Burke, K., 265
Burns, R., 251
Bush, D., 347–48
Byron, G., 268

Caballero, F., 207
Calcaterra, C., 353
Calderón de la Barca, P., 258
Calogero, G., 364
Capellina, D., 82
Caponigri, A. R., 319, 352
Capponi, G., 366
Capri, 297
Capuana, L., 202, 206
Caracciolo, A., 355, 357
Carducci, G., 151, 155, 202, 221, 251, 275
Caritt, E. E., 304, 305, 320, 326–29 *passim*
Carus, P., 321
Casamícciola, 292

Cassirer, E., 57
Castellano, G., 202, 299, 313, 324
Categories: philosophical, 113, 254, 285. *See* Forms of spiritual activity
Catharsis, 99
Catholicism, 137, 293, 297
Catullus, 75
Cavaciuti, S., 330
Cecchetti, G., 355
Celestina, La, 251
Cervantes, M., 39, 116, 216, 251
Chambers, E. K., 337
"Characterization," 109, 142–43, 151–65, 254, 290
Characters: in fiction and drama, 81, 142, 168–69; criticism of, 142
Chateaubriand, F. R., 187
Chénier, A., 251
Chérix, R. B., 328
Christ, Jesus, 147
Ciardo, M., 329
Cicero, 268
Cione, E., 299
Circular motion of forms of spirit, 20, 47, 71
Clark, H. H., 323
Classic and Romantic, 49, 54, 192, 278
Classicism, 49, 103, 192
Classicità, 193
Classification, empirical, 97, 100, 107, 109
Claudel, P., 277
Clericalism, 198
Clouard, H., 218–19
Cognition, elementary, 15, 16, 215, 222
Cohen, M. R., 330
Coleridge, S. T.: *Rhyme of the Ancient Mariner*, cited, 25, 31, 32, 43; criticism, cited, 33, 34–35, 49; philosophy, 66; mentioned, 75, 224, 288, 323
Collingwood, R. G., 57, 272, 304, 305, 306, 337
Comedia, 258
Comedy, 106, 110; new, 109
Comic, the, 112–16
Commedia dell' Arte, 118–19, 122, 306, 310
Common sense, 19, 147
Communism, 297, 354
Comparative literature, 195–96
Concepts: 17, 257, 264, 289; in poetry, 41–42, 135–37, 229; expression of, 76–77, 83, 84; functional, 186–87
Confession: literature of, 218

Constant, B., 251
Contemporary literature, 200, 218, 275, 279, 280
Content: poetic, 156, 223–24. *See also* Form and content
"Contentism," 358
"Contentual," 358
"Contentualism," 223–24
Contenutistico, 223
Context, 25
Contextualism, 68, 70, 71, 74–75
Contextuality, 288
Contini, G. F., 348
Conventions: literary, 75, 102, 138, 145, 171, 246, 254, 258, 272; theatrical, 241
Coordination and subordination, 98, 116–17
Corneille, P.: Croce's criticism of, 245–47; mentioned, 103, 159, 161, 179, 208, 258, 284–85
Correctness, 77
Corsi, M., 315
Cosmic intuition. *See* Intuition
Cosmo, U., 231
Costanzo, A. di, 342, 363
Creizenach, W., 106
Critica, La, 198–209, 295, 298, 303. *See Quaderni della Critica*
Critical vocabulary: introduction to, 209
Criticism: history of, 109, 171, 240, 282–86; literary, 140–65, 172–74, 283; psychological, 143, 148; criticism of, 158–59, 208, 245; poets', 163; technical, 164; judicial, 164; evocative and suggestive, 176; and philosophy, 283–84. *See also* Aesthetics; Historical
Croce, Alda, 295, 356
Croce, Benedetto: book reviews by, 5, 53, 308; thoughts of, 6, 10; criticism of his doctrine, 8; chronology of, 8; "system" of, 22–23; tendency to criticize accepted opinion, 171, 249; criticism by, 198–209, 227–52; life of, 293–98; bibliography of, 299–306; correspondence of, 304; philosophy of, 307–8; critical essays by, 308–11. *See also* Aesthetics and practical criticism
—"Aesthetica in nuce," 305, 358; *Breviary of Aesthetics*, 53; "Defence of Poetry," 175; *Essence of Aesthetics*, 53; *Estetica*, 5–7 *passim*; *Filosofia, poesia, storia*, 53, 303, 326; Heidel-
berg Lecture, 46–52; *Logic*, 8, 9, 21, 53, 57–58, 107, 285–86; "Memoirs of a Critic," 201–2; *New Essays on Aesthetics*, 53, 211–25; *Philosophy of the Practical*, 55–56, 215, 224; *Poesia, La*, 253–57; *Problems of Aesthetics*, 46–52, 67–69, 78–80, 83–84, 93–94, 149–50; "Reform of Literary and Art History," 160–61, 186, 189; *Theses of Aesthetics*, 16. *See also Critica, La; Napoli Nobilissima*
Croce, Elena, 295
Croce, Lidia, 295
Croce, Silvia, 295
Culture: history of, 109, 183–85

D'Annunzio, G., 72, 158, 160, 202, 206, 250, 252, 261, 275, 276, 344
Dante: Croce's criticism of, 227–36; mentioned, 25, 40, 48, 75, 82, 89, 103, 115, 128, 135–37, 138, 155, 160, 161, 169, 179, 193, 208, 216, 249, 251, 257, 260, 262, 273, 284, 330, 342
Dantisti, 227–28
Darwin, C., 104, 326
De Amicis, E., 67
De Balzac, M., 162, 189, 207
De Born, B., 251
Decadents and decadentism, 167, 206, 223, 275–81, 334
Definition, 320–21
De Gennaro, A. A., 314, 357
Della Valle, E., 354
De Ruggiero, G., 153, 199, 341
De Sanctis, F., 15, 39–40, 49, 82, 155, 168–73, 190, 195, 202, 215, 216, 227, 230, 232, 235, 237, 261, 263, 326, 352, 365
De Sarlo, F., 317
Dessoir, M., 313
Development, 189
De Vito, A. J., 355
Dewey, John, 5, 33, 306, 340, 366
Dialect literature, 206
Dialectic: of opposites, 19; of distinct forms, 19–21, 50, 151, 290
Dialogue: art of, in faction or drama, 27
Dickens, C., 25
Dictionary, 70
Didactic heresy, 40–41
Diderot, D., 251
Dies Irae, 251

Di Giacomo, S., 207, 294
Dilettantism, 200
Dionysian, 116
Dissociation of sensibility, 171
"Distincts," dialectic of, 19–21, 257. *See also* Dialectic; Forms of spiritual activity
Diversion, 270
Documents, historical, 180
Dodds, Mrs. E., 92, 327, 336
Dogmatism, 53
Donagan, A., 333
Donohue, J. J., 338
D'Ors, E., 353
Dover-Wilson, J., 177–78
Dovizi, B. *See* Bibbiena
Dowden, E., 361
Dramaturgy, 104, 244
Drière, J. C. La, 339
Dryden, J., 131, 268–69
Dubos, J. B., 104
Ducasse, J., 304
Dumas fils, A., 251
Duse, E., 118

Economic form of spiritual activity, 20, 153
Economic theory of science, 66
Education. *See* Teaching
Education, Ministry of, 296–97
Effable: only the individual is, 38
Effusion: emotional, 217–20, 267, 269, 276
Ehrenpreis, I., 314
Einfühlung, 366
Eisler, R., 321
Elder, L. W., 338
Eliot, T. S., 25, 48, 60, 134–36, 163–64, 235, 334, 349
Ellipsis, 79, 83
Elton, W., 333
Emotion, 149. *See* Effusion; *Sentimento;* State of mind
Empirical aesthetic, 132, 135, 341
Empirical concepts, 17, 113, 152, 188
Empiricism, 256, 267, 286
Encyclopaedia Britannica, 305, 322
England, 294, 295–96
English literature, 310
English Review, 211
Enlightenment, Age of, 186, 193
Entertainment, literature of, 266, 267
Epic, 101–2. *See* Genres

Erasmus, D., 268
Ermatinger, E., 338
Errante, G., 314
Error: necessary forms of, 52; critical, 66
Estrinsecazione, 90
Ethics, 20
Etymology, 331
Evolution, theory of, 182, 254
Ewing, A. C., 320, 321
Execution, Artistic, 117
Expressionism: in England, 326
Expression: of content, 8, 15; of intuition, 42–45; of emotion, 46–63; practical, naturalistic or symptomatic, 55, 77; obstacles to, 73; non-aesthetic, 264–65. *See also* Concepts
Expressions: negative, 72
Externalization, 90–95, 121

Faculties of the mind, 34
Falconieri, J. V., 360
Fancy, 194
Fantasia, 49
Färber, H., 338
Farinelli, A., 354
Farrell, R. B., 321
Fascism, 7, 198, 202, 206, 223, 276, 278, 296–97
Fate: in tragedy, 262
Faucci, D., 318, 358
Feeling, 20, 243, 254
Figures of speech: 64, 78–84, 108. *See* Ellipsis; Inversion; Metaphor; Pleonasm; Synecdoche
Filicaia, V. da, 342
Flaubert, G., 25, 26, 108, 148, 189, 195, 207, 209, 221
Flickinger, R. C., 341
Flora, F., 153, 236, 314, 352
Foerster, N., 313
Fogazzoro, A., 250, 344
Fogle, R. H., 323
Folk poetry, 250
Fontaine, J. de la, 273
"Formal" characters, 153
Formalism, 15, 143, 151
Form and content, 43, 47, 58, 183, 188, 194, 196, 317
Form: indescribability of, 155, 157–58; aesthetic, 158, 169, 214; form and content, 207, 220–23, 267. *See also* Content; Inner form

Forms of spiritual activity, 20–21, 113. *See* Categories

Formula, critical. *See* Characterization

Foscolo, U., 251

Fowler, H. W., 333

Fracastoro, G., 339, 366

"Fragmentism," 47, 251, 259

France, 294

Franchini, R., 293, 318, 319

Freemasonry, Italian, 198

Freiburg, 294

French criticism, 147–48, 168

French culture, 119

French literature, 5, 247, 309

Freud, S., 9, 12, 153–54

Freytag, G., 104

Frezzi, F., 233

Friederich, C. J., 321

Friedman, N., 334

Fubini, M., 109, 363

Fueter, E., 179, 185

Futurism, 47, 275, 278, 365

Gaeta, F., 202, 250

Galileo, G., 268

Galpin, A., 348

Garbari, R., 326

Gargiulo, A., 313

Garin, E., 325, 364

Gayley, C. M., 350

Genius, 127

Gennaro, A. A. De, 314, 357

Genres, 51, 54, 85, 96–111, 140, 244, 254, 267, 273, 288

Gentile, G., 16, 20, 126, 188, 200, 213, 214, 295, 296, 316, 324, 327

Genus and species, 98, 116–17

George, S., 271, 279, 281

Gerbi, R., 303

German: thought, 14, 119; scholarship, 167; criticism, 168; mind, 196

Germany, 249, 294, 295

Gervinus, G. G., 283

Gestalt, 36, 212

Giacomo, S. Di, 207, 294

Gide, A., 279

Giolitti, G., 295–96

Gilbert, A. H., 306

Gilbert, K., 306

Gilbert, S., 333

Giornale storico della letteratura italiana, 167, 170

Gobetti, Piero, 120

Goethe, W.: Croce's criticism of, 247–49; mentioned, 39, 40, 89, 145, 160, 161, 193, 207, 216–17, 238, 251, 260, 269, 273, 284

Goldoni, C., 115

Gongora, L., 251

Gourmont, R. de, 67

Grammar, 69, 74

Gravina, G. B., 104

Gray, T., 59–60

Grazzini, A. F., 111

Greek poetry, 136–37, 309

Greeks, ancient, 100–101

Grierson, H. J. C., 197

Gröber, G., 66–67

Grotius, H., 341

Grunebaum, G. E. von, 353

Guidi, A., 170–71

Guidubaldi, E., 360

Gullace, G., 356

Gundolf, F., 196

Gusto, 127, 345. *See* Taste

Hack, R. K., 340

Halliday, F. E., 362, 366

Hamann, 366

Hamann, T. G., 69

Hamilton, Sir W., 33

Hammond, W. A., 321

Harbage, A., 361

Harmony, cosmic, 238

Hartmann, E. von, 15

Hatzfeld, H., 359

Hebbel, C. F., 104, 116

Hegel, G. W. F., 14, 15, 16–19, 20, 66, 69, 104, 116–17, 153, 168–69, 183, 192, 213, 222, 237, 283, 300, 315, 363, 366

Hegelianism, 13, 18, 294

Heidegger, M., 76

Heidelberg, philosophical congress (1908), 46

Heine, H., 115, 207

Hemingway, E., 61

Herbart, J. F., 14–15

Herder, J. G., 69, 138, 187, 283, 366

Heresies, critical, 52, 267. *See also* Biographical; Didactic; Paraphrase

Herford, C. H., 197

Heroic poetry, 109

Heyl, B. C., 345

Historical connections of poetry, 178–79

Historical criticism, 129, 157, 206, 229, 244, 258
Historical method, 199
Historical novel, 107
Historical Review, 167
Historical scholarship, 128–29, 261
Historicism: positive sense, 23, 136–39, 280, 285–86; perjorative sense, 166. *See also* Anti-historicism
Historiography, 12–13, 15–18, 19, 21–23, 179, 185
History: ethico-political, 23; of culture, 141, 266, 331; literary, 146–97, 208, 254, 288; poet of, 155–56; of ideas, 196
Hobbes, T., 114
Hölderlin, J. C. F., 76
Holophrase, 68
Homer, 102–3, 233, 251, 269
Hooker, R., 33
Hopkins, G. M., 251
Horace, 163, 273, 322
Hospers, J., 91, 327, 333, 335
Hubler, E., 362
Hugo, V., 251
Hulme, T. E., 65, 364
Humanity, 221
Humboldt, W. von, 69, 212, 324
Hume, D., 320
Humor, 114–15, 195
Hurd, R., 322
Huxley, A., 326
Hypotyposis, 80, 82

Ibsen, H., 207, 269
Ideal: character of poetry, 30, 98, 99, 218, 259
Idealism, absolute, 15, 16, 18, 199
Ideas. *See* Concepts; History of ideas
Idyllic poetry, 109
Image: poetic or aesthetic, 24–45, 142, 252, 290; critical analysis of, 58, 142, 157–58
Imagination: creative, 37, 212, 224; imagination and fancy, 49–50
Imbriani, V., 149–50
Immaginazione, 49
Impersonality, 55, 203, 205, 206
Impression, 320
Impressionism: Croce's alleged, 128, 145; critical, 147, 167, 170, 289
Index of forbidden books, Catholic, 297

Indistinction, 215–16
Individuality, 144, 157, 210–25, 254, 287
Induction, 316
Industrialism, 278
Ineffability: of individual, 38, 134, 154–55, 344, 347; of poetry, supposed, 146
Influences, literary, 195–96
Inner form, 44, 163
Integration, principle of, 25–26, 50–51, 65, 66, 69, 94, 117, 120, 287–88
Intellect, poetry of, 247
Intellectualism: aesthetic, 15, 210, 227, 231, 232–34, 287
Intensive manifold, 65, 69, 87
Intention, 201, 227, 235, 260–63, 280, 342
Intentional Fallacy. *See* Intention
Interinanimation of words, 71
Intuition: pure, 24–29; colloquial meaning of, 31; Cartesian, 31; Kantian, 32; why pure, 39; lyrical, 46–63, 254, 283, 287; self-critical, 163; cosmic, total or universal, 210–25, 252, 253, 261–62, 276, 287; Schelling's, 213
Intuitions: how classified, 117
Intúito, 34, 356
Intuizione, 32
Inversion, 80
Irony, 113
Irrationalism, 223, 278
Isenberg, A., 336
-isms, 201, 206, 275
Istituto Italiano di Studi Storici, 298
Istituzioni di letteratura, 338–39
Italian literature, history of, 189; mentioned, 311

James, H., 84–85
James, William, 5
Jaspers, K., 104, 338
Johnson, C. F., 366
Johnson, S., 132, 164
Jonson, B., 131–32
Joseph, Sister Miriam, 333
Journal of Comparative Literature, 195
Journals, critical, 199
Judgment: and the imagination, 40; critical, 130–31, 138, 160, 173, 174, 180; historical, 179
Juvenal, 272

Kant, E., 14–15, 29, 57, 114, 135, 283, 315

Kayser, W., 338
Keats, John, 126
Keast, W. R., 361
Ker, W. P., 337, 344
Kermode, F., 349
Kinds: literary. *See* Genres
King, Bishop Henry, 60
Kleist, H. V., 108
Klibanski, R., 306
Knight, G. Wilson, 347, 361–62
Knights, L. C., 334
Korff, H. A., 324
Krieger, M., 314, 331, 344, 358
Kuhn, H., 312

La Bretonne, Rétif de, 251
Labriola, Antonio, 13–14, 16, 294, 318
La Drière, J. C., 339
La Fontaine, J. de, 273
Lalande, A., 33, 320
Lamartine, A. de, 268
Lamb, C., 175, 343
Landscape painting, 107
Langage, 73
Langer, S. K., 326–27
Language, 65, 66, 67, 69, 72, 73, 76, 77.
  See Words; Sentence; Writing;
  Grammar; Etymology; Linguistics;
  Phonetic laws; Dictionary; Teach-
  ing; Parts of speech; Usage
La Piana, A., 359
La Rochefoucauld, F., 268
Laterza, Giovanni, 200, 295, 297
Laterza, Giuseppe, 295, 299
Latinisms, 80
Latin literature, 309
La Via, P., 365
Lawrence, D. H., 310
Lazarillo de Tormes, 251
Leavis, F. R., 362
Lee, Sir Sidney, 240
Lee, Vernon, 333
Leibniz, G. W., 133, 283
Lemaitre, J., 147
Leopardi, G., 221, 234, 251, 344
Lessing, G. E., 7, 283
Levi, G. A., 46
Levin, H., 333, 365
Lewis, C. Day, 319
Lewis, C. S., 360
Liberal Party, Italian, 296

Limit, concept of, 29
Linguistics, 67, 68, 78, 175
Lipps, T., 114
Literature: theory of, 105; non-poetry,
  264–73
Literaturwissenschaft, 105
Livingston, A., 304–5, 352
Livy, 268
Lombroso, C., 12
London, 294
Longfellow, H. W., 59–60, 230
Longinus, 55
Lovejoy, A. O., 192, 364
Lubbock, P., 85
Luck, G., 325
Lucretius, 272
Lyricism: pejorative sense, 48, 51, 100;
  positive sense, 53. *See* Intuition
Lyric poetry, 105, 110

Macaulay, T. B., 342
Macchia, 93–94, 149–50
Mach, E., 18, 66
Machiavelli, N., 111
Macrobius, 82
Maggini, F., 358
Mallarmé, S., 5, 75, 76, 270–71, 277, 281
Manzoni, A., 48, 107, 108, 137, 209, 251,
  355
Marburg, 294
Marchesi, G. B., 363
Marinetti, F. P., 279
Marx, K., 16, 294–95
Mattalia, D., 358, 359, 360
Matteotti, G., 296
Matter, 29
Maupassant, G. de, 108, 152, 161, 193,
  207
Mazzeo, J., 359
Meaning, 77, 87, 265
Medieval literature, 309
Medium: artistic, 6, 91–92, 94, 123
Mencken, H. L., 347
Metaphor, 78–79, 83, 289, 357
Metaphysics: rejected by Croce, 18,
  316
Methodology of history: philosophy
  as, 21, 286
Metre, 64, 65, 86–89, 145, 150, 238, 288
Middle Ages, 186. *See* Medieval liter-
  ature

Mill, J. S., 17
Milton, J., 41, 80, 101, 236, 258
Minturno, A. S., 105
Modernity, 201, 279–80. *See also* Contemporary literature
Molière, J. B., 115, 122, 251
Molina, T. de, 109
Momigliano, A., 205, 236, 239–40, 365
Monads, 133
Monism, Croce's, 90
Monograph: critical, supersedes history, 189, 254, 288
Montaigne, M., 272
Montani, F., 104
Moralism, 219–23, 225, 287
Moral judgments in art, 337
Moral problems in literature, 149
Morbidity, 221
Mordell, A., 359
Mörike, E., 251
Morpurgo Tagliabue, G., 335
Morrissette, G. A., 332
Motif, poetic, 78, 140, 149–50, 157, 160, 224, 245
Motivo lirico, 324
Muir, K., 360
Munteano, B., 354
Musset, A. de, 268
Mussolini, B., 296
Mysticism, 155, 270–71
Myth, 272

Nahm, M. C., 94, 314, 337, 340
Naïve and sentimental, 278
Naples, 171–72, 185, 195, 208, 293–98, 319. *See* Neapolitan dialect
Napoli Nobilissima, 172
Nardo, G., 314
Nationalism, 119, 247, 366
Naturalism, 48, 193–95, 214, 275, 278
Neapolitan dialect, 304
Negri, A., 250
Nencioni, G., 330, 331
Neoclassicism, 219
Nettleship, R. C., 56–57
Neutralists, Italian, 295
Newbolt, Sir H., 340
New Humanists, 146. *See also* Babbitt, I.
Nicolini, F., 293, 299, 302
Nietzsche, F., 116
Nievo, J., 207, 344

Nominalism: Croce's alleged, 113; medieval, 222
Non-art, 54, 83, 84, 264, 268. *See also* Non-poetry
Non-definitive character of philosophy, 22
Non-poetry: poetry and, 150–51, 171, 207–9, 290. *See also* Non-art
Norms, 65
Novel, the, 85–86, 106, 204–5, 258, 273; social, 110

Objectivism, 289
"Objectivistic" critics of Shakespeare, 242
Objectivity, scholarly, 181
O'Connor, W. Van, 323, 348
Oddi, S., 339
Ogden, C. K., 323, 330
Omnipresence: of categories, 285–86
Omodeo, A., 199
Oppel, H., 338
"Oratory" (persuasive writing), 265
Organic unity, 56, 144, 288
Oriani, A., 202, 250
Ornamentalism, 25, 78, 80, 288
Orsini, G. N. Giordano, 310, 314, 325, 326, 334, 341, 342, 350, 355, 360, 366
Osborne, H., 325
Ottava rima, 238–39
Oxford, 278, 294

Padding, 257
Palizzi, F., 149–50
Panlogism, 17, 213
Panofski, E., 321, 325
Papini, G., 278, 279, 364–65
Paraphrase, Heresy of, 79, 288
Parente, A., 224, 354
Pareto, V., 5
Parole, 73
Parrott, T. M., 361
Pascal, B., 133
Pascoli, G., 89, 158, 250, 276, 278
Passmore, J. A., 315
Pater, W., 44, 343–44
Patrizio, F., 284
Pearson, N. H., 338
Penzer, N. M., 304
Periods: literary, 110, 190–95; of history, 185–87

Peripety, 82
Personalità, 324
Personality: poetic, 48, 110–11, 159–60, 188; practical, 159, 242
Persuasion, 268
Pescassèroli, 293
Pesce, D., 319, 347, 363, 366
Petersen, J., 338
Petrarch, 251, 268
Petrarchan sonnet, 88
Petsch, R., 338
Phaedrus, 273
Phantasia, 34
"Philologism," 138, 241, 254, 289
Philology, 174–79, 180
Philosophy: of history, 13, 17; of nature, 17, 18; non-definitive character of, 22; problem, single or fundamental, 22, 318
Phonetic laws, 9
Piccoli, R., 7
Picturesque, the, 113
Pietrobono, L., 236
Pindar, 272
Pirandello, L., 114
Planck, M., 317
Plato, 125, 221, 223, 268, 286
Plautus, 115
Pleasures of the imagination, 266
Pleonasm, 79–80, 83
Plot, 26, 142, 246. *See also* Agnition; Peripety
Plotinus, 91, 324
Poe, E. A., 99, 252, 258, 260
Poetic diction, 72, 77, 288
Poetics, 255, 257
Poetry: supra-national, 119, 247, 249; rarity of, 143–144; "pure", 187, 258, 269–72, 275, 277, 279
Poincaré, H., 9, 18, 66
Point of view: narrator's, 85–86; poet's, 139
Politian, A., 293
Pope, A., 268–69, 272
Porter, N., 336
Positivism, 12–17, 69, 75, 104, 138, 148, 181, 186, 198, 200, 288
Postilla, 253
Practical activity, 19, 29, 99, 106, 152, 189, 243, 265
Pragmatism, 288
Praz, M., 240
Price, H. T., 362

Primitivism, aesthetic, 21, 317–18
Prior, M. A., 361
Problem plays, 224
Problems: philosophical, 22, 283; critical, 141
Progress, 280
Protasis, 101
Proust, M., 278, 279
Providence, 262
Pseudo-concepts, 72, 112–13, 122, 140, 193–94, 337
Psycho-analysis, 153–54, 280
Psychology, 152
Ptolemaic system, 229–30, 244
Pulci, L., 339
Pullino, G., 339

Quaderni della Critica, 298, 303

Rabelais, F., 47, 272
Racine, J., 48, 193, 251, 271–72
Rader, M. M., 325
Ragghianti, C., 121
Rajna, P., 241
Ralli, A., 284
Ramat, R., 360
Ransom, J. C., 44, 60, 323
Rapisardi, M., 171
Rau, C., 329
Read, Sir H., 62, 312
Realism: literary, 113, 201; philosophical, 289
"Realistic" critics of Shakespeare, 241, 243, 244, 263
Reason, 66, 280
Re-creation, 90, 125–39, 140, 151–52, 169, 179
Recurrence, 87
Regularity, metrical, 87–88, 89
Relativism: philosophical, 22, 132–33; historical, 41, 102, 138–39, 230; critical or aesthetic, 126, 132, 147, 289
Renaissance: 80, 102, 107, 109–11, 136, 138–39, 161, 186, 250, 251, 262; drama, 118; English, 168
Representation, 33
Rhetoric, 64, 66, 74, 78, 79, 80, 82, 83, 84, 107, 244, 255, 288
Rhyme, 257
Ricciardi, R., 302
Rice Institute, 53

Richards, I. A., 35, 71, 74, 134–35, 136, 323, 330, 331, 332, 333
Richter, J. P., 115
Riedel, F. G., 138–39
Rilke, R. M., 221, 251, 279
Rimbaud, A., 271, 277
Roditi, E., 304, 321
Rojas, F. de. *See Celestina, La*
Roman culture, 103
Romantic and classic. *See* Classic
Romanticism: doctrine, 44, 108, 132, 187, 224, 277–78; literature (emotional effusion), 57, 144, 206, 209, 218, 268; discrimination of Romanticisms, 191–93
Romanzesco, 243
Rome, 13, 294
Ronsard, P. de, 251
Rosetti, A., 330
Rossi, Adele, 295
Rossi, J., 348
Rossi, M., 231, 359
Rostagni, A., 322
Rousseau, J. J., 57, 218–19
Ruggiero, G. de, 153, 199, 341
Ruggiero, O., 313, 355, 364
Rümelin, G., 241–42
Russo, L., 205, 231, 275, 294, 333, 339, 352
Ruzzante, 119. *See* Beolco, A.

Sainte-Beuve, C. A., 147
Saintsbury, G., 283, 284
Salomone, E. W., 314
Sanctis, F. de. *See* De Sanctis, F.
Sanesi, I., 339
Sansone, M., 311, 343
Santangelo, G., 355
Santayana, G., 39–40
Sarlo, F. de, 317
Sartre, J. P., 91, 329
Saussure, F. de, 73
Sayers, D., 334
Sbarbaro, P., 206
Scaglione, A., 314
Scandinavian literatures, 311
Scaravelli, L., 318
Scenario, 119, 121
Schäffle, A., 367
Schelling, F. W. J., 192, 213, 312
Schiller, F., 187, 207, 268, 278
Schlegel, A. W., 45, 324

Schlegel, F., 187, 277–78
Schleiermacher, F., 366
Scholasticism, 134
Schopenhauer, A., 104
Schorer, M., 85, 355
Schücking, L., 242, 260
Schütze, M., 321, 351
Schwinger, R., 324
Science: economic theory of, 18–19; science and faith, 206
Scientism, 28, 148
Scott, Sir W., 207
Seerveld, C. G., 11, 314, 320, 342, 355
Segni, A., 105
Self-expression, 242, 327
Semantics, 265
Senate, Italian, 295, 297
Sensation, 51–52
Sensualism, aesthetic, 15, 132
Sentence, 64, 65, 68
Sentimento, 54, 149, 243
Serao, M., 343, 344
Serra, R., 354
Sgroi, C., 325
Shaftesbury, A. A. C., the earl of, 91, 347, 366
Shakespeare, W.: textual crux in *Hamlet,* 176–78; Croce's criticism of, 240–45; mentioned, 25, 39, 40, 47, 75, 80–81, 101, 103, 104, 115, 117–19, 122, 130–32, 139, 142–43, 160, 161, 179, 193, 196, 208, 238, 260, 262–63, 284, 310, 334, 363
Sheean, V., 293
Sherman, S. P., 357
Sicily, 203–4, 214
Sidney, Sir P., 38
Signs, 76–77
Simoni, F. S., 313–14
Singleton, C. S., 359
Situation: poetic, 149–68
"Skeptical" critics of Shakespeare, 241
Skepticism: aesthetic, 126, 133; philosophical, 147, 286; historical, 342
Smith, J., 340, 345
Smith, J. A., 304, 336
Smith, L. P., 361
Smith, R. J., 367
Social ideas, 199
Socialism, 276
Socialist party: Italian, 296
Society: art in, 28, 149, 187, 278–79. *See also* Audience

Soffici, Ardengo, 325
Sophocles, 193, 354
Source hunting, 182–83, 254
Souriau, É., 62
Spain, 294
Spanish literature, 196, 311
Spaventa, Bertrando, 294
Spaventa, Silvio, 294
Speech: parts of, 71
Spencer, H., 17
Spengler, O., 5
Spenser, E., 41, 262
Spenserian Stanza, 88
Spingarn, J. E.: on the theatre, 122–24; on criticism, 146–47; mentioned, 6, 7, 87, 89, 195, 210, 262, 327, 339, 344, 349, 361
Spirit, the, 18, 19, 133
Spirito, U., 316
Spiritualism: absolute, 284
Sprigge, Cecil, 8, 111, 293, 339
Sprigge, Sylvia, 303, 319
Stabili, F., 233
Stace, W. T., 31–32, 320, 339–40
Staël, Mme de, 187
Staiger, E., 338
Standard, aesthetic, 138, 147
"State of mind," 47, 49, 56, 261
Stenberg, T. G., 345
Stendhal, 189, 207, 344
Stern, A., 329
Sterne, L., 25, 115
Stoffgeschichte, 195–96, 260
Stoll, E. E., 242, 263
Stovall, F., 323
Stowe, H. B., 268
Struckmeyer, O. K., 325
Structural parts, 256–60
Structure: poetic, 66, 91, 98–99, 255, 256–60, 267; intellectual, of the Divine Comedy, 231–34
Style, 83, 84, 145, 218, 288
Stylistics, 71, 79, 84, 157, 163
Sub-conscious, 28
Sublime, the, 112–13, 115
Suggestion, 270–71
Supranational. See Poetry
Sutton, W., 330
Swift, J., 272
Symbolism, 75, 76, 126, 201, 269, 275, 277
Symbols, 62–63, 76, 112, 265
Synecdoche (part-whole shift), 35, 83, 103

Synonyms, 83
Synthesis a priori. See A priori synthesis
Systematizations: provisional, 21, 287

Taine, H., 147, 340
Tansillo, L., 263–64
Tari, A., 14, 15
Tasso, T., 41, 102, 130, 164
Taste, 125–39, 159, 176, 178, 289
Tate, A., 333
Teaching, 71, 93, 107
Technique: literary, 64–95, 272
Téoresi, 254
Terence, cited, 214
Terza rima, 273
Textual criticism, 175, 176–78, 180
Theatre, the, 108, 117–24, 171–72
Theatrical activity, 19
"Theatricalism": critical trend, 122
Theory and practice of criticism. See Aesthetics and practical criticism
Thompson, F. J., 306
Thucydides, 133, 268
Tieghem, Van P., 324
Tilgher, A., 214, 340
Tolstoy, L., 39, 188, 269
Torraca, F., 195
Totality. See Intuition, cosmic
Touchstone of philosophy, 18, 21
Toynbee, A. J., 5
Tradition: in literature, 183
Tragedy, 104, 105, 110, 116, 258, 262
Tragic, the, 116
Transcend: to (aufheben), 9, 313
Translation, 120–21, 288
Tripartition (of genres), 96
Troeltsch, E., 316
Tropes. See Figures of speech
Trübners deutsches Wörterbuch, 321
Truth: imaginative, 136
Tuve, R., 168
Types: characters 115–16, 216. See Genres

Uberti, degli, F., 233
Ugly, the, 112, 268
Ullman, S., 330, 331
Unconscious, 44–45
Understanding, the, 66

UNESCO, 306
Ungaretti, G., 365
Unities: dramatic, 104
Unity: organic, 42, 43, 289; poetic, in general, 231, 248–49
Universality: aesthetic, 137–39. *See also* Criticism
Universals: 18, 37, 100, 112–13, 132; concrete, 18, 27, 68; and particular, 124
Usage: linguistic, 73, 74
Utitz, E., 313

Valeri, N., 293
Valéry, P., 271, 279
Vallone, A., 359
Vaughan, C. E., 344
Veblen, T., 5
Vega, Lope de, 251
Vendryès, J., 330
Venturi, L., 147, 340, 345, 350
Verga, G., 111, 193–95, 203–5, 214, 261, 344
Verismo, 203–5
Verlaine, P., 75, 279
Véron, E., 326
Vianu, T., 364
Vico, J. B., 14, 16, 39, 69, 104, 114, 173, 187, 215, 222, 235, 300, 304, 318, 319, 366
Vigny, A. de, 344
Villari, P., 294
Villon, F., 75, 193
Vinci, Leonardo da, 30
Virgil, 82, 102, 170–71, 251, 258, 273
Vischer, R., 366
Visibility: pure, 366
Vito, A. J. de, 355
Vittorini, D., 362
Vivas, E., 363
Vocabulary, 145
Vogelweide, von der, W., 251
Voltaire, F. A., 268, 272
Vossler, K.: correspondence with

Croce, 346; mentioned, 231, 302, 331, 332, 334

Walkley, A. B., 92, 123–24, 324
Walzel, O., 91, 324, 335
Warren, A., 333, 338
Warren, A. H., Jr., 336
Warren, R. P., 323, 328
Wasiolek, E., 314, 329
Weber, Max, 9
Weidlé, W., 63
Wellek, R., 189, 229, 312, 315, 329, 333, 338, 348, 349, 350, 351, 352, 353, 365
Wells, R., 330
Werner, H., 330
Weyl, H., 37, 322
Wilamowitz, U. von M., 100
Will, 19–20. *See also* Practical activity
Wilson, E., 332
Wimsatt, W. K., Tr., 44, 262, 312, 340, 347, 356, 358, 363, 366
Winckelmann, J. J., 187, 366
Winters, Y., 252, 348
Wit, 138
Wölfflin, H., 187, 335
Women writers, 218
Wood, J., 323
Woodberry, G. E., 195
Words, 64, 65, 68, 74–78, 288
Wordsworth, W., 72
World War I, 276
Worringer, W., 364
Writing, 69, 90

Yeats, W. B., 329

Zanella, G., 206
Zeno, Apostolo, 258
Zeppe, 257–58
Zeppi, S., 319, 332, 366
Zimmermann, R., 315
Zink, S., 91, 335
Zola, É., 207, 348